THE ASIAN FINANCIAL CRISIS AND THE ARCHITECTURE OF GLOBAL FINANCE

The financial crises across Asia in 1997–98 ignited fierce debate about domestic economic weaknesses and flaws in the international financial system. Some analysts blamed Asian governments for inadequate prudential supervision, widespread failures of corporate governance and even 'crony capitalism'. Others assailed the inherent instability of global financial markets and what they considered to be hasty and ill-conceived liberalization taken at the behest of Western-dominated international financial institutions. In this volume a distinguished group of political scientists, economists and practitioners examines the political and economic causes and consequences of the crisis. They ask: To what extent were domestic economic factors to blame for the crises? Why were some economies more prone to crisis than others? What are the costs and benefits of international financial liberalization?

Gregory W. Noble taught at the San Diego and Berkeley campuses of the University of California before taking his present position as Fellow in the Department of International Relations, Research School of Pacific and Asian Studies, Australian National University. He is the author of *Collective Action in East Asia: How Ruling Parties Shape Industrial Policy* (1998) and *Flying Apart? Japanese–American Negotiations over the FSX Fighter Plane* (1992).

John Ravenhill is Chair of Politics at the University of Edinburgh. Previously, he was Professor and Head of the Department of International Relations of the Research School of Pacific and Asian Studies at the Australian National University. His most recent books include *The Political Economy of East Asia* (1995), *Seeking Asian Engagement: Australia in World Affairs 1991–95* (1997); and *New Developments in Australian Politics* (1997).

CAMBRIDGE ASIA–PACIFIC STUDIES

Cambridge Asia–Pacific Studies aims to provide a focus and forum for scholarly work on the Asia-Pacific region as a whole, and its component sub-regions, namely Northeast Asia, Southeast Asia and the Pacific Islands. The series is produced in association with the Research School of Pacific and Asian Studies at the Australian National University and the Australian Institute of International Affairs.

Editor: John Ravenhill

Editorial Board: James Cotton, Donald Denoon, Mark Elvin, Hal Hill, Ron May, Anthony Milner, Tessa Morris-Suzuki, Anthony Low

THE ASIAN FINANCIAL CRISIS AND THE ARCHITECTURE OF GLOBAL FINANCE

EDITED BY

GREGORY W. NOBLE
Australian National University

AND

JOHN RAVENHILL
University of Edinburgh

CAMBRIDGE
UNIVERSITY PRESS

PUBLISHED BY THE PRESS SYNDICATE OF THE UNIVERSITY OF CAMBRIDGE
The Pitt Building, Trumpington Street, Cambridge, United Kingdom

CAMBRIDGE UNIVERSITY PRESS
The Edinburgh Building, Cambridge CB2 2RU, UK
40 West 20th Street, New York, NY 10011–4211, USA
10 Stamford Road, Oakleigh, VIC 3166, Australia
Ruiz de Alarcón 13, 28014 Madrid, Spain
Dock House, The Waterfront, Cape Town 8001, South Africa

http://www.cambridge.org

First published 2000

Printed in China by Everbest Printing Co. Ltd

Typeface New Baskerville (*Adobe*) 10/12 pt. *System* QuarkXPress® [D]

A catalogue record for this book is available from the British Library

National Library of Australia Cataloguing in Publication data
The Asian financial crisis and the architecture of global finance.
Bibliography.
Includes index.
ISBN 0 521 79091 3.
ISBN 0 521 79422 6 (pbk).
1. Financial crises – Asia, Southeastern.
2. Financial crises – Asia.
3. Globalization. 4. International finance.
I. Noble, Gregory W. II. Ravenhill, John.
332.042095

ISBN 0 521 79091 3 hardback
ISBN 0 521 79422 6 paperback

Contents

Abbreviations

ADB	Asian Development Bank
AMC	Asset Management Company
AMF	Asian Monetary Fund
AMU	Asset Management Unit
APEC	Asia–Pacific Economic Cooperation
ASEAN	Association of South-East Asian Nations
BBC	Bangkok Bank of Commerce
BCA	Bank Central Asia
BIBF	Bangkok International Banking Facility
BII	Bank Internasional Indonesia
BIS	Bank for International Settlements
BOK	Bank of Korea
CBC	Central Bank of China (Taiwan)
CCLs	Contingent Credit Lines
CCP	Chinese Communist Party
CSRC	China Securities Regulatory Commission
EFM	emergency financing mechanism (IMF)
EMEAP	Executive Meeting of East Asia and Pacific Central Banks
EMU	Economic and Monetary Union (Europe)
EPA	Economic Planning Agency (Japan)
FDI	foreign direct investment
FRA	Financial Restructuring Authority
FSA	Financial Supervisory Agency (Japan)
G–7	Group of 7
G–10	Group of 10
G–22	Group of 22
GDDS	general data dissemination standard

GITIC   Guangdong International Trust and Investment
            Corporation
HCI   heavy and chemical industries
HIID   Harvard Institute for International Development
HLIs   highly leveraged institutions
IBRA   Indonesian Bank Restructuring Agency
IFIs   international financial institutions
IMF   International Monetary Fund
IOSCO   International Organisation of Securities Commissions
KAMCO   Korean Asset Management Company
KMT   Kuomintang
LDP   Liberal Democratic Party (Japan)
MITI   Ministry of International Trade and Industry (Japan)
MOF   Ministry of Finance
MPT   Ministry of Posts and Telecommunications (Japan)
NPC   National People's Congress (PRC)
ODA   overseas development assistance
OECD   Organisation for Economic Cooperation and Development
OEM   original equipment manufacturing
OFCs   offshore financial centres
PBC   People's Bank of China
PINs   Public Information Notices
PLA   People's Liberation Army
PRC   People's Republic of China
RMB   renminbi
RTC   Resolution Trust Corporation (US)
SDDS   special data dissemination standard
SEACEN   South-East Asian Central Banks
SEANZA   South-East Asia, New Zealand and Australia
SOEs   state-owned enterprises
URR   unremunerated reserve requirement

Figures

Tables

Contributors

JENNIFER A. AMYX, Department of Political and Social Change, Research School of Pacific and Asian Studies, Australian National University, Canberra

THOMAS M. CALLAGHY, Department of Political Science and the Lauder Institute, Wharton School, University of Pennsylvania, Philadelphia

✓BENJAMIN J. COHEN, Department of Political Science, University of California, Santa Barbara

BARRY EICHENGREEN, University of California, Berkeley

STEPHEN GRENVILLE, Deputy Governor, Reserve Bank of Australia

STEPHAN HAGGARD, University of California, San Diego

NATASHA HAMILTON-HART, Department of International Relations, Research School of Pacific and Asian Studies, Australian National University, Canberra

MILES KAHLER, University of California, San Diego

ANDREW MACINTYRE, University of California, San Diego

✓GREGORY W. NOBLE, Department of International Relations, Research School of Pacific and Asian Studies, Australian National University, Canberra

✓JOHN RAVENHILL, Department of Politics, University of Edinburgh

HONGYING WANG, Syracuse University, Syracuse

Preface

The financial crisis that erupted in Thailand in 1997 and quickly spread to the rest of Asia has exerted a dramatic impact on the global political economy. The magnitude of the crisis was striking. It brought Indonesia to its knees, pushed Korea and other countries suddenly and deeply into recession and threatened the financial system of China. However, the sheer size of its impact on affected economies is only one aspect, and perhaps not the dimension that distinguishes it from other debt crises in recent decades. After all, the Latin American debt crisis of the early 1980s led to a 'lost decade' of economic retrenchment in an entire continent, and posed a greater threat at the time to the financial integrity of overexposed Western banks. The African debt crisis, while of only minor significance to the international financial system as a whole, has left already poor countries in desperate straits from which there is no easy exit.

The Asian crisis was particularly notable in other aspects. First, it occurred after a huge upsurge in the mobility of international capital. Foreign money swept into Asia in the early 1990s then, beginning in 1997, swept out again – taking a great deal of local capital with it. The crisis posed new questions about how to manage risk in an increasingly globalised financial system, the appropriate sequencing of financial liberalisation and, more fundamentally, the very desirability of capital account liberalisation in countries with little bureaucratic or political capacity to implement effective systems of prudential regulation. Second, the crisis threatened countries such as Korea, Thailand and Indonesia that had been hailed as models of development for their success in sustaining rapid growth that drastically reduced the rate of poverty. Moreover, the affected economies in Asia displayed few of the classic warning signs that had preceded financial crises in the past, such as ballooning government budget deficits and high rates of inflation. Thailand manifested a few of the other traditional symptoms, such as an overvalued currency and large and growing deficits in its current account, but Korea and Indonesia seemed less susceptible by those conventional measures. The inability of the international community to predict the crisis and prevent it from causing catastrophic damage to some economies led to moves at the global, regional and national levels to improve the monitoring and governance of financial markets, and to provide additional resources to multilateral institutions to enable them to reduce the risks of contagion. Thus, the Asian crisis raises two sets of urgent questions: what went wrong? And what can be done to prevent similar problems from arising in the future?

To address these problems, the Department of International Relations of the Research School of Pacific and Asian Studies at the Australian National University, in conjunction with the Monash Asia Institute, organised an international conference in Melbourne at the end of 1998, to which leading practitioners and top-flight analysts were invited. The conference was fortunate to receive penetrating papers from two of the leading players in the Asian drama. One was Barry Eichengreen, professor of economics and political science at the University of California at Berkeley, who served as the chief research economist at the International Monetary Fund (IMF) at the height of the crisis. The other was Dr Stephen Grenville, Deputy Governor of the Reserve Bank of Australia, which has taken an active role in the rescue process and the surrounding debates on reforms to the global financial architecture. Participants in the conference, and this book that has resulted from it, included a balance of economists and political scientists, all of whom have written extensively on the crisis economies and/or on the political economy of the global financial system.

The Asian Financial Crisis and the Architecture of Global Finance covers four broad topics. Chapters 1 and 2 introduce the evolving debate on the causes and consequences of the crisis. Next, the book looks at a number of comparisons within the region. Why did Korea prove so much more vulnerable to financial instability than Taiwan, its geographic neighbour and developmental twin? How did different types of political institutions create uncertainty in the minds of foreign and domestic investors? How do recent efforts at financial reform in regional countries such as Indonesia compare to earlier episodes? Third, the book examines the roles played by the regional giants in contributing to the crisis – and how they might possibly help its resolution. Japan is especially important in the short-to-medium term because it comprises over two-thirds of the regional economy, but in the long run the crisis may have an equally profound impact on the economic and even political development of China.

The second half of the book (chapters 8 to 11) examines efforts to reform the global architecture of finance. A central and highly controversial question is how the IMF should evolve. Should it continue to 'bail out' distressed economies? If so, what kind of conditions should it impose and how should its own performance be monitored? A related question involves the nature of the international monetary regime and the preferences of the leading economies that exert the greatest influence upon it. Private-sector actors such as international banks are also crucial players. The Asian financial crisis has revealed major difficulties in negotiating arrangements to work out debts, particularly in the private sector. Although there is a good deal of consensus on the need for many technical improvements, including increasing the availability of financial information, the transparency of the IMF's operations and the quality of domestic prudential supervision, the larger policy issues remain contested.

Underlying these debates is the unifying concern on how best to handle the risks created by the increasing international mobility of capital. How great are the risks? To what extent can local or international regulations ameliorate them? Who bears the risks – and the costs of any measures taken to reduce them? This broader concern for risk management embeds study of the Asian financial crisis in some of the classic debates in political economy: governments versus markets; mobile factors of production, such as capital (now including not only the Rothschilds and the Rockefellers, but grandma and grandpa's pension fund) versus relatively immobile factors such as labour; and the relative merits of freedom and flexibility versus security and community. More than is usually recognised, the Asian crisis has opened a wedge on these issues between the IMF, the United States and the United Kingdom, which insist on upholding and accelerating liberalisation, and the governments of the affected countries – Japan and Europe – which call for significant modifications of the international financial system. Whether or not the crisis becomes a defining moment in the political economy of Asian development, it has certainly ignited a series of debates on the architecture of global finance and Asia's place in it.

CHAPTER 1

Causes and Consequences of the Asian Financial Crisis

Gregory W. Noble and John Ravenhill

The financial crisis that erupted in 1997 and engulfed Asia in gloom through the end of the millennium came as a shock to virtually all observers. The preceding decade had witnessed the end of the Cold War and the apparent triumph of liberal capitalism. Controversies over the benefits of trade and direct foreign investment had declined, as global-isation and liberalisation seemed to expand inexorably. In the developing world, periodic financial crises were hardly new, of course, but they had typically occurred in countries with weak export sectors and obvious macroeconomic imbalances such as uncontrolled inflation, inadequate domestic savings and gaping deficits in government budgets (IMF 1998a). The Asian financial crisis, in contrast, delivered an unprecedented blow to a region that had managed to bring its macro-economic house into reasonably good order and had sustained decades of rapid growth driven by exports.

The effects of the crisis throughout East Asia were more severe than any since the great depression of the 1930s. In Indonesia, the fourth most populous country on earth, the impact was shattering. In 1998, the economy contracted by nearly 14 per cent. Korea's economic reversals surpassed anything since the Korean War of the early 1950s. Thailand and relatively affluent Malaysia experienced an abrupt reversal of long-term growth trends. Even Hong Kong and Singapore, the wealthiest and most sophisticated economies in Asia outside Japan, suffered deeply as their trading partners fell into crisis. The crisis exacerbated the financial weaknesses of Japan, whose economy remained mired in stagnation. Only China and Taiwan managed to maintain respectable, if dimin-ished, growth rates and even they were forced to resort to massive and risky programs to stimulate their economies and prop up rickety finan-cial systems. The contagious effects of the crisis spread to financial

1

systems beyond East Asia – first Russia and then Brazil suffered massive capital outflows.

Although signs of incipient recovery in most of the region's economies – particularly Korea but also Thailand and Malaysia – were visible by early 1999, growth rates were substantially below those sustained during the pre-crisis decade. Financial systems remained fragile, burdened by insolvent banks and high volumes of non-performing loans. In Indonesia, the situation was particularly grim and uncertain as economic and political turmoil generated a mutually reinforcing downward spiral. Nor were the negative effects of the Asian crises confined to the region. The World Trade Organization (1999) blamed the Asian crises for the substantial slowing in trade growth in 1998 – down to 3.5 per cent from over 10 per cent in the previous year. Imports into Asia fell by 8.5 per cent in 1998. Similarly, the World Bank (1999a) predicted that the consequences of the Asian crises – a slump in commodity prices, a slowing of world trade, and tighter long-term financing – would cause average growth rates in developing and transitional economies in 1999 to fall to 1.5 per cent, the lowest rate since 1982. The International Monetary Fund (IMF) estimated that the crisis would cause a loss of real income in sub-Saharan Africa of more than 2 per cent (Harris 1999: 15). The East Asian crisis was the severest jolt to the world economy since the early 1980s recession induced by the second oil-price shock.

Causes of the Crisis

The crisis began in early 1997, when a decline in Thailand's exports caused investors (domestic and foreign) to lose confidence that the government could maintain the pegged exchange rate between the Thai baht and the US dollar.[1] Fearing not only that the dollar value of their investments would be reduced substantially, but also that the Thai government would lack sufficient foreign currency reserves to meet all claims, investors engaged in herd-like behaviour that had elements of a self-fulfilling prophecy.[2] Although the government initially attempted to preserve the value of the baht by intervening in foreign exchange markets, Thailand's foreign exchange reserves were soon exhausted. The government consequently had no alternative but to allow the market to determine the currency's value, and to seek emergency assistance from the IMF. Currency devaluation and higher domestic interest rates, required as part of the IMF's aid package, placed enormous pressure on the country's financial system. Many companies were unable to service their loans. The consequent dramatic jump in the ratio of non-performing loans caused most of the domestic banking system to become insolvent. Financial institutions were unable to repay loans denominated in foreign currencies. The local stock market tumbled as currency depreciation, increased interest rates and a curtailment of bank lending led investors to withdraw their funds.

After the Thai baht depreciated, investors focused on other economies whose similar characteristics suggested that their currencies might be vulnerable to speculative attack. The crisis spread quickly from Thailand to Indonesia, the Philippines, Malaysia and Korea. Each of these countries (which collectively became known as the most severely affected economies) experienced to some degree the same cycle of dramatic depreciation, financial system failures and stock market collapse. The devastation of these economies then triggered a further round of contagion, through trade effects. Other economies in the region, notably Taiwan and China, faced a loss of markets in the crisis-hit countries (which, together with the stagnant Japanese market, had in recent years accounted for around half their total exports). They also faced intensified competition in third-country markets from goods produced by the crisis economies, which now had advantages stemming from substantially devalued exchange rates.

A persuasive explanation of the crises would involve two elements. First, it would identify the factors that had changed and thus made some East Asian economies more vulnerable to financial crisis in 1997 than they had been in previous years. Second, it would explain why the contagion from the financial crisis affected some East Asian economies and not others: why was Korea more seriously affected than Taiwan, and Malaysia more than Singapore?

The most fundamental change in the majority of East Asian economies in the 1990s was the dramatic increase in inflows of international capital. Net private capital flows to less-developed economies tripled between 1987–89 and 1995–97, to total more than $US150 billion a year in the latter period (Eichengreen et al. 1999: 1). In the mid 1980s official capital flows to less-developed economies exceeded private capital flows; a decade later private flows were more than seven times the volume of official flows. In Asia alone in 1996, the last pre-crisis year, total net capital flows amounted to $US110 billion compared to an annual average of under $US17 billion in 1983–89 (see chapter 2 in this book, Table 2.1).

The dramatic increase in capital flows reflected a combination of factors. On the supply side these included the growth of pension funds in Western industrialised economies with enormous capital to invest, and changing technology that made it easier for investors to move funds instantaneously around the world. The majority of the new inflows took the form of portfolio rather than direct investment, flows that could easily be reversed through the non-renewal of loans (most of which were of very limited duration). The dramatic fall in the spread of interest rates paid by developing and developed economy borrowers in the years immediately before the crisis points to an abundance of capital in search of profitable investment opportunities.

The growth in flows to Asia also reflected a combination of factors on the demand side. Rigidities in domestic financial systems, often because of government regulations, limited the range of instruments available to local investors. Moreover, financial repression at home and a typically greater abundance of capital abroad made foreign funds relatively inexpensive compared with those available in domestic markets – an annual interest rate differential as high as 10 per cent (Grenville & Gruen 1999: 6). Access to foreign funds was facilitated by two developments. One was the increasing internationalisation of the activities of East Asian firms, which enabled them not only to control foreign funds offshore but also to tap foreign capital markets. Further, most governments in the region at least partially liberalised foreign capital movements. The desire for liberalisation was partly driven by perceived competitiveness imperatives – to do what was necessary to participate in the burgeoning offshore banking industry (as seen, for instance, in the Thai government's creation of the Bangkok International Banking Facilities in 1993). Partial liberalisation of capital flows offered banks opportunities to profit from arbitrage by borrowing at low interest rates abroad and on-lending domestically (and in some instances internationally) at much higher rates.[3]

Liberalisation within a Flawed Policy Framework

Inadequate Regulation

In few instances did governments put in place an effective policy framework to cope with the new inflows of foreign capital. In part, the problem was lack of experience. Governments had neither the knowledge nor the bureaucratic capacity to cope with the regulatory challenges posed by the enormous capital inflows. Even the more developed economies such as Japan had relatively few trained bank inspectors, and throughout the region established ministries resisted attempts to create new independent regulatory agencies. Although some governments embraced the ideology of liberalisation, they ended up with an awkward half-way house that often created a perverse incentive structure.[4]

Moreover, one dimension of the problem – the predominance of short-term debt – was an externality issue, posing particular coordination problems for governments. For the domestic financial institutions involved, the incentive was obvious: short-term loans carried lower inter-est rates than their long-term counterparts, thereby increasing the institutions' opportunities for profitable arbitrage. What was rational for individual financial institutions, however, was not rational for the economy as a whole. By the middle of 1997, short-term debt accounted for a substantial portion of the total debt of several East Asian economies (the proportion ranged from 19 per cent for the Philippines to 24 per cent for Indonesia, 39 per cent for Malaysia, 46 per cent for Thailand and 67 per cent for Korea). In a relatively brief time, short-term debt expanded to exceed the total international reserves of three of the crisis economies: Korea, where the ratio of short-term debt to reserves was in excess of 300 per cent, Indonesia (160 per cent) and Thailand (110 per cent) (Goldstein 1998: Table 6). Such ratios rendered the economies particularly vulnerable to speculative attack.

The licensing of new banks that followed partial liberalisation throughout the region created its own set of problems. Many of these financial institutions were unknown to regulators who were accustomed to operating in a framework of 'relational' banking. Moreover, new financial institutions had a powerful incentive to increase market shares – and often did so by lending to companies with dubious financial qualifications.

Risky lending practices contributed to another problem: the invest-ment of increasing resources in largely unproductive activities. East Asian economies had already been saving and investing at unpre-cedented levels – in many instances, close to 40 per cent of their GNP. Even before the vast increase in capital inflows of the 1990s, rates of return on investment in several economies appeared to be low (and falling). Firms were creating substantial overcapacity in some sectors. The new inflows of foreign capital in the early 1990s exacerbated the imbalance between available capital and productive investment oppor-tunities.[5] They caused bank and non-bank credit in these economies to expand much faster than GDP. A substantial portion of the new investment flows was directed to the real estate and stock markets, fuelling speculative bubbles. Eventually much of this new lending would contribute to the non-performing loans held by local banks.

Fixed Exchange Rates

The maintenance of pegged exchange rates (usually against the US dollar rather than a basket of currencies) greatly exacerbated the vulnerability of economies to crisis.

With a system of pegged exchange rates, most governments found it impossible to shield local economies from the impact of increased inflows of foreign capital (to practise 'sterilisation', in the terminology of economists). The flows had several important consequences. With currency appreciation ruled out, capital inflow fed into the money supply, the increase of which in turn fuelled inflationary pressures. Some economies (notably Thailand, Malaysia and Korea) were already subject to substantial wage pressure because of growing shortages of skilled workers and/or the activities of trade unions that were enjoying new opportunities in democratic political frameworks.[6] Domestic inflation, in a context of pegged exchange rates, made exports increasingly uncompetitive in world markets, a problem exacerbated in 1994–95 by the appreciation of the US dollar against the Japanese yen, and the devaluation of the Chinese yuan. All countries in the region experienced lower rates of export growth in 1996 than in previous years (Goldstein 1998: Table 7). The decline was particularly precipitous in Thailand, Malaysia and Korea.

The apparent commitment of governments to the maintenance of a pegged rate created a moral hazard problem. Financial institutions and other borrowers had little incentive to insure against the exchange risk when borrowing in foreign currencies. Hedging their loans would have cut considerably into their profit margins. But unhedged borrowing put the entire financial system at risk when the exchange rate depreciated. Domestic financial institutions were simply unable to service their loans.

Distinguishing Crisis and Non-crisis Economies

Liberalisation of capital movements, vastly increased capital flows, poor prudential supervision of banking systems and unproductive investments, all within a context of fixed exchange rates, combined to increase the vulnerability of East Asian economies dramatically in the first half of the 1990s. How well do these factors distinguish the most severely affected economies from others in East Asia that did not suffer immediate dramatic falls in their exchange rates and stock markets? Differences between the economies on key economic variables are presented in Table 1.1, which also includes data on three Asian economies – China, Japan and Taiwan – not immediately subject to crisis.

Table 1.1 enables identification of the combination of factors common to the most seriously affected economies. Inflexible exchange rates alone did not cause the problem: China maintained an exchange rate that was pegged against the US dollar (albeit one that had been significantly devalued in 1994).[7] Nor does inadequate prudential regulation alone distinguish the most seriously affected economies: Japan's oversight of its financial institutions before 1998 arguably was no

Table 1.1 Key economic variables of East Asian economies

	Indonesia	Korea	Thailand	Philippines	Malaysia	Japan	China	Taiwan
Exchange rate	Crawling peg	Managed float	Peg	Managed float	Managed float	Freely floating	Peg	Managed float
Significant accumulation of short-term foreign debt in relation to foreign exchange reserves	Yes	Yes	Yes	No	No	No	No	No
Significant real exchange rate appreciation 1996	Partial	No	Yes	Yes	Yes	No	No	No
Capital account liberalisation	Yes	Partial	Yes	Yes	Yes	Yes	No	Partial
Inadequate prudential regulation	Yes	Yes	Yes	Partial	Partial	Yes	Yes	Partial
Current account deficit 1996	Moderate	Moderate	Large	Moderate	Moderate	No	No	No

superior to that of some of the crisis economies (for a discussion of Japan's banking system see chapter 6). Rather, the fatal combination was capital account liberalisation coupled with a basically inflexible exchange rate and (with the partial exceptions of Malaysia and the Philippines) largely ineffective official oversight of the financial system.

Two of the three economies that did not experience a severe financial crisis in 1997–98 – China and Taiwan – maintained restrictions on capital movements. Moreover, like Japan (which had liberalised its capital account), both China and Taiwan had accumulated substantial foreign exchange reserves and had relatively insignificant levels of foreign debt compared to reserves. They were thus far less vulnerable to a speculative panic than other economies in the region. One lesson from the crisis was that, in a world of highly mobile capital, there are advantages to maintaining sizeable foreign exchange reserves (Grenville & Gruen 1999).

The level of short-term debt in relation to foreign exchange reserves is one reason why the crisis was much worse in Indonesia, Korea and Thailand than in Malaysia and the Philippines. Also, Malaysia and the Philippines had implemented a series of reforms in the financial sector. Although by no means meeting international best practice, prudential regulation in those countries was superior to that in the other crisis economies.

Although few commentators dissent from the above explanation of how the financial turmoil was triggered, or on the major economic factors that made the economies vulnerable to crisis, they disagree on the lessons and policy prescriptions to be drawn from the unhappy events of 1997–98. Much of the enormous literature that the crises generated falls into one of two broad camps – in Miles Kahler's terminology (see chapter 11), the 'fundamentalists' and the 'panic-stricken'.[8] To fundamentalists, the root causes of the crises lay in misguided economic policies that East Asian governments had pursued for many years. Close government ties with business elites gave rise to regulation based on relations rather than rules and even to various forms of 'crony capitalism', a situation that generated moral hazard problems when states gave implicit or explicit guarantees that encouraged businesses to engage in unduly risky behaviours. Many East Asian economies were a crisis waiting to happen.

To fundamentalists, the problems of the crisis economies arose not because governments had liberalised their financial systems but because they had not liberalised them enough. Some held that the required liberalisation necessitated dismantling the East Asian developmental model. Above all, the system of relational banking and close ties between the state and private business had to be dissolved to remove the worst of the moral hazard problems. The one exception, where the fundamentalists wanted an enhanced role for the state, was providing prudential regulation of the financial system. Also, the admission of foreign financial institutions would provide a new element of competition for local institutions and foster the adoption of higher standards of financial rectitude.

The panic-stricken held that the fundamentals of the East Asian economies were essentially correct, and that the lessons to be learnt from the crisis were exactly the opposite of those perceived by the fundamentalists. Although advocates of the panic-stricken approach acknowledged that governments had made some errors, they viewed the rapid economic growth rates that East Asia had enjoyed as testimony to the underlying soundness of policies appropriate to those economies' levels of development and institutional infrastructures. Rapid economic growth legitimised governments' developmental strategy, including the close working relationship between state and private sector. If East Asian economies had recently suffered asset-price bubbles, they were due to governments' incapacity to sterilise capital inflows rather than to excessive investment encouraged by moral hazard. The roots of the crises lay in a global financial system that had escaped multilateral oversight; the principal mistake made by governments had been excessively hasty liberalisation of their financial systems, thereby generating asset bubbles and ultimately rendering their economies vulnerable to the herd-like behaviour of speculators.

To the panic-stricken, the crisis arose because of premature liberalisation of capital markets and the activities of speculators. The obvious policy implications were international surveillance of the activities of hedge funds, and measures (such as that proposed by Nobel Laureate James Tobin, for a small tax on foreign exchange transactions) to penalise short-term international capital flows. While improved prudential supervision would be helpful, less-developed economies could not be expected to match the standards of advanced industrialised states overnight. The fluctuations in the huge flows of short-term capital would have been difficult for even well-regulated systems to manage.

Even many critics of the developmental state believed that speculative flows had played a major role in triggering the crisis. Opposition to capital account liberalisation found support in unexpected quarters, including economists with impeccable liberal credentials, the most prominent of whom was Jagdish Bhagwati (1998a). Scepticism about the benefits of liberalising short-term capital inflows was also expressed by the chief economist of the World Bank, Joseph Stiglitz, and by financial authorities in Japan, some European countries and Australia.

✲ The Politics of Financial Policy: Behind the Fundamentals

Clearly, a number of Asian countries chose and maintained policies that left them highly vulnerable to a potential loss of confidence among international investors. Since financial authorities in most of those countries were trained in the same Western graduate schools as their counterparts in the developed world, the obvious question is why they chose unwise, or at least highly risky, policies.

A number of scholars have focused on the ways in which the relative strength of social coalitions and economic sectors influence financial arrangements. In Korea, for example, major conglomerates focused on promotion of manufacturing. They pressured the government to direct credit toward manufacturing and give preferential loans to exporters and favoured industries. In Korea (and Taiwan) the financial sector was never a major concern in its own right, but treated as a crucial input to manufacturing (see chapter 4; Shafer 1994). The degree of concentration of the financial sector may also affect policy choice. In Thailand, for example, before the economic boom and hasty financial liberalisation of the late 1980s and 1990s, a small number of commercial banks cooperated closely with the Bank of Thailand to create an increasingly flexible and stable financial system. Close links with the agricultural and trading sectors prevented them from developing an orientation toward investments in manufacturing (see chapter 3; Doner & Unger 1993).

In other cases, the orientation of financial policy is best explained not by the relative weights and cohesion of various sectors, but by the particular links that individual financial institutions establish with state organs, ruling parties and leading politicians. In Indonesia, as in the Philippines under President Marcos, major business groups that formed tight links with the President and members of his extended family received preference in the allocation of financial licences and in many other policies. When financial regulators tried to impose discipline on these groups, they often found their efforts stymied by political influence. Banks would shut, only to reappear under new names (see chapter 5). Such ties may be particularly resistant to liberalisation, since the introduction of competition and application of a uniform code of behaviour may threaten the interests of those with close ties to the ruling clan.

Another important variable is the degree of foreign participation in the financial sector. Countries that allow significant investment and activity by foreign banks, brokerage houses and insurance companies may face significant pressure to relax regulations on new products and the repatriation of profits, and to loosen regulations that create market segmentation. In Korea and most other Asian countries, however, foreign financial institutions remained a distinctly minor presence.

An alternative perspective emphasises not the 'demand' for financial structures but their supply. One supply-side approach focuses on the degree to which key financial agencies, typically the Ministry of Finance and the central bank, are powerful and insulated from social and political forces. In Japan, the Ministry of Finance (MOF) took primary responsibility for supervision of private financial firms. However, the key to MOF's power was its authority over the compilation of the central government budget, so it regularly sacrificed financial policy to budgetary policy. In addition, MOF's deeply embedded network of relations with private-sector financial institutions often impeded regulatory reforms (for a discussion, see chapter 6). Similarly, in Korea, the Ministry of Finance and Economy remained subject to the whims of the Presidential Office. The central regulatory agencies themselves were subject to periodic reorganisation and reshuffling. In Taiwan, in contrast, the Ministry of Finance and Central Bank of China were powerful and well-insulated, though lower-level regulators were not (on the contrast between Korea and Taiwan, see chapter 4; on Korea see Woo 1991).

The second major consideration on the supply side is the influence of parties and elections. Political parties typically strive to manipulate the financial system to gain advantages for their supporters, and often for themselves. They may also intervene in markets to further various national goals, such as the creation of a powerful military capability or insulation from foreign economic influence. Political infighting and instability can also impede reform or even set off a stampede by investors anxious to pull their capital out before chaos erupts. In Japan, for example, the Liberal Democratic Party (LDP) persistently vetoed reform efforts that would impose costs on farmers' associations and contractors, two of their most important support groups. Despite complaints from bankers, the LDP refused to privatise or reform the postal savings system, both because the national association of postmasters possessed intimate knowledge of the financial dealings of potential political supporters in every district in Japan, and because the moneys collected from the postal savings system funded a dizzying array of pork-barrel projects and quasi-governmental organisations – most of which earned miserable returns (Rosenbluth 1989; Inoguchi & Iwai 1987).

In Korea, too, the ruling party's dependence on political contributions from leading business groups made it reluctant to impose financial reforms that might have reduced the flow of funds to the highly leveraged conglomerates. When a series of scandals split and paralysed the ruling party in the run-up to the presidential election of 1997, it was unable to respond even to a virtual financial implosion. Similar problems beset coalition governments in Thailand (see chapter 3). The severest problems occurred in Indonesia, where doubts about the health of President Suharto and his ability to preside over reforms that could damage the interests of family members and other cronies undermined what had appeared to be initially successful steps to cope with the crisis, and cast doubt on Indonesia's commitment to financial sector reform (see chapter 5; MacIntyre 1998; Hill 1998b).

If parties often distort financial markets for their own purposes, unusually well-organised and disciplined parties may also preside over relatively competent regulatory structures. Singapore provides the archetypal case of a ruling party that has been able to discipline itself and has supported well-paid and aggressive regulators (Hamilton-Hart 1999). In Taiwan, the quasi-Leninist organisation of the ruling Kuomintang (KMT) and its bulging coffers enabled it to preside over a sound, if somewhat rigid, financial system. Backbench members of the party sometimes became involved in scandals at the local level or in the securities sector, but the KMT and the central regulatory agencies to which it delegated regulatory authority prevented corruption from undermining the banking system, which controlled the overwhelming bulk of assets in the financial system (chapter 4; Cheng 1993).

Even where parties have been deeply implicated in financial irregularities or systemic vulnerability, they are necessary conduits if reforms are to be implemented. Bureaucrats, academics, industry groups and consultants may perform much of the specific drafting, but only parties can cut the deals and aggregate the interests to pass new legislation. That political energy is often, perhaps usually, generated by a political or economic crisis – often a crisis arising from the failures of the old system, as in the loss of mainland China by the KMT (Dickson 1993) and the traumatic upheavals surrounding the fall of President Sukarno in Indonesia (Hamilton-Hart 1999). In other cases, economic crisis contributes to political changes that bring new social forces to power. As Geddes (1995) points out, often the popular fervour for reform and the difficulty of ousting existing elites from their privileged positions compels the new democratic forces to press for more transparent, market-based arrangements. That dynamic seems to be at work in both Thailand, where the failings of the old system energised a movement to revise the constitution and electoral system and to develop new safeguards against corruption, and in Korea, where the emerging financial crisis helped perennial outsider and would-be reformer Kim Dae Jung gain a narrow victory in the presidential election of 1997 (for a discussion see chapter 3). The Indonesian case is a powerful reminder, however, that crises alone will not necessarily deliver the desired results.

Finally, it is worth recalling that the sophisticated regulatory structures of the West evolved over a long period. Reforms were often stimulated by a long line of scandals and crises. In the United States, for example, the Federal Reserve System grew out of a reform commission that was stimulated by the panic of 1907, while the depression of the 1930s led to the creation of the Federal Deposit Insurance Corporation (Mayer 1998). As recently as the 1980s, financial crises led to the adoption of improved regulatory procedures in the United States, Australia and Scandinavia.

Even so, turning reform proposals into policy is not easy. Incumbent political machines prove remarkably adept at turning new sources of revenue to their advantage and coopting newly risen social forces (Calder 1988). Good government parties usually defeat incumbent political machines only after protracted battles (Erie 1988). Even then they may have a difficult time creating stable coalitions capable of implementing in full the reform proposals stimulated by crisis.

Political reform and prudential regulation are precisely the types of public goods that political systems tend to underproduce, particularly if they create few opportunities for political entrepreneurship. Proposals for the introduction of independent regulatory agencies and stiff prudential regulation rouse few voters to fighting pitch. In Japan, the ruling LDP and its failed financial policies angered many voters, particularly middle-class residents of large cities, but they were just as likely to become alienated from politics as to support the reformist parties. The farmers, contractors, postmasters and small business owners behind the LDP, in contrast, could be depended upon to show up at election time. Some financial reform legislation pressed by the opposition parties and opposed by MOF bureaucrats passed the Diet in 1997, but the opposition parties have not taken a consistently pro-reform stance (see chapter 6). Similarly, despite the hopeful signs in Korea and Thailand, it is too early to declare victory in the battle for financial reform.

If economic factors had made some economies far more vulnerable to crisis by the mid 1990s than at the beginning of the decade, what of political factors? To what extent had some elements of the political situation deteriorated? The picture is very mixed. Some political systems, notably Korea, the Philippines and Thailand, appeared in 1996 to be much more stable than they were a decade earlier. Indonesia stands out as an exception, as corruption and cronyism appeared to be on the increase in the mid 1990s (Robison 1997). What is very clear, however, is that inappropriate policy responses by governments in all the worst-affected economies succeeded in turning a severe challenge into a crisis. In Thailand, the critical government mistakes were its equivocation in the face of financial sector problems, and its decision to squander most of its foreign exchange reserves in defence of the baht. In Indonesia, the initial goodwill that the government earned from international markets and financial institutions through its decision to seek early consultations with the IMF soon dissolved, as President Suharto appeared increasingly unwilling to deal decisively with financial sector problems, particularly those which involved members of his immediate family or favourites (Hill 1998a). In Korea, the government failed to act decisively when faced with corporate bankruptcies; this indecision was widely attributed to corrupt relations between ruling party members (and, indeed, the President's family) and business groups. Moreover, the government failed to respond effectively to the pressure on the Korean won caused by the devaluation of the Taiwanese dollar in October 1998 (see chapter 3). In Malaysia, Prime Minister Mahathir's denunciation of international speculators and implicit threats against foreign capital, coupled with new political instability arising in part from struggles over the future course of economic policy, unnerved international markets.

Whether a more effective set of policy responses could have avoided the crises is debatable, given the economies' underlying vulnerability to speculative attack, and the contagion effect once Thailand's financial system succumbed. Some of the worst effects might have been mitigated by more appropriate and timely policy interventions. However, in most countries, coherent parties capable of drafting and implementing comprehensive financial reforms will probably emerge only after a protracted series of economic crises and campaigns for political reforms. The rate of political reform lags well behind the extraordinary rate of innovation in telecommunications and financial technology.

Domestic Responses

Governments in the affected Asian countries have considered a wide range of measures and reforms to deal with the immediate exigencies of the crisis and to prevent its recurrence. One solution to the problem of huge waves of investment pouring into developing countries then decamping at the first sign of crisis would be direct controls on capital movements.

In liberal economic theory, financial flows carry a number of important benefits for developing countries (see the discussion in chapter 8; Eichengreen et al. 1999). Just as trade in manufactured products allows countries to specialise in industries according to comparative advantage, so too should financial integration channel surplus savings to countries that can put them to best use by offering the highest returns. Since poorer countries have the potential to grow much faster than rich ones, by drawing on accumulated Western technology and by moving resources out of agriculture and into higher productivity employment in manufacturing and services, they are in an especially advantageous position to put the capital of developed countries to good use. Introduction of foreign capital allows domestic firms to invest more and at lower interest rates, leading to faster growth and alleviation of poverty.

The participation of foreign financial institutions in domestic markets also promises to bring a number of benefits, including introduction of more diverse and sophisticated financial products and demands for improved accounting and auditing standards. Foreign financial institutions prod locals to improve the efficiency of their management. By introducing greater competition and more objective standards of performance, the opening of the domestic financial system may break up incestuous or cartelistic arrangements. When combined with fixed exchange rates, capital openness effectively commits countries to controlling inflation. Governments cannot pursue an independent monetary policy with a fixed exchange rate.

However, it is increasingly apparent that financial liberalisation carries substantial risks. Less-than-robust financial systems and regulatory structures leave all but a handful of developing countries vulnerable to speculation and collapse. Huge inflows of capital, much of it aimed at short-term gains, are difficult for them to absorb prudently and efficiently, and when the capital suddenly retreats at signs of instability the domestic economy is plunged into deep recession that sours even formerly solid loans and leaves domestic banks vulnerable to collapse. Unable to renew or extend lending, domestic banks contribute to a credit crunch that exacerbates the original financial problem. Moreover, there is no evidence that in practice, unlike in economic theory, capital account liberalisation has been associated with improved economic performance (Rodrik 1999a).

In principle, exit controls should prevent a 'rational panic' by preventing investors from all leaving at once (Radelet & Sachs 1998a), and entry taxes would decrease the initial inflows of speculative money. Without capital controls, in the wake of crises governments are forced to hike interest rates to punishing and perhaps destructive levels to retain capital, both foreign and domestic (contrast Wade & Veneroso 1998a, and Eichengreen's discussion in chapter 8).

In practice, observers are sharply split on the desirability and feasibility of capital controls. For most of the postwar era, capital controls have been commonplace even in developed countries. Despite gradual liberalisation, Korea, Taiwan and several other countries still retained residual controls when the Asian crisis exploded. China's currency, the renminbi, was unconvertible. Over time, however, opposition to capital controls by the IMF and the international community grew. Just as the Asian crisis began to unfold, the IMF's Interim Committee, its principal governing body, recommended changing the Articles of Agreement to make the promotion of capital account liberalisation one of the purposes of the IMF (see chapter 8).

Analysts note the difficulties and dangers associated with attempting to reintroduce controls (see chapter 9). Improvements in technology and management have created increasingly pervasive opportunities to evade controls, rendering them – and other policies predicated upon them – ineffective. Regulations to deal with the loopholes and evasions become increasingly draconian and baroque, discouraging even non-speculative investments. Would-be evaders have a strong incentive to bribe regulators, undermining the fairness and reputation of the entire regulatory system. Some of the capital that flees a country in a crisis is domestic, and locals are often experts at evading local controls.

Experience of the reintroduction of capital controls is relatively sparse, itself perhaps a testament to the difficulties of implementation. The best-known case is Chile, which imposed a 'tax' (compulsory placement of a non-interest-bearing bond with the central bank) on incoming investments other than direct foreign investment. Entry taxes have the signal advantage of discouraging purely speculative short-term investments without trying to prevent panicked investors from withdrawing their investments in the midst of a crisis. They also seem much less prone to corruption (chapter 9). Even if they are more effective and less disruptive, entry taxes may not be politically attractive, however, since they may discourage investment and growth.

The Chilean tax is especially interesting because it emanated not from a statist regime, but from a resolutely liberal one. After the fall of Allende, the military government in Chile pushed rigorous reforms that soon led to the effective collapse of the banking system. The government was forced to nationalise most of the banks. While it responded with a new round of liberalising reforms, it learnt the necessity for retaining some controls (Hastings 1993). In 1991, the central bank imposed a one-year unremunerated reserve requirement on foreign loans, the rate of which fluctuated between 30 per cent in 1992 and 10 per cent in 1998. Opinion differs on how effective these controls have been: see, for instance, the contrasting views of the IMF (IMF 1998a: Annex IV, 'Chile's Experience with Capital Controls') and Lopez-Mejia (1999). Most observers believe, however, that the Chilean controls did contribute to shifting the mix of incoming investment away from short-term flows.

In the Asian crisis, the most noted example of the reimposition of capital controls came in Malaysia, an unusually open economy highly dependent on trade and foreign investment. By the standards of the region, the Malaysian financial system had been considered relatively sound. Because of its relatively large foreign exchange reserves Malaysia, unlike its neighbours Thailand and Indonesia, was not forced into the arms of the IMF – it voluntarily adopted a reform program similar to those imposed by the IMF elsewhere. Prime Minister Mahathir, however, fulminated against alleged speculators, whom he blamed for the problems not only of Malaysia but of other adversely affected economies in the region. In September 1998, he imposed controls on trading the ringgit and a one-year minimum stay on inward investment. At the same time the Malaysian government gave assurances that implementation of the measures would not interfere with the normal operations of legitimate investors. Imposition of the controls allowed Malaysia to cut interest rates and embark on a stimulative tax and expenditure policy. At least in the short term the policy seemed to achieve its goals without impinging on foreign investment, and the government relaxed the measures somewhat in February 1999 (Athukorala 1999).

A number of other countries, including Taiwan, the Philippines and Hong Kong, undertook more selective actions to limit trading in their currencies and derivatives or to limit some repatriation of profits. Whether capital controls will be effective and whether they will re-emerge as serious tools in the policy kit of governments remains unclear, but at the very least they have returned from the land of the heterodox (chapter 9). The domestic coalitions favouring controls may appear relatively weak in contrast to the actors that benefit from capital account liberalisation. Nonetheless, to the extent that short-term flows are judged to be a 'collective bad' and a substantial factor in recent financial crises, moves to constrain them may gain significant international support.

In the wake of the crisis virtually all countries in the region took measures to improve prudential regulation. Many analysts argued that the first and most important step was to increase the ratio of banks' capital relative to risk-adjusted assets (loans) to the 8 per cent required by the Basle Accord of 1988 or even higher, since high levels of capital can compensate for a multitude of managerial and regulatory sins, and data on capital adequacy tend to be lagging indicators (Fane 1998; chapter 8). Most countries increased provisions for reserves against non-performing loans. Japan, Korea and other countries began assessing non-performing loans with stricter standards adopted from the US Securities and Exchange Commission (SEC). In Japan, after years of delay by the MOF, the collapses in late 1997 of the tenth-largest bank and one of the four leading securities firms finally stimulated major changes in financial regulation, including the formation of a Financial

Supervisory Agency. The new agency, which proved much tougher than observers had expected, carried out its own audits rather than relying on self-assessment by the banks. It found additional dubious loans and forced banks to undertake remedial action (chapter 6). Korea, Japan and others undertook reforms intended to ensure that banks listed crucial assets such as land and stocks at current (depreciated) market values rather than at often-misleading book values. Throughout the region regulators strengthened provisions against lending to related companies, a major source of fraud and contagion. Both Japan and Korea moved to require major companies to issue consolidated financial accounts that would reveal loans and credit guarantees to their subsidiaries and affiliates, and prevent the double-counting of assets.

Progress was neither uniform nor complete. Indonesia, in particular, made far less progress than did Korea and Japan. Moreover, if banks can evade other prudential controls, it is hard to believe that those sufficiently motivated would not be able to use in-group financial transactions or other tricks to evade capital requirements (Oatley & Nabors 1998: 44–5; Rodrik 1999a). Disturbingly, evidence mounted that over the past decade or more virtually every country in the region had repeatedly run campaigns to improve prudential regulation, often to little or no effect because of political interference. Most ominous was Indonesia, where efforts to close failed banks and reimpose financial discipline fell victim to the same personalistic forces that had made Indonesia vulnerable in the first place (chapter 5; on Korea, see Smith 1998: 74–5). The degree of initial success in financial restructuring is related to a country's degree of bureaucratic capacity prior to the crisis: Japan, Korea and Malaysia have made significant progress; Thailand and the Philippines have been mired in problems. Indonesia remains in a class by itself, with few signs of successful reform. On balance, however, progress in tightening financial regulations looked impressive relative to efforts at corporate restructuring.

Most reformers called for countries to go beyond specific technical fixes, by increasing the independence and unity of oversight agencies. They hoped to effect a shift from intimate and holistic relations between regulators and individual financial institutions that often degenerated into corruption or inaction, to systems based on vigorous and timely enforcement of transparent universal rules. In Japan, Korea and China, central banks gained increased autonomy from politicians and ministries of finance and new regulatory agencies took over much of the responsibility for inspecting banks and other financial institutions. The efficacy of the new financial agencies is unproven, however, and observers note that Western countries are far from united on an ideal model for regulatory oversight (Ji 1998). Even in the United States,

Table 1.2   Crisis and recovery in East Asian banking

	Indonesia	Korea	Malaysia	Philippines	Thailand
Average banking deposits as % of 1998 GDP	46	38	104	57	94
Estimated peak non-performing loans 1998 (%)	65–75	16–23	20–25	12.5	45–55
Estimated cost of bank re-capitalisation as % of 1998 GDP	32–37	11–16	16–23	–	30–39
Role of asset management company	AMU inactive and unstaffed	Unclear if KAMCO will restructure debtor firms or sell the claims	Danaharta may restructure debtors but has yet to do so	Considered but deemed inappropriate	AMC created for finance companies but not for banks. FRA auctions non-performing loans and the buyers restructure the debts

Source: World Bank (1999b: Table 2)

generally regarded as having the most effective oversight mechanisms, Congressional opposition to reform has meant that government supervision of banks remains split among several agencies (Mayer 1998).

Even new and strengthened supervisory agencies faced a number of serious transitional problems. First and most obvious was the immense cost and political conflict incurred in disposing of bad loans, repaying depositors of failed institutions, recapitalising the financial system and stimulating weak economies (see Table 1.2). Estimates of the costs ranged from tens of billions of dollars for Korea and Thailand to hundreds of billions in China, to as much as a trillion dollars for Japan. In many cases recapitalisation meant the effective nationalisation of troubled financial institutions, leading to concerns that governments would either mismanage the banks or quickly resell them to their former owners or other politically favoured figures after recapitalisation, thus creating a giant problem of moral hazard, not to mention public outrage.

Finding enough qualified auditors to go through the tangled books of borrowers presented an immense challenge even in Japan, not to mention Thailand or Indonesia. Nor was it clear what standards auditors would apply in the interim, since strict application of regulations on capital adequacy or borrower creditworthiness could paralyse entire financial systems before they recovered from crisis (on Indonesia, see chapter 5; on Korea, see Ji 1998). Meanwhile, looming behind the massive efforts to resurrect the banking systems of the region was the inexorable shift in global finance from banking to securitisation. Even before they developed adequate skills in risk management, Asian banks faced the prospect of losing their best corporate customers to the bond and mutual funds markets, depressing profitability and creating powerful incentives to lend to riskier customers (Mayer 1998: 208–30; Lincoln 1988). Unfortunately, while securitisation may be more efficient than banking in an age of widespread information, securities markets are even more unstable (see chapter 4 on the greater fragility of the securities industry in Taiwan; see chapter 10 for the problems of foreign debt holdings by Indonesian companies).

Two years after the onset of the Asian economic crisis, the extent of financial and corporate restructuring in the most severely affected economies remained limited. Governments closed and merged a number of banks, but only a handful of banks were acquired by foreign investors. Despite huge injections of public funds, banks remained undercapitalised. Debt-for-equity swaps were extremely rare. Of the 2069 non-bank financial institutions in the crisis economies, many of them financially weak, only 242 had shut their doors by August 1999. Non-performing loans remained at the peaks of 20–70 per cent of GDP reached in 1998. Thai and Indonesian banks will not be able to grow out of their non-performing loans through retained earnings unless interest rate spreads increase to double their historical levels. Banks in Malaysia and Korea, though less troubled, remained highly vulnerable to changes in interest rates and renewed corporate distress. The governments of Indonesia, Malaysia and Korea transferred significant portions of bad debts to public asset management companies, but by mid 1999 had managed to sell only 2 per cent of the assets to new private buyers.

Corporate restructuring proceeded even more slowly. Most Asian companies are family-owned and, large or small, reluctant to surrender control or even significant oversight to outsiders (Claessens, Djankov & Lang 1999). Few cases passed though formal bankruptcy proceedings and even informal out-of-court settlements were limited. Even when 'restructuring' of corporate debt occurred, it consisted largely of reduction in interest rates and deferral of principal. In Thailand, the value of corporate debt restructured as of March 1999 barely exceeded 10 per cent of non-performing loans. Regardless of their level of debt, few large companies closed factories and offices. Smaller companies shed many workers and appealed to governments for emergency credit, but few undertook serious restructuring. In the words of the World Bank's chief economist for the Asia–Pacific region, the restructuring process 'has not yet resulted in sound, recapitalised banking systems and strong corporate balance sheets, much less a resumption in growth in bank lending and corporate investment' (Kawai 1999: 2; Claessens, Djankov & Klingebiel 1999). Despite all the talk of corporate restructuring, two years after the outbreak of the Asian crisis very few indebted large firms had closed their doors. Increases in direct foreign investment provided some relief, particularly in Korea and Thailand, but excess capacity remained endemic throughout the region. As in the US savings and loan crisis of the 1980s and the stagnation of Japan in the early 1990s, political pressures to exercise regulatory forbearance remained powerful.

The limited restructuring that did occur did not replace close links between large firms and national governments with robust capital markets and strictly market-based relations. After 1997 the Japanese government abandoned the 'convoy' approach to regulation and permitted the entry of a number of foreign investors, but many Japanese corporations became dependent on a huge increase in lending through state-owned development banks. The Chinese government reversed tough macroeconomic policies that had encouraged restructuring of state-owned enterprises, instead reiterating its commitment to retain the largest of the SOEs and working overtime to stimulate the depressed and deflationary economy (chapter 7). Clearest of all was Korea. The leading *chaebol* conglomerates responded to government demands that they reduce nominal debt levels, but did so largely by relying even more heavily on non-bank financial institutions, many of them controlled by the chaebol themselves. The government pushed 'big deals', in which the chaebol reversed scatterplot diversification by exchanging assets with each other. These deals aimed to increase specialisation, focus and economies of scale – but at the cost of greatly increased market concentration in autos, electronics and other key areas of the economy. The top five chaebol accounted for more than half of the total capital raised by Korean business in the first half of 1999. Most of it came in the form of bonds rather than new equity, but the paralysis surrounding the failure of the leading conglomerate, Daewoo, undermined the bond market – demonstrating again the intricate linkages between corporate and financial sector reforms. Asian corporations remained dependent

upon weak and badly regulated banking systems and on continuing
support from government. In many countries, real or feigned fears that
tightened oversight had created a credit crunch were used to justify
directing credit to politically well-connected companies, industries and
regions.

Proposals for reforms in corporate governance regimes aroused
considerable controversy and significant social resistance. Regulators
and academics called for changes in corporate governance, including
strengthening the oversight function of boards of directors of banks and
other corporations (Ji 1998). Including more outsiders on boards,
giving top priority to the interests of shareholders, and occasionally
overruling and even replacing management would amount to a virtual
capitalist revolution in many Asian countries. A few companies, such as
Japan's Sony, began to change, but resistance was deep and broad.
Progress in redesigning bankruptcy systems and in crafting less formal
alternatives made but slow progress (Claessens, Djankov & Klingebiel
1999; Kawai 1999).

Proposals to use the opportunity of the financial crisis to accelerate
liberalisation of capital accounts, trade regulations and labour systems
also aroused heated debate. The IMF, the US government and some
local reformers argued that systemic changes were crucial to effective
implementation of financial reform and that the shock of the crisis
offered a rare opportunity to mobilise the political energy for reform. In
practice, the US government took advantage of the crisis to push long-
sought trade goals. Some said that reform would take decades, as it had
in the West. They contended that imposition of an excessively ambitious
'one size fits all' agenda, largely tangential to the immediate task of
macroeconomic and financial stabilisation, would be undemocratic and
potentially destabilising (Feldstein 1998; Rodrik 1999a; see also chapter
2).

Governments devoted most of their attention to increasing expenditures to deal with the short-term consequences of the crisis, and
reforming regulation to prevent its recurrence. The IMF, like the World
Bank, increasingly adopted a rhetoric that emphasised the need to
strengthen the social safety net and the advantages of a relatively egali-
tarian distribution of income. The East Asian economies entered the
crisis with fairly strong public finances, so they were able to boost expenditure on unemployment relief, demand stimulus and recapitalisation of
failing banks. After years of recession, Japan's financial situation was
significantly worse, but it too poured in large sums to get the economy –
and the banks – moving again. China embarked on an aggressive infrastructure development program, while Taiwan's government poured
billions into programs to prop up the stock and property markets. In

both cases, detractors claimed that the programs would only create more bad loans and delay systemic reform. Despite the aggressive efforts, unemployment increased virtually everywhere in the region. In Thailand and Indonesia, the crisis pushed tens of millions back into poverty.

Reforming the Global Financial Architecture

Disappointment with the international community's failure to anticipate the Asian crises and to prevent their generating significant damage to world welfare – despite IMF assistance packages of unprecedented size (totalling $US117 billion) – prompted a flurry of proposals on how the international financial regime might be reformed. These proposals ranged from demands for the abolition of the IMF to suggestions for the establishment of a global central bank.

The crisis opened new fissures among key players in the international financial regime. Not surprisingly, most of the governments of the crisis economies perceived the lessons to be learnt from their experience very differently from those drawn by Washington and London. Typical of the panic-stricken view, they saw the crisis as pointing out the need for restrictions on the activities of speculative capital, for additional quickly disbursed assistance to governments whose currencies were under speculative attack (in the hope that the availability of such funds would avoid the typically deflationary consequences of IMF programs) and for cooperation on monetary affairs at the regional level. Again, not unexpectedly given its efforts over the years to promote an Asian alternative to the Washington consensus on 'getting the state out of the market', the Japanese government sided with the views of other Asian governments, as did the Australian central bank (although not its Treasury). More surprising was the bluntness with which the Japanese MOF criticised the activities of the IMF and promoted a new regional monetary fund.

European governments, while not particularly sympathetic towards the statist or clientelist practices of East Asian countries, sided with the Japanese government against Washington (and London) in decrying the excessive swings of floating exchange rates and proposing a move towards a system based on target zones for key currencies. Opinion on exchange rate systems remained sharply divided, however. The IMF and many academic economists argued that the Asian crisis provided overwhelming evidence that countries faced a stark choice between floating rates and politically demanding currency boards (see chapter 8). Most governments and some academics countered that floating rates were not risk-free, especially for less-developed economies. Their advice was that countries should choose from an array of options depending upon their level of development and economic circumstances (Grenville & Gruen 1999; Frankel 1999).

The crisis also deepened divisions between twin Washington-based financial institutions, the IMF and the World Bank. Disagreements were not unprecedented (disputes had occurred in the late 1980s over management of structural adjustment programs in Africa). What was novel was the frankness of the World Bank's public criticism of IMF views on the virtues of liberalised capital markets in less-developed economies, and on some of the components of IMF conditionality attached to its Asian rescue packages. In its scepticism about the value of short-term capital flows, the World Bank lined up with East Asian governments and some economists against what Bhagwati (1998a) terms the 'Wall Street–Treasury complex', which critics allege had captured the IMF.

Reforming the IMF

Calls for the abolition of the IMF came from a variety of neoliberal economists and think-tanks. The essence of their argument was that by bailing out countries that suffered crises, the IMF was internationalising the moral hazard problem. The ready availability of international finance encouraged governments in less-developed economies to engage in behaviour that sustained domestic moral hazard problems, and discouraged them from making the reforms necessary to set domestic financial sectors on a sound footing. Further, international bailouts had encouraged speculators to undertake dubious investments without any risk to themselves. The argument said that, unlike in the Latin American debt crises of the early 1980s, speculators had escaped largely unscathed from recent crises in Mexico and now East Asia because of international rescue efforts.[9]

To these critics of international support, the crisis economies were not big enough for their difficulties to threaten the integrity of the international financial system. Most commentators and all governments, however, dissent from this view. They fear the possible externalities for the international financial regime (and, indeed, for the security regime) from crises such as those that beset East Asia in 1997–98. Private and social costs in the financial system may diverge markedly (see chapter 8; Kapstein 1998).

Neither the abolition of the IMF nor its transformation into a global central bank is on the post-crisis agenda. But the crisis has raised various issues relating to the IMF that can be expected to generate incremental reforms. Critics from the left and from the right are agreed on the need for greater transparency in the IMF's decision-making procedures. The

IMF has moved in this direction, with its executive board agreeing to release Public Information Notices following 'Article IV consultations' (the bilateral discussions the IMF holds with member economies, usually annually, to review economic and financial developments). The presumption is that in future the IMF will publish Letters of Intent, although member economies will retain veto over publication (IMF 1999a). Within the IMF, consensus has emerged on enabling the board to participate more effectively in the formulation of IMF programs. To achieve greater transparency without sending self-fulfilling signals to the market is no mean task, however (see the discussion in chapters 8 and 11). Releasing information that points to weaknesses in a member economy may well trigger an adverse market reaction.

The conditions that the IMF attached to its assistance to the Asian crisis economies have generated a great deal of criticism, not always from expected quarters. Governments on the western Pacific rim have castigated the IMF for exacerbating the crisis through its insistence on governments introducing deflationary measures. A number of mainstream economists, especially those with detailed knowledge of the crisis economies, joined this criticism (see, for instance, McLeod 1998a, 1998b). The principal criticisms of IMF policies were stated succinctly and strongly in a speech that Japan's Vice-Minister of Finance, Eisuke Sakakibara (1999), gave at the Manila Framework Group's meeting in April 1999. He asserted that:

- the IMF applied its standard prescription of tightening fiscal policy even though the Asian crisis countries, unlike those in Latin America that had previously been crisis victims, were not running large budgetary deficits or unreasonable current account deficits. Fiscal policy tightening threw the economies into a deeper recession than was necessary;
- the IMF was far too optimistic about the growth outlook for the economies when designing the programs;
- the IMF unnecessarily raised interest rates. The objective was to halt inflation and attempt to stem capital outflows, but higher interest rates contributed to the downturn in economic activity and manifestly failed at first to stabilise the exchange rate;
- the IMF contributed to the recession by creating a liquidity crisis through its ill-timed closure of financial institutions. Indonesia provided a spectacular example, the closure of sixteen private banks prompting a run on other institutions;
- the IMF's conditionality was too intrusive, extending to many issues of economic structure far beyond what was necessary to resolve the immediate crisis.

Eichengreen (chapter 8) provides detailed analysis of the criticisms of the IMF. He makes the case that some tightening of fiscal policy was unavoidable, given the need to reduce absorption when capital inflows were reversed. He notes, however, that such measures have to consider the stage of the business cycle, and that the IMF initially considerably underestimated the depth of the recession that the crisis would generate. The IMF's own assessment of its response to the crises (Lane et al. 1999: 101) similarly concedes that the initial programs 'erred in underestimating the need for fiscal policy to support activity'. The IMF (Lane et al. 1999: 34) also acknowledges that, because the programs were not successful in restoring confidence, private capital outflows greatly exceeded the IMF's initial projections, with negative consequences for the exchange rate.

Neither Eichengreen nor the IMF accepts the argument that interest rates were raised to excessive levels. The IMF denies that monetary policy was tightened too drastically, and asserts that the settings in Korea and Thailand achieved their objective of avoiding a depreciation/inflation spiral (Lane et al. 1999: 83). Eichengreen asserts that lower interest rates would have been incompatible with a roll-over of maturing loans: the unenviable choice was between higher interest rates or exclusion from international capital markets. And interest rates fell quickly in 1998, to levels below those prevailing before the crisis.

The IMF at least partially concedes the argument that bank closures in the early stages of the crisis contributed to a liquidity crisis and to panic among depositors. Its internal assessment notes that the failure to provide guarantees to depositors when the Indonesian banks were closed was 'ill-advised' (Lane et al. 1999: 43).

Accusations that the IMF was 'overdoing it in Asia' had been widely voiced, most notably by Feldstein (1998). Some believed that the IMF had exceeded its role as crisis manager by setting out to dismantle the developmental state in pursuit of the liberalising agenda favoured by the Wall Street–Treasury complex. The IMF and its defenders, however, argue that reform in the financial sector alone would be insufficient to resolve the structural problems evident in the crisis economies. Supporting reforms are required in the real economy – in goods and labour markets – and in the relations between the state and the private sector (see chapter 8). The difficulties caused in the Korean financial system by the demise of the Daewoo group illustrate the imperative of linking corporate financial reform with reform of the financial system.

Often overlooked by the IMF's critics is the extent to which it was encouraged to broaden the scope of conditionality by other actors, including domestic technocrats and the World Bank. They saw the crisis as an opportunity to shift the balance of the domestic political economy towards those elements favouring reform. As Sadli (1998: 275) comments, IMF intervention from a nationalist standpoint can be 'humbling, but from an economic and technocratic standpoint it is a blessing in disguise'.

The IMF's preliminary assessment of its programs in the crisis economies accepts some of its critics' major arguments. It appears that some institutional learning has occurred, although the extent to which the IMF will change its standard operating procedures in the design of its programs is yet to be demonstrated.

Member countries have given the IMF additional resources to combat future crises. In January 1999 the eleventh quota increase was implemented, providing 45 per cent more finance (totalling 212 billion special drawing rights, SDRs). Agreement has also been reached on a new contingent credit line, to be made available quickly when the currency of a country that has an IMF-certified good track record comes under attack because of contagion.[10] The contingent line of credit will not be subject to the limits on member economies' overall access to IMF resources, but commitments will be expected to be 300–500 per cent of the member's IMF quota.

Improved Transparency through International Oversight

To some analysts, a central lesson of the East Asian crises was the need for increased scrutiny of the financial policies of governments and the practices of institutions. Improved transparency would achieve several objectives: it would discipline governments, encourage the adoption and observation of improved prudential standards and, by providing better information to foreign investors, enable markets to function more smoothly and thereby prevent herd-like and panic-stricken adjustments. And, as Eichengreen describes in chapter 8, the domestic implementation of agreed international standards can be an alternative to greater IMF intrusion in domestic economic management.

Agreement was reached in 1999 on strengthening the IMF's special data dissemination standard (SDDS), in particular to ensure that full information is made available on the disposition of countries' foreign reserves (the lack of transparency about this was certainly a factor in the Korean crisis). In addition, the finance ministers of the Group of 7 (G-7) industrialised economies agreed to create a 'Financial Stability Forum' to promote cooperation in the supervision of global markets. The Forum would be responsible for coordinating the activities of national and multilateral agencies. As discussed in chapters 8 and 11, a variety of international bodies in addition to the IMF provide standards for government and corporate behaviour in various dimensions of international finance and monitor compliance with these standards (see also IMF 1998a: Box 1.1).

One thrust of East Asian governments' responses to the crises has been to demand greater symmetry in the calls for transparency – to establish more monitoring of foreign private sector actors, especially heavily leveraged international investors such as the hedge funds. Despite initial resistance from the US and British financial communities, the G–7 finance ministers agreed in September 1999 to call for greater disclosure of highly leveraged financial institutions (Group of 7 1999). However, as of late 1999, no practical measures had been implemented to address these concerns.

Widespread agreement exists that, in principle, improved transparency for governments, private sector actors and international financial institutions alike is a good thing. The belated disclosure of information which documented that the financial problems in Thailand and Korea were much worse than markets had previously believed, contributed to the panic that hit both economies in 1997. For governments, demonstrating that they are complying with international best practice may not only be useful in prudential regulation but also in selling the economy as a relatively secure location in which to conduct business.[11]

Such exercises, however, demand substantial bureaucratic resources that may be beyond the capacities of many less-developed economies. Moreover, as the Group of 22 (G–22) (1998) noted, confidentiality may be warranted in some circumstances, for instance, so as not to discourage frank internal debate. And some argued that the crisis demonstrated less the need for more information than for better interpretation of information that was available. The frequent complaint of economic historians is that each new crisis generates demands for new information that would have been useful in predicting that crisis but which is seldom of much value in predicting or preventing the next one. The World Bank's chief economist, Joseph Stiglitz (1998), comments that 'much existing information seems not to be fully incorporated into market assessments, so there is no guarantee that markets will respond perfectly to perfect information … Better information is like a better navigation chart: useful but not everything'. In short, improved transparency in critical areas such as disposition of foreign exchange reserves may help avoid unnecessary problems, but in itself will be insufficient to guarantee against panic.

Improving the Capital Adequacy of International Banks

In the wake of the crisis, the Basle Committee on Banking Supervision's 1988 agreement on capital adequacy came in for considerable criticism.

Observers concurred that the standards failed to align the capital provision requirements of loans with their riskiness. For example, loans to banks in OECD countries – even Korea and Mexico, the newest and weakest members – required only one-fifth the capital provisions demanded of loans to even the best corporate customers. After much research and policy debate (and considerable tension between the US and some European countries), in June 1999 the Basle Committee announced new standards that readjusted requirements for different types of loans, including higher requirements for loans extended by banks to other banks. The Committee held off on proposals to let banks use their own credit-risk models, but suggested that the most sophisticated banks be allowed to apply their internal rating systems. It also called for greater incorporation of market incentives and encouraged national regulators to consider imposing higher requirements as necessary (Basle Committee on Banking Supervision 1998, 1999). Though the new draft standards marked an important step forward, they would not be implemented until the end of 2000 at the earliest. Moreover, the emphasis on tailoring regulations to fit national circumstances and corporate strategies threatened to conflict with the post-crisis call to increase transparency, apply universal rules and maintain a level playing field. Some observers even questioned whether international banks would reach final agreement on the proposed standards (*Economist*, 16 October 1999: 8).

Bailing the Private Sector In

The Asian crises not only raised questions about the management of risk in an environment of liberalised capital movements, but also about how costs should be shared when things go wrong in the international financial system. In particular, critics from the left and the right alike asserted that private sector actors, particularly those responsible for short-term capital movements, were not bearing their share of the adjustment costs that the crises generated. Private sector actors were perceived to have benefited from an internationalisation of moral hazard – as beneficiaries of official bailouts they did not suffer negative consequences when risky investments soured. No consensus emerged on whether the hedge funds in particular were a major cause of the crisis, and whether their activities should be limited.[12] However, almost universal agreement existed among official participants on the desirability of extending the principle of greater transparency to private sector actors, and of requiring private sector actors to participate in rescue efforts through rolling over existing loans or extending new credits.

As Callaghy illustrates (chapter 10), the coordination of negotiations on debt rescheduling in East Asia has been much more complicated than in some previous exercises where governments were in debt primarily to official creditors. Within the region, the structure of debt varied considerably. In Korea, most of the debt was owed by domestic financial institutions to their international counterparts. In Indonesia, on the other hand, most of the debt had been contracted directly between domestic firms and foreign private financial institutions (although the Indonesian case was unusual in East Asia in that it also involved a substantial quantity of official debt). Not surprisingly, a roll-over of the Korean debt was easier to arrange, although even that required substantial pressure from the US government.

Private banks, not surprisingly, have resisted efforts to involve them in formal arrangements for debt rescheduling. The private sector was pressured to contribute to the IMF's new contingent credit line. The Japanese government proposed that new IMF programs should be made conditional on the private sector's maintaining existing levels of exposure and/or providing new roll-over loans, and that with IMF approval countries in crisis might declare a temporary moratorium on external debt (Ministry of Finance 1999b). Given these complexities and the differing views of governments of industrialised economies, however, it is likely that negotiations for private sector participation in bailouts will continue to occur primarily on an *ad hoc* basis.

Regional Responses

The credibility of the principal regional institutions – the Association of South-East Asian Nations (ASEAN) and the Asia–Pacific Economic Cooperation (APEC) grouping – was seen, perhaps unfairly, as being damaged by their ineffective response to the crises that beset their members in 1997. 'Unfairly' because, in an integrated global financial system, the limits to effective regional action are readily apparent.[13]

By far the most controversial of the regional initiatives was a proposal from Taiwan and Japan for the establishment of an Asian Monetary Fund. The intention of the proposed fund (which, in the Japanese version, was to have capital of $US100 billion) was to provide quick-disbursing, low-conditionality assistance to economies whose currencies were under speculative attack. The initial proposal was killed, however, by opposition from the US government that saw it as, at worst, weakening the authority of the IMF or, at best, sending mixed signals to countries about the need to reform domestic institutions.

Although much talk has occurred on the need for a regional response to the crises, little analysis has taken place of what action might most appropriately be taken at the regional level. For country groups that are engaged in liberalising capital and labour as well as trade flows, such as Australia and New Zealand, monetary cooperation might be a logical response to problems generated by closer economic integration, just as the creation of the Single Internal Market encouraged European Union members to agree on monetary union.

Beyond these 'natural' areas for closer monetary cooperation, difficult questions arise when considering 'regional' initiatives. What is the appropriate geographical definition of the region? ASEAN has been cooperating increasingly with China, Korea and Japan in 'ASEAN Plus' meetings. But if the region is to be built around that grouping, not only will Australia and New Zealand be excluded but so too will Taiwan. Who will contribute the funds and who will set the rules? Clearly, the countries best placed to contribute funds are China, Japan and Taiwan. But Taiwanese participation is very unlikely to be acceptable to China. And China is similarly likely to be unhappy about contributing to any fund that will be largely controlled by Japan. Who will enforce conditionality on any borrowings from the fund? One of the great advantages of having the IMF impose conditions for economic restructuring is that no government has to take immediate blame for IMF policies (even if the US is often considered to be behind them). But a regional fund, controlled by the largest economies, has the potential to generate enormous political embarrassment. Could Japan effectively impose conditionality on Indonesia, for example, or Singapore on Malaysia?

It seems unlikely that the proposals for an Asian Monetary Fund will be revived in their original form. Instead, the Japanese government, under heavy criticism for its failure to revive its own economy as a locomotive of growth for the region, has implemented a number of bilateral programs with the most seriously affected economies, and is working on regional initiatives through the Asian Development Bank. The Japanese government's New Miyazawa Plan, announced in October 1998, commits up to two trillion yen in assistance to other Asian economies. The Export-Import Bank of Japan will handle most of the medium- and long-term assistance, some of which will take the form of export credits tied to the purchase of Japanese goods and services. It will also provide assistance in the form of funding, capital investment and guarantees to financing schemes such as equity and debt funds that invest in Asian private sector enterprises. This funding will include working capital to facilitate the restructuring of private sector enterprises. The MOF is coordinating the short-term assistance; this includes Japanese government guarantees of borrowing undertaken by governments and their agencies in the crisis economies (Castellano 1999). In addition, the

Miyazawa funds are financing an 'Asian Currency Crisis Support Facility' within the Asian Development Bank (Ministry of Finance 1999a).[14] The economic crisis has undoubtedly drawn East Asian economies together. Their increasing solidarity rests not just on shared perceptions that the conditionality of the IMF programs was unnecessarily harsh. It also stems from the perception that they do not have an effective voice in the governance of the monetary system. One role that a regional organisation could play, therefore, is representational. However, there is uncertainty over which institution could most effectively represent regional interests. All the original five ASEAN economies apart from the Philippines, as well as Australia, China and Korea, were members of G–22, a grouping of self-styled 'systematically significant economies' established in Washington in April 1998. The G–22, however, died an early death.[15] Another grouping, the Manila Framework Group, originated in a meeting of officials from most APEC countries in November 1997, and has lobbied for reforming the system to enable speedy mobilisation of funds in the event of crisis, and for more systematic monitoring of economies on a regional level. The Group links the East Asian, North American and Oceanic members of APEC, but excludes Taiwan. This exclusion, coupled with the inclusion of Canada and the US, raises questions of the group's utility as a regional representative. A couple of years after the onset of the crises, the issue of effective representation for East Asia in the governance of the international monetary system remains unresolved.

Probably the most feasible outcome from greater collaboration at the regional level on financial issues is for more systematic monitoring of conditions. Neighbours are comparatively well-placed to observe conditions across their borders and, given the risk of contagion effects, have a powerful incentive to apply peer pressure to ensure that other governments act with appropriate rectitude. The new collaboration among ASEAN finance ministers and central bankers in the region provides channels for monitoring and persuading.

Conclusion

The Asian financial crisis resulted from the sudden flight of large amounts of international capital from developing countries that lacked adequate systems of prudential regulation, and whose foreign exchange rates proved disastrously brittle. The crisis demonstrated that even in countries that had balanced rapid growth with macroeconomic stability, reliance on mobile foreign capital, particularly short-term loans, entailed major risks. Panic-stricken contagion spread that risk throughout Asia, threatened the financial systems of economies elsewhere, and slowed world economic growth. Unlike the crises of the 1980s, the East Asian crises occurred in a period of strong growth of the US and European economies and after the banks of most industrialised economies had strengthened their capital base. The Asian crisis was not severe enough to rattle Wall Street or the City of London.

Whether the contemporary global financial system, with its huge flows of short-term capital, is more susceptible to panics and crises than in the past is debatable (see Bordo & Eichengreen 1999). A couple of years after the Asian crisis broke out it is clear, however, that it has differed in several ways from most that preceded it. Despite the relatively strong macroeconomic fundamentals of the Asian economies, the severity of the crisis was much greater than in previous episodes since the introduction of floating exchange rates – and indeed severer than a typical crisis in less-developed economies in the pre-1914 era. The fall in output in the worst-affected Asian economies was two to three times greater than the average in previous crises (Bordo & Eichengreen 1999). Further, because of the high leverage of corporations in most of the crisis economies, the Asian crisis was unusual in two other interrelated dimensions: the extent of corporate distress and of banking sector problems. The ratio of non-performing loans to GDP in the Asian crisis economies was substantially larger than in the Latin American crises of the 1980s or the Mexico crisis in 1995 (Claessens, Djankov & Klingebiel 1999: Figures 1, 5). But surprisingly, given the depth of the Asian crisis, the initial recovery occurred faster than in most other recent crises. Unlike Mexico's bounce-back from 1995, the initial Asian recovery depended to a far lesser extent on export earnings (export volumes increased from the crisis economies in 1998 but were offset by a decline in terms of trade).

If the crisis persists long enough to break up entrenched bureaucratic and business interests, yet not so long as to devastate the region's economies, it may be recalled as a turning-point, a crucial and possibly salutary node in the punctuated equilibrium of regional development. Even then, it will probably be some years before we can tell if the region is converging, for better or worse, toward an Anglo-American pattern of financial and corporate regulation, or if the world of comparative capitalism will remain as diverse as ever. The absence of well-defined laws and procedures for bankruptcy in many of the crisis economies has hindered restructuring at the corporate level, therefore the anticipated boom in mergers and acquisitions did not materialise. Substantial volumes of foreign direct investment did flow into Korea (whose government moved to reverse a previously unwelcoming climate) and Thailand, but political uncertainties in Indonesia and Malaysia made investors reticent about those countries.

Less than two years after the crisis broke out, the impetus for reform seemed to wane as growth resumed. The domestic recession, combined with significant devaluations, brought a dramatic turnaround in the balance of trade. In 1998 imports collapsed, but a year later exports began to pick up. Foreign exchange reserves were rapidly rebuilt; currencies regained a substantial portion of the value lost in 1997.

Little fundamental change has occurred in the political systems whose weaknesses contributed to economic vulnerability. In Thailand and particularly in Korea, the emerging crisis was a factor in the election of leaders committed to serious reform, but even they faced daunting resistance as unemployment mounted and entrenched interest groups faced the prospect of losing their privileged access to capital. As economic conditions eased and new elections loomed, the temptation to pull back from reform grew. The generally acknowledged need to stimulate local economies, resuscitate loans to small companies and strengthen social support networks to deal with unemployment, somewhat perversely presented politicians with new opportunities to gain credit for distributing largesse. And, again somewhat perversely, the tasks that the state inevitably had to assume in taking over bankrupt financial institutions and in promoting corporate restructuring enhanced its role in the crisis economies.

Lack of progress in corporate reform reflected not only the economic magnitude of the task but also the conflicting political imperatives faced by governments. At least in the short run, the crisis did not strengthen party discipline or bring to power new parties based on social groups committed to reform. While the democratic character of the post-crisis political systems of Korea and Thailand may have helped them cope with promoting stabilisation and recovery (Rodrik 1999b), the systems are still vulnerable to the indecision and immobility that contributed to the crises.

The Asian financial crisis was of sufficient gravity that, in the words of Benjamin J. Cohen (chapter 9), it 'provided one of those rare watershed moments when conventional wisdom could be seriously challenged'. In the short term, crisis-hit countries and the international community undertook a number of reforms to deal with the effects of the crisis and reduce the risk of recurrence. Significant progress occurred in increasing the volume of financial data available and the speed with which the data is disseminated. Governments in the region and international institutions such as the IMF took steps to improve the transparency and accountability of their regulatory operations. In many countries, financial regulators gained increased independence, and governments committed themselves to international standards of accounting and auditing. Governments devoted substantial resources to recapitalising depleted banking systems and to stimulating local economies. The IMF promised to provide contingent credit to sound economies and to tailor adjustment packages to individual cases in future cases of financial crisis.

Yet the numerous technical improvements at the international level were not matched by fundamental structural revisions. On each of the major structural issues the government of Japan, many European governments and the affected Asian economies called for changes, but ran into doughty resistance from entrenched ideologies and interests in the United States, the United Kingdom and the IMF. Anglo-American investors interpreted the crisis as proof of the corruption and incompetence of Asian governments rather than as evidence of the need to redesign the architecture of global finance to reduce volatility and risk. The Japanese government continued to press the case for reforms but, given the structural and cyclical weaknesses of the Japanese economy, lacked the confidence, commitment and heft to effect fundamental change.

Thus, while economists and governments vigorously debated alternatives to existing arrangements in the international financial system, no consensus developed on issues such as the desirability of exchange rate bands (as favoured by the European and Japanese governments). Consequently, despite the wide-ranging discussion of possible reforms to the global financial architecture, the changes agreed have been modest. Proposals to create an Asian Monetary Fund fell on stony soil. The US dollar remained the principal reserve asset; holdings of Japanese yen and the new euro remained limited. Piecemeal adoption of capital controls was widespread, but no country rushed to join Malaysia in adopting and attempting to legitimate a comprehensive system of controls.

Two years after the outbreak of the financial crisis, the Asian economies exhibited moderate cyclical recovery but limited financial restructuring and regulatory reform. The leading financial nations and institutions have not been strongly pressured to promote fundamental change in the global financial architecture. Political reform of prudential supervision and corporate governance in Asia, as elsewhere, is a slow, painful and iterative process. In the meantime, the transformation and expansion of the international financial system proceeds apace. The resulting strains and crises may yet place the redesign of the global financial architecture on the international agenda.

CHAPTER 2

Capital Flows and Crises

Stephen Grenville[1]

There are many things that went wrong for the countries caught up in the Asian crisis of 1997, but of the myriad causes two clear central problems can be identified – the fatal combination of large and volatile international capital flows, interacting with fragile domestic financial sectors.This chapter will focus on the first of these issues, international capital flows.

International flows are now centre-stage in the international economic policy debate, certainly a higher profile than capital flows usually have. Traditionally, the focus has been on their real sector counterparts – the savings/investment balance and the current account surpluses and deficits. Both theory and practical policy-making often assume that these are the 'movers' of the action, with capital flows largely a passive, accommodating residual. But the Asian crisis suggests that the action may be in the capital flows themselves. The capital flows were certainly excessive in the sense that they were greater than could be absorbed (that is, the capital flows were substantially larger than the current account deficits: see Figure 2.1). The capital inflows into Indonesia, Malaysia, the Philippines and Thailand in the five years 1990–94 were twice as large as the current account deficits (Calvo & Goldstein 1996: 125). Capital inflows into Thailand in 1996, for example, were equal to 13 per cent of GDP. The 'excess' flows increased the foreign exchange reserves of the recipient country, in effect, being recycled back to the capital-exporting countries. But in the process they made the normal cycle in the recipient country much worse, providing the funding to make the expansion phase of the cycle stronger and longer, driving up domestic demand and asset prices. While there were both 'push' and 'pull' factors for the capital flows, it is clear that the flows were not simply a passive

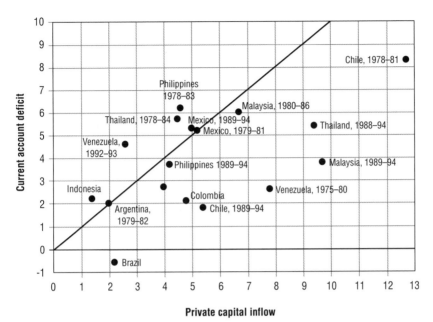

Figure 2.1 Capital inflows and current account deficits
Source: World Bank (1997: 243)

accommodating force responding to fundamental economic factors in the capital-importing countries.

First, we will look quickly at the broad facts.

Two things stand out from the picture shown in Table 2.1. First is the extraordinary increase in capital flows, starting in 1990, the increase being truly phenomenal in Asia. By the mid 1990s developing countries were taking 40 per cent of global foreign direct investment (compared with 15 per cent in 1990) and accounted for 30 per cent of global portfolio equity flows (compared with 2 per cent at the start of the decade) (World Bank 1997: 9). The second feature is the volatility of the flows, even in these multi-year averages.[2] Following the Latin American debt crisis of 1982, inflows to that region turned into outflows nearly as large, which were sustained until the end of the decade.

Just as the law begins with a presumption of innocence, economics begins with a presumption that market outcomes will be beneficial: there is an *a priori* case that international capital flows are a Good Thing. Financial flows supplement domestic saving, allowing more investment in those countries where returns are highest; they buffer the variations over time between exports and imports; foreign direct investment brings the advantages of technological transfer; savers can gain from diversifi-

Table 2.1   Capital flows to emerging markets (annual averages, $US billion)

	1977–82	1983–89	1990–94	1995	1996	1997
All emerging markets						
Total net capital inflows	30.5	8.8	120.8	192.0	240.8	173.7
Net foreign direct investment	11.2	13.3	46.2	96.0	114.9	138.2
Net portfolio investment	–10.5	6.5	61.1	23.5	49.7	42.9
Other*	29.8	–11.0	13.5	72.5	76.2	–7.3
By region						
Asia	15.8	16.7	40.1	95.8	110.4	13.9
Western Hemisphere	26.3	–16.6	40.8	35.7	80.5	91.1
Other	–11.6	8.7	39.9	60.5	50.0	68.8

Notes: * Includes bank lending
1977–89 figures exclude economies in transition and some Middle Eastern
emerging markets
Sources: IMF (1995: 33; 1998a: 13)

cation; and, to complete the case for free capital flows, we should record
the argument that even speculative capital flows can serve a beneficial
purpose.

Perhaps the classic model for the beneficial operation of capital flows
is illustrated by Singapore in the 1970s and 1980s. The flows were very
large – averaging around 10 per cent, in some years 15 per cent, of GDP.
They were used to substantially increase the rate of investment (that is,
not for consumption), and there was a substantial technological transfer
that accompanied the foreign direct investment which dominated the
flows. Following the 'stages of development' academic literature, we can
see these flows being used to partially fund the catch-up as Singapore
moved towards the technological frontier and its living standards rose to
equal those of the industrialised Western countries. This sustained
increase in living standards is confirmation that the combination of
application of capital and education produced very large and sustainable increases in production per head.[3] In a mutually reinforcing
process, the profit opportunities fostered the development of the institutional channels which, at the same time, facilitated the capital flows.[4]

This experience might give some clues to why these flows occurred
more generally, why there was a huge increase in the 1990s, and what
role capital flows played in the subsequent Asian crisis. There are two
broad groupings of factors involved:

- the presence of abnormal profit opportunities as these countries
  moved towards the technological frontier;
- an institutional structure which facilitates the flows of capital.

Profit Differentials

The countries of Asia, with their high rates of growth, provided high profit levels and many opportunities for profitable investment. Expected returns on equity in emerging markets were consistently higher than those in mature markets and their volatility was slightly lower, indicating high risk-adjusted returns (IMF 1998a: 32). Equity and stock prices were also performing strongly (IMF 1998a: 38).

Growth and foreign investment certainly went hand-in-hand, although it might be noted that there was a stronger relationship in the 1980s than in the 1990s (see, for example, BIS 1998a: 36). As well as these potential returns, there was also a question of exchange rate expectations: we will return to this issue when we look at reasons for the volatility of flows. For the moment, it is enough to record that there were *ex post* large excess returns on investment in the emerging Asian markets, taken as a whole.

While it might seem that the main action in terms of profit differentials would come from the great opportunities in the capital-receiving countries, it seems that quite a bit of the action – at least in the variability of the flows – came from changes in interest rates and exchange rates in the *capital-supplying countries* – 'push' factors rather than 'pull' factors. A powerful force encouraging greater flows was the lower interest rates in most developed countries in the early 1990s (US interest rates fell by 200 basis points between 1991 and 1993). The low rates made some investors search out higher returns overseas and, in seeking higher returns, they were ready to accept greater risks. So pervasive was this new attitude that spreads on Brady bonds were bid down sharply in the early 1990s.

As the decade progressed, an important source of capital flow was Japan. Not only was it a large saver, but the drawn-out recession meant that interest rates were extremely low (reaching 0.5 per cent) during most of the 1990s. Much of this capital flow went initially to the United States but, with the size of the US current account deficit set by the savings/investment balance, the extra inflows were recycled and, in effect, funded the outflows to emerging countries. The interest differential between major industrial countries and emerging countries was greatest for Japan, hence the rise of the 'yen-carry' trade – borrowing at low interest rates in yen and on-lending at high returns in other currencies, particularly in Asia. When local-currency borrowing rates were around 20 per cent (for example, in Indonesia), yen-based interest rates seemed extraordinarily attractive.[5]

There was another important structural change in Japan which began in the late 1980s and accelerated in the first half of the 1990s. With the very rapid and sustained appreciation of the yen, Japanese manufacturers recognised that they needed to transfer a large proportion of Japan's manufacturing production (particularly at the low end of the technology spectrum) to the lower labour-cost countries of Asia. This was a fundamental factor in driving the increase in foreign direct investment to the region.[6]

Was 'push' or 'pull' more important? In a structural sense, the high-profit 'pull' of capital-receiving countries was clearly fundamental. But short-term variation (surges and reversals) was often triggered by events in world markets. A number of researchers have found a close relationship between interest rate movements in the capital-exporting countries and capital flows (World Bank 1997: 81–3). The rise in US interest rates in early 1994 was an important trigger in the Mexican problems, and the strengthening of the yen in May–June 1997 was a factor in questioning the continuing profitability of the yen carry.

Institutional Structure

We noted earlier that profit opportunities in emerging countries were probably greater in the 1980s than in the 1990s, yet the surge of capital did not come until 1990. This would suggest that, while relative profit prospects were important, other factors were also involved. This section explores the importance of the institutional channels of transmission: did the institutions exist to facilitate, in a fairly frictionless way, flows which were attracted by the high profit opportunities? This is a chicken-and-egg issue: as the capital flowed, it encouraged the further development of financial infrastructure. In the ten years between 1985 and 1994, for example, the combined market capitalisation of the eighteen major developing countries in the International Finance Corporation Emerging Markets Index increased by a factor of thirteen. This process was spurred by greater knowledge about the countries. One measure of this was the increase in formal credit ratings given by major agencies: eleven countries had ratings in 1989; by 1997 the number had risen to over fifty (IMF 1997: 244).

Part of the increase in the 1990s reflects the conclusion of the Latin American debt crisis of the 1980s, marked by the issue of Brady bonds in 1989. With those, previous debt was settled in a way that could give new investors confidence that their debts would be honoured. Not only did Brady bonds settle the long-standing debt problems from the 1982 crisis, they also signalled that the authorities in capital-exporting countries (particularly the United States) might help to sort out problems. This would have given institutional investors some comfort.

Table 2.2 Assets of institutional investors, 1980–95

	1980	1988	1990	1991	1992	1993	1994	1995
Total ($US billion)	2454	7466	12 347	13 840	14 687	16 805	18 217	20 641
Total (% of GDP)								
Canada	35.2	52.2	60.3	66.9	72.6	81.2	85.6	89.2
Germany	20.3	37.1	39.5	37.4	37.5	42.5	44.9	48.9
Japan	23.1	50.3	77.9	75.6	79.1	84.1	85.2	87.0
UK	64.1	118.3	117.5	129.7	143.3	175.2	156.1	176.0
US	59.3	88.1	118.7	128.3	132.8	141.4	141.7	158.6

Sources: IMF (1995: 166; 1998a: 184) Figures from 1990 onwards include other forms of institutional saving outlined in IMF 1998a and include figures for France and Italy. See also BIS (1998a: 84)

One oft-cited reason for the increase in capital flows in the 1990s was the reduction in various forms of capital controls in the emerging countries. This must have been a factor,[7] but a number of the countries had an accommodating attitude to many forms of capital flows well before the 1990s (Indonesia, for example, had had essentially open capital markets since 1970).

While all of these factors played a part, the dominant new factor of the 1990s was the greatly increased importance of institutional funds managers.

With an annual increase of around $US1000–2000 billion in the portfolios of institutional investors during the 1990s, there was clearly great potential to fund flows to emerging markets, when attention turned to them. And turn to them it did. Not only were there big increases in these funds, but during the 1990s they became more focused on the need for portfolio diversification and shifted from almost no exposure to emerging countries to having significant exposure (although still substantially less than most rules of thumb for portfolio diversification would suggest).[8] At the general level, we can see the increase in international integration from measures of cross-border transactions in bonds and equities. For the United States, these were equal to less than 10 per cent of GDP in 1980, were around 100 per cent by 1989 and 200 per cent by 1997 (IMF 1998a: 187). Another general measure: non-resident holdings of US public debt were around 15 per cent of total in the 1980s, but 40 per cent by 1997 (World Bank 1997: 75; BIS 1998a: 89; IMF 1998a: 185).

In addition to institutional investors, banks have become more internationalised and are readier to lend to emerging countries. The high

42   STEPHEN GRENVILLE

Table 2.3   International bank and bond finance for five Asian countries[a]
($US billion)

	1990–94	1995 Q1 –1996 Q3	1996 Q4 –1997 Q3	1997 Q4	1998 Q1
		at annual rates		at actual rates	
Net inter-bank lending	14	43	11	–31	–31
Bank lending to non-banks	2	15	11	–1	–4
Net bond issuance	3	17	32	1	–2
Total	19	75	54	–31	–37

Notes: [a] Indonesia, Korea, Malaysia, the Philippines and Thailand
Sources: BIS (1998b, 1998a)

profile of the mutual funds, particularly the hedge funds, may distract attention from the central role of the banks. We will see that the bank flows were not only large, but very volatile.

Variability

While the general case in favour of capital flows is a powerful one, the practical problem is their variability – the surges and reversals. There has always been variation in capital flows as relative interest rates changed during the cycle, as profit opportunities opened up and were competed away, and in response to general factors of confidence and exchange rate expectations. However, for the most part, the variability is not enormous. For example, even when international financial markets lost confidence in the Australian dollar in the mid 1980s (the 'Banana Republic' episode), the exchange rate reacted significantly but capital continued to flow to Australia – enough, in fact, to fund a larger current account deficit as the crisis proceeded. The recent experience in Asia has been very different, with strong surges and major reversals of the flows.[9]

Worth noting is the different behaviour between banks and institutional investors, on the one hand, and foreign direct investment, on the other. In this episode, foreign direct investment has proven to be the most resilient inflow and bank inflows the most flighty (World Bank 1997: 31). This accords with the presumption that direct investment is harder to reverse and is more focused on the fundamentals.

It was the banks which reversed their positions dramatically as the crisis broke: having averaged $US16 billion annual inflow to the five troubled Asian countries, the flow rose to $US58 billion for most of 1995

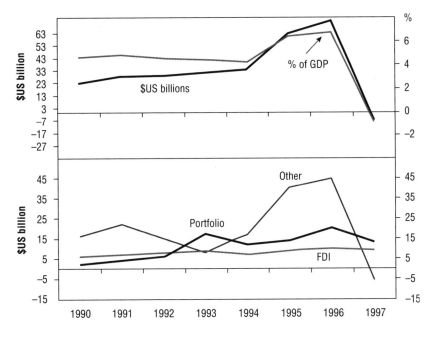

Figure 2.2 Asian private capital flows prior to the crisis
Source: IMF (1998a)

and 1996, fell to an annual rate of $US22 billion in the last quarter of 1996 and for most of 1997, and in the last quarter of 1997 and the first quarter of 1998 recorded an outflow of over $US75 billion (BIS 1998a: 122). This might give the first clue to reasons for the much sharper variation in flows in the 1990s. Not only did these institutional developments mean that the volume of capital flows increased but, with the greatly increased importance of portfolio and banking flows, the nature and volatility of capital flows changed.

This section argues that the volatility of flows was a product of:

- the tiny size of the financial markets in the emerging countries, relative to the capital-exporting countries. Size, or relative size, does matter. Minor portfolio adjustments for fund managers were large changes for the recipient countries;
- a lack of information and understanding about the emerging markets, which meant that opinion was fickle and not well anchored by the fundamentals;
- risk premiums that do not seem to follow a monotonic process, increasing steadily as risk increases. Rather, risk seems to be more like a binary (on/off) process;

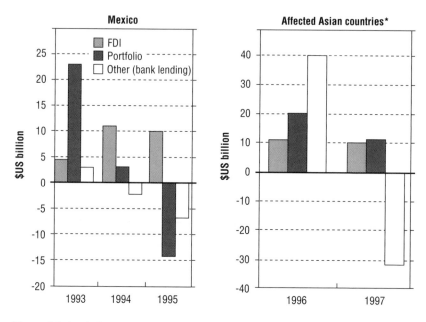

Figure 2.3 Capital flow reversals
Note: *Indonesia, Korea, Malaysia, Philippines and Thailand
Source: IMF (1998a)

- the state of transition in emerging economies, which was such that it is not sensible to think of capital flow volatility as an equilibrium process, with profit expectations continuously equilibrated across international markets. The disequilibrium manifested most clearly in the exchange rate – what Obstfeld (1998: 6) calls 'an open economy's most important price'. This central linking price, at the heart of cross-border profit calculations, was uncertain and unanchored – it could shift sharply, and there were no strong forces to return it to its starting-point. As exchange rate expectations changed, capital flows responded strongly.

Relative Size

The recipients of capital inflows were small relative to the size of the flows. While net capital inflows into the United States were over $US180 billion (measured as the sum of foreign direct investment, portfolio flows and other), that figure was little more than twice the size of the flows to Indonesia, Korea, Malaysia, the Philippines and Thailand. Compare this to the size of those economies, credit systems and share

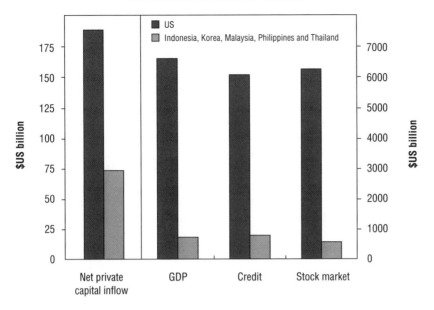

Figure 2.4 Output, credit and equity capitalisation, 1996

markets: the United States dwarfs those countries by a ratio of around ten to one.

The problem has been described by the BIS as: 'This asymmetry, coupled with the ebbs and flows that have historically characterised portfolio investment in emerging countries, highlights the potential for instability as a marginal portfolio adjustment by the investor can easily amount to a first-order event for the recipient' (BIS 1998a: 90). Also: 'The sums involved were relatively small from the perspective of individual investors, even if of dangerous size from the perspective of the recipients' (BIS 1998a: 169).

Information

Part of the explanation for the reversals is the paucity of investors' information about the emerging markets. Usually, their knowledge was so superficial that it could be (and was) overwhelmed by the arrival of relatively small amounts of new information. More importantly, investors without their own knowledge base simply followed the herd. In such a world, it is rational for any individual player to shift with the herd when new perceptions arrive. Whatever the fundamentals, when the herd is running you run with it. In its usual understated way, the BIS observed that 'highly correlated strategies across different players may have contributed to an aggravation of asset price movements' (BIS 1998a: 95). The informational problems were compounded by the biased and ill-founded nature of much of the information and commentary. In hindsight, it might seem surprising that there were not more pundits highlighting the excessive nature of the flows and the domestic policy-making deficiencies of the recipient countries. But who would these pundits be? To policy officials in the recipient countries, the flows (and the development of sophisticated financial sectors) were a sign of progress and modernity: who would want to express doubts about that? In academic circles, the dominant paradigm was 'efficient markets': who would be bold enough to question the outcome of the market? Any unexplained differential was passed off as a 'risk premium' – the academic 'fifth ace' that could square any circle and explain any regression result, no matter how different from prior results. In the financial markets themselves, who was going to bite the hand that fed them (see Fox 1998)? Some subsequent commentary suggests naiveté among investors: they 'received repeated assurances that the financial sector was well supervised ... and that there would be no changes in exchange rate policy' (IMF 1998a: 41). In hindsight, the degree of ignorance was so great as to border on the comic. *Business Week* (22 September 1998) said of a fund manager's response to the Russians' halting of trade in their domestic debt market: 'Nobody in the history of the world has ever done anything this foolish'. Some sense of history!

At the same time, it should be noted that information that was available was not used. The BIS banking data provided a comprehensive view on what turned out to be the most volatile element of the flows, but the existence of the data was either unknown or ignored (for an exception, see Radelet 1995). As far as the outcome is concerned, however, unused information was as irrelevant as unavailable information.

The Behaviour of Risk Premiums

The process of assessing and reassessing risk is captured, to some extent, in the pricing of emerging market debt, but this does not capture the full extent of the problem. As Sachs (1997) observed: 'euphoria turned to panic without missing a beat'. One of the characteristics of capital flows in the crisis was their reversal – it was not simply a matter of the capital-receiving countries being forced to pay somewhat more for the capital, because of a changing perception of risk. New flows dried up and existing capital fled, not to be lured back at any price. Considerations of risk seem to be a binary (on/off) process. In part, this was a rational response by lenders. Even well-run enterprises had their profit

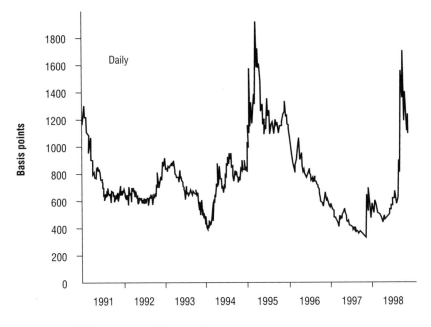

Figure 2.5 EMBI spread to US treasuries

(and repayment) prospects radically altered by the new environment of high interest rates, massive falls in exchange rates and shattered growth prospects. Once interest rates rose sharply, a different calculus became relevant – the credit risk overwhelmed any risk-premium calculation. Credit lines were cut. This follows the theory of Stiglitz and Weiss (1981), that when interest rates rise sharply, lenders recognise that the only borrowers who are willing to pay the high rates are those who do not intend to pay back.

The process was not helped by the behaviour of credit rating agencies, who went along with the general pre-crisis euphoria and exacerbated the turnaround of opinion by substantial downgradings after the crisis had occurred. As the downgrades shifted some financial instruments below investment grade, institutions with portfolio constraints on asset quality were forced to sell at any price. The fact that many of these portfolios were judged month by month, or even daily, led to strong short-termism.

It may also be useful to recall the old distinction between risk and uncertainty. It was the latter (whose characteristic is unpredictability) rather than the former that was relevant, and perhaps we should not be surprised that uncertainty premiums can shift dramatically.

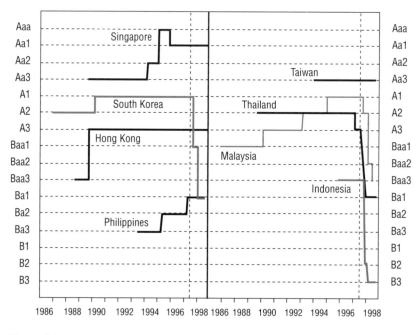

Figure 2.6 Asian credit ratings, 1986–98

A Disequilibrium Process

The capital-receiving emerging countries were being transformed so fast that it is neither sensible nor realistic to see the process in terms of the usual textbook notions of returns equilibrated at the margin and smooth allocation of resources, particularly capital. Systems were in flux, and production functions were changing continuously. This manifested in various ways, but three examples will illustrate the issue.

The first example of apparent disequilibrium in capital flows was identified two decades ago – the Feldstein/Horioka paradox (1980) – that there seemed to be too much correlation between domestic saving and investment rates in individual countries. The implication was that capital flows between countries were smaller than would occur in a well-integrated world. This perhaps offers another clue to the puzzle. It is not so much that capital flows rose suddenly to achieve abnormally high levels, but that they were less than optimal earlier, so the big increase was a move towards a more normal or equilibrium situation.[10] These are asset or stock equilibriums. When these ill-defined and changeable temporary equilibria are displaced by a shift of confidence, the flow required to

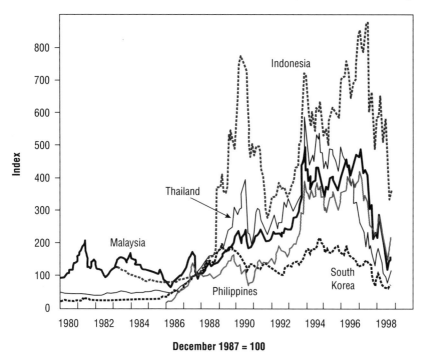

Figure 2.7 Asian share markets, 1980–98
Source: Datastream

shift from the old to the new stock equilibrium may be very large and disruptive.

Second, profits (or even expected profits) were not equilibrated across countries. Throughout the 1980s excess profits had been earned, illustrated by equity returns and high domestic real interest rates in Indonesia, Korea and Thailand.

The high interest rates were imposed by the authorities to rein in very dynamic economies, where many investors wanted to borrow to exploit the profit opportunities (interest rates were not high to support exchange rates, as is sometimes claimed; exchange rates were under upward pressure for most of the period). The capital flows which occurred were not sufficient (or could not be absorbed quickly enough) to exploit all the opportunities. There was a widespread belief, based on pre-crisis experience, that any new factory or office building would prove profitable because of the tremendous growth of the economies. No matter how much capital flowed, marginal investors did not feel that their actions had taken the last abnormal profit opportunity and that a 'normal profit' equilibrium had been reached. Investors could not tell if

Table 2.4   Average real interest rates[a]

	1980–89	1990–98
South Korea	4.6	7.7
Thailand	6.1	5.0
Indonesia[b]	5.3	6.6
Malaysia	2.7	3.0
Philippines	–6.2	2.4

Notes: [a] Average of end-month short-term real interest rates
[b] 1980–89 average for Indonesia starts from 1983.
There are thirteen monthly observations missing over the period
Source: IMF International Financial Statistics

what they were seeing were temporary abnormal profits (in which they should try to get a share of the action), or high return because of high risk. Too many assumed it was the former. To the extent that markets acted to equilibrate returns, they did so by bidding up asset prices, thus reducing the profit return of the investor who paid the higher price. But this was a knife-edge equilibration: as asset prices rose investors extrapolated the rise, so that even if the profit flow on the asset was normal, investors expected to benefit from continuing asset price increases. Investment continued until there was obvious excess capacity, and the bubble burst.

The third manifestation of disequilibrium was in the exchange rate. What is the 'right' exchange rate for a country receiving large capital inflows and likely to receive them for a protracted period of perhaps a decade or more, before investment returns are reduced to 'normal'? This relates to the old issue of the 'transfer problem' – how to bring about the current account deficit that is the real-resources counterpart of the financial capital inflow. For this, the exchange rate probably has to appreciate from its underlying value. But how far? Portfolio equilibrium would suggest that the appreciation must be enough to create the expectation of a subsequent depreciation, at a rate to balance the higher expected returns on domestic, compared with foreign, assets – to balance the differential between the domestic interest rate and the foreign rate. If this view was realistic, we would see a once-off appreciation followed by a drawn-out steady depreciation, at a rate equal to the difference between domestic and foreign interest rates. It hardly needs saying that the implication of an enduring and finely balanced calculus does not fit reality, even remotely. True, exchange rates in the crisis countries were under continual upward pressure in the first half of the

1990s but this was largely resisted (and did not happen much in real terms, via faster domestic inflation). Then, more or less once and suddenly, exchange rates experienced massive falls.

What story fits the facts better? Capital flows involve a foreign exchange risk: even hedging simply shifts the risk to another party. For the period of inflow during the first half of the 1990s, the authorities in the crisis countries maintained fairly fixed exchange rates to stop an overappreciation which would have cut into their international competitiveness and the dynamism of the tradables sector, and made them vulnerable to changes of confidence when markets became concerned about overvaluation. Investors knew this, as did borrowers in these countries, so they were prepared to take the risk of having a foreign exchange exposure without covering it (compare the yen carry), with the view that the exchange rates were more likely to appreciate than depreciate.[11] Herd behaviour was important in the capital surge, as well as in the withdrawals of capital. The smart money went to the crisis countries in response to the profit opportunities and lots of dumb money went along for the ride, financing dubious investment projects. Once there was a change in confidence, there was a rush for the exits. The leverage elements which had built up during the capital-inflow stage made it imperative that positions be unwound quickly when the reversal came – leveraged investors cannot wait for the market to return to its senses, they sell or they are sold. To make matters worse, these forced sales took place in markets which had become illiquid – when no one wants to take on the risks, the price falls a long way. In textbook markets, price falls bring out bargain-hunters; in crisis markets, price falls confirmed the worst fears.

The problem is that asset prices (whether real estate or the exchange rate) are quite random in the short run, and the short run is the investment horizon relevant to fund managers who are judged on their quarter-by-quarter (or month-by-month) performance. In a market dominated by such investors, there are no Friedmanite stabilising speculators to buy when the price falls. Even rational investors join the herd.

While we might be amazed at the extent of the movements in exchange rates (the rupiah fell to less than a fifth of its initial value, which no one at the time thought was significantly overvalued), we should not be surprised by the failure of the portfolio model – or any other model – of exchange rate behaviour. The most basic and central idea in any view relying on the efficient-markets hypothesis is uncovered interest rate parity – that interest rate differentials are the best predictor of exchange rate movements. Despite the most diligent efforts by those who have built models and academic reputations on the efficient-markets hypothesis, the data inconveniently but consistently refutes it.[12]

So is it any surprise that, once fixed exchange rates were dislodged by a combination of large adverse terms-of-trade shifts, modest overappreciation through inflation and adverse international commentary, unanchored rates could swing to absurd values? There were no accepted views on fundamentals. Investors had seen how much the yen/US dollar rate moved during the 1990s in well-understood and deep markets: it is hardly surprising that they would not stand in the way of huge swings in Asian currencies. By the time extrapolative expectations took hold, demand curves for foreign exchange sloped the wrong way: as the price became cheaper, people bought less.

Once this was teamed with large open exposures the fragile financial sectors of the crisis countries collapsed, sometimes under the weight of their open foreign exchange positions, but more often under the collapsing creditworthiness of their commercial sector borrowers (who had large uncovered foreign exchange exposure). This collapse of the financial system interacted with the real economy: even good investment projects turned sour in the face of credit withdrawal and deep economic recession. The rest is history.

Conclusion

More than a century ago, Bagehot observed, 'the same instruments which diffused capital through a nation are gradually diffusing it among nations'. He warned that while 'the effect of this will be in the end much to simplify the problems of international trade ... for the present, as is commonly the case with incipient causes whose effect is incomplete, it complicates all it touches' (Bagehot 1880: 71, quoted in World Bank 1997). This encapsulates a key insight: as countries integrate their domestic financial market with international markets, an eminently desirable process, there is a longish period of transition during which an economy is extremely vulnerable to changes in confidence.

There was plenty of hand-wringing about this issue even before the 1997 crisis. The World Bank summarised the situation:

> The world's financial markets are rapidly integrating into a single global marketplace, and ready or not, developing countries, starting from different points and moving at various speeds, are being drawn into this process. If they have adequate institutions and sound policies, developing countries may proceed smoothly along the road to financial integration and gain the considerable benefits that integration can bring. Most of them, however, lack the prerequisites for a smooth journey, and some may be so ill-prepared that they lose more than they gain from financial integration (World Bank 1997: 1).

Substantial capital inflows to emerging countries were not irrational, unnatural or undesirable. Although there are many benefits from capital flows, their variability is clearly harmful and hard to correct: 'boom and bust cycles are hardly a side-show or a minor blemish on international capital flows: they are the main story' (Rodrik 1998a: 56). As Bhagwati (1998a, 1998b: 14) notes, the 'panics, manias and crashes' that characterise capital flows have no counterpart in trade flows. The question is what to do.

Any policy that attempted to isolate an economy from international capital markets would be costly in terms of forgone growth. The need is to devise an institutional structure which can reap the benefits of capital flows while diminishing the risks to countries whose financial infrastructure is not resilient enough to cope. What needs to change?

One early response was to try to identify some technical deficiency which caused the real world not to mimic the efficient markets of the textbooks, and assume that correcting that would fix the problem. We noted that information deficiencies were one reason why opinions, confidence and critical prices such as the exchange rate were unanchored and subject to violent change. After the Mexican crisis of 1994–95, there was an argument that came very close to saying that if Mexico had revealed its foreign exchange reserve levels more explicitly during 1994, somehow the crisis would have been averted. A variant of this emerged in the early days of the Thai crisis: if only Thailand had revealed its forward foreign exchange position, markets would have operated smoothly to avoid crisis. This seems naive, but we have to be careful in pointing that out: to question the benefits of greater transparency is like arguing against peace, freedom and motherhood. So let me be quick to say that more transparency would help. But it is a different matter, in a world of complex causality, to see that as a fundamental solution. It is hard to explain the extraordinary movements in asset prices in sophisticated markets such as US equities in 1987 and the yen in 1995–98. How much more information is needed to prevent swings of that sort?

A similar fix has been suggested, in the form of elimination of guarantees and moral hazard. We have already noted that many of the so-called guarantees were, more accurately, misassessments by optimistic market players – they were guarantees only in the eyes of investors. Moral hazard is a more believable market deficiency, at least in some cases. For example, financial markets were confident, based on experience, that countries do not devalue or renege on foreign debts while they are under the tutelage of an IMF program. This gave investors in Russia early in 1999, for example, a false sense of security. The answer seems simple: make sure investors lose money from time to time. This, like many solutions, is supported in general but difficult to apply in specific cases. As Soros (1998a) has noted: 'Financial markets ... resent any kind of government interference, but they hold a belief that, if conditions get rough, the authorities will step in'. Once governments have helped, moral hazard is part of investment decisions. Certainly we should try to reduce it by requiring private sector investors to share the burden, but we should not fool ourselves into thinking that moral hazard can be entirely eliminated.

A further variant of the fix-the-market approach suggests that markets were not sufficiently open. In the early days of the Asian crisis, a common argument held that the problem was simple deficiencies in domestic policy-making, for which open capital accounts were the best discipline. There is truth in this argument – countries which do not make policy mistakes certainly stand a better chance of weathering international storms – but it is unrealistic to hope for continuously perfect policies. There must be a framework that can cope with the inevitable imperfections of the policy process. With the crisis much further developed, we can now see that even countries such as Hong Kong with good policies, sound infrastructure and high openness can come under enormous pressure. So even if policy-makers, working as they do in imperfect and politically driven worlds, were able to produce consistently good policies, it is no assurance against volatility in capital flow.

We have to accept that markets, even under as favourable conditions as are likely to be found in the real world, have not and will not consistently act as a smooth, well-informed, far-sighted Walrasian auction process to maximise the benefits and minimise the costs of capital flows. 'Given the troubling way in which economic, political and social factors interact, it is simply not prudent to assume that everything will turn out for the best' (BIS 1998a: 170). While we strive for good policy-making and urge more information disclosure (including by the private sector players in international markets), we need to explore other possibilities.

Part of the problem in coming to grips with these issues has been the insistent voice of an accidental coalition of academics, and vested interests who used the efficient-markets paradigm as an intellectual battering-ram to open new commercial opportunities. The intellectual climate is now shifting. When the doyen of hedge funds, George Soros, describes capital flows as 'a wrecker's ball', we know the debate has changed.

What measures might be explored? We will start with the least controversial possibility. Much of the focus should be on improving prudential measures – the 'rules of the game' governing the financial sector, particularly banks. Much hard work is needed to make existing rules work properly: limiting connected and government-directed lending; getting asset valuations (and hence provisioning) right; and enforcing foreign currency open position limits. The rules need to be reinforced. Banks must be made to take account of their borrowers' overall balance sheet position, so that banks are not brought down, at one remove, by the foreign exchange exposure of their borrowers. Poor credit appraisal was clearly a central factor in the Asian crisis, which has to be addressed. None of this can be done effectively without a good accounting and legal (including bankruptcy) framework and, realistically, none of it will be put in place quickly. That is the rub. It is difficult, perhaps impossible, to have fully effective supervision before financial development occurs, as the markets will be pushing ahead faster than supervisors. The deregulation process is a difficult environment in which to get this right: at the same time that one set of regulations is dismantled, another set (the prudential rules) has to be put in place. Hence the debate about sequencing has an academic ring. We must work hard on the prudential framework. It will be important. But it may not be enough.[13]

When things go wrong, as they will from time to time in even the best-managed system, there must be clear methods of rapid resolution. This should include a readiness to institute standfast and workout arrangements for private debt. Just as bankruptcy arrangements should not be too easily available for resolution of domestic debts, such international standfast and workout arrangements should only be instigated by some internationally endorsed process, for example as part of an IMF standby arrangement. We must be ready to do this promptly when circumstances warrant. Again, textbook ideas have been unhelpful in practice – the idea that private sector borrowers and lenders will work things out satisfactorily has proved naive. The collateral damage is too great. Private sector debt was and is a festering sore which inhibits the return to health of some Asian economies. This is not to argue that the private sector should have been bailed out. Rather, it should have been quickly and decisively bailed in, to bear its full share of the costs of crisis resolution, through standfast and workout arrangements.

Many of these measures will remind lenders of the risks involved. This will raise the cost of borrowing in good times, but that would be no bad thing. In the same vein, the existence of well-defined international standfast and workout arrangements, and collective action clauses in bonds which specify the possibility of workouts, may cause lenders to focus on the possibility of loss, but wouldn't that help the moral hazard problems? If more carefully designed and rigorously enforced prudential controls inhibit some short-term flows, would there be any great loss in that? Clearly, part of the capital surge of the 1990s could have been forgone, with benefit. Is the problem like advertising, that we do not know which part to stop? No. We can see elements – short-term rootless flows – which had minimum benefits and greatest costs. A case can be made that it would have been no great loss if the Asian countries had received only the foreign direct investment flow. Although it is technically true that 'speed doesn't kill – it's the stopping', the problems come from excessive inflows, so if the net result of more rigorous 'rules of the game' is smaller inflows in the boom times that will be a plus. If something has to give way in the 'open economy trilemma' (Obstfeld & Taylor 1997), limiting the variance of capital flow seems a good place to start.

The third and most controversial set of possibilities is those which smack of capital controls. Even here, the debate has shifted. Now, Chilean-type controls seem acceptable in international opinion. These are market-based, up front and *ex ante*, on inflows rather than outflows. Capital controls is still a lively topic of debate. The consensus view is changing, but slowly. Although acknowledging that temporary controls may be required in certain circumstances, the international consensus has a rather disparaging tone. Just as 'real men don't eat quiche', real countries don't resort to capital controls. If such short-term capital controls are a legitimate instrument of policy, we must define more clearly the circumstances and be readier to endorse their use in those conditions.

The alternative to implementing these ideas is inaction, in the hope that the problems will go away or because of some ideological position based on the preservation of market purity. This risks losing the very real benefits of capital flows, if it leads to emerging countries implementing ill-designed measures to isolate themselves from the problems. At the same time, the crisis tarnishes the complex international trading structure and adds to the growing voices damning 'globalisation'. Krugman (1998b) points out that Keynes considered that his interventionist active fiscal proposals were necessary to save the market system. Now, changes are needed in international financial markets to safeguard the continuance of international capital flows, with all the benefits they bring.

CHAPTER 3

The Political Economy of the Asian Financial Crisis: Korea and Thailand Compared

Stephan Haggard and Andrew MacIntyre[1]

Discussion of the causes of Asia's economic crisis has been dominated by a focus on economic, especially international economic, factors. To the extent that attention has been paid to the role of the domestic and the political, it has been in relatively broad terms, such as crony capitalism, weak leadership or autocratic government. Given the spread of the crisis across a range of geographically proximate countries in a relatively short time, emphasis on the role of international capital markets and contagion is certainly not misplaced. Nonetheless, it is at least incomplete and may in fact be misleading. Domestic political factors played an important role in the onset of financial crises in the region and in their initial management.

In particular, we are interested in showing how institutional arrangements constrained the ability of governments to respond to mounting economic policy problems and how this, in turn, contributed to rising uncertainty and ultimately panic among investors. In making this argument, we focus on two new democracies – Thailand and Korea – and the way in which they managed financial sector problems. In varying degrees, institutional arrangements in the two countries rendered them vulnerable to problems of policy incoherence. There was no single common institutional 'problem' at work; rather, different institutional configurations embodied different advantages and disabilities. In Thailand's parliamentary system, the problems were chronic, rooted in a basic constitutional design which generated weak coalition governments and incohesive parties. In Korea's presidential system, the problems were less fundamental and more cyclical, the result of a weakened incumbent and divided ruling party.

Yet despite these weaknesses, the very democratic nature of politics ultimately contributed to self-correction. In Thailand, this went so far as to involve constitutional reform designed, in part, to alter some of the conditions that gave rise to uncertainty in the first place. The democracies stand in sharp contrast to the experiences of authoritarian Indonesia, where a more fundamental process of regime change generated more prolonged uncertainty and a more severe recession.

The Role of Politics in Financial Crises

There are a number of economic factors necessary for the onset of Asia's financial crises. As with Latin America's debt problems in the 1980s, Asia witnessed a dramatic increase in international capital flows in the early 1990s, including not only the mobile portfolio capital of hedge funds and 'speculators', but extensive bank lending as well (Kahler 1998; Institute for International Finance 1999). Further, the maturity profile of the external debt was increasingly skewed toward the short run, particularly in the two cases we examine here, Thailand and Korea. This increase in capital flows was partly the result of an important policy variable. All countries in the region, including Korea and Thailand, had either opened their capital accounts some time earlier or had made moves to do so in recent years. Whatever the merits of capital account liberalisation over the long run – and they are hotly contested – most would agree that the East and South-East Asian countries did not have adequate prudential regulation to manage the inflows that they received. As a result, external crises quickly metastasised into more fundamental banking crises (Kaminsky & Reinhart 1998).

No less important were problems of exchange rate management and various difficulties in the export sectors, which affected the current account. A commitment to fixed or heavily managed exchange rates created vulnerabilities to currency overvaluation, particularly when coupled with an open capital account and a heavy weighting of the currency towards the US dollar at a time when it was rapidly appreciating. When increased export competition from China and Mexico was added to the equation, the potential for serious current account problems became increasingly sharp (Corsetti, Pesenti & Roubini 1998). Some accounts, which we will call 'fundamentalist', put primary emphasis on the unsustainability of current account deficits, but there is ongoing debate on this score and and on important differences between countries. Export growth slowed in all countries in the region in 1996, and Thailand's current account deficit was quite large at the time its crisis broke in 1997. But Korea had deficits which did not deviate substantially from levels that had been financed by private capital inflows in the past. Moreover, recent research suggests that the extent of overvaluation has been exaggerated. Using CPI-deflated trend rates, Chinn (1998) finds overvaluation of only 13 per cent as of May 1997 in Thailand; Korea shows a slight undervaluation using the same measure.

Critics of the fundamentalist view emphasise a further set of factors which all agree operated to some extent: self-fulfilling speculative attacks and contagion (Radelet & Sachs 1998b). Thailand had been hit by speculative attacks at several points before the final crisis in July. Korea was also clearly affected by a chain of events that began with Taiwan's devaluation, which led to the stock market crash in Hong Kong during the week of 20–24 October and an acceleration of foreign withdrawals and refusal to roll over loans in Korea beginning in early November.

With the exception of Krause's (1998) account, the arguments of both the fundamentalists and those emphasising self-fulfilling speculative attacks have not systematically addressed the role of political factors in generating crises. However, as Krause points out, crises typically require a trigger – which may come from uncertainty about the future course of government action. If relevant economic parameters are deteriorating and the likelihood of government taking timely and effective remedial policy action is viewed as low or uncertain, investors have incentives to exit quickly. Uncertainty about the future policy environment can thus be a trigger for financial crises and panics.

Although Korea and Thailand had quite different political systems, both were subject to institutionally induced policy paralysis that affected the perception and behaviour of investors. In Thailand the institutional problems were stark and made it extremely difficult to achieve decisive policy leadership. Thailand's particular combination of parliamentary structure and multiple weak political parties produced a consistent pattern of very shaky and short-lived coalition governments. This produced a heavy bias away from public-goods oriented policies and towards pork-barrel style particularistic policies. Not only did this contribute directly to the accumulation of economic distortions that underlay the outbreak of the crisis in Thailand, it greatly compounded the difficulty of dealing with the crisis once it began. As we will show, divisions within the ruling parliamentary coalition led by Chavalit Yongchaiyudh persistently prevented attempts to tackle mounting problems in the financial sector. The government's vulnerability to defection and coalitional collapse meant that a relatively small group within the government was able to veto plans to move against failing financial institutions. Instead of writing down bad loans and forcing shareholders to accept losses, Thai authorities kept them afloat by pumping in new funds. Not only did this paralysis undermine investor confidence about the government's ability to deal with the country's mounting economic difficulties, it greatly accentuated the country's economic predicament by contributing to rapid money supply growth. An intriguing feature is that not only did the financial crisis lead to the collapse of Chavalit's government, it paved the way for a process of constitutional reform intended to strengthen democracy and to reduce both corruption and the propensity for policy to be captured by narrow sectional interests.

In contrast to Thailand, Korea's political system is not typically considered prone to weak policy leadership. With a fixed term and substantial powers of legislative initiative, the Korean president would appear well-positioned to respond aggressively to potential crises. Moreover, Korea has an electoral and party system which has tended to generate comparatively disciplined, even hierarchical, legislative parties and the Kim Young Sam government enjoyed the benefits of unified government, with a clear majority in the unicameral National Assembly.

However, policy-making in presidential systems depends on whether government is unified or divided, that is, on whether the president's party enjoys a legislative majority or support from a majority coalition, and whether the president and party leadership have control over their own party. If divided government pertains, or if the president's party is internally weak, divided or undisciplined, then presidential systems can produce legislative gridlock.

Korea experienced both patterns in 1997–98. In 1997, Kim Young Sam enjoyed a legislative majority, but his administration fell victim to divisions within the party and ultimately between the executive and the legislature. The source of these divisions was the 'no re-election' rule – a succession struggle within the party for the presidential nomination – and subsequent efforts by both the presidential candidate and the party in the legislature to differentiate itself from a failed incumbent. As the financial crisis unfolded in the second half of the year the government was periodically paralysed, a situation that appeared unlikely to change until after the election. Investors responded accordingly. The significance of these factors was demonstrated clearly when the election re-established a strong executive and produced important policy initiatives.

Thailand

The severe economic crisis that erupted in Thailand in July 1997 with the dramatic devaluation of the baht was unexpected. Nevertheless, a slowdown in the economy and indeed a depreciation of the currency were widely anticipated in the face of mounting economic problems through the 1990s. By late 1996, Thailand was coming off a remarkable economic boom, prolonged by the inflow of foreign capital. Real GDP growth slowed from 8.8 per cent in 1995 to 6 per cent in 1996, paralleled by a sagging stock market. Two issues were of particular concern: the widening current account deficit (growing from an already large 8.1 per cent of GDP in 1995 to 8.4 per cent in 1996) and unease about overborrowing and mismanagement in the financial sector. The deteriorating current account position reflected a number of factors: sustained real currency appreciation, strongly rising real wages, declining demand in key export markets and a realignment of the yen–dollar relationship. In the financial sector, a very rapid expansion of domestic credit was funded by international borrowing (particularly short-term borrowing). By 1996, foreign-funded domestic lending was 1.8 times the size of the country's monetary base. Coupled with this increasingly vulnerable position was a growing perception that banks and finance companies were carrying worrying levels of non-performing loans and that the country's financial authorities were not overseeing the situation effectively. These factors fuelled growing speculation against the baht in the second half of 1996 (Nukul Commission Report 1998; Bhanupong 1998; Warr 1998). Despite mounting concern over the apparent inevitability of some sort of currency depreciation, Thai authorities did very little to address any of these problems, clinging to a doomed strategy of defending the pegged exchange rate – until the dam burst on 2 July 1997.

One of the most striking features of the crisis in Thailand was the government's failure to take effective pre-emptive or remedial action in the face of clear warning signals. The government formed under Chavalit Yongchaiyudh in November 1996 came to power amid much talk of new and strong policy leadership. However, this rhetoric quickly disappeared as it was subject to mounting vilification for immobilism, indecisiveness and corruption. Justified though these criticisms were, they were nothing new. Chavalit's government was no more venal or inept than its predecessors; indeed, part of the difficulty it faced was the accumulated legacy of reforms not made by previous administrations. With slight differences, this characterisation also applies to the democratically elected governments led by Banharn Silapa-archa, Chuan Leekpai and Chatichai Choonhavan. In short, Chavalit's government was fundamentally no different from any of the other elected governments stretching back to the late 1980s. All rested upon shaky multi-party coalition arrangements, all implemented little in the way of major economic reform and all were afflicted by serious and ongoing corruption scandals. The episodes of major policy change in Thailand came during the semi-democratic period in the early and mid 1980s under unelected Field Marshal Prem Tinsulanond and during two brief post-coup caretaker administrations led by the highly technocratic Anand in the 1990s.

This is not an argument that economic governance in Thailand has declined with democratisation; rather, it is an argument that Thailand's constitution and electoral system (until the constitutional overhaul in late 1997) produced serious problems of political leadership and policy-making. The indecisiveness of political leadership in Thailand resulted from the fragmentation of the party system and the tendency to weak coalition governments. With parliamentary majorities constructed of half a dozen parties, each with internal weaknesses, cabinet instability was a chronic problem. As leader of the governing coalition, the prime minister was vulnerable to policy blackmail by coalition partners threatening to defect in pursuit of better deals in another alliance configuration; indeed, all democratically elected governments except the Chatichai government, which fell to a military coup, met their end in this fashion.

The institutional root of these problems was Thailand's combination of a parliamentary structure (in which government rests on party cohesion) and a multi-member electoral system (which undermined party cohesion). As Allen Hicken (1998) has argued, Thailand's multi-member electoral system strongly encouraged candidates to campaign on the basis of individualised strategies rather than on the basis of party label, as they were compelled to differentiate themselves from competitors of the same party. Not only did this create weakly disciplined parties, but the emphasis on candidate-based rather than party-based electoral strategies ensured that politicians strove to deliver selective benefits to voters in their electorate in order to differentiate themselves from their same-party rivals (Cox 1984; Carey & Shugart 1995). This encouraged vote-buying and placed a premium on politicians being able to generate a flow of cash to cover costs while in office.

In short, the logic of the country's electoral system made it all but impossible for politicians to agree to economic reforms if such reforms threatened rent-taking arrangements they had gained for themselves or their key supporters. With weak parties and coalitions, strong action on difficult policy issues – whether exchange rate management or Bangkok's notorious traffic congestion – was always severely undersupplied. We explore these difficulties in the context of the government's management of one critical policy area that fed directly into the crisis – Thailand's ailing financial sector.

Thailand's financial sector began to diversify and deepen rapidly following the financial liberalisation of the late 1980s. An important part of this reform was the creation of the Bangkok International Banking Facility (BIBF) in 1993, which was intended to launch Bangkok as an international financial centre. Given the fixed exchange rate and substantial interest rate differentials, the BIBF functioned in practice to facilitate the inflow of capital from foreign lenders to Thai financial institutions and companies. But the international side was only one part

of the equation. Domestic financial markets were also liberalised to new
entrants, particularly finance companies, without adequate oversight or
prudential regulation. By the second half of 1997, Thailand was beset
with an estimated Bt1 trillion in bad debts held by banks and finance
companies and the government had spent an estimated Bt430 billion in
propping up failing financial institutions (roughly, $US28.6 billion and
$US12.3 billion) (*Bangkok Post*, 12 October 1997, 14 August 1997).

Early warning signs of the problems facing the country's financial
institutions came as far back as 1994 when the Bank of Thailand (the
central bank) began to examine the affairs of a struggling mid-sized
bank, the Bangkok Bank of Commerce (BBC). Extending over several
years, the BBC scandal was clearly important in denting business confidence and the reputation of the central bank in particular. More
important for our purposes, however, is what the BBC saga reveals about
the political constraints on coherent policy-making in Thailand.

After becoming concerned about the situation at BBC in 1994, the
Bank of Thailand failed in its efforts to gain supervisory representation
on BBC's board. As the extent of mismanagement at BBC and its
estimated $US3 billion in non-performing loans became public in mid
1996 following disclosure by the opposition, there was a run on the
bank. Having indulged BBC for an extraordinary period, the central
bank finally stepped in forcefully in May, taking formal control of BBC
as it crashed and its management fled. Ultimately, a total of $US7 billion
was spent to keep BBC afloat. The central bank governor was forced to
resign in disgrace over the episode, but the reputational damage had
been done. In addition to possible impropriety by the central bank
governor, suspicion was directed to several politicians within Prime
Minister Banharn's Chart Thai party, who, it emerged, had been the
beneficiaries of large loans from BBC (*The Nation*, 18 April 1997,
13 March 1997; Pasuk & Baker 1998: 105–10, 259).

In September 1996, Banharn's government collapsed after key coalition partners deserted him. After what was widely regarded as the
country's dirtiest election, and having benefited from large-scale defections from Banharn's Chart Thai party, Chavalit's New Aspiration Party
(NAP) narrowly emerged as the largest party in the parliament. Chavalit
proceeded to construct a six-party coalition comprising most of the
parties from the previous government. Notwithstanding the massive
vote-buying on behalf of his NAP (*Far Eastern Economic Review*, 28 November 1996: 16–22), Chavalit entered government with perhaps the most
promising credentials of any elected Thai government. Banharn's
government (of which Chavalit had been part) was widely regarded as
inept, hopelessly corrupt and blamed for presiding over the country's
sagging economic fortunes. Chavalit himself had strong military links,

support from big business and a reputation as a skilful politician. He quickly signalled that he would exploit these assets by appointing a cabinet built around an 'economic dream team' of highly respected technocrats, most notably Amnuay Viruwan as Finance Minister.

Despite this effort to insulate economic policy-making from the vagaries of Thai politics, the logic of the country's political structure very quickly reasserted itself. The BBC saga came to life again when it emerged that criminal charges laid against several BBC executives had lapsed because Bank of Thailand officials had failed to act before the statute of limitations came into play in early 1997. Chavalit ordered the suspension of a deputy governor at the central bank and several other senior officials over the affair, but this did little to conceal the fact that politicians who were now members of his party maintained strong links with BBC.

Problems in the Thai financial sector and the government's inability to deal with them effectively ran much deeper than BBC. The biggest area of concern was not the banks, but finance companies. The country's fifteen banks dominated the financial sector but, with entry by new banks tightly limited, finance companies played an increasingly prominent role in the financial system through the 1990s. By the end of 1996, Thailand's ninety-one finance companies (twenty-five were pure finance companies and sixty-six performed both finance and securities functions) accounted for nearly 25 per cent of total credit (EIU 1998a: 31, 50). By the beginning of 1997 their difficulties were becoming apparent to both domestic regulators and foreign investors, as several factors combined to weaken them: the end of a prolonged property boom in late 1996 (real estate was the core collateral for much of the borrowing), mounting nervousness about substantial foreign liabilities given repeated speculative attacks on the baht, and the consequences of the central bank's use of higher interest rates in an effort to help support the currency and dampen inflationary pressures.

On 5 February 1997 came the first Thai default, by the company Somprasong, on a foreign loan repayment. Later that month, it was announced that the largest of the finance companies, Finance One, was seeking a merger with a bank to stave off collapse. In the face of widespread fears of an impending financial implosion, Finance Minister Amnuay and central bank governor Rerngchai Marakanond suspended trading of financial sector shares on the stock exchange on 3 March and went on national television to announce a series of emergency measures designed to reassure nervous markets. The two key elements of the policy intervention were a requirement that all banks and finance companies make much stronger provision for bad loans and an announcement that ten of the weakest financial companies would have to raise their capital base within sixty days.

These measures did little to reassure financial markets, and when trading resumed the following day (4 March) financial shares fell heavily amid reports of a rush to withdraw funds. Underlying the nervousness of the market were doubts about the government's ability to follow through with its restructuring plans. Such fears proved well-founded. No sooner had Amnuay and Rerngchai targeted the ten ailing finance companies than a familiar political dynamic re-emerged – the plan encountered heavy resistance from within the government. Several senior members of Chart Pattana, the second-largest party in the coalition, had controlling interests in some of the ten targeted institutions. Not only did they succeed in vetoing the plan and ensuring that no action was taken against the ten companies, but the very fact that the institutions were permitted to continue trading meant that – as with BBC – the central bank had to provide liquidity in order to keep the companies afloat in the face of runs by panicked investors and depositors.

The financial market problems in March constituted a critical juncture in the development of the larger crisis in Thailand. There was a clear and pressing need for effective government action, and widespread concern among Thai and foreign investors about the scale of the bad loan problem in the financial sector. At the same time, the currency was coming under mounting pressure with money market players sensing exchange rate vulnerability. Amnuay and Rerngchai did not dare pursue the strict path favoured by financial hawks – forcing shareholders to accept big losses by allowing ailing institutions to fail. Nor were they prepared to permit foreign investors to take a controlling stake in these institutions. However, even the intermediate path they opted for – lifting capital adequacy provisions and singling out the weakest institutions for immediate attention – proved politically unattainable. These initiatives failed not because they were blocked by popular outcry or parliamentary opposition, but because they were effectively vetoed by other members of the ruling coalition. Rather than risking the collapse of his new government by alienating Chart Pattana, Chavalit preferred to gamble on compromise and delaying measures.

The finance minister's inability to follow through on even the moderate plans he had outlined had a very corrosive effect on investor confidence. In addition, there were high costs associated with delay: a side effect of injecting large-scale emergency funding into the ten failing finance companies was a substantial surge in the growth of monetary aggregates, which only served to sharpen the fundamental contradiction in the government's overall strategy with respect to the exchange rate.

At the same time as it was pumping money into insolvent finance companies to keep them afloat, the central bank was spending reserves to prop up the exchange rate. As the markets increasingly recognised, this was not a sustainable strategy. In mid May the baht suffered its heaviest assault. By then it was no longer only big Thai companies and foreign investors that were betting against the baht: middle-class Thais were also increasingly moving to dollars (Siamwalla 1997: 2).

Frustrated by his inability to persuade the coalition's leaders in cabinet to move on more extensive financial sector reforms and on other fronts such as cutting more pork from the budget, Amnuay resigned from the government on 19 June. The leader of the government's technocratic dream team had lasted just seven months in office. With a few exceptions, his attempts at major reform had been blocked by other parties within the government. As one minister lamented, 'to solve economic problems we cannot simply announce economic measures, we have to follow up on their progress' (*Far Eastern Economic Review*, 29 May 1997: 15). But with a diverse coalition and massive debts incurred by all parties in order to win office, there was little prospect of the cabinet agreeing to take tough measures that might hurt the economic interests of ministers or their financial benefactors. Even if a majority was in favour of taking action, a minority could veto the action by threatening to walk out of the coalition.

After struggling to find a prominent figure who would accept the post of finance minister, Chavalit offered it to Thanong Bidaya, head of the Thai Military Bank. Thanong fared little better than Amnuay. Seeking to seize the initiative, on 27 June he announced the suspension of sixteen finance companies (including seven of the original ten), giving them thirty days to implement merger plans. With the central bank no longer able to sustain the exchange rate, five days later, on 2 July, it was announced that the baht was being cut loose. The baht immediately fell and began a long steady descent; by the end of the year, the currency had lost 45 per cent of its previous value.

In his efforts to push financial restructuring, Thanong stumbled on the same obstacle as Amnuay: although he had won approval for the initiative, Chart Pattana leaders were able to block its implementation. Not only did Chart Pattana succeed in preventing the closure or forced merger of the sixteen finance companies, it managed to persuade the central bank to continue injecting liquidity into the institutions. In late July, in the context of negotiations with the International Monetary Fund (IMF) to obtain a rescue package, it was revealed that loans to the sixteen finance companies now totalled a staggering Bt430 billion, a figure that exceeded the total capital of the finance companies and equalled about 10 per cent of GDP. The government naturally sought to downplay its direct involvement in this scandal, and instead forced the resignation of central bank governor Rerngchai as well as another senior and respected official (*Bangkok Post*, 14 August 1997).

A week later, on 5 August, in an effort to regain the initiative and to make a necessary policy prepayment on the rescue package,[2] Thanong announced that a further forty-two finance companies would be suspended because of the scale of their loan problems and imminent insolvency. A total of fifty-eight – two-thirds of the country's finance companies – had now been suspended. Like the earlier sixteen, this batch was given a short period in which to meet tough new capital adequacy rules, merge with a stronger institution, or go out of business. In an effort to stem charges of corruption and cronyism, Virabhongsa Ramangkura, a respected technocrat newly appointed as deputy prime minister in a hurried cabinet reshuffle in mid August, replaced the official in charge of the committee established to vet rescue plans of the suspended finance companies. He installed Amaret Sila-on, the respected head of the Thai Stock Exchange (*Bangkok Post*, 26 August 1997).

However, as one section of the government was moving to force an overhaul of the financial sector, another was moving in precisely the opposite direction. With a looming deadline for deciding the fate of the suspended finance companies, the politics of reform intensified. In early October, the Association of Finance Companies vigorously courted Chart Pattana leader Chatichai as well as Prime Minister Chavalit, seeking a relaxation of the criteria for rehabilitation. The IMF responded by publicly expressing a wish that the independence of Amaret's screening committee not be undermined. A week later he resigned, after only a short tenure, declaring that he was being undercut by forces within the government (*Bangkok Post*, 12 October 1997). Further concessions were soon made to Chart Pattana and the finance companies. Announcing the creation of two new independent agencies to handle the evaluation and processing of the finance companies, Thanong also revealed that the deadline for their restructuring would be extended (no new date was set) and that earlier loans to the ailing finance companies by the central bank could be treated as equity. This move increased the probability that the public resources injected into the companies would never be recovered (*Bangkok Post*, 14 October 1997). In another successful rearguard move, Chart Pattana succeeded in delaying cabinet approval of the plans for the two new agencies announced by Thanong until the decrees included text that specifically reversed their independence from the government (EIU 1998a: 13).

By this stage, however, the government was disintegrating. On 19 October, Finance Minister Thanong resigned over the reversal of a petrol tax a mere three days after it had been announced as part of the government's long-awaited policy response to the IMF bailout. In the wake of manoeuvring prior to the formation of an expected new government led by Chart Pattana and impending defections in Chavalit's own party, the crippled prime minister announced his resignation on 3 November. Thailand was in very deep disarray.

The crisis in Thailand began to abate in 1998 when a new government under Chuan Leekpai committed itself to implement the IMF program and moved ahead with the closure of the financial institutions and some aspects of a broader process of restructuring. The new government was able to make some progress on these issues during an initial honeymoon period when it benefited from a combination of factors: a clear sense of national emergency, its status as a transitional administration in the lead-up to the introduction of the newly approved constitution, and the domestic bargaining leverage deriving from IMF conditionality. However, as 1998 progressed it was increasingly subject to the same fundamental pressures as all its predecessors.

Although our focus here is on the restructuring of the financial sector, many others would have yielded a similar picture, including the process of designing and approving the new constitution. These and other cases would also show that Thailand's combination of a parliamentary structure with multiple weak parties meant that policy-making was bound to be particularly indecisive. This was not a function of the character of particular personalities or the combination of interests represented in Chavalit's government; the same pattern applied in previous governments. Under this political structure, party and faction leaders were compelled to work assiduously to generate resources to hold their members together, and prime ministers had to struggle to keep their coalitions together. And because defection was often an attractive option for coalition members, major public goods oriented policy reforms were extraordinarily difficult to undertake. The fractiousness of the cabinet was mirrored in a constant turnover of key personnel. Chavalit's government endured for twelve months and experienced three cabinet reshuffles, three finance ministers and two central bank governors.

To summarise, Thailand's political structure exerted a powerful and negative influence over the policy-making process. Party fragmentation, intra-coalitional and intra-party conflict allowed serious economic problems to accumulate, thus contributing to the outflow of capital and setting the stage for the currency crisis. We can see the same factors limiting Thailand's ability to respond aggressively once the crisis broke. Widespread public disillusionment with the system and its alarming impotence in the face of the crisis propelled the introduction of dramatic constitutional change in the latter part of 1997. This is not the place to discuss those changes, but it is worth noting that in addition to deep and widespread economic hardship, Thailand's economic crisis has given birth to a new political system.

Korea

Before turning to the question of how political factors affected the crisis, it is important to place those events against their economic backdrop. Korea experienced a substantial terms-of-trade shock in 1996 and a worsening of its current account position, caused by slowing in export growth across a range of sectors. The yen started to depreciate against the US dollar in 1995; as the Korean won was tied closely to the dollar, this eroded the competitiveness of Korean exports. The decline of semiconductor prices also played a particularly important role in the second half of 1996, as nearly a quarter of Korea's total exports are semiconductor devices. The current account deficit increased from 2 per cent of GDP in 1995 to 4.9 per cent in 1996. With the increased deficit naturally came an increase in foreign indebtedness, which stood at $US78.4 billion at the end of 1995, $US104.7 billion at the end of 1996 and $US161.8 billion in November, when the crisis broke.

However, these problems appeared to turn around before the crisis broke. The current account deficit began to lessen in the first half of 1997, and in June the country recorded a trade surplus. Nor, as we have noted, is there a compelling case – as there was in Thailand – that Korea's problems stemmed from severe overvaluation. The composition of Korea's debt proved a particularly serious problem; at the time the crisis broke, over half of it (54.9 per cent) was short-term, which naturally created tremendous vulnerability to investor panic.[3] Failure to roll over short-term debt was the precipitating cause of the crisis and, as we will show, high corporate leveraging and domestic financial problems made Korea vulnerable. But it is important to underline that the country's overall foreign debt burden was very modest – 25 per cent of GDP, compared with 47 per cent of GDP in Indonesia and 46 per cent in Thailand at the end of 1996. There were few reasons to believe *ex ante* that Korea's debt burden was unsustainable or that debt would not be rolled over.

In respect of the short-term factors responsible for the crisis, there can be little doubt that the events in the Hong Kong and Tokyo stock markets in the week of 20–24 October played a major role in setting off the Korean crisis. Korea experienced substantial capital flight at that point, and began to feel a severe liquidity crunch. American and European banks failed to roll over short-term debts, and the collapse in stock prices constrained the ability of banks in Japan, already experiencing difficulties of their own, to extend credit. In the wake of Hong Kong's difficulties, the ratings agencies downgraded a number of Korea's banks.

However, the crucial question is whether the ensuing behaviour by investors was simply 'rational panic' (Radelet & Sachs 1998b), or whether it rested on a reassessment of other weaknesses in the Korean system, including political weaknesses. Our argument is that the impending election fragmented the ruling party and made it difficult to take measures that would weaken its electoral chances, particularly given the strength of the opposition and the revealed weakness of the ruling party's candidate. The poor performance of the Kim Young Sam government, and the potential strength of Kim Dae Jung in capitalising on that record, created divisions within the ruling party as presidential hopefuls and legislators sought to distance themselves from the government. The result was a period of sustained policy uncertainty before and immediately following the crisis that contributed to its outbreak and depth. Bureaucratic rivalries, simple indecision and wishful thinking played into the crisis, but more fundamental political factors were at work in limiting the Korean government's effectiveness in managing the external shocks that hit the country in 1997.

President Kim Young Sam's political decline and 'lame duck' status can be traced to the Hanbo scandal which broke in January. Although there were several failures of smaller *chaebol* in the second half of 1996, that of Hanbo, the country's fourteenth-largest industrial group, was more significant. The government denied allegations of impropriety following the announcement of Hanbo's collapse. However, a series of bribery arrests and above all the arrest, National Assembly testimony and conviction of the president's son, Kim Hyun Chul, substantially weakened the president's standing. Kim Young Sam's withdrawal from the political arena accelerated prior to his party's nominating convention in July. Unlike his predecessors, and partly because of his own political liabilities from the Hanbo scandal, Kim refused to actively participate in the process of choosing his successor.

Kim's apparent personal conflicts with the leading candidate, Lee Hoi Chang, contributed to dividing the ruling party before the election. Kim had appointed Lee as ruling party chairman after the Hanbo scandal in an effort to resuscitate his own reputation. Lee used his new position to build support for his presidential bid, which drew resentment from his ruling party challengers, including members of President Kim's party faction. Lee was able to capture the nomination on 21 July, but was unable to win a majority on the first ballot and garnered only 60 per cent on the second. Following his nomination, Lee showed a substantial lead in the polls and appeared on his way to victory in December. However, his popularity plummeted when it was revealed that his two sons had avoided military service for being underweight, quickly opening a debate within the party on whether he should be replaced. Another presidential hopeful, Rhee In Je, left the ruling party and launched his own campaign on 13 September, taking many of Kim Young Sam's supporters in the New Korea Party (NKP) with him – ironically, strengthening Lee Hoi Chang's control of the party. Lee's chances were improved by the formation of an alliance with another candidate, Cho Soon, but Kim Dae Jung's position was also strengthened by an unlikely alliance with conservative candidate, Kim Jong Pil; the combination of the ruling party's blunders and the alliance of the two Kims opened the possibility that Kim Dae Jung might actually win presidency.

In sum, the political background to policy-making in this period includes a severely weakened president and a divided ruling party headed by a candidate desperately trying to differentiate himself from the incumbent. Although National Assembly elections are not concurrent with the presidential elections in Korea, ruling party legislators were naturally concerned about the party's fate and, as we will see, disinclined to take actions that would damage the party in the run-up to the presidential elections.

The two key policy problems that Korea faced prior to the crisis were the management of corporate bankruptcies and related problems in the financial sector, and the problems surrounding the exchange rate and capital outflows which accelerated following the collapse of the Hong Kong market. In both cases, government indecisiveness had a visible effect on investor perception and behaviour.

The disposition of the Hanbo case sent mixed signals about the government's intentions toward failing enterprises and exacerbated uncertainty about the health of the banking system. The government made no effort to save Hanbo's management; the firm was effectively nationalised. But new money was also injected. When two more of the top thirty chaebol folded – Sammi in March and Jinro in April – the government sought to orchestrate a more concerted response to the problem of the highly overleveraged chaebol. On 18 April, thirty-five commercial and state banks announced an 'anti-bankruptcy' pact, under which they would continue to extend credit to any top-fifty chaebol at risk and defer debt payments for ninety days as long as the company was 'basically sound' and developed a 'self-rescue' package. Since the anti-bankruptcy pact necessarily called the position of the banks into serious question, the government had to supplement the concerted lending and rescheduling effort with a new initiative to inject

liquidity into the financial system. It did this through the creation of a
new bailout fund worth 1.5 trillion won, which would take over some of
the 12 trillion won of non-performing assets held by the banks.

In the weeks following the announcement of the package, the stock
market rallied sharply. However, from July Korean financial and foreign
exchange markets entered a period of marked turbulence and uncertainty, and the government's management of the Kia bankruptcy was
clearly a major cause. The Kia crisis broke on 23 June, when Kim Sun-
Hong, chairman of the group, appealed directly to the government for
assistance in persuading creditors not to call maturing loans. On 15 July,
the group's creditor banks placed it under the anti-bankruptcy pact on
the basis of a rescue plan that included a reduction in the number of
affiliates, real estate sales and layoffs. Unlike other highly diversified
conglomerates, Kia had attempted to focus its business strategy in the
automotive sector, but its entry into autos threatened substantial surplus
capacity in the sector. Samsung, which had announced its intention to
enter the industry, had an interest in seeing Kia's efforts fail. Indeed,
Samsung saw the takeover of Kia and/or Ssangyong as a way of solving
some of its own production problems.

What ensued was a highly politicised battle over the future of Kia, in
which Kia's management sought to blackmail the weakened government, locked in a tightening presidential race, into providing a bailout.
Refusing to resign, the group's chairman quickly denounced the loan
package as inadequate and mobilised support for the company from
suppliers, employees, competitors and the general public. On 21 July, a
coalition of over sixty social groups, including such unlikely partners as
the anti-chaebol Citizens Coalition for Economic Justice and the
independent Korea Confederation of Trade Unions, formed a 'save Kia'
movement (*Korea Newsreview*, 26 July 1997: 16). On 4 August, the banks
postponed their final decision on the bailout package until 29 September and withheld further lines of credit in the interim. Kia's
management quickly threatened that many of Kia's suppliers would fail,
and appealed to the government to intervene.

According to Kim Sok Tong, chief of the Ministry of Finance and
Economy's Foreign Capital Section, a number of the major Korean
commercial banks were technically insolvent after Hanbo's collapse, but
the government was doing everything in its power to stave off outright
bankruptcy (Cho & Pu 1998: 126). On 25 August, the government
announced measures to shore up the financial system, with a target of
providing at least $US8 billion liquidity for the banking system (*Korea
Newsreview*, 30 August 1997: 24–5). At the same time, the government
began to signal its impatience with Kia's open campaign for intervention
and support, and with the entire anti-bankruptcy pact, on the grounds

that the uncertainty and delay over the future of the firm was itself becoming a major source of financial market uncertainty. On 28 August, Finance Minister Kang Kyung Shik announced his intention to scrap or modify the anti-bankruptcy pact; over the next month, the government began to send stronger signals that it wanted Kia's creditors to let the firm go bankrupt when the 29 September deadline passed.

The Kia management was unwilling to submit to court receivership (*pasan*), however, under which existing management would be replaced, and exploited an important alternative in Korean bankruptcy law to avoid it. Under Korean law, firms may file for court 'protection' or 'mediation' (*hwa ui pob*). Under this procedure, management maintains its rights and, if three-fourths of creditors agree, debt payments can be postponed and new credits extended. Banks may have an incentive to go along with this option since court receivership implies liquidation and certain losses. After moving four subsidiaries toward court protection, Kia management filed for court protection for nine more on 22 September. One powerful weapon the government maintained in trying to force creditors toward the receivership option was the threat that the government would not guarantee Kia's foreign obligations ($US687 million) if Kia sought court protection. Meeting on 25 September, Kang Kyung Shik and representatives of Kia's creditors announced their intention to seek receivership for the firm. At the final meeting of creditors on 29 September, the creditors delivered an ultimatum to Korean Motors and Asia Motors to choose court protection or receivership, as further credit would not be extended. Nonetheless it was a full month – until 22 October, the day before the biggest stock market fall in Hong Kong – before the government intervened to settle the Kia issue, and that intervention was not greeted favourably by the Western financial press.

Thus, by late October the Korean banking system had been severely damaged not only by the string of corporate bankruptcies, but by a highly politicised and uncertain process which left the ultimate disposition of Kia and its creditors in limbo for months. Korea's tottering financial system was already on the verge of collapse when the shock from Hong Kong hit on 23 October, and reports from Moody's and foreign brokerages demonstrate clearly that foreign analysts were aware of it. As foreign investors began to pull out of the region, the downward pressure on the won accelerated. On 28–30 October, the government halted trading in won after it depreciated by its daily limit of 2.5 per cent, despite heavy market intervention to support it (*Korea Newsreview*, 1 November 1997: 15). On 28 October, the government announced yet another package designed to induce an infusion of foreign capital, marginally raising foreign ownership limits on the stock exchange – at a time when investors were rushing for the exit. On 1 November, the Haitai Group announced it was unable to stave off bankruptcy: Moody's, and Standard and Poor's, downgraded the credit rating of Korean banks on 3 November. Foreign banks began to refuse to roll over the short-term foreign debt of Korean financial institutions and the foreign press began to report that the Bank of Korea's foreign exchange reserves were evaporating and the BOK had committed to extensive forward contracts to defend the won for the rest of the year (Cho & Pu 1998: 91).

Whether a full-blown crisis could have been averted after the shock from Hong Kong constitutes an important counterfactual, and there are certainly good reasons to think that it could not. At that juncture, Kim Young Sam was preoccupied with charges that he was secretly backing Rhee In Je's candidacy against the ruling party's Lee Hoi Chang, and delegated the crisis issue to Finance Minister Kang Kyung Shik. Kang met the president on 10 November and outlined a strategy that included passing the financial reform legislation the government had introduced in August, initiating financial stabilisation measures, seeking alternative financing from the United States, Japan and elsewhere, and then, only after those efforts failed, turning to the IMF. Yet Korea's appeal to other lenders as well as its negotiations with the IMF were going to be heavily influenced by the government's ability to undertake a credible reform program. In secret discussions with the Korean economic team, IMF managing director Michel Camdessus expressed explicit concern about the market importance of passing the financial reform legislation and of guaranteeing that all presidential candidates would back the package. In short, Camdessus understood that the issue was not simply one of acting decisively, but of guaranteeing legislative commitment to the program that would make it credible as well.

At the end of the second week of November, it appeared that the package of financial reform bills was headed for passage. A subcommittee under the National Assembly's Finance and Economy Committee passed the package by a vote of six to two and passed it to the full committee for a vote on 14 November. However, one of the contentious issues in the reform package was the creation of a new Financial Supervisory Board which would consolidate a number of existing regulatory agencies, and whether it would be under the direct control of the Prime Minister or the Minister of Finance and Economy, where the National Assembly believed it would have more oversight powers. The labour unions representing the BOK and the four agencies targeted for elimination were particularly opposed to the potential impact on agency employees. BOK workers demonstrated in front of New Korea Party headquarters on 13 November, and employees of the Securities Supervisory Board and the Insurance Supervisory Board protested in front of the National Assembly and BOK the next day (*Korea Herald*, 15 November 1997). The employees threatened to strike immediately if the National Assembly passed the reform legislation, and a group of former central bank governors held a press conference to voice their opposition to the bills.

The ruling party could have passed the bills on its own, but Lee Hoi Chang's supporters were rightly concerned about the political cost of doing so. Kim Dae Jung did not want to alienate labour immediately before the election and could easily make an issue of the legislation; the ruling party thus preferred to consult with the opposition to secure its support. However, the opposition had few incentives to cooperate. If it signed on, it would be associated with potentially costly reforms; if it postponed its assent, any negative economic effects of postponing the reform package would most likely rest at the feet of the president and the ruling party candidate, Lee Hoi Chang. Kang Kyung Shik and his staff tried in vain to persuade the National Assembly to pass the financial reform legislation on the last day of the session, but the Finance and Economy Committee did not bother to send the bills to the floor for debate. As a result, Kang failed to deliver the reforms and the National Assembly was adjourned until after the election (although when the crisis broke, it reconvened in a failed attempt to revive the legislation). The markets were clearly adversely affected by the failure to pass the reform legislation, and Korea's only hope of avoiding the IMF was to secure bilateral support from Japan or the United States, perhaps with a relatively small amount of additional IMF support.

Kang recognised that it would be difficult to secure such support but, given the central bank's loss of reserves and the open disagreement within government on how to respond, some policy initiative was required. Kang proposed a package comprising some measures for dealing with insolvent financial institutions and widening the trading band for the won to 15 per cent, but the president decided to dismiss Kang and several other economic advisers. By this point it is difficult to disentangle the economic and political; if the dismissal of Kang was designed to restore confidence, it hardly succeeded. On 19 and 20 November, the BOK lost $US1.6 billion and $US1.1 billion of reserves respectively, and the won sank to the lowest permissible limit for the fourth day in a row despite the stabilisation measures announced by the new Minister of Finance and Economy, Lim Chang Yuel. A number of ratings agencies downgraded Korea's short-term and long-term foreign currency rating and indicated that the lack of transparency made it difficult to determine the amount of non-performing loans in the banking system (*Korea Herald*, 20 November 1997). On 21 November, Korea announced it was going to the IMF.

There is substantial debate about whether the IMF program in Korea was appropriately designed, both with respect to its demands on fiscal and monetary policy and in the closure of failed banking institutions. We find it plausible that both these criticisms are justified, and that the failure of the IMF program to stem the decline of the won was related to problems of program design. However, it is also important to point out that the initial market response to the announcement that Korea was going to the IMF was positive, even though the foreign exchange and equity markets were turbulent in the two weeks during which the program was being negotiated. Moreover, while it is true that the finalisation of the program did not stabilise the markets, the period of further deterioration between the time the program was announced on 3 December and its revision and augmentation on 24 December overlapped with the final weeks of the election campaign. Too much attention has been given to Kim Dae Jung's remarks that the program might require renegotiation; in fact, his remarks did not have that implication and in any case he quickly retreated from that position and pledged his support. Nonetheless, political uncertainties continued throughout this period, as is evident from the closeness of the final presidential vote: Kim Dae Jung won by only two percentage points of the vote, and only with a plurality given Rhee In Je's capture of 20 per cent of the vote.

We do not mean to dismiss the underlying sources of Korea's financial crisis in the overleveraged chaebol, the precipitous opening of the capital account and shocks emanating from abroad, particularly in late October. Yet how the markets responded to those problems depended on investors' views of the government, and we have attempted to show that election-year politics, particularly the divisions that the election created within the ruling party, affected the coherence of the government's response.

Conclusion

The economic crises in Korea and Thailand are part of a wider global and regional economic phenomenon and there are crucial shared characteristics in the severe economic problems they and other countries have experienced. However, theirs is not just a story of the perils of being exposed to fluctuating global capital flows or common economic circumstances. Attention must also be paid to the political capacity to manage these external constraints and policy challenges. Korea's normally decisive system was paralysed by a presidential election and splits over succession within the ruling party that allowed interest-group pressures to operate, weakened the legislature's ability to act, and led to indecision and delay. Thailand's problems were in some ways more fundamental, as the constitutional order itself was arguably to blame, creating weak and unstable coalitions. Unless the policy preferences of all parties in the coalition were aligned – not a common occurrence – policy stasis was likely to result. In contrast, the problems with Korea's institutional framework are more typical of most presidential democracies and of a cyclical nature: policy stasis was the result of the president's lame duck status, impending elections, and splits between the executive and his co-partisans in the legislature. Policy immobility was thus much more typical of the Thai system. Nevertheless, once the crisis broke, both political systems were gripped by it and their capacity to respond in an effective manner was crippled, thereby compounding investor uncertainty.

Our analysis has focused on explaining why these two quite differently configured democracies responded in a counterproductive way to the onset of the crisis. The argument could readily be extended to shed light on the handling of the recovery process. In Thailand, the new government led by Chuan Leekpai gained a strong reform mandate, powerfully reinforced by severe IMF conditionality, and was initially able to introduce significant changes. Before long, however, familiar coalitional dynamics were slowing and stalling the reform process. Significantly, the crisis in Thailand led not only to a change of government, but provided vital momentum to the stumbling process of constitutional reform. The key provisions of the new constitution included the elimination of multi-member electoral districts with plurality voting and the introduction of a new provision discouraging cabinet defections by forcing cabinet members to give up their seats in parliament. Although these provisions did not come into effect until the next election, over time they should help to mitigate some of the problems of weak multi-party coalition government.

In Korea, Kim Dae Jung had run for the presidency on no fewer than four previous occasions; each time the economy was doing well and the Korean electorate opted for conservative candidates. The crisis provided Kim with an electoral opportunity, but his victory also gave him a mandate to undertake wide-ranging reforms. Exploiting his honeymoon and cooperation from the ruling party, Kim orchestrated a wide package of reforms prior to his inauguration which were only slightly different from those that the National Assembly failed to pass in November. Once inaugurated, divided government did slow the reform process somewhat, but by the end of the year the government had gained a majority in the National Assembly and its reform record for the first year was impressive.

We have focused our political analysis on how the institutions of government affect the incentives and capabilities of politicians to act in an effective and timely fashion. However, there is an alternative tradition of political analysis that emphasises the role of interests as the key determinant of public policy. In analysing the East Asian crisis, that theory has focused on corruption, cronyism and nepotism as the source of the region's difficulties. In Thailand, close links existed between politicians and financial institutions against which the government needed to take action, and there is credible evidence that these links contributed to delay. But the role of rent-seekers depended on the institutional configuration; their power stemmed from their ability to gain political access through weak parties, the nature of coalition government and their ability to blackmail the government.

The Korean case also presents interesting ambiguities. Lending to Hanbo was clearly influenced by political calculations, but the over-leveraging of chaebol was a broader phenomenon not limited to Hanbo. Corruption did not appear to play a role in other cases. The deeper issue in Korea is whether the close connection that has long existed between the state, banks and chaebol gave rise to problems of moral hazard. We find some merit in these arguments, but the more compelling short-term problem was uncertainty over whether the government would act. A weakened government was increasingly torn between its commitment to an arm's-length relationship with the chaebol, precisely in the name of attacking corruption, and electoral and party pressures that sent signals that the government might not hold firm to that non-interventionist commitment. Our analysis naturally raises the long-standing question of the role of regime type in the politics of adjustment. We have pointed to ways in which democratic governments can generate market uncertainty; others, including Mo and Moon (1999) have gone further, arguing with respect to Korea that democratisation is partly to blame for the crisis. However, we do not believe that democratic governments necessarily have greater difficulties in adjusting than authoritarian ones; indeed, the opposite may be true. Whatever its short-term weaknesses, democracy allows voters to throw out incumbents and thus allows reformers to gain political mandates to change the policy status quo. In authoritarian systems there is no check on a failing leader, who can prolong his rule by relying on repression – at least for some time – in the face of profound economic distress. Democracies may generate corruption, but under certain circumstances they can also generate incentives for oppositions to expose its costs. Moreover, authoritarian governments are not immune from problems of rent-seeking; on the contrary, the lack of accountability and transparency may make them even more virulent. Indonesia demonstrates these problems clearly.

The financial crisis in Thailand and Korea – as elsewhere in Asia – was assuredly a multi-dimensional phenomenon. A number of factors combined to produce this stunning economic reversal. Not all the factors, however, were economic. Politics played a pivotal role. We have argued that in Thailand and Korea the institutional framework of government powerfully constrained the behaviour of political leaders and thereby generated policy uncertainty at a time when markets were craving clear and effective remedial action. The source of this policy disability differed – reflecting the differing frameworks of government – but in both cases it was ultimately institutional in nature. And as we write, Brazil provides yet another powerful illustration of the impact of political institutions in times of economic difficulty, as that country's highly fragmented system of government gives rise to policy blockage, investor uncertainty and capital outflow.

CHAPTER 4

The Good, the Bad and the Ugly? Korea, Taiwan and the Asian Financial Crisis

Gregory W. Noble and John Ravenhill

The financial crisis that erupted in Thailand had strikingly differing effects on Taiwan and the Republic of Korea, two countries previously hailed for their outstanding economic performance. In South Korea the press of investors seeking to withdraw their capital created unsustainable pressure on foreign exchange reserves, forcing the Korean government to allow a drastic devaluation of the won and to seek the support of the International Monetary Fund (IMF). In contrast, Taiwan initially appeared to have escaped the East Asian contagion largely unscathed. Its currency underwent a modest and orderly decline of about 17 per cent from the end of 1996 to the end of 1998. No major Taiwanese banks or manufacturing companies collapsed. And although the growth of Taiwan's economy slowed in 1998, it recorded a gain of just under 5 per cent, second only to China in East Asia and still one of the world's stellar growth performances.

This contrasting vulnerability to the financial shocks emanating from South-East Asia is especially striking because, by most measures, Korea's economic performance in the previous decade remained outstanding and indeed in many respects even surpassed that of Taiwan. Prices of traded goods were stable. Unemployment was low and the government's budget balanced. Over the 1990s, rates of savings, investment, productivity growth and expenditures on research and development surpassed those of Taiwan to rank near the top in the world (Table 4.1).

Many of the factors commonly adduced to explain the emergence and diffusion of financial crisis in Asia are unable to differentiate between Korea and Taiwan. For example, economists have cited the overvalued currencies and pegged exchange rate systems common to some of the countries most severely affected by the Asian financial crisis. This explanation has much less relevance for Korea. The link between

Table 4.1 Economic profiles of Korea and Taiwan on the eve of the crisis (1996, $US unless otherwise noted)

	Taiwan	Korea
Population	21.47 million	45.55 million
GDP	$272.3 billion	$484.6 billion
GDP per capita	$12838	$10639
GDP growth rate, 1990–96 annual average	6.3%	7.7%
Industrial production increase	1.8%	8.5%
Labour productivity (manufacturing), annual average increase 1990–95	5.8%	10.6%
Inflation (GDP price deflator)	2.7%	3.4%
Unemployment	2.6%	2.0%
Savings (gross savings/GDP)	24.9%	34.6%
Investment (gross investment/GDP)	21.1%	38.6%
R&D spending/GDP	1.85%	2.68%
Outstanding debt of central government/GDP	14.4%	6.5% [1995]
Inward direct foreign investment (accumulated total)	$14.721 billion	$12.775 billion
Outward direct foreign investment (accumulated total)	$12.42 billion (approved)	$10.22 billion (actual, through 1995)
Exchange rate (year-end)	27.49 NTD/USD	844.2 won/USD
Current account balance (CAB/GDP)	$11 billion (4%)	–$23 billion (–4.9%)
Foreign reserves and gold	$88 billion	$32.4 billion
Gross external indebtedness[a]	$24.45 billion	$110.32 billion
Foreign debt/foreign reserves	28%	340%

Notes: [a] Total external claims of banks in the BIS reporting area and the official and officially guaranteed or insured trade-related claims of banks and non-banks in twenty OECD countries.

Sources: For Taiwan, CEPD (1998); for Korea, Korea National Statistical Office (1997), except for:
   Outstanding central government debt/GDP: Republic of China, Ministry of Finance (1996: 446).
   Inward direct foreign investment (thanks to Eric Ramstetter): Taiwan Economic Data Center, National Taiwan University, CD-ROM, November 1998; Korea: IMF, *International Financial Statistics*, CD-ROM, November 1998 External indebtedness: OECD/BIS (1999)

the Korean won and the US dollar was weak. The won depreciated against the dollar by 5 per cent in nominal terms between 1993 and the end of 1996, a depreciation of slightly under 2 per cent of the real effective exchange rate. Nor did exchange rate policy differentiate Korea from Taiwan, which if anything maintained a tighter link to the dollar.[1]

To what extent did differences in the structures of their foreign trade affect the relative vulnerability of the Korean and Taiwanese economies to the crises emanating from South-East Asia? The rise in intra-regional trade in East Asia in the decade before the onset of the crises contributed to a contagion effect (World Bank 1998a: 11). Foreign trade was one medium through which external shocks were transmitted to the domestic economy. Dependence on markets that are growing relatively slowly or those that have contracted suddenly, following the onset of economic crisis, similarly contributes to vulnerability. Meanwhile, the extent to which domestic exports compete directly in third country markets with exports from economies whose currencies have undergone substantial devaluations because of economic crisis may also generate contagion effects from crises elsewhere.

Did Korea and Taiwan differ substantially in their trade-induced vulnerabilities? Certainly, it was not the case that the Korean economy was the more open of the two: the ratio of exports and imports to GDP in 1996 was less than 60 per cent in Korea whereas it exceeded 80 per cent in Taiwan.[2] Neither was Korea substantially more dependent on the markets of the troubled economies of the Association of South-East Asian Nations (ASEAN) grouping. In 1996, ASEAN states provided markets for approximately 12 per cent of the total exports of both Korea and Taiwan. And both economies depended equally on the stagnant Japanese economy for another 12 per cent of their exports. If trade patterns contributed to the different trajectories of the Korean and Taiwanese economies in 1997, the explanation must be sought beyond these aggregate data.

Another set of explanations for the different impact of the crises on Korea and Taiwan emphasises the deleterious effects of extensive state intervention and 'crony capitalism' in Korea. Although more plausible, these arguments have important limitations. Explanations based on excessive intervention and corruption have difficulties coping with timing and variance. Almost all observers agree that the Kim Young Sam government liberalised Korean economic policies, and that state direction of the economy declined in the 1990s. Indices of economic openness and polls of business executives on perceived levels of corruption in Asia typically ranked Korea just below Taiwan: both were lower than Singapore or Hong Kong but well above Thailand and Indonesia (Root 1996: xv; Gwartney 1996). Moreover, as Chang (1999) notes, crony capitalism has been more often assailed than specified. Few critics explain exactly what 'crony capitalism' means and why, if its effects are so devastating, Thailand, Indonesia and Korea managed to sustain decades of rapid growth before suddenly crashing in 1997.

Critics from the other end of the spectrum contend that Korea ran into trouble because the government bowed to international and domestic pressures to dismantle the very planning and coordination apparatus that had formerly guided its high-investment–high-growth economy. For Chang, Park and Yoo (1998: 739), 'it was the demise of industrial policy, rather than its perpetuation, which drove the Korean economy into crisis'. The Kim Young Sam government abandoned the practice of drafting five-year plans when it merged Korea's 'pilot agency', the Economic Planning Board, with the Ministry of Finance (MOF) in 1993. This abandonment of a coordinating role for the state, critics assert, had two particularly deleterious consequences. In the industrial sphere, it produced serious problems of overinvestment and surplus capacity as the large corporations rushed to further diversify their investments. In the financial sphere, liberalisation encouraged the entry of new merchant banks that were largely responsible for an explosion of Korea's short-term foreign debt – from negligible levels at the beginning of the decade to $US160 billion at the onset of the crisis (Wade & Veneroso 1998a: 10). In Taiwan, in contrast, Weiss (1998) asserts, the state retained its 'transformative' capacity. The Council for Economic Planning and Development continued to play an active role, the Ministry of Economic Affairs continued to target specific industries for future development and the Central Bank of China (CBC) contin- ued to exercise tight control over the financial sector.

We have some sympathy for these arguments (although we believe they are far more relevant to the financial sphere than to manufacturing industry, especially in their interpretation of the current planning capa- bilities of the Taiwanese state). Lack of effective regulation certainly underlay the crisis in the financial sector in Korea. On the other hand, we find the counterfactual they imply – that Korea could have main- tained a pilot agency to play a traditional coordinating role in the economy in the mid 1990s – to be unpersuasive and grounded in ahis- torical and apolitical analysis. As is often remarked, Korea Inc. may have been a more accurate characterisation of the relationship between state and business in Korea in the 1970s than Japan Inc. was for its counterpart in Japan. But the changing balance of power between the state and *chae- bol* (large, predominantly family-owned business groups), a relationship complicated by democratisation in Korea from the mid 1980s, and the influence of pro-market ideas in key agencies, greatly constrained the opportunities for the state to continue to play a directive role in industry policy.

An Alternative Approach: The Legacies of Developmental Statism

Accounting for the striking difference between Korea's and Taiwan's vulnerability to contagion from the South-East Asian financial crises, we believe, requires a perspective that is both longer-term than the explanations offered above, and explicitly political. The differential impact of the crises in 1997 reflected divergent legacies of government–business relations and markedly different approaches to the allocation of capital. Certainly, Korea and Taiwan shared many important geographic, historical and geopolitical similarities. Both countries were highly statist in the 1960s and 1970s and both gradually and somewhat reluctantly liberalised in the 1980s and 1990s, in response to international and domestic pressures as both countries underwent successful democratic transitions. Yet Korea's political economy was decisively structured by the 'big push capitalism' that directed massive amounts of bank lending to chaebol.

The growth of chaebol began in earnest in the early postwar period with the sale to favoured corporations of Japanese assets, often at prices well below market value. Import and production monopolies, guaranteed by the government in exchange for political contributions, solidified the dominance of these groups in the Korean economy.[3] The heavy and chemical industries (HCI) drive announced by President Park in January 1973 decisively cemented the dominant role of chaebol in Korea's economy, even at a time when the government evinced increasing concern at their economic power. The government decided that the licensing of a monopoly or oligopoly in targeted sectors would be the most effective means of encouraging rapid growth in industries characterised by economies of scale, a small domestic market and huge capital requirements. The HCI drive, while successful in transforming the economy, laid the foundations for the periodic crises that the Korean economy was to experience over the next quarter-century, of which the most recent, in 1997, was the most severe.

The elements of imbalance and vulnerability reinforced by the HCI push embraced both financial and industrial aspects. The financial system was severely repressed; banks were directed to lend to favoured corporations, often at negative real interest rates.[4] One consequence was a tradition of very low returns on capital for commercial banks, a problem compounded by high rates of non-performing loans. Small and medium-sized enterprises that did not receive 'policy' loans had to rely on the curb market where interest rates were substantially higher.[5] Chaebol competed mainly on the basis of size: even more than their Japanese counterparts, chaebol put growth before profits. But whereas many Japanese companies were at the leading edge of technological

KOREA AND TAIWAN   85

Table 4.2 International comparison of average debt:equity ratios in manufacturing (%)

	Korea		US	Japan	Taiwan
	Manufacturing	*Top 30 chaebol*			
1991	307	403	147	209	136
1992	319	426	168	202	138
1993	295	398	175	202	133
1994	303	403	167	196	131
1995	287	388	160	196	138
1996	317	450	154	187	n.a.

Sources: IMF (1998b: Table 6) except for Taiwan where the source is Central Bank of China (Zhongyang Yinhang) (1996)

innovation, chaebol typically relied heavily on imitation rather than innovation, their competitive edge derived from their efficiency in mass production. Chaebol continued to depend heavily on imported technology.[6]

The Industrial Sector

As family-owned firms, chaebol had few obligations to shareholders. The availability of low-cost policy loans in the 1970s and 1980s encouraged reliance on debt rather than equity, a tendency reinforced by the desire of family owners to avoid dilution of their control. In the 1990s, chaebol came to depend increasingly on funds that local banks borrowed offshore. An investment binge was driven by the availability of relatively low-cost foreign funds: production capacity in the manufacturing sector grew by a quarter in the three years to 1997 (OECD 1999: 25). The chaebol's continuing heavy reliance on debt is reflected in the data in Table 4.2, which compares debt:equity ratios across four economies. The contrast with Taiwan is particularly marked.

The chaebol's heavy dependence on debt, coupled with their reliance on imported technology, capital goods and critical components, had a profound effect on the vulnerability of the Korean economy to economic downturns, including externally generated crises. A much higher percentage of Korean companies' sales revenues was devoted to debt servicing than was true of their counterparts in other economies, including Taiwan (Table 4.3).

Moreover, an unusually large portion of the total costs of production for Korean companies was consumed by royalty payments and licensing fees to foreign companies. Between 1962 and 1996, total royalty

Table 4.3 International comparison of interest costs to sales ratio in manufacturing (%)

	Korea	Germany	Japan	Taiwan
1986–90	4.8	1.2	1.9	2.0
1991–95	5.8	1.7	1.7	2.2

Source: IMF (1998b: Table 7)

payments made by Korean firms were estimated by the Ministry of Finance and Economy at $US13.2 billion. The volume of payments increased substantially in recent years, jumping by 52.5 per cent in 1995 and a further 18 per cent in 1996 to an annual total of $US2.3 billion, roughly half from the electronics and electrical industries. More than two-thirds of the total was paid by the top thirty chaebol (*Korea Herald*, 24 October 1996, 6 December 1997). In contrast, in Taiwan total imports of technology (including consulting and training services) barely exceeded $US500 million in 1993 (Republic of China, NSC 1995: 165–9, 252). Royalties paid by a typical Korean semiconductor firm in the mid 1990s amounted to close to 15 per cent of total costs, compared with only 2.6 per cent for a typical Japanese firm. Interest payments by the Korean firm contributed a further 13 per cent of costs, compared with less than 6 per cent for Japanese firms (Mathews forthcoming). An inflexible labour market in Korea, where firms faced restrictions on laying off workers, further added to the cost problems of chaebol.

High debt-servicing costs and reliance on imported technology, compounded by export specialisation in a few industrial sectors, contributed to the generally low levels of profitability of Korean corporations and rendered them (and the Korean economy in aggregate) vulnerable to periodic, externally induced crises. The first occurred in the early 1970s, and another in response to the world recession triggered by the second round of oil price rises in 1979. It is notable that since the economic shocks emanating from the US decision to open diplomatic negotiations with the People's Republic of China, which were compounded by the first round of oil price increases in 1973–74, Taiwan's economy has never displayed the same vulnerability to external shocks as its Korean counterpart. In all years, Taiwan has avoided economic contraction (which occurred in Korea in 1980 as well as in 1997).[7]

The dominance of chaebol in Korea produced an economic structure far less flexible than that in Taiwan. Although bankruptcy in Korea was by no means unknown, even among the larger corporate groupings, the complex pattern of cross-subsidisation within chaebol enabled many unprofitable companies to survive. The lack of transparency in privately owned companies, facilitated by chaebol's control of non-bank financial institutions, stymied government efforts to restrict cross-subsidisation. And banks, which had high volumes of loans to individual chaebol, had powerful incentives to continue lending rather than to force companies into liquidation (for an example in the period leading up to the crisis, the anti-bankruptcy pact of April 1997, see chapter 3 in this book). Contrary to the expressed intentions of successive governments, chaebol increased their control of the economy so that by 1987 sales of the top five groupings contributed 75 per cent of manufacturing GDP (Kim 1997: Table 6.2, 183). Moreover, the ranking of the top companies was relatively unchanged over two decades. Of the top ten chaebol in 1994, only four had not been in the top ten in 1975: the same companies – Samsung, Hyundai and LG – occupied the top three spots (although not in the same order) in 1975 and 1995; Samsung and LG had been the two largest groupings in 1965 (Kang 1996: Table 3.1, 54).

The imbalances in the structure of the economy severely constrained the policy options available to governments. Repeated efforts at economic restructuring from the mid 1970s, all designed to limit the role of chaebol in the economy, were frustrated by the conglomerates' growing economic and political power. Moreover, the central role that industrial policy had played in directing industrial development placed governments in a difficult position – they felt compelled to provide additional assistance to corporations and banks that had encountered financial difficulties because of previous state-mandated 'policy' loans. A 'too big to fail' syndrome also existed, with governments concerned about the effects on employment, economic stability and the financial system should one of the larger corporate groupings or commercial banks be permitted to go bankrupt. Problems in the manufacturing sector thus necessitated a government bailout of the financial sector. In the financial reforms of the mid 1980s, for example, a core government objective was to prevent corporate failures from weakening the financial system. Under the Industrial Development Law of 1985, the government exerted pressure on private banks to provide supplementary finance to companies in difficulty, and provided additional preferential loans and favourable tax treatment. The consequence was that the state appeared to be providing a sovereign guarantee to the finances of the corporate groups. Only one large chaebol was allowed to go bankrupt in the 1980s – the Kukje group, the seventh-largest chaebol, in 1985. However, the primary motivation appeared to be political rather than economic. The group's chairman had publicly complained about the government's demands for contributions to the Ilhae Foundation and the New Community Movement.[8] The dominant role of chaebol greatly complicated the task of economic liberalisation. Successive governments feared that liberalisation, especially of the financial system, would have the unintended consequence of enabling chaebol to carve an even more dominant role in the economy.[9] In an economy as lopsided as that of Korea, market solutions would not necessarily produce a flatter playing field.

In contrast to the big push of Korea, Taiwan followed a pattern of 'bifurcated capitalism'. Rather than sponsoring the growth of giant private conglomerates, the government in Taiwan maintained a stronger state sector and provided more space for small private firms. Publicly owned enterprises comprised a significant share of manufacturing output, particularly for basic commodities, and dominated many service sectors, including finance, transportation and telecommunications. When the government moved to strengthen the heavy industrial base in the 1970s, it relied upon state-owned enterprises rather than fostering large private conglomerates. When the second oil shock hit at the end of the decade the government was able to shift quickly to promoting cleaner, less energy-intensive industries based upon high technology, without worrying about the financial vulnerability and political interests of conglomerates. The government founded a variety of quasi-public research organisations such as the Industrial Technology Research Institute (ITRI) and the Institute for the Information Industry, which played important roles in the development of Taiwan's dynamic electronics and computer industries. Similarly, the government planned and managed the extremely successful Hsinchu Science-Based Industrial Park. The government avoided policy loans, instead relying primarily upon alternative tools such as tax incentives, research subsidies, land planning and labour immigration. Rather than favouring large companies, this approach systematically lowered entry barriers to favour small and medium-sized firms. ITRI, for example, conducted contract research and organised research and development consortia that made it possible for small manufacturers to compete in high-tech industries (Noble 1998).

Over the years, Korean and Taiwanese companies have followed distinctive paths to corporate success, especially in the modalities through which they have integrated into international production networks. Generalisation is hazardous, of course, and exceptions can be found in both countries to the patterns suggested here. Taiwanese companies have concentrated on computer products, often relying on original equipment manufacturing (OEM) contracts for products sold under the brand names of US and Japanese computer giants. Linkages with these corporations have provided ready access to technology and marketing outlets. In contrast, Korean chaebol set out to manufacture a much broader range of products on a mass scale, and to market them under their own brand names in direct competition with companies from industrialised economies.

In the past, OEM production was considered a sign of weakness. Taiwan's firms missed out on the high profits associated with branded marketing, and in recessions were not shielded by brand loyalty. However, Korean brands in various sectors – especially automobiles and consumer electronics – acquired a negative reputation in the North American market in the late 1980s that hindered their efforts to penetrate the world's largest single market. Markets in less-developed economies assumed increasing importance for Korea in the 1990s. Whereas the share of developing countries (including China) of Korea's exports rose from 26 to 51 per cent between 1990 and 1996, the share of industrialised countries fell from 70 per cent to 43 per cent. Korea's exports to the centrally planned economies, to Latin America and to the Middle East together accounted for 14 per cent of its total in 1996. For Taiwan, the comparable figure was only 5 per cent. Some might see the penetration of developing markets by Korean companies as a sign of their competence and versatility. Other commentators (for example, Ernst 1998) view Korea's growing dependence on developing country markets and the rapidly declining US share of its total exports as evidence of Korean companies' inability to sell their consumer products in markets where sophisticated consumers demand products that are on the technological frontier.

Reliance on different markets affected the two economies' relative vulnerability to economic crisis. Korea's concentration on slow-growing markets was one reason why its exports fared less well in the mid 1990s than those of Taiwan. In electronics, almost 60 per cent of Korea's exports were directed towards markets where demand was declining or stagnant (Japan, East Asia, other Asia, Latin America and Eastern Europe); in contrast, about 55 per cent of Taiwan's electronics exports went to the rapidly growing US market and to the European Union (Ernst 1998: 61–2).

The structure of production also contributed to differences in economic vulnerability. Whereas three leading sectors contributed almost equally to Taiwan's exports (computers, electronics and textiles each provided slightly over 15 per cent of the total), for Korea, one sector (electronics) constituted fully one-quarter of the total. Computers comprised less than 5 per cent of the total. Textiles and clothing provided another 15 per cent, autos 10 per cent and shipbuilding 4 per cent. A large part of Korea's exports were thus concentrated in sectors (memory chips, autos and shipbuilding) characterised in the mid 1990s by world overcapacity and declining prices.

Of course, Korean companies themselves had contributed to this surplus capacity. Semiconductors constitute over 40 per cent of Korea's exports of electronics, and of this figure well over 80 per cent of exports are of DRAMs. By the mid 1990s, Korean firms had captured roughly one-third of the world DRAM market and were sufficiently significant that their own production decisions affected their export prices.[10] Korean companies ignored the softening demand for 4 MB and 16 MB chips in the mid 1990s and continued to expand production capacity. Taiwan's electronics/computer industry is more diversified than its Korean counterpart: Taiwan accounts for only 3 per cent of world production of semiconductors and its output is far less concentrated in DRAMs.[11] Korea's concentration on exporting goods in which worldwide surplus capacity was growing was the major reason why its terms of trade turned negative in 1996. From 1995 to 1996, Korea's terms of trade deteriorated from 101.8 to 90.3 (1987 = 100). In contrast, Taiwan's terms of trade remained remarkably stable from the late 1980s and actually improved from 1995 to 1996 and again from 1996 to 1997 (in the latter year from 98.7 to 103.7; 1991 = 100) (Council for Economic Planning and Development 1998).

In 1996, although the volume of Korea's exports rose by more than 20 per cent their value increased by less than 5 per cent.[12] The two economies entered the period of the financial crisis with markedly different trajectories in trading performances. Korea did not rely more than Taiwan on weak trading partners in South-East Asia and Japan, but it did export more mass commodities into glutted markets.

Difficulties in penetrating the markets of industrialised economies, coupled with excessive debt burdens, severely depressed the profitability of Korean companies. In Korea, the profitability of business groups ranked between sixth and thirtieth in assets slumped dramatically during the 1990s. Even during the boom years of 1994 and 1995, the peak of the business cycle, chaebol ranked between eleventh and thirtieth were earning a negative return on assets (Table 4.4). The fragile state of chaebol finances was partly masked by the boom in semiconductor exports: in 1995, the year before the start of the crisis, the top three semiconductor companies (Samsung Electronics, Hyundai Electronics and LG Semiconductors) reportedly contributed 70 per cent of the total net profits of all the top thirty chaebol (IMF 1998a: 5–6). With the collapse of semiconductor prices in 1996, those companies too became vulnerable. In the words of Borensztein and Lee (1999: 7), the picture that emerges in analysing Korea's economic performance in recent years 'is one of economic growth sustained by higher and higher levels of investment even in the face of declining productivity of capital and almost vanishing corporate profitability'.

Table 4.4 Comparative rates of profitability
Return on assets of the top 30 chaebol in Korea (%)

	1993	1994	1995
1–5	1.86	3.54	4.86
6–10	0.87	1.17	1.10
11–30	–0.40	–0.06	–0.08
Mean for top 30	1.11	2.19	3.15

Source: Shin & Hahm (1998: Table 1.4)

Profitability in the manufacturing sector in Taiwan
(return on net worth, %)

1992	1993	1994	1995	1996
7.60	6.74	7.53	7.99	8.26

Source: Republic of China, Ministry of Economic Affairs
(Jingjibu) (1996)

Although profitability remained dangerously low in Korea in the 1990s, it actually improved from higher levels in Taiwan. We do not claim that an economic crisis would inevitably have occurred in Korea in 1997 had it not been for the contagion from South-East Asia. Indeed, the worst effects of the crisis might have been avoided had the government not attempted to prop up the won in the second half of the year (Park & Rhee 1998). However, there is overwhelming evidence that the Korean economy was more vulnerable to contagion than was its Taiwanese counterpart. In this context it is important to note that six of the thirty largest chaebol (Hanbo, Sammi, Jinro, Kia, Haitai and New Core) filed for court protection in bankruptcy proceedings in 1997, before the collapse of the Korean won. The IMF reports that, collectively, chaebol ranked between ten and thirty by size of assets posted losses in each year since 1992. Kia, the seventh-largest grouping, made losses in each year since 1994. The chaebol were in considerable disarray even before the currency collapse triggered by contagion from South-East Asia. Korea's crisis was thus much more than a financial crisis; it was rooted in problems in the 'real' economy – but these problems inevitably spilled over to the financial sector (Smith 1998). The chaebol's investment binge was responsible for a doubling of external debt in 1993–96.

In Taiwan, the near-absence of directed lending led to patterns of corporate finance very different from those of Korea. Lower levels of investment, coupled with respectable profits, meant that firms could fund much of their growth through retained earnings, leading to much lower debt:equity ratios. Lower interest burdens allowed firms to concentrate more on profits and less on cash flow and market share. Surplus savings also enabled smaller and medium-sized firms to borrow from banks. Popular perception notwithstanding, Taiwan's firms were not all small – Korea had just as many small manufacturers in proportion to the overall size of its economy – nor did they all serve niche markets: a handful of medium-sized firms from Taiwan, such as Tatung and ASUSTech, dominated world output in a number of industries, such as computer monitors, mice and motherboards. However, access to capital at reasonable but not subsidised rates encouraged them to specialise and form dense production networks with local and foreign firms rather than trying to create huge and diversified conglomerates.

Government financial policy helped ensure that private business conglomerates remained smaller, less leveraged and much less diversified than in Korea. Facing less discrimination in bank lending than in Korea, small and medium-sized enterprises remained more independent, accounting for a larger share of exports and establishing more links with foreign companies. A more open attitude toward foreign direct investment opened opportunities for small local firms to supply parts and components at the same time that it crimped the development of large conglomerates. For example, all of Taiwan's major automobile assemblers and manufacturers of telecommunications switching equipment depended upon investments and technology from foreign multinationals. In sum, compared to Korea, Taiwanese government policy, particularly financial policy, led to an industrial structure with greater roles for both state and market – and much less private oligopoly.

The Financial Sector

Government control over bank lending was the principal instrument through which the Korean state attempted to shape the economy's developmental trajectory. Government reliance on concessionary lending exerted a profound influence on the vulnerability of the Korean economy to externally induced financial crises. It weakened equity markets and encouraged business groupings to rely on debt rather than equity. Moreover, government interference weakened the financial system and generated moral hazard problems.

Although most banks in Korea were largely in private hands in the 1960s and 1970s, they were de facto public enterprises (SaKong 1993: 27) because legislation introduced in 1961 limited the voting rights of private shareholders. The government had the power to dictate lending guidelines, which it used to great effect in the policy loans directed to favoured industrial sectors and conglomerates. Policy loans constituted close to half of total domestic credit in the 1970s. Through most of that decade, the real interest rate on policy loans was negative. Continued government controls on bank interest rates led to a significant growth first in the curb market, then in the share of non-bank financial institutions as they were encouraged by the government as a means of restricting the curb market. By 1980, non-bank financial institutions accounted for more than a third of all deposits, a share that was to double in the course of that decade.

In the wake of a financial scandal in 1982, bank shares held by the government were privatised and the limits on private shareholders' voting rights were repealed.[13] Bank loan rates were unified. The banking sector was opened to foreign joint ventures and non-bank financial institutions were deregulated. Governments, however, continued to meddle extensively in bank policy. The government appointed senior executives, often from the ranks of former regulators, in a Korean variant of *amakudari*. In 1984, the government set ceilings on bank credit for each chaebol. It also continued to direct banks to lend to particular companies or for specified purposes. Policy loans still constituted between 40 and 50 per cent of total lending through 1992. Only later did their share fall substantially, to under 15 per cent by the mid 1990s.

Policy loans left two significant legacies. First, they spawned a large quantity of non-performing assets, estimated at more than 10 per cent of all loans in the mid 1980s. At the time, many of Korea's commercial banks arguably were technically insolvent (Park & Kim 1994: 209). Attempts to deal with the problem of non-performing assets led to further entanglement between banks, companies and the government. In 1985, a law provided tax privileges to banks for the sale of non-performing assets, and for special low interest loans to be extended by the Bank of Korea (BOK) to commercial banks to enable them to lend to the business groups that were interested in taking over non-performing assets. These arrangements, details of which were not made public, were intended to prevent bankruptcy of banks and firms alike.[14] By 1995, the ratio of non-performing loans of the commercial banks still stood at 5 per cent (Shin & Hahm 1998: Table 1.1). Korea's criteria for classifying loans as non-performing were lax by international standards, so that figure understates the actual share of bad loans.

Second, policy loans and consequent non-performing assets contributed to the low profitability of banks. Korean banks' return on assets averaged 0.56 per cent from 1990 to 1993; by 1996, that already low ratio had slumped to 0.26 per cent (OECD 1999: Table 14). Government involvement in credit allocation generated a typical moral hazard problem. Banks paid little attention to the creditworthiness of companies. Apparently secure in the belief that the government would intervene to rescue both company and bank should problems arise, they extended additional credit to companies to finance overdue interest payments. Equally important, rather than developing a capacity to assess the credit worthiness of borrowers, banks simply relied on property as the principal collateral for loans. Korean banks were judged by a leading bank rating agency to be among the least efficient in Asia (Delhaise 1998: Table 5.3), substantially worse not only than their counterparts in Taiwan but also those in Indonesia and China. The World Bank estimated that Korean banks in the first half of the 1990s had the highest percentage of non-performing loans, highest cost:income ratio and lowest returns on equity and on assets of the various Asian banking systems it surveyed (World Bank 1998a: Figure 3.3, 37). The bankruptcies of large chaebol in early 1997 severely weakened several commercial banks even before the onset of the crisis. Non-performing loans jumped to more than 7 per cent of the total.

Attempts to liberalise the financial system were complicated by fears that chaebol would be able to capture financial institutions and use them to reinforce their dominant position in the economy. Institutional investors were barred from owning more than 8 per cent of the shares of major city banks, a regulation that the chaebol circumvented through the purchase of shares by individuals associated with their companies. They were not barred, however, from ownership of merchant banks.[15] Nine new merchant banks were given licences by the Kim Young Sam government in 1994 and a further fifteen in 1996, adding to the six in existence before liberalisation of the financial sector began in earnest in 1993. Merchant banks, in principle, were regulated by the Ministry of Finance and Economy (rather than the BOK) but the ministry had fewer than ten officers to supervise the thirty merchant banks (Ji 1998: 3). The ministry failed to establish even a minimal regulatory framework such as capital adequacy ratios for these banks (Shin & Hahm 1998: 28). In the early 1990s, non-bank financial institutions replaced commercial banks as the principal source of loan funds for the corporate sector (Borensztein & Lee 1999: Table 3, 13).[16]

Liberalisation was accompanied not only by government failure to implement an appropriate framework of prudential regulation but by government policies that perversely encouraged short-term rather than long-term borrowing in foreign markets. The thirty merchant banks, together with twenty-eight foreign branches of commercial banks opened between 1994 and 1996, were allowed to engage in short-term borrowing without restriction (ostensibly to enable corporations to finance imports of capital goods). Long-term borrowing, in contrast, required approval from the Ministry of Finance and Economy, which also maintained restrictions on inward direct foreign investment.

Government policies thus directly encouraged the mismatch between short-term borrowing in foreign currencies and long-term domestic lending that triggered the financial panic that produced the collapse of the won.

Moreover, liberalisation of regulations on capital outflows, coupled with high domestic interest rates and low profitability, prompted banks to pursue high-risk international investments – a classic example of 'gambling for redemption'. The IMF reports that Korean financial institutions purchased 40 per cent of the first Eurobond issue by the Russian Federation, an entire Deutschmark issue by the Colombian government and more than 20 per cent of total bonds issues by Mexico and Brazil. Korean financial institutions also began to speculate heavily in derivatives, including substantial volumes of domestic Indonesian debt. Many of these instruments proved to be illiquid once the financial panic began in South-East Asia (IMF 1998a: 55). Underlying the banks' reckless investments was a belief that the government would bail them out if they got into difficulties.[17]

In contrast to Korea, the Kuomintang (KMT) has been able to maintain crucial boundaries between central and peripheral parts of the financial system. Central regulators such as the Ministry of Finance and the Central Bank of China are widely respected and relatively immune to political pressures. Standard and Poor's and Moody's singled them out as major reasons why Taiwan's banking system is relatively sound compared to the rest of Asia (*GSSB [Gongshang Shibao]*, 29 October 1998; see also Kuo & Liu 1998). Bank managers were promoted on the basis of seniority and avoidance of mistakes (bad loans) rather than on their contribution to marketing loans. As a result, bank loans flowed primarily to publicly owned firms and those with collateral, especially land. The Ministry of Finance required banks to limit loans to 70 per cent of value of land or stocks. Policy loans were largely limited to loans from the central government's Bank of Communications (*Jiaotong Yinhang*) to upgrade technology. Despite widespread contention that industrial policy inevitably leads to politicisation and bad loans, the Bank of Communications registered one of the lowest rates of non-performing loans in Taiwan at just 1.6 per cent at the peak of the country's financial instability in 1998 (*Caixun*, December 1998: 388). Unlike Korea, where merchant banks and non-bank financing grew explosively in the 1990s, in Taiwan traditional bank intermediation remained dominant (Cho 1994: ch. 6). Banks were neither aggressive, as in Korea, nor oriented to close relationships with customers, as in Japan.

Until late 1991, a decade after privatisation of Korea's banks, virtually all banks were publicly owned.[18] The Ministry of Finance then issued a raft of licences for new banks, but used administrative oversight to ensure that the growth of private banks remained slow and steady. In the 1990s, banks were only beginning to develop skills in credit analysis, risk management, product innovation and project financing. The influx of new banks encouraged innovation and customer service. Profitability and financial stability declined slightly, but remained far superior to Korea. From the end of 1993 to the end of 1997, return on assets at domestic banks declined from 1.1 per cent to 0.8 per cent, still many times higher than in Korea. Non-performing loans increased from a low 1 per cent to just under 3 per cent. The ratio of Tier 1 capital to risk-weighted assets fell from 16.8 per cent to 9.9 per cent, still well above the requirement of 4 per cent suggested by the Bank for International Settlements (BIS) (Central Bank of China [Zhongyang Yinhang] 1997: 36). Non-bank financing, including venture capital, grew rapidly, but from a small base. The financial system became somewhat more flexible and a bit more vulnerable to panic, but the change was limited.

Prudential supervision by Taiwan's provincial government, which actually owned more financial institutions than did the central government, was significantly weaker, but still far more stringent than in Korea. The 'big three commercial banks' traditionally owned by the provincial government have a huge first-mover advantage in the large network of branches in prime locations. Nevertheless, their return on assets has been only average and they have been plagued with non-performing loan rates nearly twice as high as those of the private banks (unweighted average of 5.37 per cent as of the end of July 1998: ZGSB [Zhongguo Shibao], 14 August 1998). When the crisis hit, their capital adequacy ratios failed to reach BIS standards. Taiwan Provincial Assembly members routinely used authority over budgetary authorisations of provincial banks to exert pressure on every aspect of their operation, from loans to personnel and procurement. However, individual politicians, rather than large conglomerates, were the major beneficiaries of public ownership. For many years the Provincial Assembly resisted the attempts of the central government to privatise provincial banks, but constitutional revisions passed in 1997 led to the effective dissolution of the provincial government and smoothed the way for privatisation in 1998.

In sharp contrast to the financial institutions regulated by Taiwan's central and even provincial governments, local financial institutions, especially community and agricultural credit cooperatives, have been plagued by endemic problems of politicisation, inefficiency and incompetence (Li & Zhuo 1997; Zhang 1998; Ho & Lee 1998). Responsibility for regulation of credit cooperatives lies with the Ministries of Interior, Construction and Agriculture. All are highly political agencies with intimate links to local public works and local politics. Given Taiwan's numerous local elections, cooperatives and agricultural associations are

crucial to local electoral success (*ZGSB*, 19 June 1998; on cooperatives
and factional politics in Taichung, including the link to the Speaker of
the Legislative Yuan, see *Shangye Zhoukan*, 14 December 1998: 54–8).
Cooperatives have received major regulatory advantages. They are
exempt from the minimum requirements that banks must meet on
capital and reserves and they do not pay taxes; partly as a result, they
have proliferated. In the mid 1990s, bad loans increased rapidly at both
cooperatives and agricultural credit departments. Over 20 per cent of
agricultural credit departments had (admitted) non-performing loans
rates of over 5 per cent. The government always bailed out depositors
(*GSSB*, 4 May 1998; see also Zhang 1998: 61). Though the KMT engaged
in extensive political manipulation of local financial institutions, they
remained a distinctly minor part of the overall financial system. Agricultural credit cooperatives controlled two-thirds as many branches as
domestic commercial banks but accounted for only a little over 4 per
cent of assets of financial institutions. Similarly, credit unions accounted
for 12 per cent of branches but only 5 per cent of total assets in 1994
(Republic of China, Ministry of Finance 1996: 16–17, 6–7). Government
policy and market pressures are converting many of the credit unions
into banks, which are subject to much tighter regulatory oversight.

Savings, Investment and the Balance of Payments

These contrasts in financial policy and industrial structure left Korea
more vulnerable to financial panic at every level. After the transition to
export orientation in the early 1960s, the economies of both Korea and
Taiwan maintained high rates of economic growth powered by high
levels of savings and investment. Over the next three decades Korea's
savings rates gradually increased to very high levels, but investment generally remained even higher, averaging 37 per cent of GDP throughout
the 1990s. With savings lagging behind investments, Korea ran persistent current account deficits. Foreign borrowing covered the deficits;
direct foreign investment, long discouraged by the government and
unwelcomed by chaebol, remained extremely limited. Korea's heavy
dependence on foreign loans was the foundation of sporadic balance of
payments crises when downturns in the global economy triggered debt
servicing problems. With gradual liberalisation of foreign borrowings,
Korea's debt snowballed after 1990. Total foreign debt rose from
$US32 billion in 1990 to more than $US110 billion at the end of 1996.
As a percentage of GNP, total foreign debt rose from 13 per cent at the
start of the decade to more than 20 per cent at the end of 1996. Neither
this figure nor Korea's debt service ratio (5.8 per cent in 1996), however,

was high in comparison either to levels previously prevailing in Korea or to those in some South-East Asian and Latin American economies (Chang, Park & Yoo 1998: 738). They fell well below the levels regarded as dangerous by the international financial institutions, but nonetheless rendered Korea vulnerable to financial panic. What was particularly problematic about Korea's debt was its maturity structure, with close to 60 per cent of the total at the end of 1996 being short-term – the consequence of the perverse incentive structures for financial institutions discussed above.

In the 1960s and 1970s, Taiwan also maintained very high levels of investment. However, unlike the case in Korea, savings were even higher, leading to persistent current account surpluses (and to lower rates of inflation and real interest). Beginning in the early 1980s – even before Taiwan's democratisation pushed government spending into the red and before the Plaza Accord and US pressure led to a significant revaluation of the New Taiwan dollar – Taiwan's economy departed fundamentally from the high-investment–high-growth pattern maintained by Korea. From 1980 to 1986, gross capital formation fell by almost half, from 33.85 per cent of GNP to 17.12 per cent. In the next couple of years capital formation recovered just over a third of that loss, to 23.10 per cent in 1988. For the next decade investment fluctuated closely around that level. Labour-intensive manufacturing no longer propelled investment, but after the unsettling experiences of the two oil shocks the government declined either to expand the state-owned sector or to use directed lending to spur massive investment in capital-intensive industries by large business groups; indeed, in some cases, such as petroleum refining, it continued to block them. By 1986, investment fell below half of savings and surplus savings exceeded 20 per cent of GNP, leading to an unsettling bubble in property and equity markets that forced the government to relax capital controls (DGBAS 1998: 36–7). By the late 1980s, share and bond markets began to contribute to corporate financing, but traditional bank intermediation remained far more dominant than in Korea.

Savings also declined, but more slowly. After peaking at 38.54 per cent of GNP in 1987, savings slid by a little over one-third to an average of 25 per cent from 1994 to 1998. In 1986–87 alone, Taiwan's foreign reserves swelled by more than $US50 billion (CEPD 1998). While current account surpluses declined from the peaks of 1986–87, the sharp decline in investment left Taiwan with comfortable surpluses, for example, in 1996, on the eve of the Asian financial crisis, almost $US11 billion (DGBAS 1998: 36, 46). As in Korea, Taiwan's foreign debts were short-term and unhedged, but because of the surplus of domestic capital they constituted only a trivial fraction of Taiwan's GDP and foreign exchange holdings – indeed, Taiwan became a net international creditor in the 1990s.

Political Sources of Financial Policy

The differences in financial structure and macroeconomic policy between the two countries stem from fundamental differences in their political structures. While both countries were conservative and pro-growth, the leading political institutions and the social groups that supported them differed in fundamental ways.

In Korea, big push capitalism rested on a coalition of the military and large business, a 'sword–won alliance', in the words of Tun-jen Cheng (1990). The military gave big business access to economic rents in exchange for political donations. An able bureaucracy, in part a legacy of Japanese colonialism, serviced the ruling coalition. The military, however, never succeeded in institutionalising its rule. Early attempts to consolidate a military-led political party gave way to personal rule largely based on the suppression of opposition, by a well-developed police apparatus. Presidential government was punctuated by occasional popular uprisings led by students, by factionalism and by declarations of martial law. Korean military regimes, however, partly because of pressure from US sponsors, maintained a democratic facade, the most important manifestation of which were national elections both for the presidency and for the National Assembly. Government was extremely centralised. Local officials were appointed from Seoul rather than being elected.

In the thirty-five years that the military ruled Korea after the end of the civil war, it never succeeded in gaining widespread popular legitimacy despite the impressive economic performance of the country under its stewardship. The military failed to construct a broad coalition of support. Agricultural interests often felt neglected by the regime's emphasis on industrialisation, and most urban elements were hostile. Workers were suppressed. Students and churches were opposed in principle to military rule. The middle class often questioned whether the benefits of big push capitalism justified the suppression of democratic rights. Military candidates for president succeeded in elections, however, not only because of the suppression of opposition parties by the state security apparatus but also because of divisions within the opposition, largely based on regional loyalties. In the first truly democratic election in 1987, for instance, the military candidate, Roh Tae Woo, won with only 37 per cent of the popular vote because his civilian opponents were unable to forge a united front. The lack of legitimacy of the military regimes in turn affected popular attitudes towards big business, which at best were ambivalent. Pride in the achievements of

Korean companies was tempered by resentment at the cosy relations between the military and the chaebol, and at the suppression of workers' rights.

Democratisation greatly complicated governance in Korea. The essence of big push capitalism had already come under challenge not just by pro-democratic elements but also by institutions staffed primarily by economists trained in North America.[19] By the early 1980s, the principal government coordinating agency for industrial policy, the Economic Planning Board, had become a strong proponent of internationalising the economy by exposing it to the rigours of the marketplace. It was supported by the most influential of the government-financed think-tanks, the Korea Development Institute. Industrial policy became an arena for struggle between various ministries; bureaucratic politics in the sector were complicated by the emergence of an independent electoral arena.

Efforts to rein in chaebol in the 1980s foundered for several reasons. One was their increasing ability, given the growing internationalisation of the economy and of their own operations, to circumvent government policies. Another was the vacillation in government policies: enthusiasm for confronting the chaebol waned when the economy experienced a downturn – and when elections were looming. In the period since the first democratic elections in 1987, the economic power of chaebol continued to increase. In 1986, the four largest chaebol contributed 5.7 per cent of Korea's GNP; by 1995 their share had grown to 9.3 per cent.

Big business enjoys substantial leverage in any political system, a reflection of the structural power of capital. In few industrialised economies, however, is economic power as concentrated as it is in Korea. Democratisation arguably strengthened the political power of big business in Korea. Korean national elections are very expensive, and the parties have no independent funds on which to draw.[20] The Federation of Korean Industries (FKI), the chaebol's principal lobby group, has been the largest source of political funding in Korea since its establishment in August 1961 (Lee 1996: 168). Additional funding came from individual businesses: it is evident that large firms withheld contributions if candidates were perceived to be anti-chaebol.[21]

Governments in the democratic era before the 1997 crisis were no more successful than their predecessors in constraining the chaebol. Policy failures in this domain were typical of the gridlock that has characterised Korea since democratisation. Mo and Moon (1999) attribute this policy gridlock to political culture, especially the legacy of authoritarianism and the 'unruly and irresponsible behaviours' of societal actors unwilling to accept compromise. We believe, however, that policy gridlock is better explained by structural features of the Korean polity.

Two of these structural features have already been noted: the structural power of big business, and bureaucratic rivalries. These rivalries were reinforced by different world views on economic policy, and exacerbated by democratisation, which led to far greater penetration of the state by societal elements (Lew 1999). In addition, however, Korean politics post-democratisation has been marked by the same divisions that were prominent during the military era. Unlike Haggard and MacIntyre (see chapter 3), we do not believe Korean parties can generally be characterised as 'strong, disciplined, even hierarchical'. Rather, political parties have been weak, divided from each other and often within themselves on regional lines, and organised around personal cliques. Conflict between the president and the legislature has been frequent. And presidents themselves have seldom enjoyed a strong mandate: no president in the democratic era has been elected with a majority of the votes cast. Typical of the fluidity and instability of Korean politics is the fact that the chief economic minister, the deputy prime minister, was replaced no fewer than seven times in the Kim Young Sam administration (Shin & Ha 1999: 67).

In contrast to Korea, the ruling Kuomintang (KMT) party in Taiwan was unusually well-organised and autonomous. On the mainland the KMT developed as a revolutionary party and in the 1920s it received organisational assistance from the Soviet Union. Under Chiang Kai-shek the KMT moved to the right, competing with but also learning from the Chinese Communist Party. Internal strife, corruption and the Japanese invasion weakened its discipline in the 1940s but immediately after removal to Taiwan the KMT managed to reorganise itself (Dickson 1993) and impose unquestioned leadership throughout society, including such rice-roots institutions as farmers associations and credit cooperatives (Chen 1995). As a result, analysts referred to the KMT of the authoritarian period as a 'quasi-Leninist' party (Cheng 1989). The wide range of enterprises inherited from the Japanese upon the retrocession of Taiwan enhanced the party-state's already impressive capabilities. The outbreak of the Korean War convinced the US government to resume aid to the KMT, but by that time the party had established a firm foundation in Taiwan and it was able to resist recurrent US pressure to reform and open up the political system. While Taiwan hosted US bases from the mid 1950s to the end of the 1970s, there were no unified military forces and the KMT rebuffed efforts to curtail the political commissar system through which the party controlled the military. In perhaps the biggest contrast with Korea, Taiwan had virtually no national elections until the 1990s. Taiwan did conduct local elections (unlike Korea from the 1960s to the mid 1990s), but the KMT was able to use its ubiquitous organisation and the revenues from party-owned enterprises to supervise local politicians and factions. The KMT lacked the incentive to find or create a big business partner and, indeed, feared that big business could compromise its goals and structural integrity. The strength and autonomy of the KMT ensured that Taiwan's economic policy was largely immune from the need to attract voters and campaign funds.

It is often suggested that the government's decision not to encourage the growth of large conglomerates reflected an ethnic split between a government dominated by mainlanders and a business class dominated by long-time residents of the island. This argument is unconvincing. Even while on the mainland, the KMT did not form a close relationship with businesses though both were based in the Shanghai area. After the move to Taiwan the business class was not entirely local. Plenty of mainlander firms such as Yu Long and Far Eastern were available to serve as partners had the KMT been so inclined (Noble 1998: 177–8). Government–business relations and credit allocation diverged from Korea because of differences in political organisation – the strength and autonomy of the quasi-Leninist KMT, the need of the Korean government to create capitalist partners – rather than ethnicity.

Deliberate repression of large business groups contributed (along with land reform and labour-intensive exports) to a relatively equitable distribution of income and wealth and to a much more fluid class system than in Korea. When Taiwan began democratising at the end of the 1980s, the economic agenda was dominated by debates over privatisation and expansion of the welfare state rather than economic concentration and financial policy. Nor was big business in a position to block financial reform.

If the KMT was stronger domestically than were ruling parties in Korea, its external situation was considerably weaker. Taiwan's small size and open economy rendered it potentially vulnerable to instability and manipulation by the much larger mainland, and its diplomatic isolation meant that it could not hope for aid from the IMF, Japan or the United States. The KMT feared not only the inflation and financial impropriety that had destroyed its political base in China's coastal cities in the 1940s, but also capital flight and infiltration by investors acting on behalf of the mainland. The KMT created a strong and highly conservative central bank, headed through much of the rapid-growth period by a long-time retainer of the Chiang family. Macroeconomic policy consistently placed priority on fiscal probity and control of inflation. If necessary, as after the oil shocks, the KMT sacrificed growth to stability (Cheng 1990).

Taiwan also placed severe restrictions on the overseas activities of local financial institutions. Considering Taiwan's level of economic development and dependence on exports, its financial activities

remained surprisingly domestic. Until the late 1980s, outward investment was strictly controlled and banks established few overseas
branches. In the 1990s, as Taiwan's manufacturers were forced to move
abroad to seek cheaper land and labour, some internationalisation of
finance began, but the Ministry of Finance exercised close supervision
over risk management: banks that expanded too rapidly in a particular
country or industry faced delays in obtaining permits to open valuable
domestic branches (MOF interview, May 1998). The government
refused to allow banks to open branches on the mainland to service the
huge influx of investment from the island's manufacturers. If, in 1997,
Taiwan proved less vulnerable than Korea, then it was largely because
the KMT government retained the political incentive and the policy
tools to enforce conservative financial practices in the heart of the financial system.

The exception that proved this political rule and illustrated the
bifurcated nature of Taiwan's financial system was a series of stock scandals that erupted in the latter half of 1998. Slumping prices hammered
traditional commodity industries such as steel, dealing an especially
heavy blow to Kaohsiung and the south, where non-performing loans
spiralled. The stock market fell from over 10 000 points in the summer
to under 6500 points at year's end. A number of stock speculators were
unable to meet margin calls, which in turn threatened many securities
financing companies and created fears of a downward spiral of declining
stock and land prices. Almost all cases involved excessive diversification,
stock speculation and dependence on non-recurring income. Many
involved contacts with KMT legislators and local politicians (*ZGSB*, 6
October 1998; *GSSB*, 29 October 1998; *Shangye Zhoukan*, 16 November
1998, 14 December 1998; *Caixun*, December 1998). Looming legislative
elections worried the KMT. President Lee and Premier Siew imposed a
highly interventionist bailout plan upon reluctant officials at the
Ministry of Finance and the Planning Council. The plan called for
administrative guidance and a multi-billion dollar package to prop up
the stock market and provide relief financing to troubled but 'deserving'
companies. Analysts complained that bailout funds would surrepti-
tiously flow back into the stock market, prolonging the speculation.
After announcement of the plan, Yin Naiping, one of Taiwan's leading
scholars of finance, concluded that 'Taiwan is no longer qualified to say
that its economic fundamentals are sound' (*GSSB*, 13 November 1998).

Politically, though, the KMT evidently made an astute judgment: with
the stock market temporarily stabilised, the KMT won a majority in the
legislature, recaptured the mayorship of Taipei and barely lost in Kaohsiung (*Shangye Zhoukan*, 16 November 1998: 92; *ZGSB*, 4 November
1998; *GSSB*, 13 November 1998). The irregularities in the securities

sector exerted downward pressure on stock prices and undermined the quality of loan assets held by banks, but they did not fundamentally undermine the financial system. The government accelerated efforts to merge weak credit unions and convert them to banks, which were subject to closer supervision. Non-performing loans edged up to about 5 per cent, but with large injections of public funds the stock market recovered to between 7000 and 8000 points. In the wake of the diplomatic turmoil surrounding President Lee Teng-hui's statement in July 1999 that Taiwan should conduct relations with mainland China on the basis of 'special state-to-state relations', Taiwan's Central Bank of China (CBC) took firm action to prevent fluctuations in the value of the New Taiwan dollar from undermining confidence in the local economy and stock market (*Shangye Zhoukan*, 12 August 1999). Similarly, in the aftermath of a massive earthquake in September 1999 that killed more than 2000 people and caused billions of dollars in damage (and in anticipation of the upcoming presidential election), the government resorted to aggressive use of deficit financing. Although some observers worried that the government was not doing as much as the more deeply affected Asian economies to reform Taiwan's financial system (*Far Eastern Economic Review*, 11 March 1999), in the short-to-medium run the government was able to rely on huge foreign exchange reserves, a legacy of prudent budgeting and active management of markets to prevent the emergence of financial crisis.

As in Korea, politics exerted powerful pressures on the financial system but at a lower level and with much less dire implications for the overall financial situation. The KMT's dual strategy of using central regulators such as the CBC and the Ministry of Finance to impose conservative financial and economic goals while allowing local organs to be used for political purposes, proved more successful and less costly than the centralised 'politics of the vortex' that pervaded and eventually undermined the entire Korean financial system.

Conclusion

Decades of directed credit allocation and big push capitalism saddled Korea with a bevy of highly leveraged conglomerates, a chronic deficit on the current account and huge, unhedged short-term foreign debts. While Taiwan was not entirely invulnerable to financial pressures, as the stock scandals and corporate failures of 1998 demonstrated, the KMT's strategy of bifurcated capitalism protected the heart of the banking system and allowed Taiwan to ride out the worst of the Asian financial crisis.

This comparison may seem to strengthen the case for a 'fundamentalist' rather than 'panic-stricken' account of the crisis. Our position is between these extremes. The financial collapse that beset Korea in November 1997 was not inevitable. Had it not been for the South-East Asian crisis (and, indeed, for serious policy errors by the Korean government immediately before the collapse of the won), the Korean economy might have muddled through without the significant reverse suffered in 1997–98. However, Korea really did have much more serious economic and financial problems than did Taiwan, despite Korea's impressive growth record and generally sound fiscal and monetary policy. The declining rates of profitability among chaebol suggest that structural reform was long overdue and Korea's financial system, generally judged as among the least efficient in Asia, had recently experienced a partial liberalisation that provided perverse incentives to poorly regulated financial institutions. On the other hand, even conservative Taiwan had an increasingly difficult time implementing prudential regulation as the financial system grew more complex and open. This suggests that the IMF's position that the unfettered movement of international capital is safe and desirable as long as prudential regulation is adequate may be excessively optimistic about the capacity of most developing (and even fairly developed) countries to implement the requisite regulatory framework. Taiwan's success in riding out the storm also suggests the wisdom of slow careful liberalisation – and of keeping $US80 billion worth of foreign exchange in the bank.

The divergent responses to the strains of 1997–98 clearly reflected the legacies of markedly different approaches to capital allocation and government–business relations more broadly. Of course, even path-dependent approaches allow for the possibility that political and economic crises can cause countries to head in new directions. The crisis in Korea, coupled with the election, for the first time, of a president from the opposition parties, opened new political space for reformist elements. Moreover, the involvement of the IMF, through the conditionality attached to its massive bailout package for Korea, provided a scapegoat that at least initially could be blamed for the politically unpopular aspects of the restructuring program.

The government's immediate response to the crisis was impressive, as, indeed, was the rapidity of the economy's recovery. The Kim Dae Jung administration introduced a comprehensive package of reforms that embraced restructuring of the financial sector, the corporate sector and labour markets. The government closed insolvent banks and set aside 64 trillion won (14 per cent of GDP) for bank recapitalisation and the purchase of non-performing loans. A new independent regulatory authority, the Financial Supervisory Commission, was introduced. Corporations were required to reduce their debt:equity ratios to 200 per cent, to reduce the number of subsidiaries and to abandon the practice of cross-subsidising subsidiaries. New regulations provided for improved corporate governance with more rights for minority shareholders, mandatory inclusion of outsiders on boards of directors, and greater transparency in the presentation of financial statements. The government abolished ceilings on foreign shareholdings in individual companies and permitted all forms of mergers and acquisitions, including hostile takeovers. Firms were permitted to lay off surplus workers; the government established agencies to assist workers find temporary employment and greatly expanded the coverage of the unemployment insurance system.[22]

The Korean economy bounced back far more rapidly than the crisis economies of South-East Asia. By the end of 1998 the economy had stabilised, laying the foundations for growth in 1999 that exceeded 8 per cent. The collapse of imports contributed to a current account surplus of $US40 billion (equal to 12.5 per cent of GDP) in 1998. Together with loans from international financial institutions and new flows of foreign direct investment, the trade surplus replenished Korea's foreign exchange reserves. By the end of 1998 reserves stood at $US50 billion, substantially higher than the country's short-term debt. A budget deficit of more than 3 per cent in 1998 not only boosted the social security net and helped recapitalise the financial system, but provided much-needed finance to small and medium-sized enterprises.

Despite economic success and the president's undoubted commitment to fundamental economic restructuring, all-too-familiar features of the political economy reappeared. In Korea, the hand of the past weighs heavily. Efforts at reform have repeatedly fallen victim to a 'tarbaby' effect: despite its rhetorical commitment to liberalisation, strong government action was required to tackle the cumulative effects of previous interventions. And enthusiasm for reform has waned now that the immediate crisis is past, especially if efforts at reform appear likely to generate a political backlash.

The dominant role of chaebol in the economy continues to present the most significant challenge to restructuring in the corporate and financial sectors. To reduce excess production capacity, the government negotiated directly with chaebol leaders to forge 'Big Deals' in eight major industries, aiming to force greater specialisation through mergers of subsidiaries. Government intervention, however, has had a number of perverse consequences beyond creating a further moral hazard problem (if the merged companies fail, will the government not be obliged to bail them out?) In particular, implementation of the mergers will lead to greater concentration in the various sectors, a move from oligopoly to monopoly or duopoly. The government appears to lack the political will to enforce the hard decisions necessary to reduce excess capacity, given the opposition of labour unions to the mergers. In the semiconductor industry, managers of the new enterprises have promised not to lay off any workers for at least two years. In the car industry, the government reportedly initially pressed Daewoo to continue to produce the unprofitable Samsung car for two years after its takeover of the Pusan plant, then extended the period to five years. It reportedly also insisted that Daewoo's bank creditors share the losses from the continued production of the cars.[23] The reorganisation of industries through the merging of subsidiaries also suggests to foreign investors that the government is reluctant to allow acquisitions in these key sectors.

As with previous economic crises, the Korean economy has bounced back remarkably quickly. Too quickly, according to many advocates of reform. With the crisis receding into the background, the removal of the IMF scapegoat and the approach of parliamentary elections, the political incentives for pursuing radical economic restructuring disappeared. As in previous administrations of the democratic era, the president has had to battle an often-hostile National Assembly and resort to familiar Korean parliamentary tricks to get his legislation through. Any national consensus on the need for fundamental economic restructuring in response to the crisis soon evaporated.

The chaebol have been able to use their dominant economic position to continue to evade government efforts at reform. Cross-subsidisation of subsidiaries continues even after some of the subsidiaries were spun off under supposedly independent ownership.[24] Although government efforts to push the chaebol to reduce their debt:equity ratios have enjoyed some success, the move has also had unintended consequences. Some chaebol have aggressively marketed stock investment funds that observers suspect have been used to subsidise affiliates.[25] Meanwhile, the largest chaebol dominated issues in the local equity market, the five largest conglomerates accounting for 55 per cent of total funds raised by rights offerings in the first half of 1999. The problems that the insolvency of the Daewoo group caused for the financial sector in mid 1999 suggest that the government will continue to consider that the chaebol are 'too big to fail'.

In Taiwan, the financial shock was much smaller and the elections of December 1998 left the KMT in control, ensuring considerable continuity of policy. The slow privatisation of the three main commercial banks continued, but Taiwan backed away from its previous commitment to remove all capital controls. The legacies of Korea's big push capitalism and Taiwan's bifurcated capitalism continue to exert a profound influence on the countries' developmental trajectories. So far, at least, the Asian financial crisis has not fundamentally transformed the political economies of either of these East Asian countries.

CHAPTER 5

Indonesia: Reforming the Institutions of Financial Governance?

Natasha Hamilton-Hart

Indonesia: Regulatory Failure and Reform

As Indonesia's currency crisis deepened from late 1997, the country's well-known regulatory weaknesses began to assume greater significance in the eyes of domestic and foreign reformers. As a result, Indonesia, like Thailand and Korea, adopted an IMF-led program of bank restructuring, structural economic reforms and changes to the legal framework governing banking, bankruptcy and corporate governance. Indonesia's currency collapse was by far the most severe of all the crisis-hit countries; its economy contracted the most and signs of recovery were slow to emerge. Nonetheless, for the optimistic, the very depth of the crisis in Indonesia offered prospects for real reform, as the rotten core of the country's political and administrative system was conclusively exposed. In May 1998, President Suharto was forced to resign after thirty-two years in power. He was succeeded by his deputy, B.J. Habibie, who assumed office as an interim president.[1] Habibie voiced support for legal reform, removed controls over the media, released political prisoners and scheduled open elections for June 1999. In addition, the new government stated its commitment to financial sector reform, with the support of the International Monetary Fund (IMF) and other external agencies.

The failure of financial governance cannot account for the timing and extent of the currency crisis, but regulatory weakness did make Indonesia vulnerable to a sudden reversal of capital flows. Private external debt had been grossly underreported and prudential bank regulation was largely unenforced, aggravating the inherent instability of a post-deregulation financial sector (Nasution 1992; McKinnon & Pill 1996). The self-defeating attempt at maintaining restrictive monetary policy and a crawling currency peg that ensured progressive devaluation in the context of large capital inflows was also a factor behind the currency crisis (McLeod 1998a). This policy mistake was itself a product of Indonesia's underlying political economy.[2] Thus, even if the crisis cannot be explained without reference to external factors, domestic governance was also relevant.

This chapter asks whether the financial sector reforms that have been proposed and partially implemented as of September 1999 address the causes of regulatory failure in Indonesia. After reviewing the development of the financial crisis, the chapter describes the financial sector reform agenda. The main features and failings of Indonesia's earlier record of financial reform are then summarised. The final section assesses the post-1997 reforms in the light of the earlier failure of financial governance.

The main conclusion is that although the conditions attached to the use of IMF funds have provided reformers with a considerable source of leverage, the reform process has done virtually nothing to improve financial governance even though the reforms have brought changes to the law and upgraded the technical qualifications of those administering it. Both these tactics were employed by the previous government and are unlikely to solve problems of poor enforcement, corruption and the manipulation of public policy by governmental and non-governmental actors. The reform agenda explicitly targets 'weak governance' but it largely misdiagnoses the sources of regulatory failure in Indonesia, with the result that many reforms fail to achieve their stated aims and some are actually perverse. The limits to reform in Indonesia are often not the result of determined resistance by government actors, nor can they be wholly accounted for by the depth of the economic crisis itself, although both these factors have played a role. We argue that many of the paradoxical or nugatory aspects of crisis management and reform in Indonesia stem from the very nature of the reform blueprint, together with deep-seated features of the Indonesian governing system. The model of crisis management and financial governance promoted in Indonesia follows fairly closely the template set out in global blueprints for a new financial architecture. However, that template is one that, in practice, demands a large role for public authority and public resources. This makes it difficult to apply in a country such as Indonesia, where the government has rarely been able to deploy either authority or resources in a disciplined manner for public purposes.

The significance of this type of government indiscipline depends on external factors and the public policy goal at issue. After all, Suharto's regime was always corrupt but it presided over many developmental achievements for thirty years (Hill 1996). Oil revenues, generous foreign aid and the locational advantage of being part of an increasingly integrated and rapidly growing region were all external factors that supported growth in Indonesia during that period. And although the government was corrupt and often administratively weak, it was not the equivalent of the Marcos regime in the Philippines or what Peter Evans has termed 'predatory' states such as Zaire (Evans 1995: 43–7; Schwarz 1994: 147). The presidential family did not simply move billions of dollars offshore; development spending did produce roads, schools and agricultural infrastructure, and repression was efficient and restrained enough to secure order rather provoke widespread insurgency.[3] But even if patrimonial government was compatible with capitalist development (Robison 1986), the government often failed on tasks that required the active enforcement of policy against powerful interests. This failure had ramifications across a wide range of issues – from forest management to bank supervision to justice for ordinary Indonesians (Dauvergne 1997: 60–9; MacIntyre 1993; Hendro Sangkoyo 1999) – but few adverse effects, at least in the medium term, for overall economic growth.

A government's ability to deliver economic growth is thus not a good predictor of its ability to supervise and regulate a modern financial sector. Nor is a government's ability to carry out liberalising financial reforms a good predictor of whether it can manage the consequences of competition and development in the financial sector. Post-liberalisation financial crises can be expected on both theoretical and empirical grounds (Diaz-Alejandro 1985; McKinnon & Pill 1996). Indonesia, which implemented a technocrat-led program of financial liberalisation in the 1980s, did not have the capacity to supervise its liberalised financial system. Prudential supervision and financial liberalisation entail not only different administrative capacities but different political preconditions. A simple model of collective action explains why: the benefits of financial deregulation in the context of an open capital account are relatively concentrated, while the costs and risks are diffuse. Conversely, the costs of compliance with prudential regulation are concentrated and the benefits diffuse. Therefore, deregulatory reforms, at least in the financial sector, are politically easier than prudential regulation, particularly if circumstantial factors (such as balance of payments crises) make the status quo untenable.[4] Indonesia's record of financial liberalisation, described in a later section, provides evidence to support this logic: rapid growth in the deregulated private banking sector sustained rather than eroded a patronage-based political economy. The private interests favoured prior to financial reform also gained most under deregulation (Hamilton-Hart 1999: 131–4), especially since the state bank sector, while rapidly shrinking, remained significant enough to absorb the transitional costs associated with other economic reforms.[5]

As long as significant regulatory weaknesses persist, a financial sector that is simultaneously developed, liberalised and stable is unlikely in Indonesia.[6] This raises the question of whether, given the regulatory context, financial liberalisation was a mistake on the part of the Indonesian and foreign economic technocrats who advocated it from the 1980s. That is a larger question than can be answered here, since it depends on how one theorises the relationship between financial liberalisation and growth, as well as how one weighs the efficiency losses of financial controls against the costs of financial instability. Suffice it to say that both theory and evidence on the costs of various types of financial control are contested[7] and that most analyses fail to take into account the practical difficulties of providing the supporting regulatory infrastructure on which successful financial liberalisation depends. For developing countries in particular, there may be reasons to constrain competition in the financial sector (Hellmann, Murdock & Stiglitz 1997). As economies mature, controlled financial systems that had positive or neutral effects on growth appear to become more unwieldy and costly (Patrick & Park 1994). In the Indonesian case, a financial system that was heavily state-controlled until the mid 1980s was significantly inefficient and prone to abuse (MacIntyre 1993). Nonetheless, the attempt to create a modern and liberalised financial sector was probably premature: compared to countries such as Korea and Japan when they began financial liberalisation, Indonesia's per capita income was lower, its industrial structure less mature and the government's institutional capacity for supervision much weaker.

Financial Crisis 1997–1998

Poor-quality bank loans and pressures on monetary policy due to large inflows of capital were evident prior to 1997 (Nasution 1992; Dean 1996; Siregar 1996). On the whole, however, optimism about the financial sector was high. Deregulatory reforms were considered successful (Cole & Slade 1996), the stock market was buoyant (if occasionally turbulent) and bank stocks were particularly favoured. Reports by three foreign securities houses on Indonesian banks reflected the mood among investors. In November 1996, the Credit Lyonnais billing of the sector was 'Rise and Shine', the W.I. Carr March 1997 assessment was positive, although predicting greater competition, and although the March 1997 Jardine Flemming report did express concern about Indonesian banks the report predicted difficulties, not major instability. Indonesia's macroeconomic fundamentals, it said, looked very good. The Jakarta

Stock Exchange index continued to rise until 8 July 1997 (Evans 1998: 19).

Then in August 1997, in the wake of Thailand's forced devaluation, the Indonesian stock market began to fall and the crawling peg exchange rate was abandoned in favour of a relatively free float. The currency continued to slide despite raised interest rates, which began to cause problems for Indonesian banks. Indonesia began negotiations with the IMF, with which it reached an agreement on 31 October. The central bank, in cooperation with the Monetary Authority of Singapore and the Bank of Japan, intervened to support the rupiah in the first week of November. With the IMF-led support package of $US37 billion, these measures contributed to stabilising the rupiah at around 3200 to the dollar, down from 2400 at the start of 1997 (Soesastro & Basri 1998: 9–13).[8]

Success, however, was short-lived. The currency fell steeply in December and dramatically in January, reaching Rp16 500 to the dollar that month before recovering somewhat in March and April, only to crash again to nearly 16 000 in June. The decline from early 1997 to early 1998 amounted to a real devaluation many times greater than any Indonesia had experienced before.[9] By mid September 1998, the stock market had lost 60 per cent of its July 1997 value – 91 per cent in US dollar terms (Evans 1998: 20). Although stock and currency values improved towards the end of the year, the banking system remained effectively bankrupt. Corporate indebtedness, unemployment and poverty were not receding and concerns about political stability were increasing. Street riots in Jakarta in May 1998 had already resulted in about 1000 deaths and violent outbreaks continued in 1999, mainly in the outer islands but also in Java, including the capital itself in late 1998. The economy contracted by about 14 per cent in 1998, a decline that dwarfs the country's last recession in the 1960s (Evans 1998: 5). By March 1999, the central bank classified 59 per cent of all bank loans in Indonesia as non-performing (Bank Indonesia 1999a: 105). By April 1999, private bank claims on the private sector had been written down to Rp134 trillion, from 202 trillion a year earlier (Bank Indonesia 1999b: Table I.8).

The Reform Agenda

Financial sector reforms announced from November 1997 fall into three categories: crisis management and bank restructuring, policy reform and institutional reform. This section summarises the initiatives and outcomes in each area.

Crisis Management

Crisis management efforts provide a window on the financial sector political economy in Indonesia as it is unfolding. The first significant development was the closure of sixteen 'unviable' banks on 1 November 1997, a day after Indonesia concluded its agreement with the IMF. The IMF press release stated that the Indonesian authorities 'are determined that only a small portion of the costs of the restructuring will be met from the public purse. The government will compensate small depositors only, and not private shareholders and creditors. The government will not guarantee any liabilities of private non-financial companies, domestic or foreign' (IMF, Press Release no. 97/50, 5 November 1997). The sixteen banks closed in November were small, but some had connections to the Suharto family. Rather than generating credibility through resolute action, the closures provoked a run on bank deposits and exacerbated capital flight. Any gains accruing to the government for resoluteness were lost when one of the closed banks associated with the Suharto family reopened shortly afterwards under a different name (Soesastro & Basri 1998: 19–20).

Under pressure from massive currency falls, the government submitted a revised set of structural reforms and financial policies to the IMF in January (GOI 1998a). The report stated that Indonesian banks were required to submit rehabilitation plans to the central bank. Banks had already been weakened by the currency collapse, increased interest rates, deposit runs and capital flight. The result was a huge increase in Bank Indonesia liquidity support to the banking system. In response to depositor panic and the refusal of international banks to accept letters of credit issued by Indonesian banks, Bank Indonesia announced on 27 January that it would guarantee all deposits and liabilities of local banks for two years – effectively assuming banking sector risk (Johnson 1998: 46–50). Central bank emergency support to the banks amounted to around Rp140 trillion by the end of 1998.

Earlier statements on limiting the public costs of rescue thus gave way to the need to restore confidence. The government stated that this task was its top priority, to which end it was working with the IMF, the World Bank and the Asian Development Bank (GOI 1998a). Bank Indonesia actions, however, created opportunities for banks to take advantage of the situation. Up to Rp60 trillion of central bank liquidity support was allegedly diverted by bank owners to settle overseas debts (*Jakarta Post*, 29 July 1999), to invest in high-yielding central bank bonds or simply to invest offshore. Central bank emergency advances, therefore, 'were providing the funds that fed the run on the rupiah. No effective action was taken to prevent the banks from funding capital flight' (Cole & Slade 1998: 64).[10]

The situation was exacerbated by a rift between President Suharto and his economic advisers. Suharto pursued the idea of a currency board system, sacked the governor of the central bank and resisted action that would have damaged the business interests of his children and associates (Robison & Rosser 1998). In February, a leaked letter from the IMF's managing director threatened the withdrawal of financial support and on 6 March the IMF announced the suspension of the second instalment of Indonesia's bailout package (Johnson 1998: 27–8). Suharto soon backed down: the currency board idea was dropped, a projected tax on foreign exchange trading was discarded and monetary policy was tightened. A revised agreement with the IMF in April kept the structural reforms of the January agreement but expressed a new willingness to consider government aid in solving the private offshore debt problem (Johnson 1998: 31). From this time, the government occasionally stalled on some issues but largely acceded to the IMF-led reform agenda.

The main organisation given the task of managing the banking crisis was the Indonesian Bank Restructuring Agency (IBRA), created on 27 January 1998 and granted extensive powers. Within a few months IBRA had fifty-four banks, representing 40 per cent of banking assets, under supervision (Johnson 1998: 47). It had taken over most of the country's large private banks, including Bank Central Asia (BCA), owned by Suharto crony Liem Sioe Liong and two of Suharto's children.[11] By July 1999, IBRA declared that it had assets worth Rp600 trillion under management, in the form of twelve nationalised banks, other bank shares, non-performing loans transferred from state and private banks, and corporate assets pledged by former bank owners and private debtors (*Jakarta Post*, 2 July 1999).

IBRA was thus a critical actor in Indonesia's financial reform program, responsible not only for nationalised banks and non-performing loans but for determining whether and how former bank owners and delinquent debtors (categories which overlapped considerably) would be held accountable. In July 1999, an Indonesian analyst made detailed allegations of bribery involving IBRA staff, the ruling political party and one of the banks receiving government recapitalisation funds (*Business Times*, 4 August 1999). The affair, which became known as the 'Bank Bali scandal', prompted the IMF, World Bank and Asian Development Bank (ADB) to suspend loan payments to Indonesia.[12] IBRA's chairman pointed squarely to politicians from President Habibie's Golkar party (and indirectly to the president himself) as the actors behind the irregular payments (*Kompas*, 14 September 1999). The incident made it plain that, if not corrupt itself, IBRA was unable to prevent abuses.

Well before the Bank Bali scandal broke, however, several question marks hung over IBRA and the bank restructuring process. Bank Indonesia and a large number of foreign accountants carried out audits of all Indonesian banks during 1998, ostensibly to provide an objective basis for deciding which banks would be closed and which recapitalised to bring their risk-weighted capital adequacy ratios up to 4 per cent, as called for in the third agreement with the IMF (Johnson 1998: 57–8). Thirty-eight banks were closed in March 1999 and a further seven which failed to meet the recapitalisation criteria (having capital adequacy ratios below –25 per cent) were nationalised on the grounds that their size made that the less costly option. The delay in reaching this decision was widely interpreted as the result of lobbying by bankers and government attempts to muster support for particular bank owners (*Australian Financial Review*, 4 March 1999; *Business Times*, 18 March 1999). Bank owners whose banks were closed or nationalised included a number with ties to Suharto or Habibie. This meant that the recapitalisations and closures could be taken as a sign of increased decisiveness and reduced political interference.

In fact, the restructuring suggested that the politics of banking under Habibie would not be clean or decisive. While some former cronies and members of the Suharto family lost their banks (*Business Times*, 16 March 1999), most of the 'casualties' of the plan were injured only to the extent that, by losing banks with negative worth, they were relieved of obligations to depositors and the central bank. Further, the government announced that it would not manage the nationalised banks and that their former owners would be given the option of buying them back (*Business Times*, 17 March 1999).

Confusion and the perceived politicisation of the bank restructuring process meant that both official support and official pressure raised allegations of impropriety. For example, the central bank justified an early allocation of recapitalisation funds to Lippo Bank, owned by the Riady family, on the basis that it had submitted the most viable business plan. This was an attempt to counter rumours that the funds were a special favour to James Riady, who was known to meet regularly with President Habibie (*Business Times*, 30 January 1999). Parliament revoked the government's plans for recapitalisation on the grounds that it smacked of corruption (*Business Times*, 19 February 1999). Yet when the government took action against bankers, it was sometimes considered to be acting unfairly. For example, the Widjaja family members who controlled Bank Internasional Indonesia (BII) were forced to resign their board positions on the grounds that they were not 'fit and proper', even though the family was raising private funds to recapitalise the bank and no legal process had been launched against them.[13] When IBRA published lists

of debtors owing money to state banks in June 1999, the intended effect
of demonstrating transparency was undermined by the agency's
inclusion of two businessmen known to be under pressure from Habibie
in a list of twenty-six 'non-cooperative' debtors. Of the hundreds of
debtors owing money to the state banks, these were by no means the
largest.[14]

Given the lack of transparency, it is difficult to judge whether the government was 'bailing out the owners of banks while disproportionately
punishing the real sector' (*Asian Wall Street Journal,* 30–31 July 1999: 10)
or attempting to impose a degree of accountability on Indonesian
bankers. It is clear that the public bailout of the banking sector was
huge. In June 1999, the revised figure for the total public cost of bank
recapitalisation was Rp550 trillion – over three and a half times government domestic revenue for 1998–99 and over 50 per cent of 1998 GDP.
Most of that amount would be funded by government bonds at market
rates of interest, issued to the recapitalised banks. Moody's Investor
Services estimated that the government could spend over Rp732 trillion
restructuring the banking sector (*Business Times,* 11 September 1999).

The government is unlikely to recover more than a fraction of those
costs. On the broader question of accountability, the evidence is mixed.
Liem Sioe Liong disposed of some assets in Indonesia, reportedly in
order to repay Bank Indonesia emergency credits and regain control of
his bank, BCA (*Business Times,* 19 December 1998, 28 January 1999).
Some bank owners, for example the owner of Bank Danamon, Indonesia's second-largest private bank, appear to have minimised their
obligations.[15] The extent of the overall bailout in this and other cases
will depend on IBRA's asset recovery actions. As noted above, IBRA's
credibility has been damaged by its inability to prevent (or uncover) the
Bank Bali scandal and in other respects it has performed poorly, at best
non-transparently.

After its first year of operation IBRA was described as a paper tiger,
unable or unwilling to advance the process of recovering bank debts
despite its extensive extrajudicial seizure powers (*Far Eastern Economic
Review,* 22 April 1999: 68). By the end of June 1999 it had realised only
Rp1.4 trillion from its loan recovery efforts, mainly from small retail
credits. Former bank owners and some of the largest bad debtors of state
banks were meant to have pledged assets to IBRA to cover their debts.
Even though most of these bank owners were known to have grossly
exceeded legal limits on related party lending, none had been prose-
cuted for abuses of the banking law. The owners of five large
private banks taken over in 1998 were reportedly given immunity from
prosecution in return for an agreement with IBRA to hand over shares

in their non-banking assets (*Far Eastern Economic Review*, 22 April 1999: 68).

IBRA announced that it had 'recovered' over $US10 billion in such assets, but it also said that the assets were still under the day-to-day management of the original owners (IBRA 1999). An internal IBRA source said that at the end of June IBRA had over Rp175 trillion (about $US27 billion at prevailing exchange rates) in pledged assets but that ownership of the assets had not been transferred to IBRA (interview, Jakarta, June 1999). A World Bank official insisted that full ownership rights had been transferred to IBRA, but refused to reveal any details about the kind of assets transferred, the basis for their valuation or who was responsible for their management (interview, Jakarta, July 1999). Some pledged assets are encumbered by significant debt.[16] IBRA has announced plans to sell some of the assets transferred to it but has yet to make any sales (*Jakarta Post*, 16 July 1999; *Business Times*, 16 July 1999). It is likely that politics will affect any disposal of IBRA assets. IBRA's head said that the agency would consider social issues such as employment and distribution when disposing of assets, and that the agency might have a role in creating 'a new entrepreneurial class' (*Business Times*, 20 November 1998) – probably a reference to political calls to support non-Chinese business interests.

IBRA's internal management was also flawed.[17] The fee structure negotiated with its consultants (Lehman Brothers, J.P. Morgan and Danareksa, a state-owned Indonesian firm) was criticised as overly generous, insufficiently tied to IBRA's performance and creating incentives for IBRA to overvalue the assets it takes over. The agency had paid Rp650 billion (over $US90 million) to its consultants over a period in which it realised only Rp1.4 trillion in gross income. As well as budget funds, IBRA received a World Bank loan of $US10 million for such fees, which have the potential to increase many times. Press reports also noted an apparent conflict of interest – IBRA's chairman was concurrently the president of Danareksa. Further, IBRA's non-consultant staff were largely recruited from the banks it took over – at least some of which are still traded on the stock exchange, despite being 99 per cent owned by IBRA.[18]

Overall, two features of the bank restructuring process stand out. First, despite transparency being the watchword of the day and despite the close involvement of external agencies, the process was opaque and confused, making it impossible to impose any credible accountability on bankers, debtors or officials. Second, it was impossible to avoid an enormous public bailout of the banking system.

Policy Reforms

The October 1997 IMF agreement called for trade liberalisation, the deregulation of monopolies and privatisation to enhance domestic competition. In mid January the government's letter of intent to the IMF (GOI 1998a) noted that the rehabilitation of state banks was under consideration with technical support from the World Bank, with the aim of eventual privatisation. The banks were not to be recapitalised except in conjunction with privatisation. Competition was to be enhanced by levelling the playing field for foreign investors, lifting restrictions on foreign-owned banks and foreign ownership of local banks. The government announced in December 1998 that most of the state banks were to be merged into a new entity, Bank Mandiri, as a prelude to privatisation (*Business Times*, 5 December 1998).

Foreign banks acquired controlling stakes in two Indonesian banks and a third was under substantial foreign management by mid 1999. However, any immediate plans for reducing government ownership were entirely reversed by the recapitalisation program, which made the government the majority owner (in theory) of all major banks in Indonesia. In addition, the government established a new export financing bank to provide subsidised export credits, guarantees and working capital facilities for exporters (*Asian Wall Street Journal*, 30 November 1998: 11; *Jakarta Post*, 5 July 1999: 8). The commitment to privatise state-owned banks remains but the scheduled privatisation of Bank Mandiri is distant enough (sometime in 2001) to be completely uncertain – and a plan to sell the major nationalised banks by the end of 1999 is falling behind schedule. Full divestment is unlikely to occur quickly unless these banks are sold for far less than they have cost the government to rescue.[19]

Policy reform after the crisis also aimed to improve prudential regulation. Bank capital requirements, after being greatly increased, were reduced in the April 1998 IMF agreement, which nonetheless set them higher than they had been prior to the crisis (Johnson 1998: 50). An amendment to the banking law to eliminate restrictions on foreign investment in listed banks, amend bank secrecy laws and enable state bank mergers and privatisation was submitted to parliament on schedule in August 1998 (GOI 1998c). Another new banking law was passed, to increase disclosure requirements and rationalise prudential regulations and penalties. The condition of Indonesia's banking and corporate sector, however, made increased capital requirements and meaningful prudential regulation almost impossible. Industry analysts reportedly said that Bank Indonesia's monitoring efforts showed 'no signs of improvement' (*Australian Financial Review*, 16 March 1999).

One reform which might have significant results is the establishment of a better capital account monitoring system. Before the crisis, Indonesian authorities imposed minimal reporting requirements on capital transactions and private foreign liabilities later proved much higher than officially reported. Plans to remedy that deficiency first surfaced in Indonesia's October 1998 letter to the IMF, which envisaged IMF advice on procedures for monitoring capital flows (GOI 1998d). Like other initiatives in the reform process, it was surrounded by a degree of confusion. On the one hand, the government made repeated statements that any form of capital control was out of the question. On the other hand, an adviser to the central bank governor said that the monitoring mechanism 'could well be the beginning of some form of management of capital movements' – even though the governor denied this (*Business Times*, 5 February 1999). Later, a central bank director announced that some kind of tax on short-term flows might accompany the monitoring system, to be in place by June 1999. That too was denied by another director the following day (*Business Times*, 23 March 1999, 24 March 1999).

The new capital account monitoring system is yet to work in practice. As of July 1999, no decision had been taken on the minimum transaction size that would be subject to reporting requirements (*Jakarta Post*, 6 July 1999: 8). Overcoming the underlying reasons for poor monitoring will be crucial to the success of the new monitoring regime. The central bank will at least partially gain what it was previously denied – legal authority to investigate the foreign liabilities of Indonesian companies – but the authority could be ineffective. The policy may not be actively enforced, or it may be enforced but prove counterproductive because investors suspect it opens the way for intrusion and abuse. After all, a major reason for Indonesia's exceptionally free capital account regime since 1970 was the necessity to maintain the confidence of foreign and domestic investors (Hamilton-Hart 1999: 152–61). Sino-Indonesians in particular have good reason to doubt that the new kind of monitoring regime will be administered impartially.[20] As this example makes clear, successful policy reform, like crisis management, depends on underlying institutional capacities.

Institutional Reform

Obstacles to effective regulation in Indonesia exist at the organisational level, in personalised and institutionally weak administrative structures, as well as in the wider political economy. The post-crisis reform program reflects some recognition of the institutional causes of regulatory failure in Indonesia but envisages only limited institutional reforms.

In January 1998, the government committed itself to improving the supervision of the banking system, introducing new penalties for breaching prudential rules and upgrading Bank Indonesia's capacity for supervision with support from the IMF and the World Bank (GOI 1998a). From March, international experts provided active support in a number of government agencies, including the central bank and IBRA. As part of the April 1998 IMF agreement, 'high-level foreign advisers' on monetary policy were agreed to, as well as systematic monitoring of reforms by an Indonesian body committed to the use of independent auditors and to working in close cooperation with the IMF, ADB and World Bank (Johnson 1998: 32). In July, the government's memo to the IMF noted that high-level foreign advisers had been appointed to Bank Indonesia and that Bank Indonesia's supervision department was being strengthened (GOI 1998b: 15).

As well as attempts to increase skills at the central bank, its position and responsibilities were changed. In July 1998, the government agreed to have a new law on central bank autonomy submitted to parliament by the end of September. The law was prepared with the assistance of Bundesbank experts (GOI 1998b: 14) and was enacted in 1999. It formalises central bank autonomy, removes Bank Indonesia's ability to take shares in commercial banks and removes the task of prudential supervision from the central bank.[21] Not much is known about the structure and authority of the new supervisory agency, to be established over a two-year period. What is fairly certain is that a new institution on its own will only move problems of corruption and political interference to a new set of offices – with the possible adverse effects of disruption, expense and loss of morale. Similarly, the benefits of formal central bank independence are doubtful, particularly in the Indonesian context. To the extent that central bank independence is meant to control domestic inflation, it is a solution in search of a problem.[22] For most of the last thirty years, Indonesia's macroeconomic policy was prudent and relatively successful. Monetary policy in the years leading up to the crisis was perverse but it was not simply too loose (McLeod 1998a).[23]

The legal system was also the target of institutional reform in 1998. One of President Habibie's declarations on assuming power was that wide-ranging legal reforms would be pursued. The previous government had already promised to overhaul the bankruptcy system and to establish a special court for commercial disputes (Johnson 1998: 34–5). The court opened in August 1998 but its results were disappointing. Given that Indonesia had limited jurisprudence to draw on and that the judges had only a month of hasty training by foreign experts, the outcome was predictable (Lindsey 1998: 119). By the end of the year, few cases had been submitted to the new court and its judgments were seen as 'bizarre or simply wrong' (Lindsey 1998: 121). Only three bankruptcies had been declared; of these, one was overturned by the Supreme Court (*Financial Times*, 8 December 1998). By early 1999, the court itself was described as an obstacle to the resolution of banking and corporate governance problems and the press were reporting concerns about private influence and corruption in its operations (*Australian Financial Review*, 16 March 1999; *Business Times*, 4 January 1999).

Earlier Experience of Reform

Previous Reforms

Indonesia had already carried out two earlier programs of stabilisation, rationalisation and financial reform. The first episode occurred in the early years of the Suharto regime, from 1966 to the early 1970s. It was aimed at dealing with hyperinflation, currency collapse and the effective bankruptcy of the country's banking system. With renewed support from foreign creditors, stabilisation policies successfully brought monetary policy under control (Arndt 1984: 135–59). As well as ending the previously unchecked central bank credit creation, the reforms entrenched a virtual prohibition on domestically funded public debt, closed several small private banks and opened the commercial banking market to ten foreign entrants. High real interest rates in the state banks mobilised savings deposits (albeit at the cost of negative interest spreads), foreign currency denominated bank accounts were introduced for retail clients (Arndt & Suwidjana 1982) and, as part of a drive to attract foreign investment and the return of flight capital, capital account controls were lifted in 1970. The central bank was reorganised and the governor arrested. Over two years, the bank underwent an almost complete change of senior management, followed by increased attention to personnel training (Hamilton-Hart 1999: 117–22). The state-owned banks were also reorganised.

   The second episode of reform was initiated in 1983 and accelerated in 1988 and 1989. Precipitating factors were the collapse in oil prices in the mid 1980s, pressure from foreign aid donors and balance of payments crises in 1983 and 1986 (Soesastro 1989; Winters 1996: 155–84; Chant & Pangestu 1994: 269). Financial sector reforms in the 1980s consisted of deregulation and liberalisation, followed by prudential regulation from the early 1990s. The latter attempt manifestly failed, for reasons that are discussed below. The deregulatory reforms, however, were extensive. Although qualified with cautions about political interference, academic opinion was almost unanimous in applauding Indonesia's financial reforms as genuine and successful (McLeod 1994; Chant & Pangestu

Table 5.1   Change in financial indicators

	Pre-reform	1990	1996
Subsidised credit[a]			
% bank lending	87	15	7
Number of banks[b]			
Total	108	168	239
State	7	7	7
Private	74	134	205
Bank assets[c]			
Total % GDP	42	63	73
Total Rp	63 284	132 924	387 477
State Rp	42 297	71 109	141 314
Private Rp	18 376	57 911	236 549
Stock exchange[d]			
Index	83	418	637
Capitalisation	100	14 186	215 026

Notes: [a] Subsidised credit through Bank Indonesia, comprising liquidity credits and direct credits, as a percentage of bank lending. The pre-reform figure is for 1980. *Source:* Bank Indonesia, *Indonesian Financial Statistics*, various issues
[b] Total number comprises state, regional development, local private, foreign and joint-venture banks. State excludes the twenty-seven regional development banks (of minimal importance). Private comprises local, foreign and joint-venture banks. The pre-reform figures are for 1988. *Sources:* Cole & Slade (1996: 114); Bank Indonesia, *Indonesian Financial Statistics*, January 1997
[c] Bank assets, in billions of rupiah. Private comprises local, foreign and joint-venture banks. State excludes the regional development banks. The pre-reform figures are for 1988. *Sources:* Cole & Slade (1996: 108); Bank Indonesia, *Indonesian Financial Statistics*, January 1997; IMF, *International Financial Statistics*, 1998
[d] Jakarta Stock Exchange. Capitalisation in billions of rupiah. The pre-reform figures are for 1987. *Source:* Jakarta Stock Exchange (1996: 108)

1994; Cole & Slade 1996). Interest rates were freed, subsidised lending reduced, barriers to entry significantly reduced, branching restrictions for domestic banks virtually eliminated and the role of state banks greatly reduced.

The reforms of the 1980s were a deliberate attempt to minimise abuses in the banking system through liberalisation, competition, reduced credit subsidies and a significantly reduced role for state banks. The reforms also included prudential measures covering limits on loans to a single borrower or business group, limits on related-party lending, capital requirements (set relatively low), foreign exchange exposure limits, prohibition of underwriting by commercial banks and prohibition on ownership of non-financial companies by banks (Chant & Pangestu 1994: 238). From 1991, new prudential regulations included the phased introduction of increased capital adequacy ratios, risk management systems and guidelines on asset quality (Cole & Slade 1996: 91–5). Training schemes were stepped up for banking industry personnel and supervisors (Cole & McLeod 1991; interview, Bank Indonesia official, Jakarta, March 1997).

The reform episodes of the 1960s and 1980s went beyond policy change to include the development of technocratic skills in economic agencies. The 'technocratic' element in the economic bureaucracy was singled out by many analysts of Suharto's government as illustrative of his (intermittent) commitment to orthodox economics and as a rational pole in the Indonesian state (Liddle 1991; Root 1996: 97; Winters 1996). The promotion of technocratic skills, particularly the training of economists and the importation of foreign expertise, was a priority under the New Order. Both the World Bank and the Harvard Institute for International Development (HIID) had large permanent missions in Indonesia. They often played leading roles in drawing up economic plans, evaluating development projects and drafting legislation.[24] From the 1970s they were also involved in training Indonesian officials (Mason 1986: 46–8). In the central bank, external staff training, recruitment of graduate economists, and internal training and rotation systems were either introduced or intensified from the late 1960s. By 1980, the Ministry of Finance had sixty-five relatively senior officers with postgraduate degrees, out of a total of ninety-nine listed in the *Financial Directory of Indonesia*. In the early 1990s, a World Bank document noted that a loan of $US6.6 million had been disbursed to the government for 'technical assistance' (World Bank 1991: 141). Indonesia possessed a sizeable pool of trained individuals, particularly economists, by the 1980s.

Efforts by the World Bank to regularise systems and upgrade skills at the Indonesian Development Bank (Bank Pembangunan Indonesia, more often known as Bapindo) illustrate the extent of attempts to remedy Indonesia's institutional deficiencies through human resources development and the rationalisation of regulatory frameworks. Reform of Bapindo from the late 1960s was fruitful in many ways.[25] The organisation shed excess staff, increased the educational level of its staff, spent millions of dollars on training in Indonesia and overseas, and instituted a series of internal reforms that were drawn up and monitored by external consultants approved by the World Bank. The repeated need to recapitalise Bapindo as a result of poor lending decisions and borrower defaults, culminating in a major scandal that broke in 1994, testifies to the complete failure of those methods to eliminate the abuse of public resources. The details of the 1994 scandal show clearly that the problems did not stem from ignorance on the part of Bapindo officers or from a regulatory framework that allowed the abuses to occur.

The situation was little different at the other state banks, which had been recapitalised in 1992 as part of a package to set them up as more independent commercial entities. The recapitalisation included a World Bank loan of $US307 million for injection into the banking sector, as well as Rp200 billion from the state budget (*Far Eastern Economic Review*, 1 April 1993). Bad loans at state banks were an explicit focus of central bank attention – and public discussion – from then onwards. Bank Indonesia announced plans to prosecute bad debtors in 1994 and set up a team to look at the fifty largest debtors of state banks. Of the 71 per cent of debtors behind in repaying loans, the central bank said it would prioritise repayment from those who refused to pay (*Indonesian Observer*, 9 June 1994). Yet problems at the state banks showed no signs of receding and in 1996 state banks received substantial off-budget funds (McLeod 1997).

Supervision was no more effective for private sector banks. As early as 1989, the Finance Minister acknowledged there were a number of weak banks and said their exit from the market was necessary (*Far Eastern Economic Review*, 12 October 1989). Apart from a few mergers of small banks and the closure of a mid-size bank in 1992, no rationalisation occurred. According to the president of Thomson Bankwatch Asia, an affiliate of a major New York bank rating agency, disregard of prudential lending limits was routine, incestuous lending was rampant and the concealment of bad loans by lending to customers in arrears was common practice (*Jakarta Post*, 10 January 1996). All the abuses were unquestionably against banking laws, as were the abuses behind the two most prominent instances of private bank instability – foreign exchange losses by Suharto-controlled Bank Duta and excessive related-party lending at Bank Summa, which led to its closure in 1992. Yet, apart from the token prosecution of a Bank Duta executive, no bank managers or owners were brought to task for breaches of the law.

Underlying Causes of Prudential Failure

The central bank's failure to enforce its own regulations was not mainly the result of inadequate skills or flawed written regulations, though both those factors may have aggravated the situation. The prudential regulations implemented from 1991 were excessively complicated and it is arguable that the central bank should have focused simply on capital adequacy ratios (Fane 1998). The fractured structure of authority over the financial sector also impeded prudential regulation, as most banks had subsidiaries that were officially under the purview of the Ministry of Finance or other agencies. Finally, there was a perception that Bank Indonesia did not have the expertise to cope with growth in the sector after deregulation (*Far Eastern Economic Review*, 12 October 1989, 20 December 1990). However, none of these factors can account for the ineffectiveness of central bank supervision. Capital adequacy ratios may have been too low, but when the timetable for their increase was introduced it was criticised as demanding too much too soon of the private banks (Cole & Slade 1996: 93). Doubts about the central bank's expertise did exist, but many bankers also believed that central bank staff were competent enough. According to one Indonesian banker, 'central bank examiners were very capable and thorough, and aware of the weaknesses of banks' (Cole & Slade 1998: 65). The Thomson Bankwatch executive who commented on the widespread disregard of banking law also said that blame for not doing more to address banking problems did not lie with Bank Indonesia (*Jakarta Post*, 10 January 1996). There is little doubt that Bank Indonesia was aware of many breaches of the law by state and private banks. But just as in the pre-reform era it had been unable to stop the channelling of loans on the basis of political connections, despite standing at the centre of the banking system (Mac-Intyre 1993), in the post-reform years a lack of information or expertise was not the fundamental reason for the failure of prudential efforts.

What, then, were the fundamental reasons for Indonesia's consistent regulatory failures? The question goes to the heart of the recently revived debate on the sources of government capacity: why do some countries have 'governments that can govern' (Huntington 1968: 8) and others have governments that lack authority or that are bent entirely to the private purposes of governmental actors? Various theories ascribe primary importance to different causal factors.[26] With the caveat that the subject is contested terrain, the rest of this section discusses some of the more important determinants of capacity and relates them to Indonesian conditions.

Government may be ineffective because of a lack of authority and the comparative strength of societal actors (Migdal 1988), an analysis which corresponds with a weak state, societal mobilisation and ineffective government in Indonesia in the first two decades of independence (Anderson 1990: 99–109). On the other hand, government strength and autonomy are often accompanied by unbridled excesses (Evans 1995: 45). Indonesia's governing institutions under Suharto are a case in point: Suharto's New Order was a state-dominated polity in most respects but it allowed the manipulation of public policy in the interests of regime maintenance and private agendas of those with personal ties to the president.[27]

The quality of state institutions is important, as are the resources or power of state personnel. As put forward in Weber's formulation about 'rational legal' governing systems, an organised, disciplined and skilled

bureaucratic apparatus run according to rule-based rather than personalised precepts is an important element of effective government in
modern capitalist systems (Weber 1947: 329–36). Socialisation and insti-
tutionalisation, through which an organisation 'acquires value' as an
institution not merely an instrument, is probably necessary to sustain
such governing systems (Huntington 1968: 8–32). Why they get developed in the first place remains open to question. Analytic histories of
state formation in Europe and Japan, as well as contemporary accounts
of capacity-building in third world states, show that the incentives of
political actors are crucial. For example, incentives to create efficient,
relatively independent bureaucratic organisations will vary with the
domestic political cleavages confronting rulers, their need to mobilise
military resources and the extent to which windfall gains such as oil
revenues replace the need for domestic resource extraction (Geddes
1994; Silberman 1993; Tilly 1985; Chaudry 1989).

Indonesia under Suharto faced no external threats, and abundant aid
and oil revenues created few incentives to develop the domestic extrac-
tive institutions which are the 'base of administration, without which
regulation and redistribution are impossible' (Chaudry 1989: 113–14).
Instead, Suharto developed the governing institutions that suited his
needs: an effective domestic security apparatus and a reasonably effective system for distributing largesse, ensuring access to foreign aid and
meeting the developmental goals necessary for political stability. A
personalised patronage system was consonant with meeting those
objectives.

Failure to implement the law consistently is an unsurprising outcome
of such a system. The failure was not confined to one sector but was
endemic in a state that 'has been infused with patrimonial distributional
networks linking officials and business people' (MacIntyre 1994: 244).
The banking system was, however, particularly vulnerable, as loan
allocation was 'a central plank in the patronage networks that sustain
political power and cement networks of support' (Robison 1994: 68–9;
see also MacIntyre 1993). As noted in the first section of this chapter,
financial deregulation in the 1980s did not signal fundamental change
in the governing system.

The basic nature of New Order political economy created a
secondary problem: that even when powerful interests were not at issue,
the central bank was hobbled by the known politicisation of banking.
Any attempt to enforce regulations immediately looked selective. For
example, according to a former Bank Indonesia governor, once the
sector was opened to new entrants it was impossible to deny requests for
licences because to do so would create the impression that the central
bank was favouring special interests (Hadi Soesastro, seminar,

Australian National University, June 1998). As an earlier study of law in Indonesia found, when the myths behind the formal legal processes are tested too often and found to be exactly that – myths – even an 'upright judge, acting according to the "rational-legal" norms of his profession, is suspected anyway of corruption and bias, not only because there are in fact corrupt and biased judges, but more importantly because politics and administration are generally known to be filled with corruption' (Lev 1972: 260). This was the situation of Bank Indonesia and the other regulatory agencies.

A third factor that impeded prudential and regulatory efforts was internal to the regulatory agencies in manifestation if not origin. That is, the failure of these organisations to develop working administrative systems that could deliver efficient services. Even when political intervention and high-level corruption were not at issue, supposedly technocratic state organs were surprisingly inept. Despite efforts at human resources development in the agencies (and in the wider civil service), they never developed as institutionalised centres of expertise but remained dependent on key individuals and outside advisers. The reasons for this state of affairs are many: the continuing orientation of Indonesia's technocrats towards outside agencies due to the need to ensure a ready supply of foreign aid financing (Anderson 1990: 112; Winters 1996: 52–82); low pay scales that, if they did not engender out-right corruption, virtually required staff to moonlight; the absence of attempts to create an organisational ethos in technocratic agencies; and the persistence of patrimonial ties and norms reflecting traditional Javanese notions of *bapakism* and personalised authority.[28]

Conclusion: Prospects for the Reform Agenda

The post-crisis reform agenda has yielded few positive results. Given that it mirrors earlier reform episodes in two fundamental ways, it is unlikely to produce better outcomes in the future. The first similarity to earlier reform episodes is the emphasis on policy changes that will address specific failings of financial supervision but leave the wider political and institutional structure of government largely unchanged. Second, institutional upgrading is mostly limited to skills development through training and the hiring of foreign expertise. The basic continuity in political and administrative practices is reflected in the way bank restructuring has proceeded and in the failure to create a rationalised bankruptcy court.

The limited and reluctant moves to investigate and prosecute those believed to be the most corrupt actors in the Suharto era – including the Suharto family – suggest that the government will not act decisively on corruption, despite reports of spectacular corruption-related losses in government agencies. Members of the Suharto family and some close associates have been investigated but progress in bringing anyone to trial for corruption or breach of banking law has been slow. Perhaps this is inevitable, but President Habibie's actions did not create confidence that the government was making anything other than instrumental use of anti-corruption efforts. Habibie was taped urging the attorney-general to soft-pedal the ongoing investigation of Suharto for corruption and to place judicial pressure on two businessmen the government had accused of corruption, both of whom were funding the pro-democracy movement (*Business Times*, 10 March 1999).[29] Thus, while the government has been 'slow to investigate Soeharto's wealth, it has been remarkably quick to use the tax bureaucracy and the legal system to harass opposition figures' (Forrester 1999: 16). Another twist was added to the saga when the attorney-general himself was accused of taking bribes. He resigned, but the investigation into the matter languished in the hands of the military police (who at one stage announced it would be dropped), while the individual making the accusations was reportedly subject to intimidation and official investigation (*Tempo*, 13 June 1999: 18–22; *Jakarta Post*, 21 July 1999). Overall, initiatives on corruption and public accountability look similar to the largely ineffective anti-corruption drives instituted in the first decade of the New Order (Mackie 1970; *Straits Times*, 4 November 1977, 23 February 1979).

In this situation, the 'persistence of structural flaws will mean the failure of piecemeal reforms, possibly even aggravating existing problems' (Lindsey 1998: 123). Like changes to a banking law that was never consistently implemented, institutional innovations such as the bankruptcy court and the mooted creation of a separate bank regulatory agency cannot achieve much without sustained efforts at creating organisational capacity. The new government's approach to institutional reform follows a path well-trodden by its predecessor, one that involves training Indonesian officials and importing foreign skills.[30] Indonesia's earlier record shows that this approach is effective in getting the aid tap turned on in a time of crisis (Anderson 1990: 112; Winters 1996: 52–82). It also provides direct benefits to those who will assess and monitor Indonesia's reforms. But the involvement of skilled outsiders is no guarantee against corruption. Reports leaked to the press reveal the World Bank's assessment that corruption in Indonesia was often glossed over, that 20–30 per cent of the $US24 billion in World Bank lending to the country since the 1960s was diverted, and that self-seeking staff mixed strongly worded policy notes with praise for the government which was among the Bank's best customers (*Business Times*, 8 December 1998, 11 February 1999). An internal memo of October 1998 stated that the

World Bank's crisis-related lending was still subject to 'significant leakage' – an outcome that was hard to avoid given that 'practically all key institutions of government are involved [in corruption]: judiciary, civil service, security forces, even internal and external audit firms' (*Financial Times*, 8 December 1998).[31] The World Bank was aware in March 1999 of some aspects of the transactions that later surfaced in the Bank Bali scandal (World Bank 1999c).

Dealing with high-level corruption is more a political than an administrative problem, but one reform that could be pursued without wholesale political change is the upgrading of the bureaucracy in terms of salary, prestige and insulation. Government departments have systems for siphoning off aid funds and extorting fees from outsiders partly because the funds are essential to basic departmental needs – a phenomenon that was noted decades ago by Harold Crouch (1978: 274, 322) and which continued in the 1990s. However, bureaucratic funding and standing received little attention in the aftermath of the crisis. A World Bank official stated that the Bank was committed to seeing an increase in civil service salaries by at least 50 per cent in the near future (interview, Jakarta, July 1999). However, the feasibility of this program, particularly given the costs of bank restructuring, appears remote. A senior Indonesian planning official did not anticipate any such support for the bureaucracy. Rather, he predicted an increase in political interference and further deterioration in morale partly due to the presence of foreign advisers and short-term consultants in many Indonesian agencies (interview, Jakarta, July 1999).

In the absence of bureaucratic efficiency and impartiality, the legal system lacks the systematic support necessary for its maintenance, as the courts cannot implement or enforce their rulings (Lev 1972: 279). As Lev also notes, the functional incentives of private economic activity will not lead automatically to the creation of rationalised bureaucratic and legal systems. The development of such systems will depend on 'whether private and public businesses find judges or fixers more accessible and efficient'. If, as in the past, formalised legal and administrative systems in Indonesia are unable to provide efficient services they will frequently be bypassed in favour of informal and extra-legal processes as a result of 'a kind of institutional Gresham's Law, in which formal processes tend to be eschewed in favour of more familiar and accommodative ones' (Lev 1972: 280–1). Almost all signs from 1999 in Indonesia indicate that informal processes remain the more familiar and accommodative ones.

These continuities are not surprising. No new political elite came to power during the period of post-crisis reforms discussed here. There was a breakdown of the previous centralisation of the patronage system (Mackie 1998) but Suharto's New Order was still largely in power

(Forrester 1999: 13). The reshuffling that brought some faces to higher levels of prominence used familiar New Order mechanisms of physical coercion and bribery (Aditjondro 1998). The business interests and past careers of those in power did not give them any incentive for action that might uncover their complicity in earlier abuses. These factors, and the organisational disarray of genuine reformist groups, mean that the preconditions for wholesale reform are weak (Robison 1998).

In addition, Indonesia faces obstacles to reform that were not faced by the New Order. First, the economic crisis and the diversion of government resources to the immediate task of dealing with its worst manifestations (including the need for ongoing negotiations with the IMF) make attention to basic bureaucratic reform almost impossible. Second, political change has decentralised the previous tightly held power structure and created room for political contest. National elections in June 1999 and the selection of a new president by Indonesia's highest representative assembly in October saw a decisive shift in power away from Golkar and President Habibie. Habibie's Golkar party performed poorly in the election, and Habibie was also affected by the Bank Bali scandal and his perceived weakness in dealing with foreigners over East Timor. Habibie resigned his candidacy before the vote for a new president on 20 October, leaving the assembly to choose between Abdurrahman Wahid, the leader of Indonesia's largest Islamic group, and Megawati Sukarnoputri, daughter of Indonesia's first president. Despite her party (the PDI-P, Partai Demokrasi Indonesia-Perjuangan) having gained a higher share of the popular vote in June than any other group, Megawati lost the contest for the presidency. The following day, after large protests in Jakarta and elsewhere in Indonesia, she was elected vice-president. In one sense, the new leadership represents a real break with the past. Both Megawati and Abdurrahman Wahid are self-declared moderate reformists, committed to clean government and the restoration of the economy. However, they were both elected with the support of Golkar and military representatives in the assembly. As pointed out by Pratikno, a professor of politics at Gadjah Mada University, this means that Golkar and the military are likely to ask for concessions in the form of government positions 'which could save them from past sins' (*Jakarta Post*, 22 October 1999). The new government could well reproduce many of the features of the New Order in more plural form.

The new pluralism is unlikely to bring about fundamental reform. Open elections and a relatively free press may promote less corrupt and more efficient administrative and judicial systems, but Indonesia's tumultuous years of parliamentary democracy in the 1950s show that this is not always the case. Historically, institutions such as democracy, the rule of law and transparency have followed rather than preceded the development of effective government organisations. They are absent or only weakly present in countries such as Singapore, where government capacities are nonetheless high. The persistence of corruption under conditions of political liberalisation in countries such as the Philippines is a reminder that parliamentary democracy does not necessarily lead to efforts at bureaucratic capacity-building. In some countries, such as South Korea, the incidence and scale of corruption increased with the advent of democratic politics (Root 1996: 18–31). It is possible that post-election Indonesia will follow something like a Thai path to relative stability, where elections play an important role in regulating political competition despite political corruption. The preconditions for such 'bourgeois electoralism' in Indonesia, however, are weak in comparative terms (Anderson 1998: 265–84). One problem is that the indigenous business class remains reliant on special favours (Robison 1998), while much of the locally owned modern business sector is in the hands of Chinese Indonesians whose political vulnerability remains great. A further problem is that a precondition of elections that have 'real policy outcomes satisfactory to substantial sections of the voting population' is 'a coherent civil bureaucracy capable of enforcing electorally generated polices: that is, a strong state' – something that is hard to build 'after the spread of mass electoralism' (Anderson 1998: 293–4).

CHAPTER 6

Political Impediments to Far-reaching Banking Reforms in Japan: Implications for Asia

Jennifer A. Amyx[1]

Ever since the collapse of a speculative asset bubble in 1991, Japanese banks have been burdened with enormous amounts of non-performing loans. The failure of Ministry of Finance (MOF) officials to tackle the problem aggressively had grave repercussions as macroeconomic policy mistakes sank the economy into prolonged recession and exacerbated the magnitude of bad bank loans. A full-blown financial crisis hit in 1997, following the collapse of the nation's tenth-largest bank and fourth-largest securities firm, and continued into late 1998. At the beginning of 1999, the amount of non-performing loans held by Japanese banks neared a trillion dollars.

This chapter argues that the financial crises in Japan and greater Asia were related in many ways. Japan's response to the Asian crisis was negatively affected by the incapacity of policy-makers to resolve the nation's own financial system woes in the years between the collapse of the bubble economy and the onset of the regional crisis in 1997. More specifically, the simultaneous presence of a financial system crisis in Japan meant that the Japanese government's proactive role in assembling aid and funding packages for the region was not matched by a similarly positive role by Japan's private sector. Japanese banks, corporations and consumers were reluctant – or simply incapable – to serve as major catalysts for regional recovery. Further, Japan's domestic policy choices for its own financial crisis have affected capital flows and investment patterns in Asia. Large flows of capital into the region and the depreciation of the yen were trends encouraged by domestic policies and they helped set the stage for regional crisis in the period leading up to 1997. Similarly, the Japanese government's more aggressive stance toward the resolution of banking sector problems since late 1998 had the side-effect of encouraging Japanese private sector capital to withdraw from the region at a critical time. In short, Japan's domestic policy solutions have had considerable international repercussions.

The chapter further argues that the Japanese government's efforts to deal with its financial system problems were significantly affected by the Asian financial crisis. The region's financial meltdown and market contraction exacerbated problems within Japan by adding large amounts of non-performing loans to existing mountains of bad debt. In addition, the Asian crisis further dampened already low consumer confidence and domestic demand in Japan just as the nation was showing signs of possible emergence from its most prolonged postwar recession. In conjunction with other domestic developments in 1997–98, the crisis thereby served as a catalyst in bringing Japan's financial sector problems to a head and effecting change which had not been forthcoming from within.

The chapter first gives an overview of Japan's economic weight in Asia. Second, it analyses the reasons why Japan's own post-bubble financial system crisis was unresolved when the greater regional crisis began. The section includes an examination of the political tensions in the Japanese system of financial governance and how those tensions shaped policy outputs. Third, the situation in Japan in 1997–98 and the role the Asian crisis played in helping to spur change in the institutions and modes of financial governance in Japan are examined. The fourth section analyses the responses of Japan's public and private sectors to the Asian crisis and considers what the responses have meant in the context of international efforts to address the crisis. Finally, the chapter concludes with a discussion of theoretical implications and persisting political impediments to far-reaching financial reforms.

Japan's Economic Weight in Asia

Japan's geographical and historical ties to Asia mean that any turmoil in the region is automatically of concern. The nation's heavy economic involvement in the region at both the government and private sector levels, however, is what makes Japan's links to the crisis especially strong.

Japan's private sector maintains involvement in the region as export absorber, import supplier, investor and creditor. Although not the top absorber of Asian exports, Japan is nonetheless an important market for the region. In 1990, Japan's share in the exports of the major South-East Asian countries ranged from a high of 43.9 per cent for Indonesia to a low of 8.9 per cent for Singapore. Between these two extremes were Japan's shares in the export markets of Malaysia (15.9 per cent), Thailand (17.9 per cent) and the Philippines (20.4 per cent). Although these shares steadily decreased in most of the countries over the 1990s, Japan continued to play a significant role as export absorber.[2]

Japan also serves as the largest source of imports for all East Asian economies except South Korea and Vietnam. Japan-bound exports from Malaysia comprise 12 per cent of that country's GDP and Indonesia has consistently maintained a trade surplus with Japan (Sugisaki 1998). Further, Japan is the single largest source of foreign direct investment (FDI) for the region (Whittaker & Kurosawa 1998: 769). Japanese investments are particularly large in Thailand, Indonesia and Malaysia. Japanese banks are also the largest creditors in the region, providing 30 per cent of all international loans to Asia. In Thailand, the influence of Japanese banks is especially strong, accounting for over half of all international lending (Sugisaki 1998).

The Japanese government has also invested heavily in Asia in the form of overseas development assistance (ODA).[3] Japan's institutional and ideological influences in the region carry considerable economic weight as well. As a prominent player in the International Monetary Fund (IMF) and Asian Development Bank (ADB), Japan had the potential to significantly shape the international community's response to the crisis.[4] Japan's economic influence is also ideological, since many countries in the region have, to varying degrees, modelled their economies after Japan's.

In these ways, Japan is an essential piece of Asia's economic architecture and responses to the crisis by Japan's government, corporations, banks and consumers significantly affect the region's prospects for recovery.

Japan's Financial System Crisis: Why the Delay in Resolution?

In order to understand the nature of Japan's response to the Asian crisis in 1997 and thereafter, it is critical to first understand the reasons behind the irresolution of Japan's own financial system crisis. The contributing factors have been many, but political choices played a key role. And the tensions shaping the choices prior to 1997 were those present when the greater regional crisis hit. These choices produced regulatory forbearance, overreliance on monetary policy measures and delay in the execution of financial system reforms. These policies, in turn, not only had implications for the capacity of Japan's financial system to deal with exogenous shocks, but also had significant implications for capital flows and currency values in the region.

Institutions and Modes of Financial Governance in Japan

Policy outcomes in Japanese finance have long reflected bargaining among actors within the context of institutionalised informal network associations. The MOF sat at the intersection of these networks, serving as the locus of policy-making and implementation.[5] Three key factors affected the MOF's capacity to adapt policies to meet changing needs: its relations with elected politicians in the Diet (Japan's parliament), private sector financial institutions and other government actors. Let us examine each of these briefly.

While the Diet must approve legislation related to private sector finance, the structure of the nation's electoral system and paucity of legislative staff give politicians incentives to focus their political resources on more locally based niches of the economy such as agriculture, small and medium enterprises and construction. Nonetheless, relations with politicians were always critical to the MOF's regulatory influence, if only in an enabling way. The number of former MOF officials serving as elected representatives remains strong, despite a general decline in aggregate numbers of bureaucrat-turned-politicians in the Diet over the postwar period.[6] MOF officials on temporary assignment regularly occupy positions in the legislative bureaus and standing committee offices of both houses, as well as in the prime minister's office, cabinet, ministers' secretariats and the cabinet legislative bureau. These points of regular contact give the MOF numerous points to obtain information helpful in gauging the receptivity of elected officials to policy proposals, and gives it numerous opportunities to influence the policy-making process once legislation leaves the ministry and enters the Diet.[7]

Although the MOF's relations with the Diet are highly institutionalised and important, the majority of financial governance actually circumscribed the Diet. Until the mid 1990s, Japanese private sector finance was governed by very few pieces of legislation. The MOF had a high degree of discretion to fill in the details of broad and vaguely worded laws through cabinet ordinances, ministerial regulations and administrative notices. Instruction of private sector actors through written notifications or informal verbal instructions – a practice known as 'administrative guidance' – was one of the most notable characteristics of regulation of the sector and gave rise to close relations between individual financial institutions and the MOF.[8]

The All Japan Banking Federation (*Zenginkyo*) served as one conduit for instruction to banks and represented the industry as a whole on particular issues, but the highly compartmentalised nature of the financial sector meant significant divergence in interests across the membership and facilitated the development of particularistic relations. These relations included daily face-to-face contact between bank employees designated as MOF-*tan* or 'MOF-handlers', in each bank and officials in the Banking and International Finance bureaus. These relations included the assumption of posts in many banks by retired MOF officials (a practice known as *amakudari*, 'descent from heaven') and the temporary assignment of private sector bankers to positions within the MOF (*amaagari*, 'ascent to heaven').[9] Through these relations, unofficial communication between banks and the MOF was ongoing and a means both for the MOF to make its desires known to banks and for banks to convey concerns and troubles to the MOF without alarming depositors or other sector actors. As the 'grey' areas in finance – business activities not falling clearly under existing rules – became more numerous from the 1970s, this mode of communication also gained importance as a means for banks and brokerages to gain tacit prior approval of new financial instruments.

The MOF's relations with other government agencies are a third pillar of its relational network. The MOF regularly sends officials to assume temporary posts in the agencies attached to the prime minister's office, as well as exchanging small numbers of personnel with other ministries. Most salient to the MOF's capacity for effective policy adaptation in finance in the 1990s was its staffing of posts in the Economic Planning Agency (EPA), an agency that produces the government's economic projections. MOF officials consistently served as the agency's deputy vice-minister, coordinating policies and views of all EPA bureaus. Its influence reaches all of the EPA's five bureaus, but the presence of MOF officials in key posts in the coordination and planning bureaus has been particularly noticeable. The former bureau is responsible for formulating the basic policies steering the economy as a whole, and the annual economic program. The latter bureau is in charge of policies and legislative proposals concerning the long-term planning of the economy, and measurement and analysis of the nation's overall potential (Japan, Government of 1996: 41).

Latent Tensions

In the system of financial governance pivoted on the MOF, two tensions are particularly important to our understanding of policy decisions in the 1990s. The first is the tension between a state empowered by its embedded relations with other actors and, conversely, constrained by its embeddedness. Conventional wisdom is that utilisation of informal relational networks was important to the government's earlier policy successes. Yet in the 1990s those same relational networks exacerbated inertial tendencies and constrained more than empowered the government in its policy options and decisions.

The second tension is intricately related to the first. It is the tension arising from a single regulatory institution simultaneously overseeing fiscal policy and private sector finance. From these two policy domains emerged a set of distinct decision-making principles that underscored all MOF policy decisions. They were a balanced budget principle, reflecting MOF's prioritisation of fiscal policy concerns, and the convoy approach to financial regulation providing implicit guarantees against bank failure.

Finance ministries or national treasuries in most countries exhibit conservative tendencies, placing a priority on the balancing of budgets. In Japan, the MOF's persistent articulation of a 'sound budget' (*kenzen zaisei*) or 'balanced budget' (*kinko yosan*) principle has been a particularly prominent feature of MOF rhetoric. Since bond issues give rise to debt servicing expenditures that legally must be paid before any other expenditure, an unbalanced budget erodes the Budget Bureau's room for discretion in the budget-making process. Evoking the principle permits the MOF to legitimately refuse demands from politicians that it does not wish to entertain.

The balanced budget principle was first breached in Japan in 1965 and encroached upon more severely in the late 1970s and early 1980s. And, as Japan's current massive levels of public debt suggest, the MOF was unable to adhere to the principle in the 1990s. Nonetheless, the balanced budget principle has remained a strong undercurrent in all MOF policy discussions.[10]

At the same time, the so-called convoy approach ensured that no financial sector actor was left behind and that no actor moved forward so fast as to endanger the viability of others. This principle served a multiplicity of interests. The stability it facilitated in the financial sector ensured constant flows of credit to industry as the nation focused on economic reconstruction in the immediate postwar period. Through its support of the banks, the government cushioned the impact of economic shocks on borrowers. Importantly, the convoy approach also served the interests of banks, as it gave rise to a cartel-like arrangement that benefited all members. Further, the practice of amakudari noted earlier meant that this principle reflected self-interested MOF behaviour. Any bank that went under meant one fewer potential depository for officials retiring from MOF.

The dual principles of a balanced budget and the convoy approach worked well during the earlier era of rapid economic growth, but proved dangerous partners in the 1990s.

Another byproduct of the tension inherent in the MOF's formal organisation was the pattern of intra-ministerial resource flows. With the Budget Bureau holding the nation's purse-strings, it naturally became the power centre of the MOF and intra-ministerial resources flowed in its direction. Bureaus overseeing private sector finance received relatively few resources – something that was not clearly a problem in the rapid-growth period when a system of bank self-regulation functioned effectively in the form of a main bank system.[11] However, the scarcity of resources allocated to formal monitoring had deleterious effects in the 1990s.

At the conjunction of these two tensions – the tension from a mode of financial governance reliant on relational networks and the tension from an institution of financial governance with such expansive authority – is a final noteworthy pattern. The 'point men' in the MOF's relational networks extending to the Diet and other government agencies have almost always been officials with strong backgrounds in fiscal policy bureaus. Thus, relational networks have disproportionately reflected fiscal policy concerns – concerns that increasingly came into conflict with prudent policy choices in the regulation of private sector finance in the 1990s.

Three Policy Options not Taken

We now turn to how these tensions affected policy decisions between the collapse of the bubble economy and the onset of the Asian financial crisis. Although the government did not totally ignore the nation's financial sector problems, official responses fell far short of what could be described as aggressive bad loan disposal, heightened prudential regulation, aggressive macroeconomic stimulus or accelerated financial system reform. Yet those were the types of measures needed to address problems of the magnitude faced in Japan. We will now examine why these policy options were not taken.

Aggressive Disposal of Bad Loans and Heightened Prudential Supervision

In the aftermath of the bubble's collapse, the MOF could have responded by requiring banks to aggressively dispose of bad debt. Doing so would have helped to restore bank capital ratios and thereby decreased the possibility of systemic risk triggered by bank collapse. The sheer amount of debt, however, would have required the securing of public funds to create an institution similar to the Resolution Trust Corporation (RTC) established by US authorities to dispose of bad debt in the wake of its savings and loan crisis.[12] In recognition of the heightened moral hazards for bank management when capital approaches zero, the MOF might also have heightened formal prudential regulation.[13]

The MOF did not pursue either option. Indeed, it refrained from acknowledging the magnitude of the non-performing loan problems in 1991 and permitted financial institutions to adjust accounting standards and manipulate accounts in the years thereafter, thereby avoiding accurate public disclosure of problems.[14] As the decade progressed and asset values continued to fall, the magnitude of non-performing loans continued to rise. The government then lowered the official discount rate, to assist banks in absorbing bad loans out of profits gained by the interest rate spread. In 1995, the rate was dropped to a historic low of 0.5 per cent. The MOF also encouraged banks to expand lending, in the hope that they would grow out of their problems.

For banks that could not survive even under these lenient conditions, the MOF drew upon its informal relations with banks to arrange rescue mergers, a procedure which was the pillar of the convoy approach to regulation in the earlier high-growth period. Rescue mergers minimised labour market repercussions. Amid heavy regulation and only the occasional emergence of problems in particular banks, the MOF easily enticed stronger banks into cooperating in this informal resolution procedure. In the 1990s, however, the procedure became increasingly more difficult to execute because all banks were burdened with non-performing loans and partial deregulation of the sector had removed many incentives to cooperate. Rather than close essentially insolvent banks, the government began to draw on funds from the Deposit Insurance Corporation to make rescue mergers more attractive for the absorbing bank.

The regulatory delay and forbearance in the above measures reflected the influences of the three relations noted earlier. Liberal Democratic Party (LDP) politicians were particularly reluctant to allow banks to go under, because of the effect on electoral constituencies. In the 1980s, the health of financial institutions of various sizes and types became increasingly interdependent through joint investment in non-banks and real estate enterprises. In particular, the *nokyo* (agricultural cooperatives) and commercial banks had invested huge amounts in these ventures, which suffered severely with the collapse of the bubble. In many cases, the rolling over of bank loans to these enterprises was the only thing preventing outright default on the nokyo loans. Bank support was therefore a means of buffering the locally based and electorally influential agriculture cooperatives. The LDP itself and the construction industry – a mainstay of its support – were some of the 'deadbeat borrowers' weighing down the banks. The party, which was in power during this period except for a brief 1993–94 interlude, therefore had little interest in seeing an RTC-like institution recover delinquent loans.[15] Finally, it would be difficult for any LDP Diet member to take credit for stopping a crisis after having participated in its creation.

Banks supported government policies because a publicly funded bailout of the sector would expose dubious lending practices and probably mean the closure of banks that were effectively insolvent. Cross-shareholding arrangements and a main bank system of delegated monitoring and risk-sharing among banks meant that the collapse of one bank would have serious repercussions on the health of many others.[16] No bank had an interest in seeing another closed. Further, greater public disclosure would have revealed accounting procedures that seriously understated the magnitude of problems. Greater scrutiny of balance sheets might then expose capital inadequacies, forcing some banks to withdraw from international operations due to inability to meet Bank for International Settlements' (BIS) standards.

Other government agencies failed to provide any significant resistance to MOF policies in this period because the ailments of the financial system were not yet clearly linked to the real economy. Low growth in the first years after the collapse of the bubble was touted by many as merely a cyclical correction. Also, banks served as a buffer between the collapse of the bubble economy and the numerous firms which had invested heavily in land-related enterprises in the bubble period. For agencies such as the Ministry of Construction or Ministry of International Trade and Industry (MITI), therefore, protection of the banking sector meant a continued life-line to their private sector regulatory constituencies.

Prolonged loose monetary policy, however, had a negative effect on domestic consumption and led to huge increases in money flows into Asia. Interest income for Japanese individual savers dropped by approximately a trillion yen annually from 1995, accounting for a 2 per cent drop in GDP and lower spending (Kikkawa 1998: 159). The historically low interest rates pushed money abroad, where greater returns on investment were possible. In early 1994, Japanese had a total of $US40 billion in loans outstanding to Asia; by 1996 the amount had ballooned to $US265 billion (Whittaker & Kurosawa 1998: 761).[17] The low interest rate also pushed the value of the yen down, decreasing the competitiveness of the Asian exports competing with Japanese goods in third markets. Japanese domestic policies thereby fuelled an asset bubble within Asia and slowed the exports of countries such as Korea, Taiwan and Malaysia. Both effects were cited later as contributing to the regional crisis.[18]

Macroeconomic Policy

Macroeconomic policy measures in the form of aggressive fiscal stimulus were another option that might alleviate the crisis. Massive deficit spending could be expected to help lift the economy out of recession through stimulating demand and thereby reversing the cycle of rising bankruptcies generating additional bad debt. Such an approach was antithetical to attempts by the MOF's fiscal policy bureaus to reduce the government deficit. Macroeconomic expansion was not seriously tried, as only one-third of the announced stimulus packages of 1992–97 were actually undertaken (Posen 1998). Growth in government expenditures was negative in 1992 and 1994, at –0.2 per cent and –2 per cent (Japan, Government of, MOF 1996).

In addition to the dearth of 'pure water' (real net new) spending, the composition of spending in this period proved problematic. The distribution of public works projects by prefecture revealed significant disparities between the nation's urban districts and rural districts controlled by LDP powerbrokers.[19] Had the government directed more spending to urban areas where infrastructure needs were greater, the multiplier effects of this spending would likely have been higher. Multiplier effects of fiscal policy measures might also have been raised through permanent tax breaks rather than increased expenditures.[20]

This period was arguably the most volatile for Japanese political parties since the early postwar period. The LDP – having enjoyed uninterrupted single-party rule since 1955 – fractured, was temporarily bumped out of power in 1993, and faced stronger and more numerous opposition challengers than ever before. The MOF simply could not get away with putting a hold on public works spending, the life-blood of LDP politicians, or disrupting the flow of funds to key LDP constituencies. In the end, fiscal stimulus half-measures and the skewed allocation of projects to rural districts did little to resolve banking sector problems and resulted in an alarming increase in government debt. Japan went from having the strongest fiscal position in the world in 1990 to having one of the weakest.[21]

The MOF utilised its relations with other government agencies to counter potential demands for more aggressive fiscal policies. More specifically, through staffing key posts in the EPA with officials from the MOF's Budget Bureau, it encouraged the significant overprojection of growth rates for every year from 1991 to 1998. In 1993, the gap between the estimated and actual growth rate was particularly large, at 3.7 per cent.[22] Although economic predictions made by the OECD and other international institutions in this period were consistently below those of the EPA, suggesting a systemic bias, other agencies such as the MITI failed to openly dissent from MOF's optimistic projections. Sensitive to US pressure to reduce the bilateral trade deficit, MITI officials feared that lower growth estimates would spur heightened emphasis on export-led growth and thereby exacerbate trade frictions (interview with MOF official).

The MOF met little resistance from the banking sector to using monetary policy as the primary policy tool for dealing with the crisis. Although significant fiscal expansion might have been expected to alleviate bank pain by halting the rising number of souring domestic loans, this positive effect would be cancelled out to some degree by lowered yields on government bond holdings accompanying any large issue of deficit bonds. In the meantime, Japan's prolonged recession translated into slowed demand for Asian goods and further supported the depreciation of the yen.

Financial System Reform and a Shift to Universal Financial Institutions

In the longer term, only deregulation could be expected to bring the needed growth in domestic demand. Segmentation and heavy regulation of the sector minimised competition and served as an important component of the convoy approach to regulation. However, compartmentalisation of finance was also a main cause of the sector's extremely inefficient return on capital.[23]

Nearly a decade before the bubble economy burst, the MOF had laid the groundwork for breaking down business barriers between types of bank and between banks and brokerages. Brokerages had little to gain and a monopoly on commissions to lose if the industry opened up to banks, however, and therefore mobilised in opposition. Changes in the political funding laws and the stock market's increasing importance as a conduit for political funds led politicians to take up the cause of brokerages and oppose encroachment into the industry's territory. The inflation of the asset bubble temporarily provided greater profits for all, even without the planned reforms. With the bubble's collapse, however, reforms again became critical. Although stock compensation scandals weakened the political clout of the securities industry, interests remained divided within the banking sector. Large commercial banks would benefit disproportionately from the breaking down of barriers between operations. The nation's three long-term credit banks, however, were among the staunchest opponents. To them, integration of the banking sector simply meant loss of their monopoly rights to the issue of bank debentures. The three long-term credit banks had strong ties to powerful politicians, as well as a long history of hiring high-ranking MOF retirees.

Other government agencies also failed to support the MOF in moving toward system reform. Strong opposition came from the Ministry of Posts and Telecommunications (MPT), which oversees the nation's postal savings system, because any discussion of system-wide reform to promote greater returns on capital would certainly point out the need to privatise the postal savings system as well. Privatisation would translate into the loss of MPT authority over what was essentially the world's largest bank.[24]

The stalling of significant financial reforms in this period, however, was another factor encouraging Japanese funds to flow heavily into Asia. Because the domestic financial system failed to make efficient use of funds, investments were best sent abroad. Although former Prime Minister Ryutaro Hashimoto initiated the so-called 'Big Bang' financial reforms in November 1996, implementation of large-scale reforms occurred after the onset of the domestic and greater Asian crises.

In summary, the MOF – embedded in a web of political, bureaucratic and private sector interests – produced a policy mix of forbearance, ineffective spending directed to LDP districts and slow-motion financial reforms. The side effects, both in Japan and in Asia, were significant.

Japan at the Onset of the Asian Financial Crisis

The onset of crisis in Asia was not the main factor in Japan's financial sector problems coming to a head in 1997–98, but it did exacerbate problems by further weakening internationally active Japanese banks and Japanese consumer confidence. At the start of the regional crisis in mid 1997, Japanese banks accounted for approximately one-third of total BIS exposure to the five most deeply affected Asian countries. Increased loan activity in the region had been a means to greater profits, in which bad loans at home could be absorbed. The onset of regional crisis not only ended this, but contributed to existing bad debt levels. MOF estimates of bad loans were ¥30 trillion in early 1996 but nearly triple that amount (¥83 trillion) in 1998 (Boyd 1998). The rapid rise in value was primarily due to the introduction of stricter non-performing loan definitions by the MOF and the burgeoning amounts of domestic bad debt brought on by the economic recession and plunging asset values. Nonetheless, unrealised loan losses from Asia for the top nine Japanese commercial banks in fiscal year 1998 were expected to total approximately ¥750 billion ($US6.5 billion) – not a trivial amount. Those same banks had only ¥300 billion in reserves allocated for non-performing loans in the region. Thus, the crisis further hampered the ability of Japanese banks to meet BIS capital requirements.

The Asian crisis also stymied the MOF's efforts to persist in its convoy approach. As noted earlier, deposit insurance funds were insufficient to prevent the collapse of major banks; therefore, continued adherence to the convoy approach required private sector cooperation. However, exposed banks in the region were unwilling to cooperate in the injection of funds or rescue mergers of domestic institutions on the verge of collapse. In November 1997, Hokkaido Takushoku Bank (*Takugin*), the tenth-largest commercial bank in the nation, collapsed. Although its financial difficulties were not directly related to the crisis, the MOF's failure to arrange its rescue – despite many attempts – reflected rising costs to cooperation within the banking sector as a whole.

The collapse of Takugin, as well as that of Yamaichi Securities, the nation's fourth-largest brokerage, in late 1997 came as a shock to Diet members and the general public. The perception that the MOF was in control had been supported by MOF support of the stock market and the very process of forbearance which permitted accounting procedures and regulatory reporting to minimise the publicly disclosed magnitude of the problem. Legislation to create a new independent Financial Supervisory Agency (FSA) to assume regulatory authority over private sector finance from the MOF had been passed in June 1997, prior to the failures,[25] and criticism of the MOF's handling of the Takugin and Yamaichi failures, as well as the emergence of scandals surrounding the MOF, set the stage for further institutional and legislative changes. By focusing on the MOF as the source of the problem, Diet members helped deflect criticism from themselves and thereby made the public more receptive to the use of public funds to resolve the crisis.

The collapse of Takugin and Yamaichi also heightened concern in the international markets about the stability of the Japanese financial system. This gave rise to an increase in the Japan premium in international capital markets, increasing capital costs for Japanese banks procuring funds in overseas markets. The Takugin failure also brought large drops in stock prices for the industry as a whole. For these reasons the banking sector itself became more receptive to the injection of public funds, despite the associated greater public scrutiny of operations.

The Asian crisis did not affect only banks, it reinforced already low Japanese consumer spending patterns. In many respects, the timing of the Asian financial crisis could not have been worse. The July 1997 meltdown in Thailand came just as Japanese consumers were reeling in the wake of an April 1997 consumption tax increase from 3 to 5 per cent, the end of a special income tax cut and an increase in health charges (Kikkawa 1998: 158). After 3.6 per cent growth in 1996, the Hashimoto administration had plunged the nation into financial retrenchment and the MOF's Budget Bureau – in charge of assessing probable effects of raising the consumption tax – grossly underestimated the adverse effect of the elevated tax on personal consumption, which comprises approximately 60 per cent of Japan's GDP. Elected officials, usually unreceptive to tax hikes, had been brought on board by the fact that Japan was increasingly being compared with Italy as its government deficit approached 5 per cent of GDP (interview with

MOF official). Japan's central government debt, officially at 87 per cent of GDP, was also at an all-time high.[26] A further step towards fiscal retrenchment came with the Hashimoto administration's passage of the Fiscal Reconstruction Law in the fall of 1997. The law prescribed that spending levels of the 1998 budget could not exceed those of the 1997 initial budget and came just as the economic turmoil in South Korea and the ASEAN nations deepened. Japanese consumers had plenty of reason to be anxious.

Against this background of depressed consumer spending, the real economy effects of the financial sector's woes intensified in 1998. With negative growth came the emergence of constituencies for whom the banking sector problems became more salient. This altered legislative policy preferences further. In April 1998, the government announced a massive fiscal stimulus plan. A tax cut plus a second and larger injection of public funds into the banking system suddenly became inseparable concepts as the year progressed.[27] Many construction companies had aided developers in obtaining loans in the bubble period by extending collateral or guarantees (Whittaker & Kurosawa 1998: 764). Until 1998, the construction sector was kept afloat by periodic fiscal stimulus packages despite the souring of these loans. Now, however, public sector spending could no longer make up for the drop in private sector demand.

The undeniable effect of the financial system crisis on the real economy also spurred MITI into action in defence of its regulatory constituencies. The MOF's protection of banks had simultaneously supported MITI constituencies in the past, but that was no longer the case. In mid 1998, as upper house elections approached, the LDP worked with the MITI to come up with a tentative bridge bank scheme to relieve the perceived credit crunch. The LDP's poor performance in the elections, however, gave the opposition much leverage in deciding the final form of legislative response. In October, the Diet established a credibly funded infrastructure for dealing with insolvent financial institutions. On the heels of that legislation came a decision by the newly established FSA to temporarily nationalise the Long-Term Credit Bank, which had been teetering on the edge of collapse for some time. In December 1998, more proof of a change in the mode of financial governance came when the FSA nationalised the Nippon Credit Bank – against the bank's loud protests – upon finding it insolvent.[28] Thus, both the MOF's balanced budget principle and its convoy approach fell by the wayside in 1998. Ironically, however, the heightened prudential regulation of Japanese banks from 1998 made Japanese financial institutions more sensitive to financial risk in Asia than they were at the onset of crisis.

Japan's Response to the Asian Crisis

Domestic policy choices in the 1990s left the Japanese private sector poorly positioned to play a proactive role in solving the Asian financial crisis. As a result, the contributions of Japan's private sector, particularly Japanese banks, might be better categorised as contributing to the problem rather than to the solution. We will examine the private sector responses before turning to the more positive and proactive government-level response.

Private Sector Responses

Japanese banks exacerbated the crisis in Asia by selling even fairly good loans to Asian companies in a desperate attempt to shore up their financial positions.[29] When the Asian financial crisis hit in 1997, Japanese banks were in a capital pinch and criticism of the banking sector was at a peak within Japan. As shown above, the public rejected the idea of a bailout until after the collapse of Takugin and Yamaichi Securities in November of that year. Given the hostile public sentiment and growing exposure of scandals in the sector, any significant domestic recall of loans would have branded banks as pariahs. Ironically, the banks had been sustaining large numbers of Japanese deadbeat borrowers since the bursting of the bubble, and would continue to sustain them while recalling fairly healthy loans from abroad – recalling loans extended overseas rather than those extended domestically incurred far less wrath from Japanese politicians and the general public. Although customer links in Asia were important in the long term, the time horizon of Japanese banks had shrunk considerably. Further, Japanese banks financing in the Asian markets and in relatively strong positions were being pressured by the MOF – which had yet to abandon its convoy approach – to cooperate in the rescue of ailing banks and credit unions through the injection of funds.

The role of Japanese banks was also prominent in the failure of major lenders to the region to reach agreement on forgiveness of loans to Indonesia. Japanese banks refused to write off significant amounts of debt because doing so would not only have jeopardised their ability to maintain BIS capital requirements, but would have brought some to the verge of insolvency.[30] Japanese banks held 38 per cent of Indonesia's private sector foreign debt at the end of 1997, a far greater share than any other country (H. Sender 1998a). This BIS figure far understates the true magnitude of Japanese bank exposure, since it includes neither lending to Japanese companies in Indonesia nor bank exposure to the Suharto family and its related enterprises through off balance sheet loans. The refusal of Japanese banks to write off any debts, however, led to a stalemate in debt write-off by other major international banks and thereby impeded the delivery of new capital to Indonesia (J. Sender 1998).

In the wake of the crisis, loans to five worst-affected countries from Japanese banks fell much more sharply than from other BIS institutions, negatively affecting the ability of those economies to finance new projects (Sugisaki 1998). The regional crisis also spurred a drop in Japanese FDI, particularly in Thailand, Malaysia and Indonesia. FDI from Japan to Indonesia, Malaysia, the Philippines and Thailand declined conspicuously from the latter half of 1997 and fell further in 1998 (JETRO 1999). Japanese manufacturers in the region were negatively affected by the crisis in two ways: the drop in local demand hurt firms producing primarily for the domestic market and the recession in Japan dampened demand for exports to Japan.

Exports to Japan from the crisis-hit countries of Korea, Malaysia and Thailand were down by 15–20 per cent in the first half of 1998 from the year before, as Japan's economic malaise and subsequent slowdown in production meant decreasing demand for construction materials and outsourcing (Sugisaki 1998). Although Japan is not the major absorber of the region's exports, trade relations with Japan have always been a major source of those nations' overall balance of payment deficits. Japan's exports to the region also fell sharply with the onset of crisis, spurred by the region's drop in demand for Japanese exports and the cutback in production necessitated by Japan's own economic malaise.

As the FDI, export and import figures suggest, the continued stagnation of the Japanese economy has negative implications for Asia's recovery. IMF officials estimated that Japan's economic downturn would lower GDP in the worst-affected countries by 1 per cent in fiscal year 1998 (Sugisaki 1998). Without spurred domestic demand, Japan will be unable to absorb more exports from Asia and assist in the revitalisation of regional trade. And although current Japanese policy measures for revitalisation of the domestic economy focus on internally generated growth, continued stagnation in Japan heightens the possibility that Japan might turn to externally generated means, such as exports, for growth. US–Japan trade frictions over heightened Japanese steel exports to the United States in 1999 demonstrated the perception in some US circles that Japan's exports already crowd out those from elsewhere in Asia.[31]

Government-level Responses

Unlike the Japanese private sector, the Japanese government has played a prominent role in responding proactively to the Asian financial crisis.

148   JENNIFER A. AMYX

When Thailand was first hit by crisis in 1997, the Japanese government proposed the creation of a $US100 billion Asian Monetary Fund (AMF), a multilateral scheme intended to stabilise regional currencies. After facing opposition from the United States and the IMF, the Japanese government abandoned the plan (at least in the short term) and shifted to a strategy of bilateral support.[32] Since then, the Japanese government's prominence in coordinating initial government-level responses has varied. It was particularly large, for example, in Indonesia, which is a major source of Japanese oil imports. There the Japanese government assembled a $US2.3 billion package of loans in February 1998, with more to follow.

On 3 October 1998, Japanese officials announced an initiative that would frame much of Japan's support to countries in the region. The initiative, commonly referred to as the New Miyazawa initiative, entails a pledge of financial support totalling $US30 billion to the five crisis-hit countries in Asia. It differs from the proposed AMF in that the pledge is composed primarily of bilateral rather than multilateral support. The initiative has made available $US15 billion in short-term funds, with the remaining $US15 billion to be made available as medium- to long-term financial support. The money has been committed in the form of direct official financial assistance and through the use of guarantee mechanisms and interest subsidies to support regional economies' attempts to raise funds from international financial markets. As of May 1999, approximately two-thirds of the assistance had been committed.

The establishment in March 1999 of an Asian Currency Crisis Support Facility, administered by the ADB, was a component of the New Miyazawa initiative. The Japanese government has provided the funding for this facility's interest payment assistance, technical assistance grants and guarantees to co-financed ADB loans and bonds issued by crisis-affected countries. In addition to the $US30 billion initially pledged by Japan, ¥20 billion in support has been pledged to Vietnam under the rubric of the New Miyazawa initiative, to support economic reforms there.

In addition to the New Miyazawa initiative, the Japanese government has worked with the United States to develop an Asian Growth and Recovery initiative. This initiative, announced on 16 November 1998, is to be carried out in conjunction with the World Bank and the ADB. Its intended focus is on revitalising the region's private sectors – the next priority in dealing with the crisis now that the currency situation is relatively stable. The Japanese government's participation in this initiative is particularly important in light of the fact that Japan's stricter supervision of its banks since late 1998 has accelerated withdrawal of private sector capital from the region. The government's aid to locally based Japanese firms and their customers has also been a means of compensating for the drop in funds available to such firms and their customers, due to the FSA's heightened loan loss reserve requirements on Japanese banks. The FSA stipulation of withdrawal from overseas operations was a prerequisite for many Japanese banks seeking recapitalisation from public funds in March 1999.[33]

In 1999, the Japanese government established a scheme for the partial guarantee of sovereign bonds in the region, as a lower-cost means of boosting the credibility of issuers in the region. This plan included creation of a $US3 billion guarantee fund in the ADB, as well as ¥27.5 billion ($US230 million) to subsidise interest payments. As part of the plan, the Diet passed legislation in April 1999 to permit the Export-Import Bank of Japan to guarantee sovereign bonds issued by emerging economies and to purchase such bonds directly. With these develop-ments, it is hoped that institutional investors in Japan and elsewhere will be more willing to reinvest in the region.[34]

Japan has committed a greater amount of total bilateral support to global efforts to contain the Asian crisis than has any other country. By offering support in the form of bilateral aid, Japanese officials can consider the progress of reforms within each nation's historical and socio-economic context, something which the IMF has been heavily criticised for not doing. The bilateral extension of aid also enables the simultaneous promotion of the yen in the region by granting yen-denominated funds. The introduction of the euro in 1999 under-standably heightened Japanese concerns over the marginalisation of the yen in global capital markets, and the New Miyazawa initiative clarifies Japan's intention to promote the yen while supplying aid to the region. Recent moves to revive the AMF proposal are seen as another means of promoting the internationalisation of Japan's currency.[35]

While the Japanese desire to promote the yen is understandable, yen-denominated aid may not be best for the recipient countries because the vast amount of international dealings and obligations to which they are tied remain dollar-denominated. Thus, the ability of yen-denominated loans to meet financing needs can fluctuate significantly with changes in the yen/dollar exchange rates. Nonetheless, the Japanese government's efforts to address the crisis and its consequences are laudable.

A major irony in Japan's provision of regional aid lies in the fact that much of the vast sums pledged have been directed at the disposal of bad loans and the easing of credit crunches within the region's economies, yet Japan continued to face mounting bad loans and a worsening credit crunch at home and, until late 1998, showed little progress in overcom-ing its domestic problems. Indeed, tensions between Japanese and US leaders when they have arisen have stemmed largely from the US Treasury's unrelenting criticism of Japan for not putting its house in order. The political challenges of assembling government aid packages for the region, however, paled in comparison to the political challenges involved in efforts to resolve the financial crisis at home.

Conclusion: Implications and Political Impediments to Full Reform

The conjunction of Japan's financial crisis with the crisis in Asia and the emulation of the Japanese model of development by many countries in the region naturally leads to a hypothesis that common systemic defects might be to blame. After all, the underlying problems in Japan of weak supervision, political paralysis and collusion certainly resonate in many ways with regional cases of financial breakdown. Could the strong relational character of policy-making and regulation pervading the systems of Japan and Asia lie at the heart of both the endogenously generated Japanese crisis and externally generated Asian crisis?

Crisis has not hit all regional economies, however, and this suggests that neither Japan's crisis nor the greater regional crisis was inevitable. The experiences of Japan and Asia in the 1990s offer strong evidence that modes and institutions of financial governance heavily reliant on and embedded in relational networks may provide contingent conditions for breakdown. In other words, these characteristics heighten the probability of breakdown in the presence of other factors, such as sudden exogenous shocks. In short, the findings suggest that relationally based regulation has implications for the adaptive capacities of governments and the way economies change.

We might have expected Japan's difficulties in transition to a more transparent rules-based system to be mirrored in countries such as South Korea, Thailand and Indonesia, which similarly faced crisis. Their net debtor status, however, meant that with the onset of crisis they faced possible national bankruptcy in the absence of external aid. Because aid assistance was conditional on fundamental reforms, the nations had little choice but to begin transition to more transparent and rules-based systems. The situation has been very different in Japan. As a net creditor with a huge pool of individual private savings, Japan is not in a position to have change imposed upon it in the same way. While Japanese officials are quick to note the nation's move toward a more transparent rules-based system, they are also quick to add that they seek not to emulate the Anglo-American model but to create a third model. Whether Japan creates a model of financial governance which is neither distinctively Anglo-American nor Asian, the FSA's progress in dealing with banking problems provides evidence that an independent regulatory agency is key to prudential regulation even in Japan.

The transition to a more transparent rules-based system in Japan still faces substantial political impediments. A rules-based system requires more resources for formal supervision. Although the FSA's 1999 budget provides for a 50 per cent increase in inspectors, the gain still leaves the agency with only 540 inspectors to oversee approximately 1100 banks. Approximately 8000 inspectors inspect 12 000 banks in the United States. Another persistent political impediment to accelerated resolution of problems surrounds the need to cut off funds to unworthy loan customers. This issue is particularly salient in the management of banks under temporary government control or in receivership. Decisions to cut off loans to delinquent borrowers are not politically popular, especially if the borrowers are mainstay LDP support groups. Thus, transparent lending rules and avoiding undue political influence on loan decisions are critical to whether Japan succeeds with reforms.[36]

The speed and extent of Japan's economic recovery will depend heavily on the rapidity with which it restores its financial system to health. That, in turn, will be one of the major determinants of whether the Asian economic crisis is contained or its effects transmitted further. Yet the role of Japan must not be exaggerated. Japan's demographics militate against rapid growth, even in the absence of financial problems. Further, the United States, not Japan, has traditionally absorbed the majority of Asian exports.[37] Nonetheless, with an estimated potential growth rate of 2 per cent (Posen 1998) Japan has significant room for improvement, and improvement would be a welcome and positive development for Asia.

CHAPTER 7

Dangers and Opportunities: The Implications of the Asian Financial Crisis for China

Hongying Wang[1]

The Asian financial crisis of 1997 has had a major impact on regional and world economies. This chapter discusses the implications of the crisis for China. Just as the Chinese word for 'crisis' is made up of two characters, danger and opportunity, the Asian financial crisis presented China with both dangers and opportunities.

The chapter begins by examining the short-term consequences of the crisis for China. China has avoided the immediate effects of the crisis, but the economic recessions in neighbouring countries have led to a slow-down in China's economic growth. On the other hand, the crisis has provided an opportunity for the Chinese government to enhance its political image both domestically and on the international stage. Next, the chapter explores some long-term implications of the crisis. Although China has avoided the financial shock and economic meltdown in the short run, it shares some of the institutional problems at the root of the crisis elsewhere in Asia. What happened to other Asian countries has alerted Chinese leaders to the urgent need for change. At the same time, the economic slowdown caused by the crisis has complicated the task of economic restructuring. The chapter analyses the political dynamics of financial and enterprise reforms, focusing on the politics of redistribution and on state preferences and capacity. In both areas, there is only limited room for optimism about the outcome of the reforms. The chapter ends with a brief discussion of possible political consequences of the financial and enterprise reforms the Chinese government proposes to undertake.

Short-term Implications

In the short run, China has avoided the financial chaos that engulfed many other Asian countries thanks to its capital account inconvertibility, large foreign currency reserve and reliance on direct foreign investment rather than debt financing. But China has not been immune to the secondary impact of the crisis. Reduced foreign investment from other Asian countries, more severe export competition and a shrinking international market in the aftermath of the crisis have led to a slow-down of China's economic growth. However, the Chinese government has gained political benefits at home and abroad. It has won praise from the West as well as from its Asian neighbours for its responsible exchange rate policy and support for Hong Kong's economic stability.

Financial Immunity

The origins of the Asian financial crisis have been a matter of contro-versy. Roughly speaking, there are two theories – the fundamentalist story and the panic story, discussed in the preface to this book. As will be discussed below, China has many of the institutional problems identified by the fundamentalist approach. But so far, it has been immune to the contagion of the financial crisis highlighted by the panic approach.

First and most obviously, the Chinese currency, the renminbi (RMB), is not convertible for capital account transactions. Therefore, investors cannot rush in and out of China with hot money. This is not to suggest that the Chinese system of capital control is perfect. In fact, it has many loopholes. Companies legally or illegally take advantage of these loop-holes to move foreign currencies overseas.[2] In 1997, China's balance of payment data shows $US22.7 billion in 'errors and omissions'. In 1998, despite a trade surplus exceeding $US30 billion and an inflow of $US31.4 billion of new foreign investment, China's foreign exchange reserves were unchanged from the beginning of the year (*Far Eastern Economic Review*, 29 October 1998; *Washington Post*, 27 October 1998: A16).[3] However, the leak has been minor in the context of a foreign currency reserve that is over $US140 billion.

Second, in contrast to South-East Asia where much of the foreign investment has been hot money, the capital inflows to China have been predominantly foreign direct investment (FDI) (Noland et al. 1998: 17). Compared to portfolio investment, FDI tends to be much less volatile. This is because companies making direct investment often seek to gain access to resources, take advantage of cheap labour and establish market shares rather than make short-term profits. Furthermore, direct invest-ment ultimately takes the form of factories and equipment. Even if investors want out, it is not easy to liquidate their investment quickly. In response to the impact of the Asian financial crisis, the Chinese govern-ment has further tightened control of foreign debt – its scale, its structure and its usage. Meanwhile, control over foreign transactions has become more rigid. Violations of foreign exchange regulations are punished by criminal codes.[4]

Economic Slowdown

While China has been spared the direct effects of the financial crisis, the economy has not escaped secondary damage. In the last couple of years, the financial crisis has devastated many economies in Asia, bringing down local currencies and stock markets, bankrupting corporations, creating massive unemployment and driving large portions of the middle class back to poverty. These factors have put serious constraints on China's economic growth.

Foreign trade has been an engine of China's economic miracle. Exports account for 30 per cent of Chinese GDP and 3 to 4 percentage points of China's GDP growth (Noland et al. 1998: 56). The decreasing demand for imports in countries directly or indirectly hit by the crisis means a shrinking international market for Chinese exports.[5] Also, the dramatic devaluation of the region's currencies generates increased competition for Chinese exports not only in neighbouring countries but also in the broader international market. China's refusal to devalue the RMB has caused tremendous difficulties for Chinese companies exporting footwear, textiles, garments and electronics.

Foreign direct investment has been another driving force of China's growth. The currency devaluation and economic recession in South-East Asia have caused a significant reduction in investment in China. As the repercussions of the Asian financial crisis spread to countries outside the region, such as Russia and Brazil, investors have turned away from emerging markets in developing countries to the safer havens of developed countries. Moreover, a large portion of foreign investment in China is export-oriented. Since China will not devalue the RMB, its attractiveness to such foreign investment projects has greatly diminished.

In response to the Asian financial crisis, the Chinese government has implemented expansionary fiscal and monetary policies to prevent China being dragged into a recession. It announced in February 1998 that it would spend $US1 trillion on new infrastructure projects, housing and high-tech industries over the next three years (*Renmin Ribao*, 2 March 1998: 10).[6] In terms of monetary policy, the People's Bank of China repeatedly lowered short-term interest rates.[7] Banks also lowered their lending standards (*New York Times*, 15 November 1998: 6). To attract foreign investment, the Chinese government reinstituted tariff and tax waivers on equipment imports for foreign investment projects (*Zhongguo Maoyi Bao*, 4 February 1998). To reduce the competitive pressure on China's exports, the government provided subsidies to offset the high value of the RMB. These include expanded loans and rebates to assist Chinese enterprises export their products.[8]

However, so far these measures have not been highly effective. China's export growth began to slow in the second half of 1997. Exports in 1998 rose only 0.58 per cent, down from 21 per cent growth in 1997 (*China Monthly Statistics*, January 1999). For the first eight months of 1999, exports fell by 0.2 per cent (Saywell 1999). The growth rate of FDI actually utilised by China declined from 8.4 per cent in 1997 to a mere 0.07 per cent in 1998 (*China Statistical Yearbooks* 1998; *China Monthly Statistics*, January 1999). For the first seven months of 1999, actual FDI fell 10 per cent (Saywell 1999). As a result, China's economic growth rate dropped from 9.7 per cent in 1996 to 8.8 per cent in 1997 and to 7.8 per cent in 1998.[9] Accompanying the slowdown of the economy has been a sustained period of deflationary drift. By August 1999, retail prices had dropped for a twenty-third consecutive month (Saywell 1999). Unemployment has gone up. Although the official figure is 3–4 per cent, experts estimate it to be 8–9 per cent in urban China.[10] In other words, although China has escaped the worst of the Asian financial crisis for the time being, it is far from safe. The dangers of further economic slowdown and rising unemployment remain.

Political Gains

Politically, the Asian financial crisis has been beneficial to the Chinese government. The sense of crisis, along with the fight against floods in the summer of 1998, has rallied the public around the government. It also offers the government an excuse for the slowdown of the economy, which had begun before the crisis. Furthermore, the crisis has drawn Hong Kong closer to mainland China. Beijing's determination not to devalue the yuan has been seen as crucial to Hong Kong's capacity to hold onto the peg between the Hong Kong dollar and the US dollar. China's readiness to support Hong Kong with its huge foreign currency reserves has added to the confidence in Hong Kong's financial and economic stability. More broadly, Hong Kong's economy is so closely intertwined with the Chinese economy as a whole that if China's economy falls into recession, Hong Kong will also suffer.[11] The financial crisis has served to increase Beijing's influence over Hong Kong.

On the international stage, the Asian financial crisis provided an opportunity for China to improve its image.[12] Soon after the outbreak of the crisis, the Chinese government declared to the world that it would not devalue the RMB. So far, in spite of the pressure on Chinese exports of the high yuan, China has stood by its promise not to devalue.[13] This is largely a self-interested policy. As the Chinese government recognises, if China devalues its currency it will make Chinese exports temporarily more competitive. But it does not offer a lasting solution. In fact, it may lead to inflation at home and instability in Hong Kong, as well as another round of devaluation of Asian currencies, which will negate the effect of RMB devaluation. Moreover, half of China's exports are based on imported equipment and materials (China News Service [CNS], 23 September 1998). Despite the self-interest in resisting devaluation, China's position has won high praise internationally. During Zhu Rongji's visit to Europe in April 1998, for instance, the European Union pointed to China's continued determination not to devalue its currency as a highly responsible position during the Asian financial crisis (*South China Morning Post*, 3 April 1998: 1). At his summit meeting with President Jiang Zemin in June 1998, President Bill Clinton praised China for its 'statesmanship and strength' (*Straits Times*, 28 June 1998: 1). Chinese leaders have repeatedly contrasted China's willingness to take risks and pay a price for the region's stability with Japan's reluctance to use its economic strength to the same end. Likewise, President Clinton's praise of China was accompanied by criticism of Japan's slow pace in reforming its financial institutions and ensuring the stability of the Japanese yen (*Straits Times*, 28 June 1998: 1).[14] The Asian financial crisis has boosted China's status in the world at large and in the region in particular. Singapore's Minister of Information and Arts similarly praised China and warned that the role individual nations play during the Asian financial crisis would determine how much say they have after the crisis is over (*Straits Times*, 23 April 1998: 2).

Long-term Implications

Although China has avoided financial shock and economic meltdown in the short run, it is plagued by the same problem of crony capitalism that is at the root of the financial crisis from Thailand to Indonesia and from Korea to Malaysia. The fate of China's Asian neighbours drives home the necessity for and urgency of making fundamental changes in the financial system. Unless the reforms are carried out reasonably soon, China will slowly but surely move toward its own financial and economic crisis. In this sense, the Asian financial crisis constitutes an opportunity for reformers in the Chinese leadership to advance their agenda. In the meantime, the economic difficulties inflicted by the financial crisis have complicated the implementation of reforms.

Financial Reforms

A modern financial system consists of a banking system and a capital market, which serve to channel financial resources and to discipline the use of those resources. Like other former socialist countries, prior to the economic reforms China did not have such a financial system. It had a monobanking system, with the People's Bank of China (PBC) acting as the central bank as well as the only commercial bank. The PBC carried out financial and monetary plans made by the government to meet planned economic targets. It used cash plan to control income and consumption purposes and credit plan to control inter-enterprise and inter-governmental transactions. The PBC was nothing more than the government's cashier for the implementation of economic plans.

Since the beginning of the economic reforms in the late 1970s, the old financial system has shown serious limitations. Financial reforms during the last two decades, especially in the 1990s, can be classified as development in three areas – institutions, instruments and markets (Mehran et al. 1996). The marketisation of finance has been the area of least progress, with the exception of the foreign exchange market. But there have been significant changes in the other two areas.

The most visible progress has taken place in institution-building. Beginning in the mid 1980s, a two-tier banking system has replaced the monobanking system. The PBC has taken on some of the tasks of a central bank. The government has tried to enhance the independence of the central bank; for example, beginning in 1994 the PBC refused to lend money to the Ministry of Finance to cover the state's budget deficit. This practice became codified in the Central Bank Law of 1995 (Lardy 1998a: 174). Between 1994 and 1996, the central bank established a framework to shift from credit policy to monetary policy (Lardy 1998a: 138).

The government has established or restructured a number of specialised banks – the Industrial and Commercial Bank of China, the China Construction Bank, the Agricultural Bank of China and the Bank of China – which it hopes will operate on a commercial basis. In 1994, the State Council approved the creation of three new policy banks – the State Development Bank of China, the Import-Export Bank of China and the Agricultural Development Bank of China. The plan is to have these banks finance policy-oriented projects, leaving the four existing specialised state-owned banks to become profit-oriented banks (Lardy 1998a: 176–7).

Financial reform has also created room for additional commercial banks, urban cooperative banks, urban credit cooperatives, rural credit cooperatives, financial firms, securities firms, insurance companies and trust and investment companies (Dai et al. 1997; Kumar et al. 1996). These new financial institutions have introduced competition into the financial sector.

In terms of financial instruments, China has developed a nascent capital market, which includes government securities and corporate bonds, and stocks. The stock markets in Shenzhen and Shanghai opened in 1990 and 1991. Individuals comprise a small portion of investors in the capital market; three-quarters of the stocks are held by the state, the companies themselves and, to a much lesser extent, foreign investors (Lardy 1998a: 133).

Despite these positive changes, the financial system in China remains deeply flawed. Banks continue to dominate China's financial system, accounting for 90 per cent of all financial intermediation between savers and investors (Lardy 1998b: 79). Furthermore, contrary to the goals proclaimed by the government, neither the central bank nor the commercial banks operate according to market principles. The PBC lacks independence and policy resources, and its operations remain under the political control of the State Council. It has few instruments to carry out monetary policies and to supervise commercial banks (Mehran et al. 1996: 20–2). On the other hand, commercial banks in China follow policy needs rather than market principles. By the mid 1980s, faced with declining revenues, the government decided to use bank loans to replace budgetary grants to support state industry. Bank loans have since grown exponentially. Since they lend mostly to unprofitable state-owned enterprises, banks have become heavily burdened with deadbeat loans. Many banks have long been technically insolvent (Lardy 1998a: 59–127).

China's nascent capital market is small and has many pitfalls. Chinese securities markets lack regulation and discipline. Insider trading is rampant.[15] Accounting standards are a fantasy (*Wall Street Journal*, 30 April 1998: R16). To counter these problems, the government plans to expand the capital market and improve its regulation, with the help of international organisations and foreign companies.[16]

The problems with China's financial system are very similar to those in Thailand, Indonesia, Malaysia and Korea – bank dominance of the financial system, lack of central bank autonomy, policy and political lending, accumulation of bad loans, and absence of a strong and disciplined equity market. In fact, the role of banks in China's financial system is even greater and banks are in even worse shape than in other countries in the region. In 1997, non-performing loans accounted for 16 per cent of bank assets in South Korea, 11 per cent in Indonesia, 7.5 per cent in Malaysia and 15 per cent in Thailand (Noland et al. 1998: 10). Estimates of non-performing loans in China vary, but it is certainly no exaggeration to estimate them at over 20 per cent of the assets of state banks (*Economist*, 2 May 1998: 65–7; Lardy 1998a: 195). If China is to avoid the fate of its neighbours, the government must urgently carry out market-oriented reforms.

The Chinese government seems to have received this message unequivocally (*Washington Post*, 17 January 1998: A22). Although Chinese researchers and policy-makers lament the power of international financial capital and its threat to national sovereignty and national economic security, especially in the developing world, they acknowledge that the financial crisis was deeply rooted in the domestic institutions of the affected countries (Zou 1998; Gong 1998; Zhong & Hu 1998). Furthermore, they recognise the inevitability of the move toward economic and financial globalisation. The only way for China to prevent a crisis is to improve its management of its own financial system (Yang & Xu 1998; Y. Wang 1998).[17]

In the immediate aftermath of the Asian financial crisis, the government announced several important policy initiatives for financial reforms. To strengthen the autonomy and efficiency of the central bank, the People's Bank of China restructured its internal organisation, reducing the number of bureaus and offices as well as personnel (CNS, 29 September 1998). More importantly, the government declared that in the next three years the central bank of China would restructure itself, replacing thirty-two provincial branches with nine cross-province regional branches and local branches. The new structure would resemble the US Federal Reserve System (*People's Daily*, 8 March 1998: 3). By early 1999, according to government claims, the restructuring had been successfully implemented. Compared to the old regime, it grants far more autonomy to the central bank, especially from the intervention of local governments.[18]

With regard to commercial banks, the government set out the following steps for immediate implementation. First, commercial banks are to be managed autonomously, making independent decisions about loans for investment projects. Second, the credit quota ceiling is to be removed, replaced by management based on the ratio between assets and liabilities. Third, the total capital of state-owned commercial banks is to be increased to 8 per cent to meet the Bank for International Settlements' (BIS) standards on capital adequacy. Fourth, China will adopt a system of auditing to classify loans according to their quality. Fifth, China will adopt prudent accounting principles and establish provisions for bad debts (*People's Daily*, 8 March 1998: 3). To help relieve the burden of the past and enable commercial banks to begin operating under the new rules, in 1998 the Chinese government issued 270 billion yuan in domestic bonds, which will be used to recapitalise the four state-owned commercial banks.[19] In addition, the government plans to establish a financial asset management company to deal with non-performing loans of state-owned banks.

Since the beginning of the Asian financial crisis, the Chinese government has shown determination to crack down on financial irregularities. It has closed or suspended a number of institutions. The most notable case has been the closing and then bankruptcy of the Guangdong International Trust and Investment Corporation (GITIC), China's second-largest trust and investment company.[20] The government has enhanced measures to increase transparency and discipline in the financial sector, including separating accounting, auditing and credit rating agencies. These include agencies adopting new accounting rules to reveal hidden costs, and the establishment of Sino-foreign joint venture credit rating companies. In December 1998, the National People's Congress promulgated the long-awaited Securities Law of the People's Republic of China. In February 1999, the State Council issued new regulations regarding the punishment of illegal financial activities.

Parallel to its policy of centralising power in the banking system, the government has taken action to strengthen central regulation of the rest of the financial system. In June 1998, the Chinese Communist Party (CCP) Central Committee established a Financial Work Commission headed by politburo member Wen Jiabao. The commission is designed to ensure vertical leadership of the financial system. The CCP Central Committee has also set up a financial discipline commission to enhance the fight against corruption. In the securities industry, the government has strengthened the vertical control of the securities market through China Securities Regulatory Commission (CSRC).[21] In November 1998, the Insurance Supervision and Regulation Commission was established.

Even as the Chinese government seeks to rectify the existing financial system, it has continued with cautious liberalisation measures. For instance, in 1998 China gave approval for nine additional foreign bank branches and four foreign insurance companies to operate in China. On the domestic front, China issued regulations on mutual funds. By the spring of 1998, there were nearly eighty funds investing in domestic securities markets (Saywell 1998). They provide investment vehicles for small to medium investors, and are expected to attract more investment and stabilise the market.

The Asian financial crisis has made Chinese leadership more aware of the importance of a modern financial system and the urgency of reforms. However, the economic difficulties brought on by the crisis have created formidable obstacles to the implementation of reforms. In the words of an economist in the State Council, 'Maintaining growth and fighting unemployment had to get the top priority. Unless these two goals are met, you can't address the other problems like banking and state enterprise reform' (quoted in *New York Times*, 15 November 1998: 6). As the government pumps hundreds of billions of dollars into the economy, much of the money is spent to prop up state-owned enterprises that are inefficient but provide employment to most urban residents. In that process, the commercialisation of financial institutions is sacrificed (*Business Week*, 27 July 1998: 44).

In the aftermath of the Asian financial crisis, the spotlight has been on China's financial system. But financial reforms are closely related to reforms of the enterprise system. Banks cannot operate like commercial entities if their major clients – state-owned enterprises – continue to rely on bank subsidies. In other words, the establishment of a viable and efficient financial system requires not only reforms within the financial institutions but reforms of the socialist enterprise system.

State-owned Enterprise Reforms

State-owned enterprises (SOEs) are formally owned 'by all the people', but are actually controlled by the government. On the eve of economic reforms, SOEs dominated the Chinese economy, accounting for over 77.6 per cent of the national industrial output in 1978. However, since 1980 SOEs have lost their dominance. In 1997, they made up only 26.5 per cent of total industrial output (CNS, 30 September 1998). In other words, today, non-state enterprises make up close to three-quarters of China's industrial output. They have been the driving force of China's economic growth in the last two decades.[22]

The relative decline of SOEs is mainly attributable to their lack of efficiency. The Chinese government has tried to restructure the incentive structures and to enhance the role of market competition. The limited reforms of SOEs have gone through several stages. In 1979–80, the key policy was profit retention. Until then, enterprises had handed over all their earnings to the government. In turn, they received government funding for their expenses and investment. The new policy allowed enterprises to retain some of their profits for investment and bonuses. In the mid 1980s, SOEs signed long-term contracts with their bureaucratic superiors about the division of profits and taxes. The third stage of reforms began in 1993. Small SOEs have been converted into collective or private companies, large and medium SOEs are being converted into limited liability or shareholding companies (Lardy 1998a: 22–3).

However, none of these reforms has improved the efficiency and profitability of state industry. In fact, the financial performance of SOEs, especially asset:liability ratios, has declined in the last two decades (Lardy 1998a: 25–47; Steinfeld 1998: 18–22). This has been the result of a number of factors, including the loss of abnormal profits, excessive wage payments, heavy welfare burdens and theft of state assets by managers and other insiders (Lardy 1998a: 47–52). In 1996, over 50 per cent of China's SOEs declared losses, and the Chinese government acknowledged that the state industrial sector as a whole had posted net losses for the year, the first time since 1949.[23]

As the burden of keeping SOEs afloat shifted from budgetary alloca-tion to loans from state-owned banks, bank lending to SOEs expanded dramatically. Outstanding loans, mostly to SOEs, increased from 53 per cent of GDP in 1978 to 100 per cent in 1996 (Lardy 1998b: 80). With more than half of SOEs officially in the red and even more undeclared money-losers, the majority of loans made to them are not likely to be collected. Indeed, these non-performing loans have been a major source of the fragility of China's banking system in particular and its financial system in general. To establish a viable financial system, there must be fundamental changes to SOEs.

The Politics of Reform

The trajectory of China's financial and enterprise systems will depend on the political dynamics of reform. Focusing on the politics of redistri-bution and on state preferences and capacity, this section analyses the forces for and against reforms and projects the likely result of the balance.

Politics of Redistribution

Market-oriented reforms inevitably lead to a redistribution of benefits among different groups in society. There are bound to be winners and losers, and the conflicts over who gets what play an important role in government's choice of policies. The reform measures that have been proposed and/or carried out have varying distributary effects on differ-ent groups in society.

A healthier and more efficient financial system would benefit money-saving households, competitive enterprises and society at large. Households in China save an average 40 per cent of their income, and most of the savings are deposited in state-owned banks that pay below-market interest rates (Lardy 1998a: 91). As many of the banks are technically insolvent, unless fundamental changes take place many households will lose their deposits altogether. Households need a viable banking system to maintain their wealth. As banks and other financial institutions improve their efficiency and competitiveness, households stand to gain not only safer deposits but better financial service and more profitable returns.

Since state-owned banks make most of their loans to SOEs, there are very limited financial resources available for other types of enterprises.[24] Collectively owned enterprises and private enterprises have long suffered from shortages of credit. In general, non-SOEs are more efficient and profitable than SOEs. If China's financial institutions become commercial entities rather than policy and political instruments, they will extend credit to the more competitive enterprises in the non-state sector rather than to SOEs, enabling collective and private enterprises to expand even faster and to absorb more workers from the SOE sector.

Reforms will also benefit society at large. A healthy banking system is essential to maintain the confidence of households, whose high savings rate has been crucial to economic development. Improvement of bank efficiency and the development of a sound capital market will enable more efficient allocation of financial resources. Reducing wasteful subsidies and increasing financial support for the most competitive economic actors will lead to long-term growth.

However, not everyone will gain from further reforms, at least not in the short term. As discussed earlier, the establishment of a viable financial system depends on reforming SOEs. The most important task for the next stage of reform is to impose hard budget constraints and to force insolvent SOEs into bankruptcy.[25] However, under hard budget constraints, SOEs will have to improve efficiency by downsizing their workforce and shedding many of their welfare functions. Those that fail to make profits will have to be taken over by other enterprises or closed. For managers, this means loss of resources, power and even their own jobs. For many workers, it means unemployment. As of 1995, SOEs employed 65 per cent of the urban population in China (Steinfeld 1998: 16). When they downsize or go out of business, the impact will be felt by tens of millions of people. What makes it especially difficult is the lack of a social safety net. For decades, SOEs have served as total institutions, providing benefits for their employees from cradle to grave. When workers lose their jobs at SOEs, they also lose housing, medical care, children's schooling and so on. The political implications are very serious.

Even without fundamental restructuring of SOEs, unemployment has been rising because of the poor performance of SOEs. In 1995, official Chinese urban unemployment reached 5.2 million or 3 per cent of the urban labour force, but a much larger number of workers not classified as unemployed had been put 'off post' with minimal or no pay.[26] Unofficial estimates of the present unemployment rate range from 20 to 28 per cent in some cities (*New York Times*, 20 January 1998: 1; *Business*

China, 30 March 1998). In 1998, the government declared that it would revamp its 5500 debt-laden large and medium-sized SOEs in the next three years, which would lead to many more workers losing their jobs.[27]

Although the government has tried to ease the pain by extending some unemployment benefits and helping laid-off workers find other job opportunities, the measures have had limited effect. There is now a great deal of discontent, anger and political alienation among Chinese workers. There are no official statistics on demonstrations and riots, but anecdotal evidence suggests they are quite serious and widespread.[28] The Chinese government is very aware of the political dangers of massive unemployment (*People's Daily*, 5 November 1998: 10).

The number of people who will benefit from financial and enterprise reforms is likely to far exceed the number of people hurt by the reforms, but their influence over government policy choices is not commensurate with their number.[29] Money-saving households are dispersed. Many of them do not fully understand the threat of insolvent banks or the benefits of a more healthy financial system. The fact that the benefits will occur in the long run makes them even less likely to resort to any kind of collective pressure on the government. Non-state enterprises have achieved increasing structural autonomy and economic importance, but the political influence of private entrepreneurs remains limited and they are not organised in a way to exert pressure on policy-making (Pearson 1997).

In contrast, the losers from reforms are relatively concentrated in the most inefficient SOEs. The costs they are asked to pay – unemployment and dramatic reduction of their living standards – are unambiguous and immediate. Consequently, they are highly motivated and willing to act collectively to defend their interests. In 1989, alongside students demanding political freedom, workers in a number of cities organised demonstrations to voice their discontent at inflation, corruption and lack of independent representation. At that time workers' living standards had improved steadily, despite some setbacks by inflation. Institutional control of factories had weakened from pre-reform days, but was nowhere near the low point of today (Walder 1991; Walder & Gong 1993). Given that the issues are now more serious and the government is even less able to control workers, it seems reasonable to expect a great deal of political struggle by workers.

On balance, the politics of redistribution does not bode well for the prospect of further financial and enterprise reforms in China. The conflict of interests among different groups in Chinese society and the potential for political turmoil that is likely to result from conflicts, are going to be major deterrents to quick and decisive reform measures.

State Preferences and Capacity

The state is important because it not only filters societal influence through its own perceptions, interpretations and calculations, but has policy preferences of its own. In addition, the institutional structure of the state shapes the capacity of the state to act (Haggard & Kaufman 1992: 18). This is very true in China, where political liberalisation has been limited and a great deal of political contest occurs within the state.[30]

The top leadership of the central government consists of a small group of twenty-five to thirty-five people who are members of the politburo of the CCP, the CCP military affairs commission, the National People's Congress (NPC) and the State Council. At the apex of the Chinese political system, they come closest to being the 'owners' of China. Because their interest and power are closely tied to the prosperity and influence of China, they are concerned about the country's overall economic development and long-term growth.[31] Moreover, as the moral and ideological appeal of communism diminishes, they see economic development as the regime's last basis of legitimacy. Consequently, they are highly motivated to carry out financial and enterprise reforms, which they recognise as vital for system maintenance. To China's top leaders, the only major deterrent to further reforms is the threat of immediate political turmoil. Their assessment of its likelihood will determine the pace of reforms, but there is little doubt about which direction they would like to move China.

In contrast to the generalists at the very top of the Chinese political system, the bureaucracies in the central government are more interested in the immediate costs and benefits of reforms for their respective sectors. Different bureaucracies have somewhat contradictory policy preferences. For instance, the Ministry of Finance, Ministry of Foreign Trade and Economic Cooperation and the PBC are likely to benefit from a healthy financial system and more competitive enterprises. On the other hand, the State Planning Commission, the State Economic Commission and various line ministries are likely to suffer from such reforms. They were designed for a planned economy and derive much of their influence from controlling the state sector of the economy. Reduced subsidies and increasing bankruptcies of SOEs will seriously cut into their resources and power. However, this source of resistance may have dwindled significantly due to the dramatic bureaucratic restructuring announced by Zhu Rongji in 1998. Since then, according to a government report, the number of ministries and commissions under the State Council has been reduced from forty to twenty-nine. The number of officials has been cut by about 50 per cent (CNS, 5 October 1998).

Last but not least, the Chinese state consists of provincial and local governments. Unlike the top national leadership, these organisations and officials are primarily concerned about the short-term and local consequences of reforms. From their point of view, the financial and enterprise reforms announced by the central government can be threatening. For one thing, reforms of the financial market, including the centralisation of the PBC system and the securities supervision system, will remove important power from their hands. The new regime will not allow provincial and local governments to use political pressure to direct financial resources to pet projects, and will make it more difficult to cover up the widespread corruption in local economies.

In addition, financial reforms entail enterprise reforms. The reorganisation and bankruptcy of SOEs can cause serious political problems for local governments. However, not all provincial and local governments are in the same situation. Generally, inland provinces have the biggest and most problematic SOEs and are going to be especially adversely affected by massive layoffs of SOE workers. The governments in those places have to deal with the tremendous economic burden and political instability that has developed and that will continue to increase. The coastal provinces are less vulnerable, given their high percentage of non-state enterprises and relatively ample economic opportunities.[32]

While state preferences have a direct impact on policy choices, the institutional structure of the state is also important in that it determines the state's capacity to act on its preferences. There are two issues here. First, is national leadership capable of overcoming the resistance of many provincial and local governments and effectively implementing its reform initiatives? Second, is the state capable of maintaining an effective institutional framework in which the market can function?

During the reform era, Beijing has granted substantial financial and economic power to provincial and local governments. As intended, decentralisation has provided great incentives for the latter to promote local economic prosperity. It has also fostered competition among different locales. This type of fiscal federalism has been crucial to China's remarkable economic success (Montinola et al. 1995). In the process of decentralisation, the central government has lost much of its traditional power over the provinces and locales, although it was never very effective in monitoring local activities. For instance, Chinese statistical agencies lacked independence from local governments. As channels of information for the central government, they were much less effective than their Soviet counterparts (Huang 1996a). As central planning gives way to local competition, their capacity has been further eroded. Moreover, the increasing economic resources in the hands of local governments combined with the decreasing share of revenues in the hands of Beijing have reduced local dependence on the centre, and the ability of the centre to reward or punish local governments.[33] As a result, the central government's capacity to implement its decisions has declined considerably (Goodman & Segal 1994).

In the 1990s, the central government took important steps to recentralise some of the power it had granted to local governments. There are indications that these steps have been reasonably successful. First, in 1994 Beijing instituted a new tax system that replaced the old system based on contract and negotiations. The new system separated central taxes from local taxes and increased the tax revenues of the central government.[34] Second, from 1993 to 1996, the central government under Zhu Rongji's leadership successfully reined in an overheated economy. The achievement of a soft landing testifies to the political credibility and economic power of the central government.[35] Third, in June 1998 the central government ordered the People's Liberation Army to withdraw from commercial activities. Given the scale of the PLA's businesses and the amount of income it generates through commerce, it is not hard to imagine tremendous resistance from the military.[36] That the central government has been able to make and announce such a decision indicates it has considerable political power (although some question whether the PLA will comply with the order: see Tomlinson 1998: 28).

In addition to the power balance between different parts of the state, the fate of reform also depends on the capacity of the state to establish the rules, mechanisms and expertise required by a market economy.[37] These include, for example, an effective legal system to regulate the behaviour of government organisations and market actors, officials knowledgeable about the functioning of a market economy, and ways and means for the government to exercise macroeconomic control without administrative intrusion.

The prospect for reform is especially dependent on the quality of China's legal system. Legal reforms in the last two decades have brought dramatic improvement in the area of codification. Hundreds of laws have been promulgated at the national level and thousands at the lower levels. Today, law theoretically governs almost every aspect of economic activities, but in reality the legal system is seriously flawed. The interpretation of law is highly discretionary and its implementation remains erratic. Incompetence and inefficiency plague the Chinese court system. Most importantly, the ideal of the rule of law remains elusive. On the one hand, the government is too strong in that it continues to exercise arbitrary political power at the expense of law; on the other hand, the government is too weak in that it fails to prevent localism, personalism and corruption from eroding the legal system (H. Wang forthcoming: ch. 2).

The political dynamics present a mixed picture of the prospect for reforms in China. In the aftermath of the Asian financial crisis, the central government exhibits a strong impulse to undertake financial and enterprise reforms, but there are strong forces against reforms. The political balance is delicate and the challenge of market institution-building is enormous. In such a complex situation, much depends on creative political leadership. If the government takes advantage of the crisis in neighbouring countries, it may be able to mobilise sufficient support for reforms. It must also provide sufficient welfare benefits to cushion the drop in living standards of the unemployed and to seriously crack down on the official corruption in China's financial and enterprise systems.

Conclusion

Assuming the Chinese government carries out its proposed financial and enterprise reforms, what political consequences may they have? Financial reforms consist of strengthening the independence of the central bank, converting state-owned banks into genuinely commercial entities and fostering a disciplined capital market. Enterprise reforms involve imposing hard budget constraints on SOEs, forcing inefficient enterprises into bankruptcy. At first sight, such reforms will increase the role of the invisible hand of the market in the allocation of resources, at the expense of the visible hand of the government. In other words, they are likely to weaken the state. But that is only one side of the coin.

In some important ways, financial and enterprise reforms will actually strengthen the government. Although the government loses much of its direct control over financial institutions and enterprises, it gains indirect control of the overall national economy. Relieved from the burden of propping up individual banks and SOEs through subsidies, the government will be in a better position to exercise general macroeconomic control through fiscal and monetary policies.

Finally, the replacement of subsidies by macroeconomic control is likely to have significant implications for China's political system, since 'each type of policy tends to develop its own distinct political structure and process' (Lowi 1985: 75). First, macroeconomic control is more transparent and universalistic than subsidies, so is less conducive to patronage politics and corruption. As the Chinese government becomes more engaged in control of the macroeconomic environment than in the allocation of subsidies, China's political system is likely to become more open and more institutionalised.

Second, while subsidies encourage decentralisation of state power, macroeconomic control tends to enhance vertical linkages (Lowi 1985). As is already obvious, further reforms in China involve partial reversal of the decentralisation process of the last two decades. Beijing is trying to recentralise some of the power granted to local governments. Reforms will increase the resources and power of the central government *vis-à-vis* lower levels of governments.[38]

Third, unlike subsidies, macroeconomic control requires the state to develop professional expertise and strong capabilities in the areas of information, communication and supervision. Similar to the logic of the 'orthodox paradox', this suggests that reforms will lead to the restructuring and strengthening of the state rather than to its dismantlement. Politically, macroeconomic policies will increase the influence of technocrats.

China has escaped the Asian financial crisis *per se*, but has suffered from the secondary consequence of economic slowdown. The plight of its neighbours has driven home the necessity of financial and enterprise reforms in China, since many of the problems at the root of the crisis in Thailand, Indonesia, Malaysia and Korea exist in China as well. But the politics of reform are complex and delicate, involving long-term risks and short-term difficulties brought on by the economic slowdown, so the balance between the forces for and against further reforms allows only limited optimism. If the reforms are successful, they are likely to bring about important changes in China's political system.

CHAPTER 8

The International Monetary Fund in the Wake of the Asian Crisis

Barry Eichengreen[1]

The economic and financial crisis that erupted in Asia in 1997 and that had by the end of 1998 engulfed virtually the whole of the developing world has not embellished the reputation of the International Monetary Fund. The IMF has been chastened, challenged and castigated for its response to the crisis. In practice, many of the criticisms to which it is subjected are contradictory and incompatible. Some observers have criticised it for pushing currency devaluation on its developing-country members, with generally disastrous consequences, and for resisting the idea of currency boards. Others have denounced it for demanding that crisis countries hike interest rates to defend their currencies on the grounds that doing so only precipitated deeper recessions and more serious financial problems, and have argued that the IMF should insist that its developing-country members adopt more flexible exchange rates. Some criticise the IMF for lending too freely, thereby weakening market discipline and increasing the likelihood of future crises; others conclude that the prompter provision of larger loans, perhaps under the aegis of a new 'precautionary' facility, is needed to avert 'self-fulfilling' crises. Some criticise the microeconomic and structural conditions that the IMF includes in its programs as meddling in the internal affairs of countries – meddling which undermines political support for necessary reforms and therefore has the perverse effect of undermining investor confidence – while others insist that the IMF has no choice but to press for institutional reform because that is essential both for the restoration of confidence and for stability in a financially integrated world.

This chapter sorts through the controversies surrounding the IMF's response to the crisis and offers suggestions for how it might go about its business differently in the future.

170

The Essential Role of the IMF in a World of High Capital Mobility

In a world where not all information problems can be remedied, crises will occur. And in a world of highly levered institutions, crises can spread and in the worst case threaten systemic stability. These are convincing grounds on which to dismiss the extreme recommendation to abolish the IMF. To be sure, the financial safety net the IMF seeks to provide is a source of moral hazard, but moral hazard, while a problem, cannot be the sole concern of policy-makers. Moral hazard risk must be balanced against meltdown risk. We do not abolish central banks' discount facilities or national deposit insurance schemes because they create moral hazard for domestic financial institutions. We do not prohibit motorists from using seatbelts because their installation encourages some to drive faster. For drivers, as for financial markets, we worry about more than just moral hazard. We worry also about the sudden stop.

This means that there will remain a role for IMF lending to countries pursuing sound policies. Like the liquidity provided by a domestic lender of last resort to a fundamentally sound bank, IMF resources can help such a country resist for a time the effects of a temporary loss of investor confidence. The limit of the domestic–central bank analogy is that the IMF does not, and inevitably will not, have the resources to lend freely to contain a crisis. This constraint can be loosened but not eliminated if national governments supplement the assistance the IMF provides and if it convinces commercial and investment banks to contribute. The best-case scenario will be one in which the IMF encourages a country's private creditors to supplement its resources, as it did in South Korea.[2] The IMF can facilitate this by pressing for the creation of standing committees of creditors, so that governments have a counterpart with which to negotiate. But formidable collective action problems will remain, and it cannot be assumed that these efforts will always succeed.

For all these reasons, it will not be possible for the IMF, even working in concert with other lenders, to follow Bagehot's classic advice for a domestic central bank – that it lend freely against good collateral at a penalty rate. Lending freely will not be feasible, irrespective of the rate at which the IMF lends and the collateral it demands. Compared to a domestic central bank, its resources will be too limited, as will its leverage over the policies of the recipient.

Exchange Rate Policy

The Asian crisis raised obvious questions about the wisdom of the IMF's advice regarding the management of exchange rates. The view of the

Wall Street Journal, that only pegged exchange rates are compatible with monetary and financial stability, is vulnerable to the criticism that pegged rates are strongly associated with crises. Pegged rates create one-way bets for speculators, making sitting ducks of central banks and governments. At the same time, the prevailing academic view that high capital mobility should and will lead most countries to float their currencies must confront the fact that floating was a disaster in Asia, where currencies, rather than adjusting smoothly, collapsed abruptly, bankrupting financial and non-financial firms with foreign currency denominated debts.

Why did the Asian devaluations have such devastatingly negative effects? If there is one explanation for this disaster, it is that governments failed to prepare the markets for the change in the exchange rate. The currency peg having been the centrepiece of their economic policy strategy, jettisoning it was a heavy blow to their policy credibility. Giving in to market pressures raised doubts about their competence and commitment to stated policy goals. Their stated commitment to the currency peg lulled banks and firms into the mistaken belief that there was no need for costly insurance against exchange rate fluctuations. Debtors saw no need to use forward and futures markets to hedge against exchange rate fluctuations. Hence, when the inevitable adjustment came, it was devastating not only to confidence but to the solvency of banks and corporations with unhedged foreign exposures. Investors, having been lulled into complacency by official assurances that the exchange rate was fixed, scrambled for the exits once they realised that those promises were empty. Banks and corporations with unhedged foreign liabilities scrambled for cover, purchasing the additional foreign exchange needed to service their debts and hedge against further currency fluctuations. Both responses pushed the exchange rate down still further, which pushed additional banks and firms into bankruptcy. This fed investor fears, further weakening the exchange rate and thereby aggravating the difficulty of servicing private sector debts.

It is disingenuous to recommend that countries operating exchange rate pegs avoid these landmines by warning the markets that the pegged rate can be changed, thereby encouraging banks and corporates to hedge their exposures. Any government operating a peg which sends the message that it is prepared to change the rate invites a speculative attack. The first priority of any government seeking to peg the currency is to convince the markets that it is committed to maintaining that peg. To protect its reserves, it will be forced to deny that it is contemplating a change in the exchange rate or a change in the regime. Inevitably, its statements will discourage banks and corporations with foreign currency denominated liabilities from undertaking transactions in currency forward and futures markets to hedge that foreign exposure. Consequently, when a change in the exchange rate comes, its effects will be devastating.

It follows that in a world of high capital mobility there are only two feasible approaches to exchange rate policy: currency boards (and dollarisation), and more flexible rates.

The Currency Board Option

The first option is not just to peg the exchange rate but to lock it in – the Argentine strategy. In this case it matters not a whit whether banks and firms hedge against exchange rate fluctuations because there is no prospect that the exchange rate will change.

Credibly locking in the exchange rate is easier said than done, as doing so involves abolishing the central bank and its discretionary powers and making that change irreversible. Currency boards have a long and distinguished lineage. One sourcebook lists more than a hundred instances in which this monetary arrangement has been applied (Hanke, Jonung & Schuler 1993). To some, this makes currency boards the natural solution to the exchange-rate problem for countries whose financial markets are too shallow and whose policy-making institutions are too fragile for them to cohabit comfortably with exchange rate volatility.

In fact, currency boards are economically feasible only as part of a broader set of policy reforms, and they are politically viable only for countries prepared to deploy that entire panoply of policies. Most obviously, adopting a currency board means that the country must conform to the monetary and financial conditions prevailing in the rest of the world. Rising international capital mobility sharpens the implications. Once upon a time, transaction costs provided countries maintaining fixed exchange rates and open capital accounts with limited insulation from financial conditions abroad, but this is no longer the case.[3] In today's world of high capital mobility, the scope for discretionary monetary policy by such countries is nil.

Second, countries which adopt currency boards effectively eliminate all scope for the domestic authorities to act as lender of last resort to the domestic financial system. This makes it essential to develop alternative arrangements for backstopping the banks. Typically, this means internationalising the banking system. Internationalising the banking system diversifies the banks' asset base and is a way of importing state-of-the-art asset and liability management techniques. Perhaps most importantly, it provides domestic banks with a proprietary lender of last resort in the form of the foreign head office, which is essential for financial stability when the hands of the government and central bank are tied. It is no coincidence that the vast majority of currency board countries have been actual or former colonial dependencies of the major financial powers, where foreign bank presence is considerable.

Foreign bank presence is similarly prominent in all today's successful currency board countries. The Argentine banking system is half foreign-owned. Estonia's banking system is roughly 70 per cent foreign-owned. Bulgaria seems prepared to move in the same direction as the privatisation of its banking system proceeds. Given the fragility of small, localised, poorly regulated banking systems, selling domestic financial institutions to foreign buyers is essential if a currency board arrangement is to work.

However, selling domestic financial institutions is politically sensitive. Governments accustomed to using banks as instruments of development policy are loath to hand over the reins to foreign owners. Industrialists accustomed to receiving preferential credits will be similarly resistant. There may be sound arguments for moving away from these arrangements in favour of a more market-driven approach to the allocation of financial resources, but the political reality is that many governments and societies are reluctant to cede control of domestic financial markets to foreign banks.

In addition, having forsworn the exchange rate as an instrument of adjustment, a currency board country must implement alternative mechanisms for adjusting to macroeconomic disturbances, notably flexible labour market arrangements. This is relatively straightforward for Hong Kong, given the porousness of its border with mainland China, and for Estonia, given the absence of Western European-style labour market institutions in the aftermath of its transition from central planning. But in Argentina, which is hardly a paragon of labour market flexibility, maintaining its currency board peg in the face of the Tequila Crisis and the Asian Flu has meant persistent high unemployment, sometimes exceeding 20 per cent.

That is a level of pain that few countries are prepared to endure. By implication, countries should start down the currency board path only when there is broad and deep support for putting monetary policy on autopilot, and there is low probability that a majority of the disaffected unemployed and other special interests can be marshalled to reverse the policy. Otherwise, when times are tough, currency speculators will anticipate mounting public opposition to monetary austerity, perhaps leading to abandonment of the currency board and the exchange rate peg and giving rise to the generic pegged-rate problem of self-fulfilling speculative attacks.

Thus, only countries in which investors harbour exceptional distrust of discretionary monetary policy, where the domestic economy is sufficiently flexible to adapt to whatever monetary and financial conditions are implied by a fixed exchange rate, and where there is deep-seated public support for the policy however painful its consequences, can sustain the currency board alternative. Argentina can, given the deep distrust of discretionary policy inherited from the country's repeated bouts with hyperinflation, which provides broad public backing for its 'convertibility law'. Hong Kong can, given investor fears that a managed Hong Kong dollar would actually be managed from Beijing, and given the Hong Kong Monetary Authority's insulation from political pressures (because Hong Kong is neither a sovereign country nor a true democracy). But in few other places is support for putting monetary policy on autopilot realistically as deep and broad.

In particular, that level of support was not obviously present in Indonesia in 1998, when some advisers recommended the adoption of a currency board. There was fear of inflation and distrust of the monetary authorities, but few of the other preconditions were in place. For one thing, the banking system was weak, and if investors tested the authorities' commitment to the peg the government might not be able to sustain the higher interest rates needed to defend it at the price of further bank failures and financial distress. There was also the question of whether the public would support these official efforts, especially if exchange-rate stabilisation were seen as a temporary expedient to support the rate only until the ruling elite removed their assets from the country. Indonesia's flexible exchange rate was a disaster, but even with the benefit of hindsight there is reason to doubt that a currency board was a viable alternative.

More Flexible Exchange Rates

Given the demanding preconditions for establishing currency boards, the vast majority of countries will have no choice but to follow the other route of allowing the exchange rate to fluctuate. For them, the advantages of greater exchange rate flexibility can be considerable. In particular, if the rate is allowed to move regularly, banks and firms will have an incentive to hedge their foreign exposures and will acquire insurance against the negative financial effects of unexpected large currency fluctuations.

This does not mean that countries that reject the currency board option will have to allow their exchange rates to float freely; they can still intervene to damp temporary fluctuations and limit the volatility a freely floating exchange rate entails. What they should not do is commit to an explicit exchange rate target that would force them to issue misleadingly reassuring statements likely to lull banks and firms into a false sense of complacency and set the stage for an ugly crisis. Floating, even dirty floating, is uncomfortable because of the volatility that it tends to entail; witness the case of Mexico, whose currency declined against the US dollar by more than 20 per cent in the final quarter of 1998. But the Mexican depreciation did not precipitate a crisis. Surely most countries, given a choice between Mexico's situation and the desperate straits of the Brazilian authorities seeking to defend their currency peg at the end of 1998, would prefer the former.

Some otherwise strong proponents of greater flexibility, both in and outside the IMF, concede a temporary role for pegged rates in countries that are trying to bring down high inflation (Fischer 1997; Sachs 1998a). A stabilisation plan that involves pegging the exchange rate can decrease high inflation at a lower cost in terms of output and employment forgone (see Bruno & Fischer 1990). But the problem is the same as with using heroin or morphine to treat a patient in agonising pain – after the source of the suffering subsides, the patient will be hooked. Open markets offer no padded cell into which to place a patient 'hooked' on pegged rates. However attractive it is as an expedient, it is better to avoid this addictive medicine in the first place.

Implications for IMF Exchange Rate Advice

This means that the IMF should push more of its members to adopt policies of greater exchange rate flexibility before they are forced to do so in a crisis. In the context of Article IV consultations and program negotiations, it should pressure them to abandon simple pegs, crawling pegs, narrow bands and other mechanisms for limiting exchange rate flexibility before they are forced to do so by the markets. Even if this evolution is inevitable it will be associated with financial distress, as in Asia, if it is forced on reluctant governments that fail to prepare banks, firms and households for it. On the other hand, if the authorities move gradually toward greater exchange rate flexibility while capital is still flowing in, banks and firms will hedge their exposures and not suffer catastrophic losses if the exchange rate moves by an unexpectedly large amount. If the government does not link its entire economic policy strategy to the maintenance of a fixed currency peg but develops a more diversified portfolio of intermediate targets and anchors, it will not lose all credibility when it bows to the inevitable.

Not only should the IMF push more of its members to adopt more flexible exchange rates, it should press them to harmonise prudential regulation with exchange rate policy. Countries seeking to limit exchange rate flexibility must subject their financial systems to exceptionally strict prudential standards. Central banks and governments operating a currency peg have little capacity to conduct lender of last resort operations, as already noted, while internationalisation of the banking system is a gradual process. Hence, such countries need to limit the need for last resort lending by holding their banks to higher prudential standards. This means imposing higher reserve, capital and liquidity requirements despite the negative implications of those measures for the competitiveness of the banking system. Argentina illustrates the point. Following the Tequila shock, it adopted a 15 per cent across-the-board liquidity requirement for all deposits of less than ninety days. It adopted risk-adjusted capital asset requirements nearly half again as high as the Basle standards. It announced a program of limited, privately financed deposit insurance to reduce the risk of bank runs due to a contagious loss of depositor confidence. Although both self-financed deposit insurance and exceptional liquidity and capital requirements reduce the international competitiveness of the banking system, the price had to be paid by a country whose entire economic policy strategy was organised around a rigid currency board peg.

Argentina's experience is not alone in suggesting that the Basle capital standards may not be an adequate basis for managing banking risk in emerging markets. The relevant distinction, however, is not just between mature and emerging markets but also between countries operating more and less flexible exchange rate regimes.

Monetary and Fiscal Policies

The IMF came under fire for asking Thailand, Indonesia and South Korea to raise interest rates and tighten fiscal policies following the onset of their crises. It was accused of blindly taking a page from its Latin American debt crisis cookbook, where the setting was one of budget deficits and inflation, making monetary and fiscal retrenchment necessary parts of the solution. It was said to have neglected the fact that Asian countries entered their crises with high savings, low inflation and government budgets in balance or surplus, hardly suggesting that excessively expansionary policies were at the root of the problem and that monetary and fiscal austerity were needed for its solution. In fact, the critics argue, the IMF should have encouraged Asian governments to employ all their available macroeconomic policy instruments to prevent the onset of recession or to minimise its severity.

Fiscal Policy

There is no question that absorption had to be reduced once capital stopped flowing in and it became necessary to eliminate the current account deficit. It being undesirable for the entire burden of adjustment to fall on the private sector, there was a presumption in favour of fiscal cuts. In addition, there was a need to recapitalise the banking system. Bonds might be issued to spread those costs over time, but additional tax revenues would still be needed to service the additional obligations. Business-cycle considerations notwithstanding, these concerns pointed to the need for tighter fiscal policy.

The problem was with the qualifier in the last sentence – 'business-cycle considerations notwithstanding'. As capital stopped flowing in and started flowing out, the Asian economies were plunged into acute recessions. There may have been an argument for balancing the budget over the cycle, but not in a recession. The IMF's failure to anticipate the severity of the recession and the fiscal conditions it applied made that downturn significantly worse. The IMF erred, in other words, by interfering with the operation of countries' fiscal stabilisers.

Eventually this realisation dawned, and the IMF modified its advice. Adjustments to its programs acknowledged the need for governments to use fiscal policy to provide countercyclical stimulus to neutralise the deepening recession and to provide a social safety net for the poor. In Indonesia, for example, the program of January 1998 revised the target for fiscal policy from a 1 per cent of GDP surplus to a 1 per cent of GDP deficit; the second revision widened it to 3 per cent of GDP and the third to 8.5 per cent. The 4 March 1998 revision of the Thai program excluded the 3 per cent of GDP interest costs of the financial sector cleanup. Successive revisions of the Korean program adjusted the deficit target from essentially 0 to 2 per cent of GDP. There is reason to hope, in other words, that the IMF has learned the appropriate lessons regarding fiscal policy.

In its package for Brazil at the end of 1998 the IMF again insisted on fiscal cuts, despite forecasting that the country would succumb to recession in 1999. Does this mean that the IMF has still failed to learn the fiscal lessons of the Asian crisis? In fact, the Brazilian and Asian situations are different. Brazil entered its crisis with large budget deficits (about 7 per cent of GDP), in contrast to Asian governments, whose budgets were broadly balanced. Brazil's history of fiscal excesses was very much on the mind of investors, in contrast to the admirable fiscal reputation of most Asian countries. Thus, it can be plausibly argued that fiscal cuts were needed in Brazil to restore investor confidence. Indeed, there was a possibility that reductions in public spending (and, to a lesser extent, increases in taxes) would in fact stimulate consumption and investment by heading off the otherwise inevitable fiscal crisis.[4] The situation in Asia was different, since there was no reason to anticipate a looming fiscal crisis. The lesson for the IMF, then, is not to ignore fiscal policy but to avoid giving one-size-fits-all advice.

Monetary Policy

In each country, the IMF recommended sharp increases in interest rates to restore investor confidence, stem capital flight and stabilise the currency. This, it argued, was the only way for authorities to quickly reassure investors, given the time needed to implement other reforms. Only if authorities signalled their resolve to defend the exchange rate by rendering short-term money market instruments more attractive could confidence be restored.

That the medicine did not work is clear; why it didn't work is less so. The IMF's rationalisation is that governments did not raise interest rates and hold them there with adequate resolve. Indonesia raised rates to 30–40 per cent in August but reduced them to 20–30 per cent in September despite the rupiah's continued decline. Korea maintained an official ceiling on interest rates as late as December 1997 despite the continued deterioration of the foreign exchange market. These half-hearted measures, it is argued, were insufficient to restore confidence.

The IMF's critics argue that interest rates were not too low but too high. High rates plunged Asia's highly geared firms into bankruptcy. As failures cascaded through the manufacturing sector and banks were rendered insolvent by the inability of customers to service their loans, the exchange rate weakened, reflecting further damage to the financial system. Flight capital, rather than being attracted back by higher yields, was repelled by additional defaults. Thus, higher interest rates weakened the exchange rate rather than strengthening it as the IMF had forecast.

The effect of interest rates on the exchange rate is an empirical question, but not one of which there has been much systematic analysis. Kraay (1998) analyses 313 speculative attacks (defined as instances when the nominal exchange rate depreciated by 10 per cent and/or reserve losses exceeded 20 per cent in a month; a successful attack is one in which the first of these two conditions obtained). He fails to find any correlation with the stance of monetary policy around the time of the attack (measured by the level of the discount rate relative to the US or by the rate of growth of domestic credit), but his analysis has limitations. For one thing, devaluations and attacks are not the same, and Kraay fails to distinguish between them. He also fails to look for the interest rate/exchange rate 'Laffer curve' suggested by theory. While modest interest rate increases are likely to strengthen the currency, if taken to excess they may so damage the financial condition of banks and firms that confidence deteriorates and the currency weakens. A convincing analysis would look for these non-linear effects of interest rate increases and allow the turning point to be lower in Asia than in less debt-dependent parts of the world.

Furman and Stiglitz (1998) conduct a similar analysis, without constructing a control group. They consider thirteen episodes where high interest rates were used to defend a currency under attack. Combining various measures of interest rates with the initial inflation rate (they could as easily combine them with a dummy variable for Latin America), they find some evidence that the interest rate defence limits the extent of the currency crash for high-inflation countries (where the signalling effect of higher interest rates is likely to matter most) but not for low-inflation countries. This is a step in the right direction, in that it allows the effectiveness of the interest rate defence to vary with initial conditions, but the critical condition (the debt or gearing ratio at the time of the attack) is not considered. In any case, it is hard to know what to make of regressions run on only thirteen observations.

Many critics of IMF policy, while insisting on the need for lower interest rates for domestic reasons, acknowledge that these would not have lured back flight capital and strengthened the exchange rate. On the contrary. Although the right choice may have been to reduce interest rates to relieve the distress among heavily indebted firms and to reflate the economy, there would have been a price, namely the need to restructure the external debt and impose Malaysian-style exchange controls. Lower interest rates might have been the right remedy for Korea, for example, but they would have rendered the country unable to roll over its maturing debts. Wade and Veneroso are explicit about this trade-off. 'Why should not Korea, for one, not just declare a debt moratorium and set about exporting its way out of trouble?' and 'The vast increase in the servicing and repayment costs of foreign loans due to the devaluation is a national disaster, the costs of which should be borne collectively. Let belts be tightened, to the extent of refusing any new reliance on external finance' (Wade & Veneroso 1998a: 17).

This is the unfortunate reality: there was a choice between reducing interest rates and maintaining capital market access, and governments could not have it both ways. Lower rates might have facilitated much-needed domestic reflation, but would have required countries to suspend service on their external debts. And that last step was something that governments, in their wisdom, were reluctant to take. They believed that debts, once suspended, are difficult to restructure and that, in the interim, access to working capital and trade credits can be severely disrupted. Thus, calls for the IMF to amend its advice to encourage lower interest rates in crisis economies will remain impractical without other changes in capital markets to make the process of restructuring and renegotiation more efficient.

Measures to Encourage Debt Restructuring

If there will always be crises, there will always be the need to clean up after them. This is where the existing international financial architecture most obviously falls short. The international community has two ways of responding to crises: running to the rescue of the crisis country with a purseful of funds, or standing aside and letting nature run its course. Both have been tried and found wanting. For two years following the Mexican rescue and for a year following the outbreak of the Asian crisis, the IMF was subjected to a firestorm of criticism for bailing out governments and international investors. Its actions, in the view of critics, only reduced the incentives for meaningful policy reform and, by shielding the private sector from losses, encouraged more reckless lending and set the stage for further crises. Then, in the summer of 1998, Russia provided an alarming illustration of the alternative when it devalued and suspended debt service payments, with devastating impacts on the Russian economy and global financial markets. Confidence was destroyed, the country's access to international capital markets was curtailed and financial markets were roiled in Asia, Eastern Europe, Latin America and even Europe and the United States. This is not an experience anyone wishes to repeat. We cannot avoid concluding that both alternatives – bailouts, and standing back and letting events run their course – are unacceptable.

Avoiding both routine rescues and devastating defaults will require a more orderly way of restructuring problem debts. Radical reform – the creation of an international bankruptcy court – is unrealistic, yet something must be done to create an acceptable alternative to massive international rescue packages.

In fact, a number of modest steps might be taken to make debt restructuring a viable option. Majority voting and sharing clauses could be added to loan contracts. This would prevent isolated creditors from resorting to lawsuits and other means of obstructing settlements that improve the welfare of the debtor and the vast majority of creditors. Other desirable changes to loan contracts include collective representation clauses (making provision for an indenture trustee to represent and coordinate the creditors in the case of sovereign debts) and clauses providing that a minimum percentage of bondholders must agree that legal action be taken. The addition of such clauses to bond contracts is the only practical way of creating an environment conducive to flexible restructuring negotiations. It can be done by legislators and regulators in the United States and the United Kingdom, the principal markets in which the international bonds of emerging economies are issued and traded, without ceding any jurisdiction or authority to a super-national agency. This approach is infinitely more realistic than imagining the creation of some kind of super-national bankruptcy court for sovereign debts empowered to impose settlement terms.[5]

This is a task for national regulators, but IMF lending policy can also play a role. By lending at relatively favourable rates to governments that incorporate such provisions into loan contracts and require domestic banks and corporates to do so, the IMF can provide a financial incentive for contractual innovation. By lending after a country has suspended debt payments and before it has cleared its arrears, the IMF can encourage recalcitrant creditors to come to the bargaining table. In so far as the large number of creditors, and rules requiring the unanimous assent of creditors to the terms of any restructuring plan, create problems of collective action that hinder negotiations, lending into arrears can jump-start the process. Lending into arrears should only be done when a government is willing to make a serious adjustment effort and to engage in good-faith negotiations with its creditors.[6] But in so far as sovereign debtors and the international community generally see the temporary suspension of payments as too difficult and costly a route to pursue, the IMF needs to use its lending power to tip the balance, opening up restructuring negotiations as a viable alternative to regular IMF rescues designed to avert default.

International Standards as a Basis for IMF Conditionality

Once upon a time, long long ago in a place far far away, currency crises were caused by recklessly expansionary monetary and fiscal policies resulting in excess demand, overvalued exchange rates and unsustainable current account deficits. Preventing them meant restoring monetary and fiscal balance before the excesses got out of hand. For the IMF, crisis management meant providing temporary financial assistance so that macroeconomic retrenchment did not produce or aggravate recessions. It meant conditioning assistance on the restoration of monetary and fiscal discipline. It was not necessary for those whose objectives were the maintenance of exchange rate and macroeconomic stability to concern themselves with a country's financial nuts and bolts – bank supervision and regulation, auditing and accounting, bankruptcy procedures, and corporate governance. We can question whether things were ever so simple, but there is some truth to the notion that for its first half-century the IMF rightly focused on countries' monetary and fiscal policies and was only tangentially concerned with their domestic institutional arrangements.

In Asia (and in its other recent programs), the IMF has become more deeply enmeshed in countries' internal affairs. It has sought to encourage authorities to improve prudential supervision, root out corruption, eliminate subsidies, break up monopolies and strengthen competition policy. In virtually every program country this has incited a backlash against the IMF, which is resented for its intrusiveness. Feldstein and others have questioned whether such intimate involvement in the internal affairs of sovereign states is really required for the restoration of currency stability (see Feldstein 1998). What business is it of the IMF, Feldstein asks, to demand that Indonesia scale back its national car program or break up its clove monopoly? The IMF, in his view, should focus on the monetary and fiscal imbalances at the root of balance-of-payments problems. Not only does the IMF lack a secret formula for how every country should organise its internal affairs, but its advice is more likely to receive domestic backing and be politically sustainable if it does not infringe on the sovereignty of its members.

This view sits uneasily with the fact, widely acknowledged – not least by Feldstein – that monetary and fiscal profligacy was not endemic in Asia in the period leading up to its crisis. Since monetary and fiscal excesses were not at the root of the crisis, how can it make sense to recommend focusing on monetary and fiscal variables when devising a response? The problem and the solution must lie elsewhere.

A hint to the location follows from the observation that high international capital mobility has all but erased the line between domestic and international financial systems. This makes it impossible to 'fix' the international balance of payments without also 'fixing' the domestic financial system. As long as the domestic and international financial systems were strongly segmented by capital controls, balance of payments deficits arose from current account deficits that were financed with international reserves. Restoring balance of payments equilibrium meant restoring balance to the current account, which implied the need to restrict monetary and fiscal policies. But now that capital is so internationally mobile, stabilising the balance of payments means stabilising the capital account, which involves restoring investor confidence. And restoring investor confidence means restoring confidence in the stability of the domestic financial system.

Inevitably, this draws those seeking to prevent and limit the severity of crises into involvement in the supervision and regulation of banks and corporates issuing publicly traded securities. It directs attention to auditing and accounting, the disclosure of financial information and corporate governance. Recent models cite banking system weaknesses, the opacity of balance sheets and moral hazard from government guarantees as the causes of currency and financial crises.[7] Guarantees encourage excessive foreign short-term funding of the banking system, while directed lending leads banks to invest in low-return projects that ultimately damage their balance sheets. The fragility of the financial system then prevents the authorities from mounting a concerted defence of the currency. Inadequate auditing and accounting prevent investors from distinguishing good banks from bad and set the stage for economy-wide banking crises, while poorly designed or enforced insolvency procedures precipitate creditor grab races and cascading debt defaults. The implication is that macroeconomic policy adjustments are insufficient to restore economic and financial stability; rather, far-reaching institutional reforms are needed to root out the causes of financial crises.

The problem is that neither the IMF nor other international financial institutions have sufficient staff and expertise to proffer advice in all these areas. The IMF cannot realistically master the regulatory particulars of banking systems in all 182 member countries. The problem grows more severe when we turn from bank regulation to auditing and accounting, insolvency codes and corporate governance, issues in which macroeconomists have little formal training or experience. Yet problems in these areas are too pressing to do nothing. If the Asian crisis has taught us one thing, it is that countries cannot restore exchange rate and balance of payments stability without rectifying deficiencies in their domestic financial systems.

The only feasible approach to this problem is for national governments and international financial institutions to encourage the public and private sectors to identify and adopt international standards for minimally acceptable practice. National practices may differ, but all national arrangements must meet minimal standards if greater financial stability is to be attained. All countries must have adequate bank supervision and regulation. All must require financial market participants to use adequate accounting and auditing practices. All must have transparent and efficient insolvency codes. The particulars of these arrangements can differ – countries can reach these goals by different routes – but any country active in international financial markets must meet internationally accepted standards.

An advantage of this approach, in addition to its ability to accommodate variations in national traditions and economic cultures, is that the burden of setting the standards need not fall primarily on the IMF, multilateral institutions in general or even national governments. In most cases, the relevant standards can be identified or defined by private sector bodies. Although those entities can be aided by officials, the role for international institutions should be limited mainly to recognising the standards, urging adoption by their members, monitoring compliance and – in the case of the IMF – conditioning assistance on a commitment to meeting them.

Fortunately, the relevant private sector bodies already exist. In accounting there is the International Accounting Standards Committee, comprising representatives of the accounting profession from 103 countries at last count, which promulgates international accounting standards. There is the International Federation of Accountants, with parallel membership, which has gone some way toward formulating international auditing standards. The International Organisation of Supreme Audit Institutions similarly issues auditing guidelines and standards. Committee J of the International Bar Association is developing a model insolvency code to guide countries seeking to reform and update their bankruptcy laws. For corporate governance there is the International Corporate Governance Network, which seeks to improve standards of business management and accountability worldwide.

In other areas, responsibility for setting standards has been taken by international committees of regulators. For securities market regulation there is the International Organisation of Securities Commissions (IOSCO), which serves as a forum for securities regulators and has established working groups to set standards and coordinate regulatory initiatives. For bank regulation there is the Basle Committee on Banking Supervision, composed of supervisors from the leading industrial countries, whose Core Principles for Effective Banking Supervision codify Goldstein's argument for an international banking standard (Goldstein 1996a). But even in these areas where regulators have taken the lead, there is a role for the private sector; for example, for the world's largest financial institutions to develop standards for monitoring and managing financial risks, and for the Basle Committee to utilise them when setting international standards for risk management practices (Group of 30 1997).

Multilateral institutions are already active in a number of areas, helping to identify standards or coordinating the process through which others agree to them. The Organisation for Economic Cooperation and Development issued a report in 1998 on global principles of corporate governance, focusing on the accountability of management, disclosure and transparency, and communication with shareholders (OECD 1998). The UN Commission on International Trade Law has adopted a model law on the treatment of cross-border insolvencies. The IMF itself has established a special data dissemination standard for the provision of economic and financial information by countries seeking to access

international capital markets. It has promulgated a code of fiscal transparency as a standard of good fiscal practice for member countries
and anticipates developing an accompanying code for monetary and
financial practices. In all these cases the multilaterals have solicited
guidance and advice from national officials and private sector experts.

The role of the IMF and other multilaterals would be wider than
encouraging the activities of self-organising groups. They should actively
consult with those groups (as the IMF already does with IOSCO and the
Basle Committee), seek status as an *ex officio* member, and certify the
standards they identify as measures of best practice. Active involvement
in the standard-setting process is necessary for the IMF to assume 'ownership' of the standards it helps to set. To give teeth to its advice, the
IMF should condition the disbursal of assistance on program countries
meeting those standards. It will need to encourage countries to apprise
the markets of their compliance, which the IMF would monitor in
conjunction with its Article IV surveillance. Finally, the IMF should
publicise its assessment of compliance as a way of strengthening market
discipline.

A more active role for the IMF and other international financial institutions in the promulgation of standards would be a departure from
past practice, but there is no alternative if one acknowledges that the
Bretton Woods institutions do not possess the resources to develop
standards in all these areas. The process will be complicated, but the
alternative – inaction – is no longer viable. It being necessary to pro-
ceed, there is no alternative to proceeding via public–private sector
collaboration.

The IMF and the Capital Account

During its 45-year history, the IMF has repeatedly refined its role. Origi-
nally conceived as the steward of a system of pegged but adjustable
exchange rates, the IMF transformed itself in the 1970s into the coordi-
nator of petrodollar recycling and in the 1980s into adviser and lender
to Latin American countries attempting to crawl out from an overhang
of non-performing syndicated bank debts. But with the advent of the
Brady Plan and the resumption of lending to emerging markets in 1989,
and the shift by a growing number of its members to greater exchange
rate flexibility, the need for those functions was cast into doubt. Capital
flooded into emerging markets in unprecedented quantities, relieving
countries of the need to apply to the IMF for help with financing budget
deficits and external accounts. The rationale for IMF assistance was
thus doubtful. With international capital markets anxious to lend to

developing countries, and developing countries able and willing to borrow, what role remained for official finance?

In the mid 1990s, the IMF therefore sought to reposition itself as the advocate of international financial liberalisation. In 1996, the Interim Committee requested that the IMF analyse the costs and benefits of capital flows and consider changes to the Articles of Agreement that would give it jurisdiction over members' policies toward the capital account. The following April the Interim Committee concluded that there would be benefits from amending the Articles to enable the IMF to encourage and promote the orderly liberalisation of capital movements, a view that it reiterated at the September 1997 World Bank/IMF annual meeting in Hong Kong, where it stated that capital account liberalisation should be made one of the 'purposes' of the IMF (Camdessus 1998a: 1).

The Asian crisis unleashed a barrage of criticism of IMF-led efforts to encourage capital account liberalisation. The analogy with current account liberalisation, many critics insisted, is fundamentally flawed: while the positive effects of free trade for economic growth have been extensively documented, the evidence of comparable benefits of capital account liberalisation is limited (see Bhagwati 1998a; Fischer et al. 1998). These points are controversial, but what is indisputable is that capital account liberalisation is a two-edged sword. On the one hand, there are clear benefits from being able to borrow and lend internationally. Capital mobility creates valuable opportunities for portfolio diversification, risk sharing and intertemporal trade. By holding claims on foreign countries, households and firms can protect themselves against the effects of disturbances that affect only the home country. Entrepreneurs can pursue high-return domestic investment projects even when domestic finance is lacking. Capital mobility can therefore enable investors to achieve higher rates of return, and higher rates of return can encourage savings and investment, ultimately supporting faster rates of growth (for a theoretical exposition see Obstfeld 1994).

On the other hand, international financial liberalisation heightens the risk of costly financial crises. It allows problem banks gambling for redemption and intermediaries enjoying government guarantees to lever up their bets. And the crisis, when it comes, tends to be correspondingly more devastating and expensive. Whether it is the costs or benefits of capital account liberalisation that dominate thus depends on how the process is managed – that is, on whether the benefits of portfolio diversification, risk sharing and intertemporal trade are dominated by the costs of debilitating crises.

Acknowledging this trade-off leads to the conclusion that an appropriate role for the IMF is not as advocate of capital account liberalisation but as adviser on prudent regulation of the capital account and

guardian against avoidable financial crises. Regulation of the capital
account is best understood through analogy with regulation of the
domestic financial system. In the domestic context it is understood that
banks are fragile. This recognition prompts governments to impose
prudential regulations on financial intermediaries' transactions and
positions in assets whose liquidity and risk characteristics have implications for systemic stability. Such regulations are especially strict where
the techniques of risk management are least developed, where auditing
and accounting practices leave most to be desired and where financial
disclosure is least adequate, weakening market discipline. The existence
of systemic risk has also led governments to provide deposit insurance
and lender of last resort services. Stronger prudential regulations are
then considered necessary to mitigate the tendency for financial market
participants to take additional risks in response to the existence of a
safety net.

These grounds justify the regulation of international financial
transactions even more strongly than they justify the regulation of
domestic transactions. Information asymmetries are more pervasive in
international financial markets. The difficulties of raising liquidity in
emergencies is greater, as is the scope for contagion. And in so far as the
liabilities of banks and other borrowers are denominated in foreign currency, the domestic central bank (not being able to print foreign
currency) has limited ability to undertake lender of last resort
operations.

This does not mean that international financial transactions should
be prohibited, but that their cost should be influenced by regulation to
take into account their implications for systemic risk. Banks could be
required to purchase cover in currency forward or futures markets for
their open foreign positions, better aligning the private and social costs
of foreign funding. They could be required to close their open positions
by matching the currency composition of their assets and liabilities –
when borrowing in foreign currency, making only foreign currency
denominated loans. Capital requirements, one important determinant
of that cost, could be adjusted to take into account not only the implications for systemic risk of banks' investments but also the special risks of
foreign funding. If bank capital in emerging markets is too rarely written
down, differential reserve requirements might be used to require banks
borrowing abroad to put up additional (perhaps non-interest-bearing)
reserves with the central bank *ex ante*. The problem could be addressed
from the lending side by requiring lending banks in advanced industrial
countries to attach higher risk weights to short-term claims on banks in
emerging markets, since the additional cost would be passed to the
borrowing banks.

Finally, to the extent that measures designed to raise the cost of bank borrowing abroad encourage non-banks to do the borrowing and onlend the proceeds to banks and other borrowers, leaving the risks to the financial system essentially unchanged, this provides an argument for taxes or non-remunerated deposit requirements on all capital inflows, not just on inflows into the banking system. These are the kind of policy recommendations to which the IMF has and should continue to gravitate.

Importantly, there is no contradiction between recommending the use of taxes and tax-like instruments to manage international capital flows and the need for capital account convertibility. Convertibility means shunning prohibitions and quantitive restrictions that prevent market participants from undertaking certain transactions at any price, but is compatible with taxes designed to better align private and social costs. A blanket prohibition on foreign borrowing is more distortionary than a tax, which still permits those with especially attractive investment projects to finance them externally as long as they are willing to pay a tax intended to make them internalise the implications of their decisions for the country as a whole.

This is the distinction the IMF has always drawn regarding the current account. Current account convertibility is a goal of IMF policy under the Articles of Agreement. But while current account convertibility is defined in Article VIII as freedom from restrictions on payments and transfers for current international transactions, that Article does not proscribe the application of import tariffs and taxes to the underlying transactions. Correspondingly, capital account convertibility, while implying the removal of controls and prohibitions, does not mean abjuring taxes and tax-like levies on the underlying transactions.

Amending the Articles of Agreement to give the IMF jurisdiction over the capital account would allow it to encourage members to implement this important distinction. It would put the IMF in a better position to guide members on the optimal speed and sequencing of capital account liberalisation. It could lend legitimacy to taxes and tax-like instruments designed to limit the level and shape the term structure of foreign debts. And it would give the IMF leverage to encourage countries utilising taxes on inflows to accelerate financial sector reforms.

Against this must be weighed the danger that an IMF with expanded powers might push its members to liberalise prematurely. The worry is that the IMF would oppose any and all tax and tax-like policies toward capital flows, or it might require countries seeking to adopt Chilean-style holding-period taxes to first obtain the authorisation of the Executive Board. It might authorise countries to restrict capital account transactions on prudential grounds only after it was convinced that other, more

capital account friendly, measures were not available.[8] If the amendment to the Articles of Agreement giving the IMF jurisdiction over
capital account policies regarded taxes and controls on inflows as
permissible only when adopted temporarily or for a transitional period,
IMF staff might become knee-jerk opponents to the indefinite use of
such measures for prudential reasons. The IMF might engage in legal
hairsplitting: even if countries were permitted to limit capital flows as a
form of prudential regulation, staff might argue that a measure had
actually been adopted for other reasons (for example, that a differential
reserve requirement was in fact being used to enhance monetary
control) and was therefore not acceptable. As Polak has put it, an IMF
with jurisdiction over capital account restrictions might become 'the
enforcer of the new code, making sure at every step that any policy it
recommends or endorses can pass the test of the new Article' (Polak
1998: 8).

Experience with Article VIII, which obliges members to establish the
convertibility of their currencies for purposes of current account transactions, provides some reassurance; it does not suggest that the IMF will
inevitably become the rigid enforcer of specific obligations. In enforcing
Article VIII, the IMF has recognised the validity of a wide range of miti-
gating circumstances. Still, to reassure sceptics, the IMF must articulate
its strategy for capital account liberalisation, explaining its approach to
the problem of sequencing and its policy on the taxation of capital
inflows. It needs to clarify that amending its Articles of Agreement
would not mean eliminating Article VI, Section 3, which gives members
the right to apply capital controls.

Conclusion

The Asian crisis is not welcome by any stretch of the imagination, but it
does provide an opportunity to reassess the role of the IMF. My review of
the controversy surrounding the IMF's response to the crisis has sought
to shift the focus from advice and conditions regarding monetary, fiscal
and exchange rate policies toward more fundamental issues. There are
already signs that the IMF has learned some of the relevant macroeconomic lessons, namely, the need to encourage more of its members to
embrace policies of greater exchange rate flexibility, the inappropriate-
ness of insisting on fiscal austerity where fiscal profligacy is not the
problem, and the fact that using high interest rates to defend the
exchange rate against attack can be costly for countries with high levels
of corporate debt. We can argue that the IMF must go still further in
these directions, but clearly the light has dawned.

However, more fundamental issues remain to be addressed. For the IMF, this means encouraging changes in the international financial architecture to facilitate debt restructuring so that there will be a viable alternative to the use of high interest rates to prevent liquid assets fleeing a crisis economy. It means encouraging the promulgation of international standards for acceptable financial practice as an alternative to invasive conditionality. It means repositioning the IMF as adviser on prudent regulation of the capital account and guardian against avoidable financial crises, not as rigid advocate of capital account liberalisation. This is a road which the international community has barely begun to travel.

CHAPTER 9

Taming the Phoenix? Monetary Governance after the Crisis

Benjamin J. Cohen[1]

> Ideas, knowledge, art, hospitality, travel – these are the
> things which should of their nature be international. But let
> goods be homespun whenever it is reasonably and
> conveniently possible; and, above all, let finance be primarily
> national.
>
> *– John Maynard Keynes*

Few observers doubt that the financial crisis that struck Asia in 1997–98
was a watershed event for the global monetary system. For years the tide
had been running one way – toward ever closer integration of national
financial and currency markets. Politically, governments were increasingly thrown on the defensive by the rapid growth of international
capital mobility. As I wrote a few years ago: 'Like a phoenix risen from
the ashes, global finance [has taken] flight and soared to new heights of
power and influence in the affairs of nations' (Cohen 1996: 268). The
only question, it seemed, was how much the traditional monetary
authority of sovereign states had, as a result, been compromised. 'The
phoenix has risen. Does it also rule the roost?' (Cohen 1996: 270).

Then came the fall of the Thai baht and all the contagion – the 'bah-
tulism' – that followed. For many, these events served to affirm the new
power of markets to constrain policy. The phoenix did indeed rule the
roost. Governments had no choice but to live with new limits on their
authority. But for others, choice was precisely the issue. The crisis
appeared to pose an opportunity to think again about the priority popu-
larly attached to financial liberalisation. Why should governments
meekly submit to the dictates of market forces? Perhaps the time had
come to cage the wilder impulses of the phoenix – to tame it, if not slay

192

it, by imposing limitations of some kind on the cross-border mobility of capital.

At issue is the governance of monetary relations in the global economy. The purpose of this chapter is to explore prospects for world monetary governance after the crisis, with particular emphasis on the management of international competition among national currencies. The chapter begins with a brief look at the gradual transformation of the global financial environment in the decades prior to the recent crisis, an epoch during which governments found it increasingly difficult to manage monetary affairs within their sovereign territories. As long as the tide was running toward greater mobility of capital, states assumed they had little choice but to learn to live with the consequences. Focusing on the countries of East Asia, the chapter then considers how policy calculations are being recalibrated as a result of the worst financial calamity since the Great Depression, bringing new respectability to the old case for capital controls. Once scorned as a relic of the past, limits on capital mobility suddenly looked as if they might become the wave of the future. The question, increasingly, was no longer whether capital mobility might be limited but rather when, how and under what rules controls might be implemented by sovereign national governments.[2]

The debate, however, is just beginning. The remainder of the chapter will probe the case for capital controls in more detail, in the hope of providing a useful roadmap of the main policy challenges involved. Three questions will be stressed: What kinds of capital movements, if any, should be subject to limitation? What kinds of controls might be most effective? What kinds of rules could be designed to avoid either economic inefficiencies or serious policy conflict? All three questions are essential to the effective governance of monetary relations. How they are answered will go far to determining the shape of the global financial system well into the twenty-first century.

The New Geography of Money[3]

That the global financial environment has been greatly transformed in recent decades is undeniable. The full significance of that change for monetary governance, however, has only lately begun to be widely appreciated. Prior to the recent crisis, policy-makers were just starting to learn how to cope with the rising challenge to their authority.

The postwar resurrection of global finance was truly phenomenal. Half a century ago, after the ravages of the Great Depression and World War II, financial markets everywhere – with the notable exception of the United States – were weak, insular and strictly controlled, reduced from their previously central role in international economic relations and offering little more than a negligible amount of trade financing. From the 1950s, however, deregulation and liberalisation began to combine with technological and institutional innovation to breach many of the barriers limiting cross-border activity. In a cumulative process driven by the pressures of domestic and international competition, the range of commercial opportunities gradually widened for lenders and borrowers alike. The result was a remarkable growth of capital mobility, reflected in a scale of financial flows unequalled since the glory days of the nineteenth-century gold standard.

Even more phenomenal were the implications of these changes for monetary governance and the long-standing convention of national monetary sovereignty. With the deepening integration of financial markets, strict dividing lines between separate national moneys became less and less distinct. No longer were economic actors restricted to a single currency – their own home money – as they went about their daily business. Cross-border circulation of currencies, which had been quite common prior to the emergence of the modern state system, dramatically re-emerged, with competition between national moneys gradually accelerating. This is what I have referred to elsewhere as the new geography of money – the new configuration of currency space (Cohen 1998a). The functional domain of each money no longer corresponded precisely with the formal jurisdiction of its issuing authority. Currencies became increasingly deterritorialised, their circulation determined not by law or politics but by the dynamics of supply and demand.

Currency deterritorialisation posed a new and critical challenge to governments, which had long relied upon the privileges derived from a formal monetary monopoly (in particular, the powers of seigniorage and macroeconomic control) to promote their concept of state interest. No longer able to exert the same degree of control over the use of their moneys by their citizens or others, governments felt driven to compete, inside and across borders, for the allegiance of market agents – in effect, to sustain or cultivate market share for their own brand of currency. Monopoly yielded to something more like oligopoly, and monetary governance was reduced to little more than a choice among marketing strategies designed to shape and manage demand.

Broadly speaking, four strategies were possible, depending on two key considerations: first, whether policy was defensive or offensive, aiming to preserve or promote market share; and second, whether policy was pursued unilaterally or collusively. The four strategies were:

- market leadership: an aggressive unilateralist policy intended to maximise use of the national currency, analogous to predatory price leadership in an oligopoly;

- market alliance: a collusive policy of sharing monetary sovereignty in a monetary or exchange rate union of some kind, analogous to a tacit or explicit cartel;
- market preservation: a status quo policy intended to defend, rather than augment, a previously acquired market position;
- market followership: an acquiescent policy of subordinating monetary sovereignty to a stronger foreign currency via some form of exchange rate rule, analogous to passive price followership in an oligopoly.

Strategies could involve tactics of persuasion or coercion. Persuasion involved investing in a money's reputation, acting to enhance confidence in the currency's continued usefulness and reliability – in effect, establishing or sustaining a successful brand name. Coercion could be exercised through a wide range of measures designed to regulate or prohibit diverse financial activities (in principle, up to and including the unfashionable option of capital controls). Though neither persuasion nor coercion was foolproof, each could be highly effective in influencing a currency's market position. In practice, most governments learned to use both in varying combinations, since they were not mutually exclusive.

Nothing demonstrated the challenge to monetary governance more than the financial crisis that hit East Asia in mid 1997. Governments that had taken pride in the competitiveness of their currencies suddenly found themselves unable to preserve user loyalty. Strategies that once seemed adequate to sustain market share had to be re-evaluated in the light of a worldwide 'flight to quality' by mobile capital. Inevitably, policy-makers were forced to take a new look at the option of capital controls.

Shock and Aftershock

As the first shockwaves of crisis swept over the region, the initial government impulse was to go on the defensive, investing expensively in determined efforts to reinforce confidence in their currencies – the 'confidence game', as Krugman ironically dubbed it (Krugman 1998b). The aim of the confidence game was market preservation, at almost any cost.[4] But as user preferences proved more resistant to tactics of persuasion than anticipated, a search for new approaches began. The question was whether anyone could think of an alternative.

Currency Boards

To a few, the answer seemed obvious: abandon any pretence of national monetary sovereignty and adopt a strategy of strict market followership in the form of a currency board, as existed in Brunei and Hong Kong. Long promoted by a small coterie of specialists inspired by the writings of US economist Steve Hanke (see, for example, Hanke & Schuler 1994; Cohen 1998a: 52–5), the currency board idea enjoyed a brief vogue in Indonesia in early 1998 prior to the forced resignation of President Suharto in May. In February 1998, on Hanke's advice, the government announced it was moving ahead with plans to establish a currency board system linked to the US dollar. Suharto referred to the project as an 'IMF-plus' program (quoted in *Economist*, 7 March 1998: 43).

However, the idea was abandoned under pressure from the International Monetary Fund (IMF) and other foreign creditors, who – with very good reason – sensed a disaster in the making. Certainly a currency board had not protected Hong Kong from the relentless pressures of destabilising speculation. Given the level of uncertainty in Indonesia at the time, establishment of a currency board might well have led to a rush to buy dollars, generating sky-high interest rates that in turn could have crushed what was left of the country's banking system. The Indonesian government was persuaded that it first needed to strengthen financial markets, deal with foreign debts and bolster central bank reserves before it could think of embarking on such a risky experiment. The plan was formally abandoned in late March,[5] and no other country in the region has indicated any interest in moving in the same direction.

Monetary Union

To others, the answer seemed to lie in abandoning monetary sovereignty not to a currency board but to a monetary union of some kind based on the model of Europe's new Economic and Monetary Union (EMU) – to go on the offensive with a forceful strategy of market alliance. Union would offer the benefit of numbers and thus the hope that the whole might, in effect, be greater than the sum of the parts. Who could doubt that one joint money might be more attractive than a myriad of separate national currencies? Even before the crisis broke, the idea was being actively explored by prominent economists (for example, Eichengreen 1997). Once the region's troubles began, interest rapidly spread. An observer wrote: 'Some kind of monetary regionalism in the region is … inevitable' (Mundell 1997). And another: 'Asia should … create an Asian Monetary Union' (Walter 1998). Official responses, however, were mostly distinctly unenthusiastic.[6] For obvious reasons, political as well as economic, no government was prepared to completely forsake its own brand of money.

In fact, the political preconditions for monetary union in Asia are not yet in place. The lessons of history on this issue are clear (Cohen 1993,

1998a: 84–91). To be sustainable, a joint currency among sovereign states requires one of two prerequisites – a local hegemon to enforce discipline or a broad network of institutional linkages sufficient to neutralise the risks of free-riding or exit by any participant. Neither prerequisite seems to be in evidence in Asia today.

It is clear that, as yet, Asian countries lack a broad constellation of commitments of the sort that might make a full surrender of monetary sovereignty immediately acceptable to all partners. This is not for want of trying. Even before the crisis, regional central banks had begun to build institutional linkages in a series of low-profile forums designed to promote dialogue and mutual exchange of information.[7] Many hoped that such groupings might weave the sort of fabric of related ties that could one day support more ambitious strategies of monetary alliance. But despite such efforts there is still little tradition of true financial solidarity – to say nothing of political solidarity – across the region.

A Yen Bloc

However, there is a potential hegemon in the neighbourhood: Japan. Indeed, it is fair to say that no regional initiative toward monetary alliance would have much chance without the active participation of Asia's dominant financial power. Collusion to promote market share would require determined leadership from Tokyo to create a currency bloc based on an internationalised yen. But are Asians prepared to bury historical suspicions of Japanese motivations and interests? Japan might well aspire to a strategy of market leadership, but it is unclear whether others in the area would voluntarily follow. Nor, in view of Japan's own economic travails during the 1990s, is it evident that Tokyo can sustain an effective campaign to cultivate regional use of its currency. In fact, nothing approximating a formal yen bloc is likely to emerge soon.

That does not rule out less ambitious forms of collaboration with the Japanese, as long as Japan's hegemonic pretensions remain relatively muted and within the limits of its present capabilities. In early 1996, for example, as many as nine governments were happy to sign a series of agreements committing the Bank of Japan to make yen credits available when needed to help stabilise exchange rates (*New York Times*, 27 April 1996: 20). In 1997, after the first shockwaves hit, they were even more enthusiastic about Tokyo's proposal for a new regional financial facility – the Asian Monetary Fund (AMF) – to help protect national currencies against speculative attack (Altbach 1997; Rowley 1997). The AMF proposal was by far Japan's most ambitious effort to implement a strategy of market leadership in Asian finance. Although successfully blocked by the United States, which publicly expressed concern about a possible

threat to the central role of the IMF in monetary affairs,[8] the idea
continues to attract interest (Bergsten 1998a) and Tokyo has persisted
in seeking new ways to promote its monetary role in the region.[9] The
process, however, is likely to be evolutionary than revolutionary in
nature. Was there an alternative way to deal with the immediate crisis?

Capital Controls

Throughout 1998, attention began to focus on the option of capital
controls – a strategy of market preservation conventionally based on
coercion rather than persuasion, inspired by the obvious example of
China. Though hardly without troubles of its own, including a near-
bankrupt banking system, loss-making state industries and rising
unemployment, China was spared the worst ravages of the crisis. When
other economies were being pushed into recession China's growth
barely faltered; when other regional currencies were being depreciated
in value (from 10–20 per cent in Taiwan and Singapore to as much as 80
per cent in Indonesia), the yuan held steady. One of the main reasons,
observers concurred, was China's vast panoply of exchange and capital
restrictions, which made it virtually impossible for domestic or foreign
users to bet heavily on a devaluation.

The most dramatic implementation came from Malaysia, which in
early September 1999 imposed strict controls on the convertibility of the
national currency, the ringgit, for both trade and investment uses. Kuala
Lumpur's new strategy was adopted in emulation of the Chinese, as
stated by one government minister: 'Malaysia's new currency controls
are based on China's model'.[10]

In the first year of the crisis the Malaysian economy had shrunk by
close to 7 per cent, the ringgit by 40 per cent and the Kuala Lumpur
stock market by 75 per cent. By the end of August, the country's authoritarian leader, Prime Minister Mahathir Mohamad, was no longer
prepared to tolerate the orthodox policies of his Finance Minister and
heir apparent Anwar Ibrahim, who was fired and later jailed. The
policies, the prime minister believed, were collaboration in a Western
conspiracy to ruin the Malaysian economy. The time had come to regain
control from international speculators, led by George Soros and 'the
Jews'. Henceforth trading in the ringgit would be carefully controlled,
the exchange rate would be rigidly fixed and capital invested in the
country would have to remain for at least one year before it could be
repatriated. The idea was to provide room for more expansionary
domestic policies than had otherwise seemed possible. Monetary
policy was immediately eased and interest rates cut sharply, and in October a new budget combined substantial tax cuts with heavy new public

spending programs. 'The plan', Dr Mahathir told legislators, 'aims at freeing Malaysia from the grip of the Asian financial crisis and to place Malaysia's economy on a stronger footing' (quoted in *New York Times*, 24 October 1998: B15).

That the prime minister's radical controls would prove controversial was hardly surprising. Though easy to ridicule for his conspiratorial views, Dr Mahathir posed a difficult challenge for conventional views on international financial management, which assumed the primacy of capital mobility. For decades, emerging nations had been lectured on the virtues of financial market liberalisation – yet here was a government that was doing just the reverse. Early signs suggested that Malaysia's economy was responding positively to the regime's expansionary policies. Dr Mahathir's audacity could have a powerful demonstration effect. What if Malaysia recovered more quickly as a result of its new insulation from international speculation? The experiment was carefully watched, though the jury remains out on a final verdict. Within six months growth was restored, permitting the prime minister to claim victory for his strategy (*Economist*, 1 May 1999: 73). However, most neighbouring countries also recovered during the same period, some even more rapidly than Malaysia, suggesting that the controls might have done more harm than good (Lum 1999). During 1999 restrictions were gradually eased, though not eliminated.

Nor was Malaysia alone. Some countries in the region, including South Korea and Taiwan, have always maintained residual controls to limit the volatility of capital flows. Even before Dr Mahathir acted Taiwan and others had resorted to new restrictions, albeit none as draconian as Malaysia's. One example was the Philippines, which in mid 1998 reintroduced limits on selected transactions involving repatriation of capital or remittance of profits. Another example, rather more startling, was Hong Kong, long considered the region's last bastion of true *laissez-faire* capitalism, where in late summer a broad program of new regulations was instituted to limit speculation on the local stock and currency exchanges.

With these initiatives, capital controls were no longer a forbidden topic in policy circles. As one source commented, 'capital curbs are an idea whose time, in the minds of many Asian government officials, has come back' (Wade & Veneroso 1998b: 23). A policy approach once dismissed as obsolete, left over from a more interventionist era, was back on the agenda.

Shifting the Discourse

Capital controls are controversial. Critics oppose them as inefficient and unworkable. Advocates defend them as a tonic for stricken economies.

For decades the burden of proof was on those who tried to block the seemingly irresistible tide of financial globalisation, but with the crisis in Asia came a new respectability for limits on the cross-border mobility of capital. Both theory and history suggest that the burden of proof has shifted to those who defend the conventional wisdom rather than those who attack it.

For and Against Controls

The traditional case against capital controls is simple: it is the case for free markets, based on an analogy with standard theoretical arguments for free trade in goods and services. Commercial liberalisation is assumed to be a mutual-gain phenomenon, so why not financial liberalisation? Like trade based on comparative advantage, capital mobility is assumed to lead to more productive employment of investment resources, as well as to increased opportunities for effective risk management and welfare-improving intertemporal consumption smoothing. We are all presumably better off as a result. In the words of Federal Reserve chairman Alan Greenspan, an authoritative representative of the conventional wisdom:

> The accelerating expansion of global finance ... enhances cross-border trade in goods and services, facilitates cross-border portfolio investment strategies, enhances the lower-cost financing of real capital formation on a worldwide basis, and, hence, leads to an expansion of international trade and rising standards of living (Greenspan 1998: 246).

All these gains would be threatened by controls, which would almost certainly create economic distortions and inhibit socially desirable risk-taking. Worse, given the inexorable advance of financial technology, restrictions might not even prove to be effective. 'We cannot turn back the clock on technology – and we should not try to do so' (Greenspan 1998: 249). Any government that prefers controls is, in effect, simply living in the past.

Against these arguments, which have long dominated thinking in policy circles, two broad lines of dissent may be found in the literature. One approach focuses on the assumptions necessary to support the conventional wisdom, which are as demanding for trade in financial assets as they are for exchanges of goods and services. Strictly speaking, as a matter of theoretical reasoning, we can be certain that free capital movements will optimise welfare only in an idealised world of pure competition and perfect foresight. In reality, economies are rife with distortions (such as asymmetric availability of information) that prevent attainment of 'first-best' equilibrium. 'It has long been established that capital mobility in the presence of significant distortions ... will result in a misallocation of the world's capital, and indeed can even worsen the economic well-being of the capital-importing country (Cooper 1999: 105; see also Eichengreen, Mussa & Staff Team 1998; Lopez-Mejia 1999).

A plausible case for controls may be made on standard 'second-best' grounds. Judicious introduction of another distortion in the form of capital restrictions could actually raise rather than lower economic welfare on a net basis. For every possible form of market failure, there can be a corresponding form of optimal intervention.

The logic of this kind of argument is not disputed. An omniscient government dealing with one clear distortion could undoubtedly improve welfare with some form of capital market restriction. What is disputed is the value of such logic in the real world of multiple distortions and imperfect policy-making. As Dooley (1996) has noted in a comprehensive survey of the relevant literature, the issue is not theoretical but empirical. The assumptions necessary to support an argument based on second-best considerations are no less 'heroic' than those underlying the more conventional *laissez-faire* view.

The second line of dissent, much more relevant to today's circumstances, looks not at isolated economic distortions but at the very nature of financial markets, which even in the absence of other considerations are especially prone to crisis and flux. At issue are the interdependencies of expectations in the buying and selling of claims, which unavoidably lead to both herd behaviour and multiple possible equilibria. Financial markets are notoriously vulnerable to self-fulfilling speculative bubbles and attacks. They also have a disturbing tendency to react unpredictably slowly to changing fundamentals – and then to overreact, rapidly and often arbitrarily. The resulting flows of funds, which may be massive, can be highly disruptive to national economies owing to their amplified impact on real economic variables. A logical case may be made for judicious intervention by state authorities, this time to limit the excessive instabilities and contagion effects endemic to the everyday operation of financial markets. In the words of a former governor of the Bank of Mexico:

> Recent experiences of market instability in the new global, electronically linked markets ... have made the potential costs of massive speculative flows difficult to ignore or underestimate ... The assumed gains from free capital mobility will have to be balanced against the very real risks such mobility poses.
>
> Some form of regulation or control ... seems necessary to protect emerging-market economies from the devastating financial crises caused by massive capital movements (Buira 1999: 8–10).

Admittedly the value of this sort of argument may be open to challenge on empirical grounds, but less so in the midst of a global emergency when the disadvantages of unconstrained mobility are obvious. In fact, the latest research demonstrates that financial liberalisation is almost always associated with serious systemic crisis (Williamson & Mahar 1998). It is the explosion of these costs that has been decisive in shifting the terms of discourse on capital controls. Increasingly the question is posed: why should freedom of capital movement be given absolute priority over all other considerations of policy? Why, in effect, should governments tie one hand behind their backs as they seek to shape and manage demand for their currency?

Perhaps most influential in this regard was a widely quoted article by economist Jagdish Bhagwati, which appeared in May 1998. After Asia's painful experience, could anyone remain persuaded by the 'myth' of capital mobility's benign beneficence?

> it has become apparent that crises attendant on capital mobility cannot be ignored ... When a crisis hits, the downside of free capital mobility arises ... Thus, any nation contemplating the embrace of free capital mobility must reckon with these costs and also consider the probability of running into a crisis. The gains from economic efficiency that would flow from free capital mobility, in a hypothetical crisis-free world, must be set against this loss if a wise decision is to be made (Bhagwati 1998a: 8–9).

In a similar vein, Krugman decried the failure of the confidence game – orthodox strategies of market preservation that he labelled Plan A. 'It is time to think seriously about Plan B', he contended, meaning controls. 'There is a virtual consensus among economists that exchange controls work badly. But when you face the kind of disaster now occurring in Asia, the question has to be: badly compared to what?' (Krugman 1998c; see also Krugman 1999: ch. 9). Within months, Soros wrote that 'some form of capital controls may ... be preferable to instability even if it would not constitute good policy in an ideal world' (Soros 1998b: 192–3). Even the World Bank joined the chorus, arguing that 'The benefits of capital account liberalisation and increased capital flows have to be weighed against the likelihood of crisis and its costs' (World Bank 1999: xxi).

By the fall of 1998, not much more than a year after the crisis began, the momentum had clearly shifted toward reappraisal of the conventional wisdom.[11] As Bhagwati concluded, 'despite the ... assumption that the ideal world is indeed one of free capital flows ... the weight of evidence and the force of logic point in the opposite direction, toward restraints on capital flows. It is time to shift the burden of proof from those who oppose to those who favor liberated capital' (Bhagwati 1998a: 12).

Back to the Future?

Reappraisal of the conventional wisdom could also be justified on historical grounds. Many people fail to remember that the IMF's original design did not call for free capital mobility. On the contrary. Reflecting an abhorrence for the sort of 'hot money' flows that destabilised monetary relations in the 1920s and 1930s, the charter drafted at Bretton Woods made explicit allowance for the preservation of capital controls. Virtually everyone involved in the negotiations agreed with the influential League of Nations study, *International Currency Experience*, that some form of protection was needed against the risk of 'mass movements of nervous flight capital' (Nurkse 1944: 188). The option of controls was explicitly reserved to the discretion of individual states, provided only that such restraints were not intended to restrict international commerce.[12] The idea was to afford governments sufficient autonomy to promote stability and prosperity at home without endangering the broader structure of multilateral trade and payments that was being constructed abroad. It was a deliberate compromise between the imperatives of domestic interventionism and international liberalism – the compromise of 'embedded liberalism', as Ruggie (1983) later called it.

Pivotal in promoting that compromise was none other than John Maynard Keynes, universally respected as the greatest economist of his day and intellectual leader of the British delegation at Bretton Woods. To Keynes, nothing was more damaging than the free movement of speculative capital, which he viewed as 'the major cause of instability ... [Without] security against a repetition of this ... the whereabouts of "the better 'ole" will shift with the speed of the magic carpet. Loose funds may sweep round the world disorganising all steady business. Nothing is more certain than that the movement of capital funds must be regulated'.[13] Keynes carefully distinguished between genuinely productive investment flows and footloose 'floating funds'. The former were vital to 'developing the world's resources' and should be encouraged. Only the latter should be controlled, preferably as a 'permanent feature of the postwar system'.[14] After Bretton Woods, Keynes expressed satisfaction that his objectives in that regard had been achieved: 'Not merely as a feature of the transition, but as a permanent arrangement, the plan accords to every member government the explicit right to control all capital movements. What used to be heresy is now endorsed as orthodox' (quoted in Pauly 1997: 94).[15]

However, that achievement did not last. Over the next half-century, as the phoenix of global finance rose from the ashes, Keynes' strictures were largely forgotten and what had been endorsed as orthodox again became heresy. Increasingly, controls came to be regarded as wrong-headed if not anachronistic. Less and less were states thought to have rights to resist the preferences of the financial marketplace. By the 1980s, financial liberalisation had become the goal of every self-respecting industrial or middle-income country. By the 1990s, the tide was moving toward free capital mobility as a universal norm. Perhaps the high-water mark was reached in early 1997 when the Interim Committee of the IMF approved a plan to begin preparing a new amendment to the organisation's charter to make the promotion of capital account liberalisation a specific IMF objective and responsibility.[16] Evidently insensitive to the irony, Camdessus asserted that the IMF's plan amounted to a mandate to add the 'unwritten chapter' of Bretton Woods (quoted in *IMF Survey*, 12 May 1997: 136).

Then came the fall of the Thai baht. Even the IMF changed its tune, dropping active discussion of a new amendment and talking instead of the possible efficacy of selective restraints (see, for example, Adams et al. 1998: 79, 150; Eichengreen, Mussa & Staff Team 1998: 2–3, 29) – a tentative step back to the future envisaged by Keynes and others when the IMF was created. Clearly, the pressure of events had conspired with a reawakened sense of history to put the case for capital controls in a new light. Limitations on capital mobility thus seemed to gain new legitimacy as an instrument of monetary governance.

Three Critical Questions

Shifting the burden of proof was only the start of the story, not the end. Even granting that a case for restraint might be made, important technical questions must be resolved if monetary governance is to be improved rather than disrupted. The three most critical questions are: What kinds of capital flows should be subject to limitation? What kinds of controls might be most effective? What kinds of rules might avoid major inefficiencies or serious policy conflict? The debate on these questions is just beginning (see, for example, Kahler 1998).

What Kinds of Flows?

Not all capital flows, to paraphrase the US Declaration of Independence, are created equal. In thinking about what flows might be limited, three key distinctions are important – differences involving the direction of capital movement, the type of capital movement and the identity of the actors.

Direction

The key distinction is between inflows and outflows of capital. In the midst of a currency crisis, when confidence in a nation's money suddenly collapses, attention naturally turns to the latter. The issue seems simple: how to stop the haemorrhaging. To many the solution seems equally simple: restrict the flight of funds in any or every way possible, as Malaysia has tried to do.

Capital outflows, however, are notoriously difficult to block, particularly at times of panic when the motivation to get out of a currency is highest. One of the more pernicious byproducts of financial globalisation has been the creation of a vast network of private institutions and intermediaries, backed by the latest in financial technology, that can be used – legally if possible, illegally when felt necessary – to evade even the most draconian public controls. As many governments have learned to their regret, restrictions may merely cause market actors to find new routes of escape. Cooper puts the point well: 'it is probably true that anyone determined to export private capital from a country can find a way, at a price, to do so' (Cooper 1998: 17).

A prime example occurred during the 1980s when several Latin American countries separately tried to suppress capital flight by imposing exchange controls, forcibly converting foreign currency accounts in domestic banks into local money. These included Bolivia and Mexico in 1982 and Peru in 1985. In all three cases, the immediate response was a decisive vote of no confidence, a clandestine flight of funds into accounts abroad that undermined rather than bolstered the market position of national money. Studies indicate that overall, taking into account deposits held in foreign as well as domestic banks, capital outflows increased rather than decreased after the restrictions were instituted (Savastano 1996). In all three countries, the failed measures were ultimately abandoned.

Experiences like these do not mean that such controls are inherently unworkable, as critics often charge. In practice restrictions may indeed work quite effectively, at least for a time, to limit flight from a currency. Much depends on institutional matters of policy design and administration – the degree to which governments can develop the technological sophistication and financial skills needed to beat the markets at their own game. Much depends on other policy initiatives that accompany the controls to restore confidence in the local money. Experience does suggest that, once imposed, limitations on outflows may have to be expanded if their impact is not to be gradually eroded.[17] The dyke must be built ever higher and wider to contain turbulent liquidity. It appears, therefore, that barriers to outflows might work best if imposed for relatively short periods to cope with temporary emergencies, rather than as a permanent element of a government's strategy of monetary governance.

Barriers to inflows, in contrast, might be sustainable for much longer periods, since it is easier to keep capital out than in. Restrictions on outflows drastically reduce the choices available to a currency's users, sowing frustration and creating incentives for evasion. Restrictions on inflows limit only one option among many, leaving foreign capital free to look for profitable outlets elsewhere. Champions of controls point to the example of Chile where, in the early 1990s, surging inflows generated growing conflict between the government's internal and external policy objectives. The problem was how to maintain a tight monetary policy without generating an exchange rate appreciation that might hinder export competitiveness. The solution was a program of administrative measures designed to discourage various forms of borrowing or portfolio investment from abroad – an approach that, with some caveats, apparently achieved its main goals before being largely dismantled in 1998 (see, for example, Adams et al. 1998: 176–9; Cooper 1999: 116–18). Similar measures have been implemented in a number of other countries, with varying degrees of success (Reinhart & Reinhart 1998: 117–19).

Limitations on inflows do little good in the midst of a panic, when the problem is too little interest in a currency rather than too much. In calmer times, however, much benefit might be derived if restrictions could succeed in reducing exposure to a reversal of sentiment. Most analyses of the current crisis in Asia concur that a key factor was a flood of capital into national financial systems that were unable to handle so much liquidity properly (Goldstein 1998; Radelet & Sachs 1998b; Wade 1998). Perhaps some form of program to limit inflows, in emulation of the Chilean model, might help prevent history repeating itself.

Type

The key distinction is between varying degrees of volatility. If the challenge confronting governments is vulnerability to self-fulfilling bubbles and attacks, the solution can hardly lie in restricting something like foreign direct investment (FDI) in fixed assets, which can be assumed to be relatively unresponsive to transitory variations of market sentiment. A more appropriate target would be the more impatient categories of capital that are most liquid and prone to contagion and overreaction – those that are most easily reversed in a short time.

Reversibility is most characteristic of investments that focus on price rather than yield, seeking to maximise capital gain rather than accrue dividends and interest over time. These include purely speculative currency transactions that bear no direct relation to underlying trade or production decisions. That means not only the traditional spot and forward segments of the exchange market but also swaps, options and the exotic forms of currency derivatives that have become fashionable. Also included would be most other categories of purely portfolio investment – equities as well as marketable debt – that can be bought and sold at a moment's notice. In the light of Asia's recent experience, a compelling case can be made for imposing some kind of limit on any or all of these types of activity. In contrast, little would appear to be gained – and much might be lost – by restrictions on FDI or FDI-like flows such as long-term bank lending (World Bank 1998b: ch. 3).[18]

What about short-term bank lending? A central cause of the Asian crisis was overreliance on foreign borrowing at short maturity – not a problem when creditors continued to refinance or roll over their claims, but very much a problem when expectations shifted. A sudden demand to make good on outstanding debts can be as damaging to a currency as sales of assets. A case could be made for some form of intervention or regulation to discourage excessive external exposure at short term.

Identity

The key distinction here is that of citizenship – whether the same rules should apply to all market actors or whether distinctions should be made between members of the national community and others. The argument cuts both ways.

Citizens are the only market actors that can legitimately hold a government accountable for its actions. Hence, one might reasonably conclude, citizens should be the only actors whose behaviour may be formally restricted by public authority. In practical terms, this would imply controls over borrowing or investments by nationals but freedom of action for non-nationals – a distinction sometimes rephrased in terms of residents versus non-residents. Foreigners (non-residents) would be allowed to move funds in and out at will; citizens (residents) would not.

Non-citizens are market actors with the least tenable claim to preferential treatment by a national government. Hence it might seem reasonable to limit the behaviour of foreigners (non-residents), if anyone, rather than one's own people (residents). Commentator Samuel Brittan (1998) evidently had that idea in mind: 'controls on inward

movements are inherently less sinister than those on outward movements designed to prevent citizens from sending funds abroad'. It is
certainly what Hale (1998: 11) means when he suggests that 'capital
controls represent a form of command economy intervention which
could have implications for a country's political freedom, not just its
economic freedom'. Brittan (1998) puts the point most bluntly: 'The
most basic argument against exchange control ... is that it is one of the
most potent weapons of tyranny which can be used to imprison citizens
in their own country'.

Is the tyranny of free capital mobility any less sinister than that of
intervention by the state? Might there not be some reasonable trade-off
between support of the property rights of money's users, whether
foreign or domestic, and defence of a government's sovereign right to
act in the nation's interests? States have long since abandoned absolute
laissez-faire as a proper guide to economic policy. In this sense, capital
controls would be no different from any other form of intervention by
public authorities intended to balance the desires and demands of the
public and private sectors.

What Kinds of Controls?

Not all controls are created equal, either. In thinking about what kinds
of controls might be the most effective, two key distinctions are important – duration and tactics.

Duration

The key distinction is between temporary and permanent. Controls that
are imposed for unlimited duration, critics argue, are insidious for
several reasons. Not only do they create powerful incentives for evasion,
they might require an onerous amount of paperwork and an ever-
expanding bureaucracy to administer them. Worst of all, they could
invite corruption and cronyism, as market actors use bribery or political
favours to obtain what is no longer legally available. Cooper (1998: 12)
cites the risk that controls 'will favour scofflaws over law-abiding citizens,
with corrosive effects on public morality'. The implication is that if
restraints are to be used, they should be imposed only at times of emergency and then only temporarily, until more stable conditions return.

The force of such arguments has been acknowledged for measures
designed to limit panicky capital flight. But are all other forms of
restraint equally susceptible to the same kinds of risks? If that were so,
states would have abandoned every kind of restriction or regulation of
market activity – domestic business as well as international, commercial

as well as financial – whereas the reverse is true. History amply demonstrates that permanent governmental interventions are not necessarily inconsistent with public morality, nor are they inevitably vitiated by widening leakage and circumvention. Again, much depends on policy design and administration as well as on the broader economic, political and social environment. There seems no reason to exclude the option of permanent controls in some circumstances.

Tactics

The issue here relates to the key distinction between persuasion and coercion. Most critics of capital controls seem to assume that restraints must be coercive in nature, involving strict quantitive limits on or outright prohibitions of specified transactions – borrowing or investment ceilings, exclusions, proscriptions and the like. Hale insisted that 'capital controls represent a form of *command economy* intervention' (1998: 11, emphasis added). But this assumption ignores the powerful role of persuasion as a tactic for preserving or promoting the market share of a currency. Much more market-friendly measures are also feasible, such as interventions that aim to alter actor incentives, via taxes or equivalent policy instruments, rather than formally suppress particular activities. That is obviously what Eichengreen (in IMF 1998c) had in mind in commenting recently that 'capital account convertibility, while implying the removal of controls and prohibitions, need not mean abjuring taxes and tax-like levies on the underlying transactions' (see also Eichengreen, Mussa & Staff Team 1998). In principle, it ought to be possible to devise effective limits on capital mobility that do not involve overt coercion.

The classic example is Chile, whose oft-cited control program mainly comprised such market-based measures, the central of which was the so-called unremunerated reserve requirement (URR) on most forms of external financing other than FDI. Any investor or lender wishing to enter the Chilean market was required to leave a sum equal to a specified percentage of the transaction on deposit with the government for one year. (The percentage was raised to as high as 30 per cent then reduced to 10 per cent in 1998, before being phased out.) Since no interest was received on the deposit, the requirement acted like a tax to discourage short-term movements in and out of the country. But since no transactions were expressly prohibited, market actors could make decisions based on their assessment of potential risks and returns. Variations in the rate of the URR gave the government a convenient instrument for influencing flows through the capital account, thus demonstrating that a well-designed program of persuasion could work as well as more coercive currency strategies.

What Kinds of Rules?

The key question is the locus of authority, an inherently political issue. Where should ultimate jurisdiction over capital controls reside – at the national level or at a higher multilateral level? To some observers, there is no question. In a system of sovereign states responsibility must remain with national governments, which are presumably best placed to determine the needs and interests of their people. Cooper expressed the representative view in a recent public forum (IMF 1998c): 'Each community should decide for itself the balance it wants to strike between corruption and scofflaws and so forth. Those are all legitimate national choices'. In effect, the trend toward oligopoly in monetary governance might be best resisted unilaterally. States should be free to limit capital mobility, if and as they wish, in an effort to restore some degree of monopoly control over their national currencies.

What of the risks of inefficiency and corruption that could result from an unrestrained use of controls? Worse, what about the risk of serious policy conflict if governments are tempted to retaliate in kind? In financial markets, as in markets for goods and services, no nation is an island. Actions in one place are bound to generate externalities that could invite damaging responses elsewhere, possibly leading to a vicious circle of beggar-thy-neighbour economic warfare on the model of the 1930s. The IMF was created to prevent a recurrence of that sad historical experience, forming the cornerstone of an edifice of norms and rules – an international regime – to govern monetary relations between sovereign states. National interest was not suppressed but, by common consent, international interests were to be taken into account. A strong case can be made for preserving the same principle as the debate over capital controls moves forward. As Mussa (in IMF 1998c) remarked in responding to Cooper's proposition:

> Dick Cooper suggests that ... this issue should be viewed largely as a national issue, an issue of national economic policy, and the choice should be left to national governments ... and I think there is something to be said for that ... [But] I think there is [also] a broader systemic interest in having capital account liberalisation handled in a manner that maximises the benefits for the world economy as a whole and limits the risks as best as possible for the world economy as a whole ... There is not only a national interest, but there is also an international interest.

How might national and international interests be reconciled? Most desirable would be a broad set of guidelines negotiated multilaterally but applied unilaterally. The guidelines should include specifications on such questions as the sort of restraints on capital mobility that may be permitted, under what circumstances and using what procedures. Within the limits set by those guidelines, governments would have wide latitude to make their own choices, with a qualified international institution – logically the IMF – designated as referee in the event of conflict or dispute. In an early analysis of the challenges of financial globalisation for monetary governance, Kapstein (1994) labelled such an approach 'international cooperation based on home country control'. More recently, Rodrik (1998b) has spoken of the need for a 'rule-based multilateral regime'. Whatever the terminology, the goal is clear – to achieve a workable compromise between national prerogatives and global considerations that will make the design and implementation of capital controls less controversial for all.

Conclusion

However, controversy is inevitable, given the distributional considerations. The Asian crisis provided one of those rare watershed moments when conventional wisdom could be seriously challenged. With economies seemingly brought to their knees by the vagaries of global finance, the time seemed ripe for reviving capital controls as a legitimate tool of public policy. Yet even if satisfactory answers are found to all the technical questions raised, there will be resistance from those most likely to be adversely affected by limitations on capital mobility. Prospective losers from controls include large industrial or commercial enterprises with sufficient creditworthiness to borrow internationally, who could be deprived of access to cheaper foreign sources of finance. They also include owners of mobile assets, typically financial service firms and high net worth individuals, who presently enjoy the privilege of investing wherever (risk-adjusted) returns promise to be highest. Potential winners include those who might benefit from a recovery of some degree of national monetary sovereignty, such as small and medium-sized businesses, retail trade, labour unions (representing worker interests) and local banks and borrowers. In practical terms, therefore, the most important question is political feasibility – how to mobilise effective support for restrictions of any kind.

Outcomes will depend on the lobbying and coalition strategies of interest groups on either side of the issue. It is difficult to predict which camp is likely to prevail in any given country, but it doesn't take much imagination to suppose that in most cases the balance of influence might tilt in favour of the bigger and wealthier anti-control constituencies, who are likely to have easier access to the corridors of power and to be better organised to articulate their interests and concerns. If governments are to reclaim any of the authority currently ceded to capital

CHAPTER 10

The Vagaries of Debt: Indonesia and Korea

Thomas M. Callaghy

Debt has been central to the Asian economic crisis and its spread to Russia and beyond. Some of the major weaknesses in the way debt was dealt with in the Latin American debt crisis of the 1980s remained serious problems when the Asia crisis struck – and were accentuated by it. This particularly related to the way that private external debt was handled. Private market actors, especially in a situation of accelerated financial globalisation, are still not well-equipped to cope with debt workouts unless the number of actors they face is relatively concentrated. Indonesia illustrates this problem in two major ways. First, its private external debt problem is particularly complicated, dispersed and serious. Indonesia's situation is further complicated by the fact that it is the only Asian crisis country to have an external debt problem large and serious enough to warrant rescheduling its public sector debt to its bilateral creditors via the Paris Club (of official creditors). Private international banks are often referred to as the London Club creditors, after the steering committees of lead syndicate banks used since the 1980s to reschedule debt owed to them by private banks and firms and debtor states.

This chapter focuses on three issues: the way the London Club banks operated in two Asia crisis countries, a comparison of that experience with the Paris Club rescheduling for Indonesia, and the complicated interplay of the Paris and London Club stories with other key actors in the Asia crisis, in particular the International Monetary Fund (IMF), the World Bank, international merchant bank advisers and international debt lawyers.[1]

Indonesia was hit by the crisis after Thailand and Malaysia but before Korea. Serious debt problems were central in each case but their characteristics varied considerably. The size of the external debt was important to the nature of its impact, but its composition was equally if not more important in determining the degree, ease and speed with which it was confronted. To illustrate this point, we compare the situation of Indonesia with that of Korea. Although Korea was hit late and last by the crisis, its serious external debt problems were dealt with first, quickly and effectively, helping to stabilise its situation then accelerate its recovery. In contrast, Indonesia's debt crisis has continued to fester, pulling the country even further down.

Indonesia: From Miracle to Contagion to Collapse

Indonesia is one of the most interesting of the East Asian miracle countries, largely because it succeeded over the last thirty years in producing a striking yet incomplete transformation. It did so despite showing many third world characteristics that make such a change difficult – a bonanza oil sector; vast, sprawling size and social heterogeneity; and weak bureaucratic capabilities. In addition, characteristics that proved to have a significant developmental impact in other Asian countries – a major role for the military in politics, heavily authoritarian forms of rule and high levels of statist intervention in the economy – did not produce positive effects in Indonesia. Instead, Indonesia suffered from particularly high, if somewhat disguised, levels of both crony statism and crony capitalism.

Indonesia sustained high rates of growth for most of the last thirty years. Between 1985 and 1996, for example, the country grew at an average of 7.1 per cent, with GDP growth of 7.8 per cent in 1996. From 1970 to 1996, the part of its population living below the poverty line dropped from 60 per cent to a little over 10 per cent. International capital of all kinds flocked to Indonesia's shores. It earned the reputation of being a rapidly rising Asian tiger.

As late as June 1997, the World Bank was saying that the Indonesian economy was still 'performing very well' (quoted in Borsuk 1998), then came the tsunami of the financial crisis. The World Bank's July 1998 report for the Consultative Group meeting best exemplifies the profound and dramatic change wrought within a year. It is worth quoting at length:

> No country in recent history, let alone one the size of Indonesia, has ever suffered such a dramatic reversal of fortune ... Indonesia is in deep crisis. A country that had achieved decades of rapid growth, stability and poverty reduction, is now near collapse ... Foreign creditors have withdrawn, investors have retreated. Capital and entrepreneurs have fled. Long-standing defects in governance, earlier camouflaged by rapid growth, have now been marked as fatal flaws.

But what a difference a year makes ... words alone cannot describe the numbing shock that has been inflicted on this country of 200 million people – the fourth largest in the world ... Few predicted the Indonesian crisis, and certainly none its severity. True, some observers expressed concern about the economy's growing vulnerability, pointing to rising external debt, slowing export growth and declining international competitiveness. But their doubts seemed petulant in the face of Indonesia's excellent growth performance over three decades and its record of poverty reduction. And besides, most macroeconomic indicators seemed in fine fettle (World Bank 1998c: I, 1.1, 1.3).

The World Bank report noted that 'Indonesia's problems began with contagion but nobody could have guessed the speed and severity of the crisis that followed. The confidence of domestic and international investors, built painstakingly over years, was shattered in months'. These new negative perceptions were a real problem. 'In this sense, then, this "crisis of confidence" has been the most damaging of all of Indonesia's crises ... and helps to explain why Indonesia has been singled out for such harsh punishment by the markets even though its economic situation prior to the crisis was no worse, and often even better, than those of other South-East Asian economies'. Finally, the World Bank noted that 'the last time this happened was in 1963 ... In one respect, Indonesia is in a more difficult economic situation today – the economic contraction expected today is much worse than in 1963' (World Bank 1998c: 1.15, 1.11, 2.1).

Nature of the Debt

At the end of 1997, Thailand, the first country hit by the crisis, had an external debt of about $US102 billion, while Korea owed $US154 billion. Indonesia's total external debt was $US138 billion, of which $US92.3 billion (67 per cent) was owed to external private creditors, primarily several hundred international banks. The government owed $US18.8 billion to various international financial institutions (IFIs), $US26.7 billion to the 'donor' countries of the Paris Club, and $US8.8 billion to private international banks. State banks and enterprises owed $US5.6 billion each, much of it to foreign banks. The total public sector debt was $US65.6 billion, 48 per cent of the total, while Indonesia's private sector owed $US72.5 billion, 52 per cent of the total. Its private banks owed only $US8 billion but almost 2000 corporations had borrowed $US64.5 billion in hard currency directly from international banks, much of it short-term and unhedged. The average maturity of corporate debt was eighteen months. In 1998 alone, debt service on Indonesia's debt was $US32 billion. The terrifying plunge of

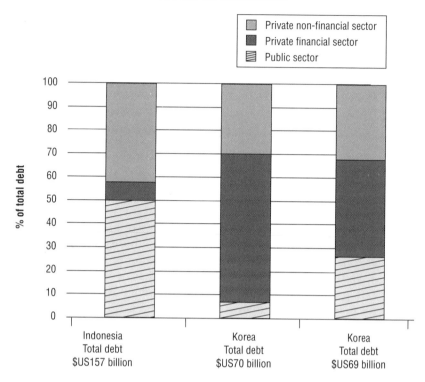

Figure 10.1 Structure of external debt by class of borrower, 1997
Source: From World Bank (1998b: 97)

the rupiah was accelerated by corporate debt, in the context of a weak and poorly regulated domestic banking sector. Together, Indonesia's state and private banks owed $US13.6 billion and its state and private corporations owed $US70 billion; the total bank and corporate external debt was $US83.6 billion. The impact of the external debt on the real economy was devastating, especially in the context of significant political and social turmoil.

Rough comparative figures sharpen the contrast with other crisis economies (see Figure 10.1). Indonesia's public sector owed 48 per cent of the total $US138 billion, the private financial sector 6 per cent and the private non-financial (corporate) sector 46 per cent. For Thailand's $US102 billion the figures were 28, 41 and 31 per cent respectively, while the figures for Korea's $US154 billion external debt were 8, 63 and 29 per cent.[2] In sharp contrast to Indonesia, Korean regulations restricted the amount its corporates could borrow directly from inter-national banks; the degree of bank intermediation was central to

Korea's debt workout. This contrast reflects the differing degrees of financial liberalisation of the two countries.

Korea: Rapid and Effective Response

In late December 1997, Korea looked as if it might default on payments on $US24 billion in short-term loans to over 200 foreign banks owed by thirty-two of its commercial and investment banks. This would have serious systemic consequences, partly because of Japan's high level of exposure and the weakness of the Japanese banking sector. Korea's situation had major strategic implications, and it was in the middle of a dramatic and historic political transition. A member of OECD, Korea was the world's eleventh-largest economy and deeply integrated into the global economy. Its foreign currency reserves were below $US6 billion and it was losing $1 billion a day in liquidity. The IMF and the United States were deeply worried. Based on close consultation between Treasury, Federal Reserve and IMF officials, the head of the New York Federal Reserve Bank called the six largest US banks to a meeting in New York on 22 December. After explaining the seriousness of Korea's situation, he indicated that the IMF and the United States could not put together a package for Korea if the international banks did not roll over and preferably restructure their Korean debt.

The New York Fed kept up the pressure by calling another meeting on Christmas Eve. Financial officials in other Group of 7 (G-7) countries began to do the same with their own banks, the British first and then the Germans more slowly. Citibank's William Rhodes, a respected veteran of the Latin American debt crisis, worked with Japanese banks and its Ministry of Finance (MOF), who were the slowest to respond. A short-term 'voluntary' roll over was agreed by 29 December, with the details and a larger restructuring plan to follow. Considerable disagreement and reluctance had to be overcome, along with resentment of the role played by the US government. The United States had much at stake, understood the larger systemic implications and had confidence in incoming Korean president Kim Dae Jung. Once the ball was rolling, the United States and other G-7 officials wanted to step into the background.

During these emergency bank talks, the Korean government was trying to put together its own negotiating team. It had already hired Goldman Sachs and Salomon Brothers as advisers. On their advice, the Koreans also hired Mark Walker, a well-known and respected US debt restructuring lawyer with substantial experience in Mexico and elsewhere. Travelling and using his extensive contacts, he began to represent the Koreans. Preliminary talks between the Korean team and its advisers with the international banks began in New York on 5 January. J.P. Morgan had put together an ambitious restructuring plan that involved Korean sovereign bonds and new loans from the banks. The Koreans had other ideas.

Considerable tension existed on the bank side, but Rhodes held the process together and became head of the official thirteen-bank steering committee. Intense and very complex negotiations took place in the last part of January, and a deal was reached in which the banks would exchange their loans to the Korean commercial and merchant banks for new one- to three-year loans guaranteed by the Korean government. It is important to point out that no *chaebol* debt was being guaranteed. The lead international banks then had to persuade more than 200 other banks to agree to the settlement.

This part of Korea's larger economic crisis was effectively dealt with in a little over a month. Korea's situation began to stabilise, and by mid February the rating agencies had returned Korea to one notch below investment grade. As a result, other forms of capital started to flow. A major crisis had been resolved by the complex interaction of state, private and international financial actors. One British banker noted: 'The sad fact is that international banks never accomplish much unless pushed by the US Treasury'. Another analyst observed: 'To the veterans of debt negotiations with Latin American countries, which dragged on for months and years, the negotiations with Korea were remarkable for their speed and intensity'. As the World Bank observed in late 1998:

> Several features are noteworthy: first, the high proportion of Korean debt owed by local banks provided a strong motivation for averting disruption to the domestic payments system. Second, the relatively small number of bank debtors and creditors helped coordination. Third, the deal, while not envisaged in the initial adjustment program with multilateral institutions, had behind it the strong support of the United States government. Fourth, the deal seems to have eased immediate pressures on the won in the foreign exchange markets. The currency stabilised and gradually strengthened in the following months (quoted in J. Sender 1998; Lee 1998: 32–7; World Bank 1998b: 100).

In the second half of 1999, Korea's debt situation focused on the ongoing restructuring or dismemberment of the Daewoo group. Korea's state-run creditor banks had taken over the restructuring effort of the firm and its roughly $US48 billion total debt, $US5 billion of which was owed to over 200 foreign banks. Those banks, represented by a steering committee chaired by HSBC Holdings, Tokyo-Mitsubishi Bank and Chase Manhattan, at first demanded they receive preference over local lenders and that the government guarantee their loans. They complained that they were being left out of the loop. By mid October the Koreans made it clear that foreign banks would be able to take part in the debt workout but that they would have to shoulder their share of the burden. The banks dropped their demands of a guarantee and agreed to equal treatment and to refrain from legal action. As in many previous private bank debt workouts in Latin America and elsewhere, smaller foreign banks were threatening to start seizing assets. Fears that similar problems might spread to other Korean firms with extensive debt problems (Hyundai, for example) clouded the negotiations. Nonetheless, high-quality negotiations took place, with very capable actors on all sides and with both immediate economic interests and longer-term political, social and regional interests in mind. This was not the case with Indonesia.

Indonesia's Private Sector Debt

As the 1997 slide of the rupiah accelerated, international banks became very uneasy and began to pull back, fearing a possible debt moratorium. In a self-fulfilling prophecy, the effect was to push Indonesian firms toward bankruptcy and to devastate the real economy. The Finance Minister announced in November that the government would not bail out the corporations. In mid December, when the exchange rate was Rp5500 to the dollar (2400 at the beginning of the crisis in July), the government appointed a committee on debt headed by Radius Prawiro. He suggested two committees – one comprising international banks and the other comprising Indonesian officials and representatives of the private sector. Neither the November nor January IMF agreements focused on the debt because the IMF believed that if it could stabilise the rupiah, the debt issue would automatically resolve itself. Although both agreements focused on Indonesia's disintegrating banking sector, neither ever really became operable as Suharto, unlike in the three previous major economic crises of the 1960s, 1970s and 1980s, refused to take serious crisis and reform measures. The IMF was able to get the government to close sixteen banks. In early 1999, however, the IMF admitted that the closures were a mistake, as they set off a major financial panic.

By 21 January, the rupiah fell to 12 000 to the dollar, partly accelerated by talk of a debt moratorium. On 27 January, Indonesia announced a 'temporary pause' in debt service. Two days later, Korea came to terms with its international bank creditors. A thirteen-bank steering committee was formed for Indonesia, headed by Britain's Standard Chartered Bank, but, despite informal discussions, it did not hold formal talks with the Indonesians until late February. Officials from the IMF, World Bank and the Asian Development Bank (ADB) also attended the meeting, as they were finally beginning to focus on debt.

Japanese banks and government were not pleased with the direction of the bank steering committee talks: they believed that Standard Chartered was offering overly generous terms that included debt write-offs ('haircuts'). In late March, at a private dinner meeting in Tokyo between Mark Walker (who was also representing the Indonesians) and Japanese bankers and MOF officials, an agreement was reached to replace Standard Chartered with a triumvirate committee leadership of the Bank of Tokyo-Mitsubishi, Chase Manhattan and Deutsche Bank. The Japanese banks held 38 per cent of the private sector corporate debt and had very serious banking sector problems of their own. The US, British and Germans held 8, 8 and 11 per cent respectively. If the Japanese banks wrote off any debt, they would have trouble meeting Bank for International Settlements (BIS) capital adequacy requirements. However, the Japanese government was both unable and unwilling to play the role that the United States had played in the Korean debt crisis. The Japanese government and its banks adhere to a lending culture that looks very unfavourably on debt restructuring, which had long made Japan a difficult Paris Club creditor. At minimum, it believed that interest must be paid, and debt stretched out only if absolutely necessary. The combination of the Asian crisis and Japan's own serious difficulties only intensified this approach. To be fair, we must also take into account the devastating situation in Indonesia, which included a government that was refusing reform, a collapsing real economy, major political and social unrest and spreading violence. Korea was almost a mirror image, introducing an element of fatalism into the Indonesia debt talks. Talks continued, however, and the committee met again in April and May.

By March, when the international financial institutions finally began to focus seriously on debt as part of the negotiations to revise the January IMF agreement, it was recognised that they and the Indonesian government were going to have to play some role in the complex private debt crisis. In the daunting list of 117 major policy measures, the government agreed to revise the 1905 bankruptcy law and to create a special bankruptcy court for workout purposes and as a lever to begin serious negotiations with firms. Variants of the Ficorca scheme used in Mexico for private debt workouts were discussed.

The result of these parallel debt discussions was a major meeting (1–4 June) in Frankfurt between the thirteen steering committee banks and an Indonesian team. IMF, World Bank and ADB officials also attended. By this time better estimates of Indonesia's foreign corporate debt put it at about $US78 billion. On the political front, Suharto had resigned and been replaced by B.J. Habibie, a transition that did not inspire the kind of confidence that the Korean one had. The Frankfurt meeting produced only a framework to handle three major issues – private corporate debt, inter-bank debt and trade credits. The major focus was on corporate debt. In line with Japanese desires, the framework required interest payments, spread them over eight years and permitted a three-year grace period on principal, but it did not write off any debt. The government was to create the Indonesian Debt Restructuring Agency to facilitate the negotiations with the roughly 2000 corporate debtors, partly by providing protection against foreign exchange risk. On inter-bank debt, the framework provided that the government would guarantee the foreign debts of Indonesian banks and that they would be replaced by new loans (after arrears were cleared) that would be extended for years but paid off at higher interest rates. Finally, the agreement renewed some outstanding trade credits.

The major feature of the Frankfurt agreement is that it was dead before it was signed, as it had very little resonance with Indonesian realities. The same holds for the parallel effort in spring 1998, with banking sector reform. The government created the Indonesian Bank Restructuring Agency (IBRA) for its roughly 200 banks in January and in April closed seven banks without incident because it guaranteed deposits; seven others were brought under its supervision. Like the debt efforts, banking sector reform made very little progress given the enormity of the problems and the complexity of the surrounding politics.

In late 1998, the World Bank summed up the Indonesian experience with private debt: 'Overall, the Indonesian experience ... is consistent with earlier expectations that orderly international debt workouts are more likely to succeed when they have strong support from governments of creditor countries' (World Bank 1998b: 100). Unlike Korea, Indonesia did not get such help as Japan was both unable and unwilling to provide it, and other major powers decided to keep their distance. The World Bank might also have pointed to the particularly challenging collective action problems posed by the Indonesian situation.

Paris Club Debt

Indonesia had a more fortunate experience with its debt to major creditor states. The idea of a Paris Club rescheduling for Indonesia was briefly raised and quickly dismissed in the fall of 1997. In January 1998, a senior international financial official in Washington was asked whether Indonesia might need a Paris Club rescheduling; the response was 'certainly not'. Even in crisis Indonesia was still considered a successful middle-income country that would be able to service its sovereign debt.

Yet Indonesia had a Paris Club rescheduling nine months later. When asked why, financial officials in Washington responded by saying that, as the World Bank put it, Indonesia had gone 'from contagion to collapse'. The following is Indonesia's Paris Club story.

The Paris Club is a complex and powerful yet rarely recognised hybrid international organisation, one that reveals a lot about the evolution of the international political economy and its governance processes. It has been one of the most powerful international organisations operating over the last several decades, directly affecting the lives of millions of people, although technically it does not exist. It is not a formal organisation with a charter, legislated set of rules, fixed membership, large bureaucracy or fancy building; it is usually described as an *ad hoc* forum of creditor countries that reschedules the public and publicly guaranteed debt of developing states. It is far more, however, and has evolved significantly since it began operations with Argentina in 1956. A small secretariat is housed in the French Treasury, and numerous officials are assigned to its operations in the creditor countries and the key international institutions linked to it. From its modest beginnings, the number of reschedulings accelerated dramatically – twenty-six in 1956–76, 150 more in 1977–90, well over 200 by the early 1990s and 308 by the end of 1997.

Indonesia is one of only two East Asian countries ever to have Paris Club reschedulings. The Philippines is the other, with five between 1984 and 1994. Indonesia rescheduled its debt in 1966, 1967, 1968 and 1970 in the period when Paris Club-style reschedulings were still in their formative period. The overthrow of Sukarno came at a time of massive social, political and economic turmoil, with the Vietnam War raging to the north. Many countries worried about the spread of communism to Indonesia. The crisis of the late 1960s in many ways rivalled the current one. 'In fact', as one observer put it in 1973, 'few countries have gone to ruin as quickly as Indonesia did, particularly in the latter part of the Sukarno regime' (Bittermann 1973: 166).

The early Indonesian reschedulings exemplify the development of both regular and extraordinary Paris Club norms. All the major elements of the international debt regime were apparent. The pattern of parallel but relatively distinct processes of handling debt and providing further assistance – what became the formalised Paris Club and Consultative Group processes – is a prime example. The debt posed a major obstacle to stability in Indonesia. It totalled about $US2.1 billion, 60 per cent of it owed to the Soviet bloc. In addition, Indonesia owed the IMF $US120 million from the aborted 1963 agreement with Sukarno. Indonesia was in arrears and thus technically in default; its debt service ratio for 1966 was 84 per cent.

The severe economic crisis of the late 1960s was only one of three major episodes of debt-related crises that plagued the dramatic transformation of Indonesia. The other two – the Pertimina crisis of the mid 1970s and the debt crisis of the mid 1980s – were successfully handled without formal rescheduling. This was possible largely because the reforms were implemented gradually and because Suharto supported the technocrats in their often stringent and unpopular policy recommendations.

The Suharto era can be characterised as a delicate and shifting balance between three loosely defined groups: the patrimonialists, those tied into key patronage networks that provided much of the regime's support; the nationalists, who supported a major role for the state in the economy; and the technocrats, initially referred to as the 'Berkeley mafia', who were responsible for the major reforms. The glues that held the system together were the consistently high rate of growth maintained during the entire period, and external advice and aid, backed by the growing confidence of the international private sector and the massive capital inflows that resulted from it. Indonesia managed to establish credibility in the fastest growing and most dynamic neighbourhood of the global economy, which in turn provided reinforcing synergies.

Underneath the surface of this shifting triangular relationship, however, much of what is now so widely referred to as crony capitalism in East Asia continued to exist. It was revealed by the crisis of 1997 and the attendant contagion brought about by increasing financial liberalisation and the ongoing development of global capital markets. During the long period of development, the technocrats did not get all they wanted; many of the reforms that they instituted were not fully or consistently implemented. Into the early 1990s, Suharto backed his technocrats during key episodes of distress. From about 1992, however, the balance in the triangular relationship tilted away from the technocrats. I would argue that the long period of sustained growth and the belief that it was not going to end shifted the balance towards the patrimonialists and nationalists, and the often crony capitalist practices that accompanied their expanding business activities. This tilt was reinforced by the growth in business activities of the presidential family, and Sukarno's age and increasing detachment from the larger economic realities being tracked by the technocrats. The discipline of crisis had disappeared.

In late January 1998, it became clear to the IMF, the World Bank and some of the Paris Club countries that, given the rapidly rising projected budget gap that the IMF was willing to accept, Indonesia was going to need a Paris Club rescheduling as well as more bilateral aid or it might be forced to declare a sovereign debt moratorium in addition to its temporary pause on private debt payments. The IMF agreed that the budget deficit would be used largely to fund social safety net expenditure on food and medicine, given the dramatically rising social tensions in the country. Primarily for status reasons, Indonesian officials were strongly averse to the idea of a Paris Club rescheduling. After all, the Paris Club was only for poor, less-developed countries that were beginning to receive special treatment. Basically, Indonesian officials were in shock and denial and, above all, embarrassed; their reluctance was palpable. Paris Club became a dirty word in Jakarta. Indonesia's Coordinating Minister for Economy, Finance and Development, Ginandjar Kartasamita, said that the government did not have any intention of going through formal Paris Club procedures because it was not in default. At first the government hoped to handle the problem on a bilateral basis, but it was soon disabused of that notion. Kartasamita said, 'We will look at other models, like what happened in Russia'.

As several international financial officials put it, Indonesia was a 'reminder' that the Paris Club was meant to deal with all countries in sovereign debt service difficulty as it had since 1956, and they were 'surprised' by the return of a middle-income country such as Indonesia. One senior official commented to his colleagues, 'Who would have thought a year ago that we would be working on Indonesia today?' Nobody had looked at the numbers carefully, and when they did many of the Paris Club countries found more aid and export credit debt owed by Indonesia – a reminder of the degree to which it was still an aid recipient, unlike most of the rest of East Asia. Besides the heavily indebted poor countries, Russia was to be the 'last frontier', and they had already rescheduled its debt and made it a member of the Paris Club.

The G-7 countries were to coordinate the Paris Club sovereign debt side while the World Bank, under the Consultative Group process, would coordinate the donor aid side. At the same time the IMF worked to reach agreement on yet another program, this time with the new Habibie government. Since the late 1980s, the G-7 countries often worked at 'precooking' upcoming Paris Club reschedulings. Senior G-7 finance officials began to exchange ideas about how to reschedule Indonesia's sovereign debt, and their deputies consulted on the details. There was substantial formal and informal contact among G-7 officials and with the IMF and the World Bank. The G-7 discussions included one five-hour conference call that included officials who had formerly worked on Paris Club issues. This process was frequently far from tranquil. In particular, considerable tension existed between the Americans, who wanted relatively generous treatment, and the Japanese about how the debt was to be handled and how much would be included in a relief package. Resolving these issues involved tough negotiation.

By the end of June, most of the Paris Club creditors, the IMF and World Bank had agreed that a Paris Club rescheduling could take place, and the Indonesians were informed. Since Indonesia had an on-track IMF program, the parallel preparations for a Consultative Group meeting for Indonesia could be finalised. On 16 July the IMF announced that it was committing an additional $US1.35 billion of its own funds to its Indonesia program and that $US6.2 billion was being added to the $US43 billion callable funds package decided upon in the fall of 1997. At the same time, Kartasamita announced the in-principle agreement to hold a Paris Club rescheduling.

On 29–30 July a formal Consultative Group meeting was held in Paris under World Bank auspices. World Bank officials said that it was likely to be the largest pledging Consultative Group meeting ever held. In the end over thirty countries and institutions pledged $US7.9 billion (see Table 10.1), a significant increase on the roughly $US5 billion of the two previous years. The fact that Korea was one of the donors was an irony that did not go unnoticed, and the Koreans were very pleased. The meeting stressed that much of the funds were to help deal with Indonesia's growing social crisis and, implicitly, its ongoing political crisis. Despite the size of the pledging and a real understanding of the implosion that Indonesia faced, fears were expressed that Indonesia would continue to be an aid junkie – after all, new bilateral aid creates new Paris Club debt.

The Consultative Group meeting was followed by an incident that reflects the increasing importance of the opinions of global markets and the odd ways in which they interact. In early August, Indonesia did not make several scheduled principal payments on $US1.25 billion of Paris Club debt. Some of the Paris Club countries and the IMF had agreed that, in anticipation of the September rescheduling, Indonesia could stop making principal payments in early August. The news rattled Indonesian and several global markets for about a week as the rumour spread that Indonesia had defaulted on its sovereign debt. The credit rating agencies noted that the incident did not affect Indonesia's ratings because they were already so low.

Indonesia's preparations for rescheduling its $US27 billion bilateral debt with its Paris Club creditors began in July when key government officials were in Paris for the Consultative Group meeting. They took the opportunity to meet with Francis Mayer, the French Treasury official who headed the Paris Club secretariat, to discuss arrangements for a meeting to be held in late September. To all intents and purposes, Indonesia was a 'first-timer' since its previous reschedulings were in the

Table 10.1 Consultative Group on Indonesia commitments ($US million)

	1996–97	1997–98	1998–99
Bilateral			
Japan	1917	1869	1500
Germany	208	66	300
US	85	74	250
Australia	51	55	75
UK	20	16	46
South Korea	39	73	30
Spain	63	63	25
Canada	21	19	25
Austria	24	20	20
Norway	n/a	n/a	10
Denmark	3	0	9
Belgium	16	n/a	6
Italy	7	0	5
New Zealand	3	3	3
Switzerland	8	5	1
Sweden	–	0	n/a
Finland	1	n/a	n/a
France	100	n/a	n/w
Total	2566	2263	2305
Multilateral			
World Bank	1200	1500	2700
Asian Development Bank	1200	1200	2700
Islamic Development Bank	100	100	400
UN agencies	37	38	144
European Investment Bank	50	100	40
Nordic Investment Bank	50	40	30
Saudi Fund	–	20	25
Kuwait Fund	25	0	25
IFAD	20	25	25
UNICEF	15	14	n/a
EU	–	n/a	n/a
Total	2697	3037	5589
Total	5261	5299	7894

Source: EIU (1998b: 36)

1960s. The government was not as fully prepared as it might have been although, as one official put it, it was far better prepared, despite its other distractions, than the Bosnian and Albanian governments. Indonesia was, at least in public, still trying to find a way around a formal rescheduling and, failing that, making a strong effort to portray any meeting as not a normal Paris Club rescheduling. In that regard, creditors were willing to take part in a charade to help Indonesia save face, but the outcome was a quite normal Paris Club rescheduling. The meeting began in Paris on Tuesday 22 September and ended, after marathon talks, before dawn the next day. A number of important issues and technical aspects had not been fully worked out before the meeting. Earlier in September, Hubert Neiss, IMF director for the Asia–Pacific region, had said, 'There are many, many details to be settled. I think with goodwill and flexibility on both sides, it is possible and feasible that the whole agreement can be reached in one meeting' (quoted in Reuters 1998a). In June, he had tried to get agreement on a deal to reschedule $US8 billion as an alternative external way to finance Indonesia's budget deficit. The proposal to reschedule a larger amount of debt would have meant more generous treatment of Indonesia by the Paris Club and met with vigorous Japanese and German resistance.

As part of the charade of not being a Paris Club rescheduling, the meeting was held at the Hotel Majestic conference centre on Avenue Kleber rather than in the conference facilities of the new French Finance Ministry building where Paris Club meetings are now held regularly. It was termed a meeting of the 'Group of Official Creditors of Indonesia', but it was chaired by Francis Mayer and involved normal Paris Club personnel, rules and procedures. Seventeen countries attended as creditors, including Korea, although it was not allowed to join regular Paris Club members on the *tour d'horizon* meeting in which creditors discuss all existing and upcoming Paris Club reschedulings.[3] In addition to the IMF and the World Bank, which always play an active role, UNCTAD, OECD and the European Commission sat in as observers.

Indonesia's total Paris Club debt was $US27 billion but the rescheduling only covered payments due between 6 August 1998 and 31 March 2000. The amount rescheduled was $US4.2 billion, of which Japan was owed between 40 and 50 per cent. Official development assistance was rescheduled over twenty years with a five-year grace period, export credits over eleven years with a three-year grace period. Japan chose an allegedly new option of refinancing its portion with new loans for the exact amount owed during the period of the agreement. It reserved judgment on whether it would refinance or reschedule remaining amounts. Japan chose refinancing for 'domestic political and legal reasons', according to Francis Mayer at the post-meeting press conference.

At the post-meeting press conference, the normal skeletal Paris Club press release was issued. The only difference was that the statement was entitled 'the Group of Creditor Countries of Indonesia Agrees to a Debt Treatment for Indonesia' ('Official Creditor' 1998). As part of the charade, Francis Mayer said that it differed from a regular Paris Club rescheduling because it involved new loans from Japan, applied only to principal, and included non-Paris Club countries, such as Korea! All the press coverage referred to it as a Paris Club rescheduling, which it was. Kartasamita called 'this agreement very important to us' and hoped it would push the rupiah towards 10 000 to the dollar by the last quarter of 1998. He also said that Indonesia would soon begin talks on the $US1.8 billion it owed the London Club banks.

International officials noted that there was some light at the end of the tunnel. The IMF's Herbert Neiss said that 'output is falling, inflation is high, the exchange rate is overappreciated, unemployment is high. However, the policies the government has agreed to put in place are making progress and the [IMF] program, which is monitored monthly, is fully on track' (AFP 1998; Reuters 1998b). Many analysts hoped that the deal would improve the world's perception of Indonesia and lead to a return of foreign capital in the medium term. One observer, however, seemed more realistic: 'This is probably just another factor that is going to put us back on the road to recovery further down the line'. And hard reality was not far away. In retrospect, the Paris Club rescheduling almost appears a brief pleasant interlude.

Indonesia's Private Sector Debt Saga Continued

A good deal of stock was placed in the prospects of creating a viable and effective bankruptcy procedure in Indonesia that would help work out the private external debt of more than 2000 corporations, or act as a lever to serious negotiation. The government was very slow to live up to its commitments on this score, and when it did the results were not those expected by the international banks and IFIs. In the fall of 1998 the new special bankruptcy court, despite World Bank special training, made a number of highly questionable rulings, usually favouring debtor firms – a vivid reminder of the difficulty of making many of the structural reforms being pushed by IFIs in the Asian crisis countries.

Despite being a major supporter of these reforms, the World Bank is brutally honest regarding the bankruptcy reforms:

> Passing legislation is one thing: developing the necessary skills, knowledge, expertise, credibility and respect for the rule of law in the day-to-day administration of bankruptcy law is a task that will take years, if not decades, to complete. Even a working bankruptcy system would not deal with the problems of insolvency in a systemic economic crisis. Thus, what will become important are orderly debt workouts – that is, less formal ways in which governments or other arbitrators attempt to achieve the same economic objectives as formal bankruptcy court proceedings by bringing together debtors and creditors to negotiate the resolution of debt problems (World Bank 1998b: 99).

The workout of private bank and corporate debt remain two of the weakest links in the architecture of international economic governance, despite over twenty-five years of experience and experimentation. After the Paris Club rescheduling in September 1998, another effort was made to reinvigorate the workout of the private external debt of Indonesia's beleaguered firms. The government launched the Jakarta initiative, which got off to a very slow start. Given the large number of firms involved, the fact that it was a voluntary process and the use of the case-by-case method, officials had a hard time being optimistic, as there would be no government bailout. The hope was that firms would negotiate workout models that could be applied to numerous other cases. By this time it was generally agreed that the amount of external corporate debt was really about $US80 billion.

A major meeting launching the initiative was held in Jakarta on 1–2 November, attended by 1200 people representing creditors, debtors and the government as well as a range of IFI, donor and investment bank observers. It was held under the auspices of the World Bank's corporate restructuring and governance group. The head of the World Bank group, Gerald Meyerman, said: 'The aim of this conference is to get these two groups talking to each other. This is the largest dating service that has ever been set up to facilitate restructuring'. The World Bank's country representative for Indonesia argued: 'If you chose to wait, you wait for collapse'.

Investment was returning to Korea and Thailand, but not to Indonesia. Nonetheless, incentives for companies to apply to the Jakarta initiative for help were few, especially given the rupiah rate. Most firms also refused to consider debt–equity swaps and believed that eventually the government would bail them out as a result of social and political pressure – if the firms did not collapse first. Some firms even felt that the crisis was an act of God, giving them the right not to honour their debts. As Jusuf Anwar, head of the Jakarta initiative, observed: 'My main obstacle is that the restructuring culture within our business and banking community is not widespread yet; we have to keep socialising what the restructure is all about' (quoted in Marshall 1998; Lee 1999).

There were two major incentives for using the Jakarta initiative. The first was the government promise to facilitate all restructuring deals. The second was the availability of a team of leading international restructuring lawyers led by US lawyer Richard A. Gitlin, head of a US–British law firm. He had earned an international reputation for his role in sorting out the collapse of the Maxwell International media empire in 1991. The IMF helped to attract Gitlin and his team. In theory they worked for the finance ministry, which asked the World Bank to fund their services. Gitlin stressed that 'you need to restructure companies, not liquidate them', but conceded that the gulf between Indonesian firms and their external creditors was huge: 'Creditors say, "We own the debt so we own this company". The debtors meanwhile say "Why should we agree to swap debt for equity when the rupiah is so low? We're not going to give away our company just because we are insolvent."' In Jakarta Gitlin earned the nickname of 'the Negotiator', referring to a US film (quoted in H. Sender 1998b, also see Shari 1999a, 1999b).

Gitlin's strategy was to chip away at the problem by attempting to negotiate deals for major firms and conglomerates, hoping to establish models, processes, precedents and personal ties. By February only 110 firms had even approached the Jakarta initiative, only a couple of major deals were being discussed and only a few minor ones with small firms were in the works. The biggest of the deals was for Bakrie and Brothers, the listed arm of the Bakrie Group conglomerate, headed by Abrurizal Bakrie, a leading and politically connected *pribumi* (Muslim) business-man. At a meeting in Singapore in early January with a committee representing many of the roughly 300 creditors, Gitlin reportedly obtained in-principle agreement on a $US1.5 billion debt–equity swap for 80 per cent of a new holding company consisting of five of Bakrie's best companies. Gitlin negotiated for three hours without the Bakrie team in the room (Shari 1999a). A preliminary deal was signed in Feb-ruary, to be finalised in June. Working out the details was still a major task, with success far from certain. Other restructuring efforts inside the group, especially for Bakrie Investindo and Bakrie Capital Indonesia, were also underway with the advice of external advisers such as Chase Manhattan. Bakrie was fighting hard to keep his own Indonesian bank afloat, a fight he eventually lost.

While key creditors such as Chase Manhattan, American Express and Dresdner Bank were at the meeting, Japanese banks, including Sanwa and Fuji, were noticeably absent. As one international banker put it, 'I see little progress anywhere else, though. The Japanese banks keep most of the debt and are not very interested in write-offs'. The major business culture gap (long apparent in Paris Club operations as well), reinforced by new structural weaknesses, will make corporate restructuring very dif-ficult for Indonesia. As one Japanese official put it, 'It is dogma. Interest must be paid'. 'Haircuts' are taboo; accepting them means lower ratings. The loans were either to be paid or left on the books of Japanese banks as performing bank assets so that the banks would not look any weaker than they already appeared, a procedure permitted under the regula-tory practice of the Japanese government. Underlying Japan's obvious structural constraints in this regard is a deeply embedded view of busi-ness relationships:

The relationship between a lender and a borrower is one of equal footing, of trust. The interest is the cost of the money that is needed for lending. If you get no interest back you are giving very benevolently. No more trustworthy relationship. *Inside a business group it is done.* If a company has invested in the other, if it is a father and son relationship, it is different (quoted in Thoenes 1999a, 1999b, emphasis added).

Ironically, one could argue that such a perspective leads to the destruction of long-term business relationships, especially in conditions such as those in Indonesia. In fact, a number of Japanese banks closed their operations in Indonesia and others pulled back, despite statements by the Japanese government that a more understanding approach to Asian debt problems was required.

The other major deal underway by early 1999 was for Astra International, a leading assembler and distributor of vehicles, mostly of Japanese origin. It sold assets to pay interest and tried to buy back some of its $US2 billion in debt to more than 100 creditors. It thought it had such a deal in January, including a moratorium on some interest and principal for a year. However, Japanese banks refused to accept the claim that Astra could not meet all its interest payments; two of them went as far as to declare it in formal default. Rini Soewandi, head of the firm, said that 'restructuring is something they're not used to' (quoted in Thoenes 1999b). In early March, Astra abandoned its efforts to get all debtors to agree to a deal. Drawing on the new bankruptcy law, it asked that creditors vote on the deal: agreement would require at least half the creditors, representing two-thirds of the debt. Astra would then make interest payments in slices tied to further agreed restructuring steps. By late 1999, all its effort had produced very little actual debt restructuring.

The Bakrie and Astra stories represented the tip of a huge iceberg. A number of international and merchant banks were attempting to work out restructuring deals with Indonesian firms but many would not even talk to them, and some of the merchant bank employees were harassed in various ways. There was plenty of room for the creativity of private actors on both sides, but the task remained herculean while the Indonesia economy continued to crumble. After twenty-five years, the market-based mechanisms for such workouts remained arduous, time-consuming and very underinstitutionalised.

It is important to remember that the attempt to restructure external corporate debt was closely tied to efforts to restructure Indonesia's floundering banking system. Banking sector reform was on the agenda from the beginning, but the government repeatedly broke promises to bite the bullet. In March 1999, for example, the government backed away from a promise to close thirty to forty banks and put others under supervision, in what was considered a highly corrupt political process. After considerable pressure by external actors, who made it a key test of Indonesia's willingness to engage in serious economic reform, the government announced in mid March that it would close thirty-eight of the 200 remaining banks, recapitalise others and supervise even more. Abrurizal Bakrie thought he had managed to save his bank – but then external pressure was applied to the government and his bank was on the final list of banks to be closed.

The summer of 1999 produced a major Indonesian corruption scandal involving senior ministers, powerful politicians, the central bank and the government's specially created banking sector restructuring agency (IBRA). The scandal involved the inappropriate approval by the central bank and IBRA of a $US70 million payment by Bank Bali to firms with ties to Golkar, the ruling party. The opposition charged that the funds were to be used for President Habibie's re-election effort. After strong external pressure the government agreed to an independent audit, which it then refused to release. Spectacular as it was, the scandal merely reflected the near-total loss of confidence by domestic and external actors in the government's economic reforms, reinforced by its actions in East Timor (that prompted rare political warnings by the IMF and the World Bank) and the highly charged atmosphere surrounding the upcoming presidential election. As the Bank Bali scandal was beginning to break and right after the IMF released a loan tranche, the government requested another Paris Club rescheduling. By mid October, however, the IMF and the World Bank had suspended disbursements due to the corruption scandal and made it clear that they would wait for a new government before trying to resuscitate economic reform.

It was also clear that any Paris Club rescheduling would have to await a new government. A peaceful transfer of power came when Abdurrahman Wahid, a moderate Muslim cleric, was elected president on 20 October and Megawati Sukarnoputri, a popular leading opposition figure to the Suharto and Habibie governments and daughter of former president Sukarno, was elected vice-president the next day. However, even with a new government, Indonesia's relations with its Paris Club creditors and donors, the IMF and the World Bank, and foreign private financial actors will not be easy. Another Paris Club rescheduling will be needed because of the lack of real progress on bank restructuring and the debt workouts tightly linked to it, and economic reform more generally. Indonesia's agony was thus prolonged as the vicious cycle of debt and banking reform continued. Despite these obstacles, however, the peaceful transfer of power provided much-needed hope and a chance for a fresh start.

Conclusion

Thus, by the last quarter of 1999, Korea and Indonesia could not have stood in starker contrast. Korea's recovery was the best among the crisis countries, despite jitters about corporate debt and fears of their spread, while in Indonesia economic reform efforts had ground to a halt, debt workouts were all but non-existent and another Paris Club rescheduling was needed.

By early 1999, the World Bank's first major report on the Asian crisis was already drawing lessons for international economic governance. It indicated:

> Left to themselves, debtors and creditors may take a long time to reach a voluntary reorganisation and ... delays in reaching agreement have real economic costs for society.
>
> The main implementation issue is collective action by creditors. Every creditor has an incentive to try to get out first or to 'free ride' on others' acceptance of workout arrangements. Negotiations are difficult to initiate, protracted and hard to enforce ... The collective action problem is much more challenging in a crisis that involves mostly private-to-private debt (as in East Asia) than in one involving public debt (as in the crisis of the 1980s). Further complicating the process is the much greater number of creditors and debtors than in the past and the centrality of exchange risk, as recent debt workouts in Korea and Indonesia show.

But how well are these lessons being learned and implemented? Despite the World Bank's striking statement that 'debtor and creditor country governments are *the* central players in orderly workouts of private debts, as well as sovereign debt' (World Bank 1998b: 98, 155, 156, emphasis added), it was unclear how a change of this magnitude was to be accomplished. By late 1999, very little progress had been made on bailing in the private sector on debt. No new major financial architecture had been created. Involvement of the private sector remained relatively *ad hoc* both in terms of norms and the cases to which they were applied. The world had not come very far since the Latin American debt crisis of the 1980s, despite the growth of market size and sophistication and the increasing recognition of the need for a role for states and international financial institutions (see chapter 8 in this book; see also Eichengreen 1999b: ch. 5). The IMF admitted the lack of progress, while saying that progress would have to be based on voluntary principles and cooperative action between the official and private sectors rather than on imposed rules (IMF 1999c).

Nonetheless, a quiet and less voluntary trend in the other direction was beginning to emerge, which produced increased tension between official and private creditors. It was linked to the insistence of the Paris

Club – under the guise of the long-held but frequently violated norm of 'comparable treatment' – that bondholders begin to share some of the burden of debt workouts. It first emerged in negotiations with Pakistan in which the Paris Club, with the tacit approval of the IMF, insisted that there would be no rescheduling unless there was a parallel workout of bond debt in addition to the normal London Club rescheduling. If this were not forthcoming, official creditors would insist that bond debt not be serviced. By September 1999, the IMF and the Paris Club were quietly giving permission for – were in fact encouraging – Ecuador to default on bond debt service as a condition for continued assistance. Private financial actors reacted to this stunning move with considerable unhappiness, but it received unexpected support from a leading business newspaper (*Financial Times* 1999).

Despite the relatively small size of its external bond debt, another Paris Club rescheduling for Indonesia might well play a role in the ongoing battle to bail in the private sector, as Indonesia will need every bit of help it can get. In addition, the new Indonesian government is likely to ask for considerably more generous debt relief. This effort is part of a larger trend in which major states and IFIs attempt to use their official power, in the service of system maintenance, to leverage more participation by private actors and markets in ways beyond voluntary cooperative action. In this sense, despite the dictates of neoliberalism, the Bretton Woods institutions and major countries are likely to continue to try to shape the global financial system in ways that fall short of a major new architecture of economic governance, and in a manner that private markets and actors perceive as an unacceptable infringement on their autonomy.

CHAPTER 11

The New International Financial Architecture and its Limits

Miles Kahler

As Morris Goldstein has remarked, 'There's nothing like a major crisis to focus people's minds on why it is important to improve the international financial architecture' (Goldstein 1998: 67). New institutions of international governance have often resulted from crises. The Bretton Woods order was designed by policy-makers who had sharp memories of the gold standard's collapse and the competitive depreciations of the 1930s. The unexpected demise of fixed parities under Bretton Woods and subsequent exchange rate volatility convinced Europeans that monetary stability required a new regional monetary design.

The Asian economic crisis, which moved rapidly from a regional disturbance to a global threat, certainly qualified as 'major'. It followed currency and financial crises in the 1990s that have repeatedly surprised those who believed that liberated capital flows would stabilise rather than disrupt the world economy. After the Mexican peso crisis, itself a sharp break in the surge of capital to emerging markets, one observer predicted with confidence that 'it is difficult to imagine another shock on the scale of Mexico's in the near future' (Cline 1996: 13). Yet less than two years after Mexico's recovery, the international economy was engulfed in an even more serious and widespread financial crisis, 'the most severe regional financial disruption since the Latin American debt crisis of 1982 and perhaps since the Creditanstalt default of 1931' (Chote, quoted in CEPR 1998: 2).

Despite the gravity of the Asian economic crisis, the official consensus on a new financial architecture has not represented a radical transformation of the global monetary and financial regime. Numerous plans for more ambitious institution-building have been set aside (see, for example, Soros 1998b). Rather than a new architecture, the current official design extends measures that have been on the international agenda since the Mexican peso crisis of 1994–95. In their extent and intent, they resemble a modest home improvement rather than a fundamentally new architecture.

Reasons for the modest proportions of these reforms are not difficult to discover. First, the Asian economic crisis has served as a drag on the dominant powers in the international financial order – the European Union and the United States – but it has not involved them directly, nor has it produced a global recession. Although it has produced substantial losses for major financial institutions in the industrialised economies, the Asian economic crisis has not threatened their solvency. Even the economic stagnation of Japan, which worsened the Asian crisis and was worsened by it, did not halt growth elsewhere. Despite the financial contagion evident during the crisis, the global financial and economic system did not prove as seamless as the apostles of globalisation would have us believe.

The major industrialised governments also evince a certain fatalism in the face of the core issues of governance in the international monetary and financial regimes – what Padoa-Schioppa and Saccomanni (1994) have labelled the change from a government-led international monetary system to a market-led international monetary system. This fundamental shift in the balance between governments and financial markets is accepted by the Group of 7 (G-7), and that acceptance sharply limits any realistic agenda for reform.

Finally, the principal governments in the international economy must work with an existing institutional inheritance, unless they wish to create entirely new and untested institutions. The new financial architecture gives central place to the Bretton Woods international financial institutions (IFIs), although only after certain (once again, modest) reforms. The International Monetary Fund (IMF) and the World Bank played a central role in managing the debt crisis of the 1980s, and the policy template that they developed was applied to the securitised capital flows of the 1990s during the Mexican peso crisis of 1994–95. Although some outside the official consensus have argued for more radical institutional reforms, such as a global central bank, those proposals have not been officially endorsed as feasible or desirable. The official consensus, at least, seems content to work with the institutions that it knows rather than craft new instruments during a time of uncertainty.

The reform proposals developed during the Asian economic crisis, however modest, must pass at least two tests. The first, their success in creating a more stable world financial order, can only be estimated in light of past crises, which may not predict future financial turbulence. The second, their political feasibility, has received little mention in official discussions. These political limits may prove to be binding constraints as the new consensus is implemented. Evaluation of the new financial architecture in light of these two criteria will determine whether, like many building plans, the blueprints adopted will eventually be set aside.

After a summary of competing interpretations of the Asian economic crisis and the implications of those interpretations for reform, this chapter outlines the evolving official consensus on a new financial architecture. The two key tests – political prerequisites and the new architecture's likely performance in future financial crises – will then be applied. Finally, the shortcomings of this apparently modest but politically ambitious model are compared to other institutional designs that might offer governments greater flexibility and autonomy in the face of a rapidly evolving financial system.

The New International Financial Environment and the Lessons of the 1990s

Driven by technological change and policy choices, financial integration has steadily increased among the OECD economies over the past twenty-five years (Herring & Litan 1995: 45). In some industrialised economies, movement toward liberalisation of capital markets and opening of the capital account spawned financial and banking crises.[1] The decade of the 1990s retraced the process of financial liberalisation among a set of developing economies whose institutional features are even less promising for dealing with the new financial environment. Banking and financial crises in the developing countries, for example, have been both more severe in economic consequences and more frequent since the early 1980s (Goldstein 1997: 3). The benefits of renewed capital flows to the developing countries, once regarded as an unmitigated benefit, are now weighed against the risks of opening to large-scale capital inflows in the presence of domestic institutional and policy weaknesses.

The Asian economic crisis offered new evidence for the ongoing debate over the causes of currency and financial crises, a debate that has influenced both the shape of the new financial architecture and estimates of its likely success in averting the most catastrophic crises. Two broad viewpoints emerged: the 'fundamentalists', who assigned financial crisis to ill-chosen national economic policies; and the 'panic-stricken', who were convinced that many crises were self-fulfilling, that is, expectations about economies that were *ex ante* unjustified were validated *ex post* by the outcome that they provoked.[2] The fundamentalist and panic-stricken accounts had implications for policy prescription. Fundamentalists were more willing to construct a shortlist of policy weaknesses that held across cases and were likely to hold in the future.

The weaknesses were also incorporated into research on warning indicators that could be applied to future crisis prevention. Key conditions of vulnerability included pegged exchange rates that became unsustainable under conditions of capital account liberalisation, fragile and poorly supervised domestic financial systems, and rapid increases in short-term debt denominated in foreign currency. To some fundamentalists, these vulnerabilities had to coincide to produce a financial crisis on the scale of those that struck the Asian economies (Krause 1998: 1; see also Goldstein 1998; Corsetti, Pesenti & Roubini 1998). If those fundamentals existed, it was more feasible to construct reliable warning indicators, policy advice could be relatively stable over time, and the costs of financial liberalisation, if that policy advice were implemented, would be lower.

Those who viewed the Asian crisis through the lens of a financial panic held a higher level of agnosticism regarding national policies. Although crises could be associated with poorly sequenced financial market liberalisation, many crises in the new financial environment surprised both official and market participants. The central puzzle was that national vulnerabilities were widespread, but only a few countries displaying them would experience financial crises (Wyplosz 1998; see also Radelet & Sachs 1998b). The panic-stricken view pointed in two directions. Since the core of this explanation rested primarily on financial market dynamics rather than the policy errors of governments, steps taken by governments to correct yesterday's vulnerabilities could not be guaranteed to prevent tomorrow's crises. Crisis management became relatively more important. This diagnosis also suggested policy prescriptions that would spare national economies as order returned to the financial markets – temporary suspensions in debt repayments, and capital controls.

As the Asian crisis was subjected to additional scrutiny, some measure of consensus was reached on a set of new fundamentals that would reduce vulnerability to financial crisis (crisis prevention). Less progress was made in understanding how to re-establish the confidence of financial markets while sparing the affected economy from a severe recession (crisis management). Worse, it was argued, the effort to win back that confidence could lead crisis managers to perversely pursue policies damaging to national economic well-being (Krugman 1998b: 25).

Despite convergence in diagnoses, the Asian economic crisis appeared to lend weight to the panic-stricken view of financial crises, for two reasons. First, *ex ante* fundamentals – at least the conventional fundamentals – were not seriously misaligned when compared to the recent history of those economies or other similar economies. The affected economies had pursued sensible macroeconomic policies and outward-oriented development policies for some time. The pattern of widespread contagion also suggested a basis in self-fulfilling speculative attacks. Although contagion was associated with trade and financial linkages in some cases, a more plausible interpretation was Goldstein's 'wake-up call', in which a crisis in one country prompted re-evaluation of other 'similar' countries (Goldstein 1998: 17–22; Wyplosz 1998).

These partly complementary explanations for the Asian economic crisis influenced the lessons drawn from the crisis by the research and policy communities and shaped the blueprints for a new financial architecture. Several characteristics of the reform consensus followed, contributing an intellectual ambivalence to the new architecture: recommendations for national policy changes were advanced, but few guarantees could be made that future financial crises could be prevented by the correction of identifiable national weaknesses. Although the panic-stricken view seemed strengthened by the Asian crisis, the interaction of financial markets and governments were not well enough understood to offer reforms that would dampen the wide swings in confidence and capital that characterised the 1990s. As a result, policy reforms fell largely to national governments in the developing countries, as they had in the past.

Lawrence Krause offered political uncertainty as a final new fundamental in precipitating currency and financial crises. Jeffrey Garten declared that 'local politics are crucial' in crisis management. However, politics was notably absent from most analyses of the crisis, although an unexpected increase in political uncertainty could provide a plausible trigger for crisis. General explanations of this kind were undermined by the same empirical shortcoming as other fundamentalist analysis, however: political uncertainty was widespread, but crises were not. Even the most seriously affected countries displayed a wide array of political shortcomings, from a weakening of bureaucratic institutions (Thailand) to succession in an authoritarian regime (Indonesia) to electoral contest and transition (Korea). In this book Stephan Haggard and Andrew MacIntyre (chapter 3) offer a more complete and politically grounded explanation of crisis than those advanced in most accounts. Since most of the existing analyses of the Asian economic crisis lack such grounding, prescriptions for a new international financial architecture were advanced in a political void. The political constraints on the new international financial architecture remained invisible, but that did not make them less binding.

Asian Economic Crisis and a New Financial Architecture

The Mexican peso crisis shook confidence in emerging financial markets and produced a flurry of reform proposals. The apparent success of US-led crisis management for Mexico and the resumption of private capital flows to emerging markets in 1996 did not obscure two lessons and one political reality learned from the peso crisis. One lesson emphasised the importance of providing accurate information to markets, as a means of crisis prevention. The second lesson underlined active crisis management to limit contagion, an ever-present threat in the new global financial environment. Opposition in the US Congress to another financial bailout on the scale of the Mexican rescue was the overriding political consequence of the peso crisis. Crisis prevention therefore assumed even greater importance. And crisis prevention post-Mexico concentrated on national policy fundamentals that would reduce vulnerability to crisis and inhibit its spread (Summers 1996: 1).

The G-7 summit at Halifax in 1995 began official efforts to address shortcomings in the existing financial order; these continued through the IMF Interim Committee meetings during the next year and the summit at Lyons in 1996. The IMF was designated lead institution for most of the reforms endorsed at these summits. The post-peso crisis agenda centred on prevention of future crises through tougher IMF surveillance of national policies and through encouraging new international standards for the timely publication of economic and financial statistics (the special data dissemination standard [SDDS] and the general data dissemination standard [GDDS]). Crisis management would be strengthened by increasing the scale of IMF resources through a quota increase and the creation of New Arrangements to Borrow, and by providing faster access to IMF resources through the emergency financing mechanism (EFM). A final aim, which achieved less short-term success, was the development of new techniques of crisis management that would involve the private sector early (bailing creditors in, rather than bailing them out) (Summers 1996: 2–3).

The new international financial architecture proposed in the wake of the Asian economic crisis can best be seen as a modification and extension of the Halifax–Lyons framework. Although the new architecture was described in different ways during the first year of the Asian crisis, IMF managing director Michel Camdessus nominated five core constituents in late 1998: transparency (the 'golden rule', 'the key for modern management, economic success and rational behavior of global markets'), 'strengthened banking and financial systems', 'involvement of the private sector' (to avoid moral hazard in crisis management), liberalisation of capital movements ('cautiously and in an orderly fashion'), and 'modernising the international markets' (internationally accepted standards and codes of good practice) (Camdessus 1998b: 310). The Group of 22 (G-22), which included representatives of systemically significant economies from industrialised and emerging markets, reported in October 1998. Its working groups reinforced the main architectural themes promoted by the IMF and other IFIs. This official consensus on a new financial architecture would be implemented in the coming months.[3]

The new architecture marked a shift from the traditional fundamentalism of the IMF. Crisis prevention became central, in light of increased demands on IMF resources and increased systemic risks posed by financial contagion. Although national policy changes remained the core of the new proposals, the policies in question were not restricted to the familiar macroeconomic at the core of past IMF and World Bank surveillance and conditionality. Rather, governments would change their interactions with private financial markets through greater informational transparency and good governance. These changes would take time and considerable advice, resources and oversight, but conventional conditionality was likely to play a smaller role. If crisis prevention failed, the new architecture looked for ways to permit an orderly negotiation between borrowers and creditors, rather than large and growing interventions using public funds, to end the crisis.

Transparency as the New 'Golden Rule'

Although delay in the provision of key data was singled out as a factor in the Mexican peso crisis, the Asian economic crisis deepened beliefs that greater availability of information between IFIs, governments and financial market participants could reduce the risk of crisis. As the IMF managing director claimed, 'Recent events have demonstrated that markets operate better when information is abundant ... Moreover, the stability of financial systems requires that sufficient attention is paid to ensuring that all market participants operate in a transparent environment' (IMF 1998e: II.6). The aim seemed to be a financial world of greater information symmetry, that would enhance financial stability.

Concrete steps to enhance transparency were centred on national governments and the IFIs themselves. The core of national government responsibilities lay in an expanded and improved SDDS monitored by the IMF for countries participating in international capital markets.[4] Given prevailing diagnoses of the Asian financial crisis, particular attention was given to improving data on international reserves, external debt and international investment, and to providing data on international reserves in a more timely way. Although the formal transition period for implementing the SDDS closed at the end of 1998, the IMF's Interim Committee and Executive Board have continued to urge further improvements in the standard.

The new financial architecture, as typified by the SDDS and GDDS, did not rely on direct data-gathering and publication by the IMF (in the manner of the *International Financial Statistics* and other statistical series). Instead, the IMF established standards for data provision and identified governments that met the new standards. The IMF's role was not to verify the data provided but to create a new and more transparent relationship between government authorities and private financial markets through the creation of standards understood and accepted by both sides.

Another transparency initiative was the Code of Good Practices on Fiscal Transparency. The Interim Committee adopted a Declaration of Principles on 16 April 1998, and the IMF prepared a manual on fiscal transparency. The Declaration of Principles clarified the deeply political character of the transparency project. The new standards, designed to encourage transparency, impinged directly on issues of domestic governance ('good governance' in the eyes of the IMF). The Declaration stipulated that 'the government sector should be clearly distinguished from the rest of the economy, and policy and management roles within the government should be well-defined', calling into question a long history of parastatals in both industrialised and developing countries. Much of the Declaration was framed in clearly democratic language: 'the public should be provided with full information', 'a public commitment should be made'. A system of independent checks and balances in fiscal policy was proposed: 'The integrity of fiscal information should be subject to public and independent scrutiny'. To many members of the IMF and the World Bank, such principles, if fully implemented, would represent a revolution in policy-making.

The agenda of transparency and code construction was extended with Interim Committee adoption of the Code of Good Practices on Transparency in Monetary and Financial Policies: Declaration of Principles, on 26 September 1999. Again, although the detailed implications were to be elaborated by the IMF, the degree of transparency in financial regulation embodied in the Code would overturn long-standing and politically embedded practices in many member states. The UK Chancellor of the Exchequer, Gordon Brown, saw a need for at least two additional codes of conduct at the centre of the new architecture: a corporate code of conduct crafted by the OECD, and a social policy code under consideration by the World Bank. His justification for this veritable industry of code construction was the same as that offered by the IMF: reducing the risk of future financial failures, increasing the ability of systems to withstand failures and building public support for economic policies of openness (Brown 1998). The G-22 crowned its recommendations on transparency by recommending that the IMF issue a Transparency Report on each economy, indicating whether the economy met internationally recognised standards of disclosure as set forth in the codes of conduct.

The private non-financial sector was central to the onset of crisis in some of the Asian economies. Its governance and transparency were left primarily to the oversight of national governments. The OECD endorsed non-binding principles of corporate governance in May 1999. International accounting and auditing standards were in the hands of private sector organisations (the International Federation of Accountants and the International Accounting Standards Committee). The IFIs had little if any leverage over or responsibility for private corporations. Private sector participants in international financial markets were encouraged by the G-22 to provide more information of greater consistency by adhering to national accounting standards, but the recommendation lacked any clear means of implementation.

More sensitive for the IMF than the transparency standards urged on national governments were new standards of transparency and accountability applied to the IFIs themselves. The opaque character of decision-making in these institutions had been a major point of attack by critics from both the right and the left. Many of these attacks were misguided: the IMF and other multilaterals operated under tight political constraints imposed by their members, who were reluctant to have the results of their negotiations and consultations made public.

At the centre of any crisis prevention response by the IMF was its surveillance of members' policies under Article IV of its Articles of Agreement and the conditions negotiated for the use of IMF resources. Following the Mexican peso crisis, intensification and broadening of surveillance were urged on the IMF; similar calls were heard as the Asian economic crisis spread. Increasing transparency through publicising the contents of IMF programs or IMF Article IV assessments of member economies remained a sensitive issue. Such information not only had an effect on market perceptions, but was politically sensitive for member governments. The IMF encouraged the release of Public Information Notices (PINs) after Article IV consultations, and in the first eight months of 1999, 80 per cent of the consultations were followed by release of PINs. A voluntary program for the release of Article IV staff reports was initiated in April 1999. The IMF also approved the release of the chairman's summary of the Executive Board's views on use of IMF resources, and in June 1999 it established a presumption that documentation for IMF country programs would be released (although the member country in question could refuse that release).

All these voluntary steps toward greater transparency did not directly confront the problem of member countries that refused the IMF's advice and threatened to create a financial crisis with international ramifications. An external team that evaluated IMF surveillance confirmed what many had suspected: 'At the end of the day, however, it was not clear to us that the authorities really paid that much attention to the IMF's advice, whether they wanted to or not ... They were all in rather difficult political situations, and the domestic politics overrode the IMF advice' (*IMF Survey*, 27 September 1999: 303).[5] External evaluators noted that in none of the four cases examined did the IMF come close to 'going public' with its advice, and few of those interviewed in the countries or at the IMF suggested that it should have. Certainly the Interim Committee had taken only a small step down that path by urging a 'tiered response', whereby countries that are believed to be seriously off-course in their policies are given increasingly strong warnings (*IMF Survey*, 27 April 1998: 120). Managing director Camdessus made it clear that public disclosure of differences between a member government and the IMF would remain rare (*IMF Survey*, 27 April 1998: 117). The IMF maintained that greater public disclosure of its country assessments would depend, in all but the most extreme circumstances, on the consent of those members. As Barry Eichengreen argues in this book (chapter 8), greater disclosure in the name of improved transparency would risk a rupture in relations with member governments (and a reduction in the quantity and quality of data received) and possibly create rather than prevent financial crises. The IMF considers those risks more significant than any potential gain in influence over national policies.

Strengthening Banking and Financial Systems

One new fundamental was central to nearly every explanation of the Asian economic crisis: a weak and poorly supervised banking and financial system. An IMF report described such a financial system, combined with an open capital account, as 'an accident waiting to happen' (IMF 1998a: 75). Even before the Asian economic crisis, others considered that the highest priority in crisis prevention was strengthening national financial systems: 'The ultimate question is how to strengthen banking systems and banking supervision in emerging markets – and how to do it quickly' (Goldstein 1996b: 58). The 1997 Annual Meeting of the IMF and World Bank endorsed Core Principles for Effective Banking Supervision that had been developed by the Basle Committee on Banking Supervision. The twenty-five principles, prepared in consultation with non-G-10 supervisory authorities, established a minimum framework for effective supervision of banking institutions 'in all countries and internationally'.[6] The IMF also developed a framework for surveillance of members' financial sectors (IMF 1998d).

As with the codes of good practice aimed at transparency in fiscal, monetary and financial policies, principles for banking regulation and supervision were certain to upset long-standing practices and the powerful political interests behind them in many emerging market economies. A second political issue arises in coordinating IMF initiatives in this area with other international institutions. Core institutional competence lies with the Basle Committee and other regulatory consortia, such as the International Organisation of Securities Commissions (IOSCO), not with the Bretton Woods IFIs. The IMF's need to forge collaborative relationships with these organisations, other international economic and regulatory organisations and the World Bank is greater in this sphere than in any other. Those outside the IMF have criticised the lack of firm deadlines for adhering to the Core Principles and questioned whether there are adequate incentives or sanctions to move member governments quickly to compliance (Goldstein 1998).

Crisis Management: From Bailouts to Workouts

Even the most optimistic fundamentalist admits that, even when national policies are corrected, financial crises can still occur. A means of managing those crises, containing both the damage to affected economies and contagion to the global financial system, is required. The official response to the Asian economic crisis first emphasised the need to increase IMF resources through a quota increase and approval of the New Arrangements to Borrow and the need to increase the speed with which financing could be provided to governments in the throes of currency or financial crises. With the increasing scale of government and IFI resources committed to rescue packages, through the Korean program of December 1997, moral hazard concerns overtook the earlier emphasis on resource adequacy. Alternatives were sought to the conventional template of debt rescheduling that had existed in some form since the debt crisis of the 1980s.

The new financial architecture is a balance between the existing model of crisis lending to governments by G-7 governments and the IMF, and a new and ill-defined model that would transfer more responsibility to negotiations between creditors in the financial markets and borrowers in the emerging markets, whether sovereign or private. Three different and not entirely compatible avenues have been opened in the search for a new template of crisis management.

The Clinton administration urged a course aimed at preventing contagion by creating a 'contingent short-term line of credit' to countries that are pursuing sound policies and are the target of self-fulfilling speculative attacks. The new supplement to the Supplemental Reserve

Facility, Contingent Credit Lines (CCLs), was endorsed by the G-7 in October 1998 and created by the IMF for a two-year period in April 1999 (*IMF Survey*, 16 November 1998: 360). Japanese Finance Minister Miyazawa indicated his government's willingness to entertain a second facility that would have lower conditionality – access determined by a 'good track record certified through regular surveillance' – and would be 'precautionary as well as quick in disbursement when needed' (Miyazawa 1998).

A second course of action, proposed by Barry Eichengreen and Richard Portes, centres on government encouragement of institution-building by the private sector so that debtors and creditors can conduct more orderly workouts (Eichengreen & Portes 1995; CEPR 1998: 35–8; Goldstein 1998: 51). Although sovereign debt was not initially at the centre of the Asian economic crisis, Eichengreen and Portes argue that the crisis in lending to non-sovereign borrowers (banks and corporations) was often transformed into a sovereign debt crisis. Their proposals include redesigning loan contracts to avoid persistent collective action problems among creditors, and developing standing steering committees of creditors for the same reasons.

A third set of innovations deals with the problem of moral hazard in the set of actors – large uninsured creditors of emerging market banks – who paid the smallest penalty of all participants in the crisis (Goldstein 1998: 39). Proponents of the panic-stricken view of financial crises have also searched for ways to reduce incentives to defect from lending at the first sign of trouble. The official consensus, beginning with the 1996 G-10 report, has tilted slightly toward borrowers in creating a template for crisis management negotiations. IMF authorisation to lend into sovereign arrears on a case-by-case basis was extended to private bondholders. The latest statement of G-7 policy also acknowledges that 'in exceptional cases, countries may impose capital or exchange controls as part of payment suspensions or standstills, in conjunction with IMF support for their policies and programs, to provide time for an orderly debt restructuring' (Group of 7 1999: para. 50 [h]).

The G-7 governments (particularly the United States) and the IMF have, on an *ad hoc* basis, implemented these shifts in the official consensus in the aftermath of the Asian economic crisis. Banks were persuaded to roll over their short-term loans as part of the Korean package in December 1997; debt relief for Pakistan has been coupled with demands for similar concessions from private Eurobondholders (see Eichengreen 1999c: 16–19). Most recently, the US government and the IMF have made it clear that they expect commercial banks to support the post-devaluation program approved by the IMF for Brazil (Phillips & Fritsch 1999). Although these cases brought some grumbling from representatives of private financial institutions, the Institute for International Finance admitted that most official interventions had remained at the voluntary end of the spectrum of possible action. Nevertheless, the default of Ecuador on its Brady bonds – the first default on this category of debt – in September 1999 placed the IMF in a difficult position, since approval of additional support for Ecuador could be interpreted as support for the default (and might not produce much-needed reforms). The Ecuador case, although expected by financial markets, highlighted the redistributional politics that would surround a more calculated stance by IFIs in debtor–creditor negotiations during crisis management.

The same political issues arise in proposals to encourage or discourage particular types of lending to developing economies. For example, Rogoff's argument that debt finance and bank intermediation, which have been at the heart of most emerging market financial crises including the Asian economic crisis, should be discouraged (or at least not favoured) in the future. Instead, equity finance and foreign direct investment (FDI) should claim a larger share of capital flows to developing countries. Although Rogoff's argument is compelling, he omits one important explanation for the current bias – the political power of banks in both lending and borrowing countries. Stock markets in developing countries are often poorly developed (and banking systems dominant) for political as well as economic reasons. Shifting the bias in policy away from banks will not occur without political conflict. The entry of foreign banks into emerging markets and the incorporation of banks in larger financial conglomerates, both likely outcomes of regulatory reforms that are underway, may paradoxically create greater political barriers to disengagement from debt finance.

The debate over the private sector's role in crisis management has obscured the emerging official consensus' clear rejection of two other options. Crisis management without intervention by G-7 governments or IFIs has been ruled out as too costly for national economies that are affected by unexpected (and in some sense undeserved) financial crises and too threatening to the stability of the international financial system. A more interventionist alternative – constructing a set of formal international bankruptcy procedures – has also been rejected. Concerns over moral hazard in this instance are directed toward developing country governments and borrowers rather than large lenders, since 'management' (the government of a defaulting country) cannot be replaced by international bankruptcy processes. Divergent models of appropriate bankruptcy procedures are evident even among the industrialised countries: without harmonisation among those economies, an international standard would be difficult to construct.[7]

International Institution-building

The official view of the new financial architecture, at least among the
G-7, is based squarely on the IMF as the central institution for prevention and management of financial crises. Apart from an increase in the
transparency of the IMF's own operations, other changes in the
organisation have been minimal: in a long-awaited change, the Interim
Committee (in existence for more than two decades) has been
transformed into the International Monetary and Financial Committee
and granted a strengthened role as advisory committee to the Board of
Governors.

Rather than reforming existing institutions or constructing new ones,
the most significant institutional innovations in the new financial
architecture are those designed to encourage collaboration between
global economic institutions. Many of the issues raised by the Asian
economic crisis require expertise that cannot be found in a single
institution. This is particularly the case in strengthening banking and
financial systems in the emerging market countries. The G-22 suggested
a Basle Core Principles Liaison Group to coordinate the international
response to improving banking and financial supervision. The
recommendation was echoed in more substantial form by Chancellor of
the Exchequer Brown, who proposed a new permanent Standing
Committee for Global Financial Regulation, to bring together Bretton
Woods institutions, the Basle Committee and other regulatory groupings (Brown 1998: 7). In February 1999, the G-7 adopted proposals
made by Bundesbank president Hans Tietmeyer that closely paralleled
the Brown plan (*IMF Survey*, 8 March 1999: 68–71). The new Financial
Stability Forum, initiated by the G-7 but designed to include emerging
market countries as well, brings together national authorities 'responsible for financial stability', IFIs and international supervisory groups.
Based in Basle, home of the Bank for International Settlements (BIS), it
is chaired by the BIS general manager Andrew Crockett. The Forum is
an exercise in coordination of existing institutions and functions; Tietmeyer's report explicitly rejected as unnecessary 'sweeping institutional
changes'.

The official consensus has rejected both the abolitionist program of
the political left and right (dismantling the Bretton Woods structure)
and proposals by others for the construction of wholly new institutions,
such as a global central bank. Rather, the new architecture has incorporated existing institutions and pressed them to collaborate more
intensively. Although the architects have chosen to centre much of the
new design on the IMF, its original mandate and mode of operation
little resemble the expanded functions proposed in the new financial

environment. The choice of Basle and the BIS as the site for the new Forum suggests incipient competition between the older intergovernmental model of monetary order and an even older (and newer) design based on central banks and their collaboration.

Private Financial Institutions, Capital Controls and Contagion

Perhaps the most important structural gap in the new architecture is a consistent set of crisis prevention proposals for private financial institutions and their lending policies. Initially, the Asian economic crisis produced some useful, if limited, suggestions: tighter regulations governing inter-bank lending and alteration of risk weightings that seem to favour short-term lending. Rather than becoming an agenda item for the Bretton Woods institutions and other global forums, however, the behaviour of major private financial institutions has been left to regulatory authorities in the G-7 countries.

Those authorities became more active after the Russian default in August 1998 and the turmoil it produced in the financial markets of industrialised countries. The failure of Long-Term Capital Management produced calls for greater scrutiny of hedge funds, particularly from Japanese and European politicians, and pressure for intensified supervision of financial institutions in G-7 countries. The G-7 emphasised three areas for attention: improving risk assessment and risk management by financial institutions, assessing the implications of highly leveraged institutions (HLIs) – a category that included hedge funds as well as other financial players – and bringing offshore financial centres (OFCs) under the umbrella of international standards. Much of this work was delegated to the Basle Committee, long the focus for regulatory coordination among the industrialised countries, and to the new Financial Stability Forum. The Forum established working groups to deal with issues arising from HLIs and OFCs as part of its initial work program (Group of 7 1999: C.22–9; Tietmeyer 1999: 23).

The discussions of regulatory tightening within the G-7 and regulatory forums were framed in technical rather than political language. The difficulties in preventing regulatory slippage, however, were as political in the industrialised world as they were in emerging markets. The Basle Committee and its 1988 agreement on capital adequacy suggested a high level of international scrutiny directed toward national regulatory standards. However, the onset of recession and banking crisis in Japan led to lax enforcement: once again, politically powerful banks were able to convince regulators to interpret international standards generously.

The Russian default of August 1998 and its financial market consequences also spurred the imposition of capital controls by Malaysia and
turned the international debate on private capital flows toward the more
contentious issues of capital account liberalisation and capital controls.
A return to capital controls threatened regulation of capital flows from
the side of borrowers rather than creditors. Official proponents of a new
financial architecture have shifted from an unblinking endorsement of
capital account liberalisation to a far more cautious stance, one that
accepts certain restrictions on capital inflows as potentially valuable
tools of crisis prevention.

A few months after the devaluation of the Thai baht, at the October
1997 annual meetings of the IMF and World Bank Group, the Interim
Committee issued the Hong Kong Statement on capital account liberalisation, placing liberalisation at the centre of the IMF agenda. The
Interim Committee proposed an amendment to the Articles of Agreement that would make liberalisation of capital movements 'one of the
purposes of the IMF, and extend, as needed, the IMF's jurisdiction
through the establishment of carefully defined and consistently applied
obligations regarding the liberalisation of such movements' (*IMF Survey*,
6 October 1997: 302). By April 1998, the Asian economic crisis had
deepened and spread, and the Interim Committee emphasised the
importance of 'orderly and properly sequenced liberalisation of capital
movements' and 'enhanced surveillance of capital flows'. That emphasis
was reflected in the IMF's study of the use of capital controls by national
governments, and the Executive Board's consensus that capital account
liberalisation remained valuable but required careful management (IMF
1999e). Some G-7 members expressed even greater tolerance of capital
controls: Japanese Finance Minister Miyazawa interpreted the IMF
review as extending not only to the less controversial restraints on
capital inflows but, in exceptional cases, to the reintroduction of
measures to prevent capital outflows (Miyazawa 1998).

The shifting official consensus reflects a lively debate on the desirability and efficacy of capital controls outside official circles. The IMF's
original proposal to include capital account liberalisation in the
amended Articles of Agreement had stimulated sharp criticism from
mainstream economists. Financial contagion in Asia lent weight to the
self-fulfilling view of currency and financial crises, encouraging a
re-examination of capital controls.[8] Few endorsed comprehensive
capital controls; some simply opposed a forceful stance by IFIs in favour
of further liberalisation. Other recommendations ranged from the use
of taxes on short-term capital inflows to controls on short-term flows that
were matched with encouragement of longer-term investment, particularly in the financial sector. Politics figured prominently in this debate:

the critics of capital controls (at least controls imposed selectively on capital outflows) pointed out their susceptibility to corruption and political manipulation. One of the advantages of Chilean-style taxes on capital inflows was their transparency and relative immunity to rent-seeking behaviour (Reinhart & Reinhart 1998; Velasco & Cabezas 1998; Radelet & Sachs 1998b; Corsetti, Pesenti & Roubini 1998: Part II, 21–6).

As Benjamin J. Cohen suggests, capital controls remain the wild card in the new financial architecture (see chapter 9). Malaysia's imposition of comprehensive foreign exchange and capital controls found few immediate imitators as the Asian crisis eased. An earlier consensus expressed by the IMF managing director ('The answers are not in restricting capital markets but in making them work better') had unravelled, but a new consensus on the desirability of controls or restrictions, of what kind and with what international oversight, had not emerged. The design and implementation of capital controls or taxes would be influenced by political as well as economic desiderata.

Political Limits to the New Financial Architecture

Although the Asian economic crisis was new, it shared a number of characteristics with earlier crises in lending to developing countries. Given that record, the apparently low level of learning by national governments was both striking and puzzling. An accumulation of short-term debt denominated in foreign currency has been a warning signal of financial crisis since the Mexican debt crisis of 1981–82, but this reliable indicator of vulnerability has usually been ignored by governments. In similar fashion, new codes of banking supervision and regulation do not represent new knowledge; they embody national practices in place for some time, available for borrowing at any time. Yet imitation of best practice elsewhere has seldom occurred in time to avoid banking crises. Exchange rate policy offers a third example. An attempt to maintain an exchange rate peg and an autonomous monetary policy under conditions of capital mobility will fail. However, many developing countries have failed to adopt monetary rules or other credibility-enhancing strategies that are not based on an exchange rate peg, even as they have opened their capital accounts (Cottarelli & Giannini 1997: 98). The risk of financial collapse has been apparent since crises struck the southern cone of Latin America in the early 1980s.

In each of these cases, a baffling unwillingness to follow simple prescriptions for crisis avoidance is best explained by an underlying political logic. Too often, discussion of a new financial architecture has taken the form of 'assume an institution' or, worse, 'assume no politics'.

The debate has been deeply concerned with governance, but it has seldom confronted issues of government institutions or the politics that underlie them. A breezy assertion of the importance of 'good governance' by the IMF managing director is only one example:

> Not so long ago, this subject [governance] was virtually taboo in the multilateral institutions; today, it is on everyone's lips, and, I hope, at the top of everyone's agenda. There can be no doubt but that good governance, including the rule of law, is absolutely essential – both in order to realise the benefits of this new global economy and to manage its risks (*IMF Survey*, 6 October 1997: 309).

This technocratic and apolitical approach to governance and the new financial architecture has blinkered its proponents. Each of the constituents of the new international financial architecture is based on political assumptions (often implicit), and represents a particular equilibrium that could be upset by future political conflict. The new codes of conduct on fiscal, monetary and financial policy, if implemented, would represent revolutionary political changes for many members of Bretton Woods institutions. Increased transparency in IMF surveillance could change the dynamics of economic policy-making, as IMF evaluations fed into domestic politics. Strengthening banking and financial systems will require tampering with regulatory and distributional bargains that involve powerful political interests. Regulatory tightening in the industrialised countries will encounter the same types of resistance. Efforts to tilt crisis management even slightly toward debtors and their interests have already produced criticisms from creditor interests. Exhortations to collaborate are unlikely to have much effect on international institutions with different bureaucratic and economic constituencies.

At its core, the new architecture is an ambitious program of policy harmonisation, involving institutional changes of central importance to many polities across different policy domains. These three features of the new architecture set political limits on its implementation. Promotion of policy harmonisation has led to a mistaken belief that the realignment of policies is a game of coordination, in which incentives for opportunistic behaviour decline after policy harmonisation has been agreed. In many of the policy domains affected by the new financial architecture, political incentives to deviate from harmonised standards and codes of good practice will be substantial. Incentives and sanctions directed to implementing and maintaining harmonised standards must be carefully designed and adequate to the goals. Although the official consensus claims broad support for the policy changes encompassed by the new financial architecture, those changes often represent an assault on established models of policy-making. Whether the reforms will be supported by plausible domestic coalitions aligned with IFIs and their program remains unclear. Finally, the scope of these changes, ranging across a large number of issue areas, requires closer collaboration between international institutions that have demonstrated little aptitude for cooperation in the past.

Incentives for Harmonisation

Few clear incentives and sanctions to induce compliance are provided in the new financial architecture. The chief architects seem to have awarded a central role to three major avenues of external influence: surveillance, conditionality and market incentives. As described earlier, the record of surveillance, where the use of IFI resources is not in question, is at best mixed. Before the onset of the Thai currency crisis, the IMF issued repeated warnings that were not heeded. In the case of Korea, warnings were apparently issued about the shaky state of the country's financial system, again to little effect (CEPR 1998: 8–9, 28). The IMF's external evaluation team documented the ineffectiveness of IMF advice in key pre-crisis situations, overwhelmed by domestic political preoccupations and weakened by the IMF's dilution of its expertise in new policy areas. Although external monitoring of an agreed program of policy harmonisation is essential, peer pressure from other member governments has not been particularly effective as a sanction, even when the threat of crisis was real. The alternative would be going public when advice was unheeded. Although debate on the wisdom of such a departure has centred on its financial market effects, the core of resistance by member governments is due to its political implications: it gives the domestic political opposition a weapon with external credibility. That political threat could give the IMF considerable leverage, but so far it has chosen not to deploy it.

A familiar supplement to surveillance is conditionality, exchanging access to IMF and World Bank resources for implementation of desired policy changes. In the wake of the Asian economic crisis, some have argued that access to IMF resources (or the scale of that access) should be linked to banking system reforms and more demanding standards of financial supervision (Dornbusch quoted in Fischer et al. 1998: 25; Goldstein 1997: 57; Goldstein 1998: 55). Eichengreen argues that such conditionality, even if credibly applied, would not affect those countries outside the club who posed systemic risks – those judged too big to fail (see chapter 8). The time required for policy changes and an ever-present possibility of slippage would also make denial of resources on these grounds very difficult. Less stringent, and therefore more credible, are proposals that would make access to certain facilities (such as the new contingency lending facility) or the terms of access (the IMF's rate of charge) dependent on compliance with the new standards. Ultimately, however, the success of conditionality is dependent on internal coalition partners, who will provide the essential political support for adopting the reforms and overseeing their implementation (see Kahler 1992). Given the complexity of the politics that underlies many of the new reforms – particularly banking regulation and supervision – careful political calculation is required to determine the feasible scope and speed of commitments that are part of IMF or World Bank programs.

The effectiveness of conditionality, whether in support of newly harmonised supervisory standards or other measures to reduce financial vulnerability, partly depends on the demand for IMF resources. A more effective and consistent tool for maintaining compliance could be market incentives, if they could be mobilised. The deployment of public warnings (or the threat of such warnings) would link IMF leverage to the financial markets but, as described earlier, the IMF is unwilling to use public warnings in any but the most extreme circumstances. Signals could be sent to the markets in a less sensitive fashion through the IMF publicly posting, similar to the SDDS and GDDS, countries that have adopted international banking standards; removal from the IMF list would signify non-compliance. IMF publication of its assessments of banking sector developments in individual countries, part of regular Article IV consultations, could also provide valuable information to the markets (Goldstein 1997: 57). These reports, issued on a regular basis, would not risk creating a financial crisis in the way that public warnings might.

Inducing acceptance of the new financial architecture through private financial markets requires discrimination and positive financial rewards for countries that have adopted the policy changes. It is unclear why large financial institutions should reward governments that pursue policies of transparency or supervise their financial institutions according to international standards. Lenders were eager to supply capital to borrowers who clearly ignored those standards in the past: is there any reason to suppose that willing lenders will not reappear (after a decent interval) even if the new standards of transparency and accountability are not observed? Perhaps calculations of risk will in the future incorporate such borrower features, rewarding with lower borrowing costs those who comply. One suspects, however, that the benefits would be relatively small.

Fear of future financial crises is a final inducement for adopting policy harmonisation embedded in the new financial architecture. If governments are convinced that policy changes will provide reliable insurance against a catastrophic crisis, they may choose to adopt the changes. Unfortunately, any benefit from the insurance is both uncertain and distant. For a politician contemplating a short time horizon, insurance costs or the benefits of opportunistic behaviour that undermines the new standards may seem more compelling than continued compliance (premium payments).

Political Coalitions and Structural Change

Whether deployed by IFIs or the financial markets, any calculation of incentives and sanctions in favour of harmonising standards must incorporate domestic political incentives for compliance or opportunism. Those political incentives are likely to be important, since the new financial architecture typifies the implications of deeper economic integration: from simple removal of barriers at the border, the demands of integration reach deeply into the policies and institutions of societies. Measures are difficult to implement, since they require governments to alter the behaviour of private actors. The status quo typically represents a political equilibrium that is difficult to move. If even conventional IMF conditionality needs significant internal support to succeed, the demands of the new financial architecture will involve even higher political requirements.

Despite the political contingencies embedded in its instruments of influence, the IMF has portrayed the new financial architecture as a means of overturning an entire style of economic policy-making that is deeply embedded in some Asian and developing societies. The managing director of the IMF bewailed 'the economic culture, which allowed unduly close links among the state, the banks, and the corporate sector. This "managed development" was simply out of tune with the demands of a globalised economy' (*IMF Survey*, 19 October 1998: 309). Although he could have been describing Germany, the target was clearly the collusive relationships between key economic actors that have characterised many Asian economies.

Martin Feldstein and others have sharply criticised the IMF for extending its conditionality to such fundamental characteristics of societies (Feldstein 1998). In this view, the IMF is impinging on national choices that worked in the past and should be able to work again. The entrapment of those countries in currency and financial crises no more proved that their underlying political and economic arrangements had failed than the Scandinavian banking crises of the early 1990s confirmed the failure of the welfare state.

As collusive relationships have been successful in the past and have produced rewards for their participants, they are not likely to be overturned easily. Consider banking supervision, often portrayed as a 'technical' policy reform. Even the IMF admits that initial implementation of an effective prudential and supervisory framework is 'easier said than done. Political pressure for regulatory forbearance is intense. The expertise required to evaluate bank balance sheets is in short supply, nowhere more so than in emerging markets' (IMF 1998a: 75). Even in the industrialised economies, with long-standing institutional investments in financial regulation and supervision, political intervention on behalf of clients is a persistent threat; examples of supervisory breakdown under political pressure are easy to find.

The IMF's experience in promoting structural reforms demonstrates the importance of internal political support that is aligned with the IFIs in favour of policy change. Paradoxically, in some Asian societies, reforms in line with the new financial architecture may draw on a reformist reservoir of political support. Attacks on collusive bargaining and demands for greater economic and political transparency could become part of democratising and even populist political programs, as they have in South Korea and Malaysia. In other instances reform will be promoted by enthusiastic technocrats, favoured by the IFIs but lacking a broad political base. The harmonising rhetoric of the new financial architecture makes little allowance for such a variable political reception and domestic pressures for and against reform.

Institutional Coordination

A final political limit to the new financial architecture is likely to be set at the international level rather than within the domestic politics of the emerging markets. Given the sweep of policy areas, implementation of the new architecture will draw on the expertise and resources of an array of international institutions. The ability of these institutions to coordinate effectively within the loose framework of the Financial Stability Forum has not been demonstrated. Their differing institutional strengths may mean that organisational and regulatory styles will clash. World Bank criticism of IMF prescriptions during the Asian crisis suggests that organisational fissures will be reinforced by intellectual ones. Competing bureaucratic and interest group constituencies within member governments may also impede policy coordination. The persistent failure of the World Bank and the IMF to collaborate effectively, a source of complaint from member governments since the 1980s debt crisis, does not inspire optimism for implementing the new financial architecture.

An emphasis on institutional coordination, all moving in step according to the new financial blueprint, fits well with the emphasis on policy harmonisation that has been described. Close coordination is less essential in a future that allows for the value of both institutional competition and policy devolution. The key international institutions, including the IMF, owe it to their members to offer clear signals on the evolving international policy consensus and requirements for financial support. However, beyond consensus on long-term policy design for reducing the probability and risks of financial crisis, some competition – between international institutions and national governments – on the ways of achieving those goals may be desirable.

The animated debate over capital account liberalisation and capital controls – begun by those outside the official consensus and by national leaders such as Prime Minister Mahathir – has produced a consensus that is far less dogmatic than the official line that dominated pre-crisis. Since the financial environment is changing rapidly, a degree of competition would appear even more valuable, as it has in the realm of macroeconomic policy coordination (Rogoff 1999: 18–19).

The official process can also be complemented by devolution to standard-setting bodies that have evolved their own procedures, often working in tandem with official regulators. (This has been the case with accounting standards in particular.) As long as the process remains open to public scrutiny and comment, devolution removes some of the direct burden of policy harmonisation from international institutions (see Eichengreen 1999c: 7–9).

Sustaining a Crisis-prone System: Will the New Financial Architecture Succeed?

The political constraints on the new international financial architecture are formidable, and there is little evidence that they have been incorporated into the design of the proposed reforms. Only one binding political constraint has received close attention – an apparent unwillingness by the major economic powers to construct new global institutions. Even if the political obstacles can be overcome, the most optimistic proponents of the new international agenda do not promise a crisis-free international financial system. However, the new architecture must promise at least a reduction in the frequency and/or severity of financial crises if it is to be judged a success. But even if the political limits just described can be overcome, at least four reasons for scepticism remain.

First, the new architecture's emphasis on transparency – Camdessus's 'golden rule' – betrays a naive belief in the power of raw information. Although definitive accounts of the crises of the 1990s are yet to be written, some observers have refused to attribute a central role to information deficits. Following the Mexican peso crisis, Arminio Fraga argued that 'most of the relevant data necessary for a diagnosis of the Mexican situation was available to the general public' (Fraga 1996: 54). Even a recent IMF report echoed this scepticism: 'The incentives to efficiently use improved information can be undermined ... unless there are clear expectations on the part of creditors and debtors that they will bear the costs of mistakes' (IMF 1998a: 150). More precisely, information available before many crises was ignored because of failure to analyse it; it was not that the information was lacking (Goldstein 1996b: 64). In this regard, those investigating the causes of financial crises might well examine the history of intelligence failures, in which signals are frequently overwhelmed by noise, and bad theories explain more than information shortages. In any case, to portray today's financial universe as suffering primarily from deficiencies in information seems a peculiar diagnosis.

The new financial architecture is distinguished from the old by its attempt to convert national governments to the religion of full and timely disclosure and to convince financial markets that a credible commitment to such disclosure should be rewarded. The new architecture almost certainly oversells the capabilities of governments, however. By promoting standards that many industrialised countries have only recently met, the new architecture is raising unrealistic expectations for many emerging market economies. Even with the best intentions (and without the political constraints already identified), transforming such economies into OECD equivalents will be a lengthy process. Even then, the ability of governments individually and collectively to comprehend and respond to changes in the ever-evolving financial markets is questionable.

Viewed from the perspective of governments, the new architecture also oversells the predictability of financial markets and what they will reward. As Joseph Stiglitz concedes, 'Although restoring [or maintaining] confidence is critical, we have little theory and perhaps even less evidence about what will restore [or maintain] confidence' (CEPR 1998: 60). The 'ever-widening list of weaknesses' described by Wyplosz will require additional government measures, in an ever-deepening cycle of surveillance–surprise–crisis, and new assessments of policy changes required by the markets. Governments may reassess whether the benefits of capital market opening compensate for the risks of an unexpected withdrawal of market confidence. These doubts have deepened due to the financial market turbulence that followed the 1998 Russian default. Global market dynamics, not only the boom and bust cycle of emerging markets, must be considered.

> The argument often heard in the aftermath of the Asian crisis was that no one could see through the opaque financial structures and markets – but the

markets and institutions that experienced the most recent turbulence were the most open and transparent in the world. Why, then, were potential dangers not more accurately perceived at an earlier stage? (IMF 1998f: 65).

Finally, the new financial architecture may have flaws that result from its global reach and its reflection of the interests of G-7 governments. Although contagion ultimately spread beyond the region, in the first phases of the Asian economic crisis regional contagion was most pronounced. Since the externalities of bad policy choices and financial market overshooting are felt first by regional neighbours, the incentives for peer pressure and financial support may also be larger within a region. Nevertheless, a new regional initiative, Japan's proposal of an Asian Monetary Fund in late 1997, was fiercely challenged by the United States and the IMF. Regional alternatives were later revived in a more inclusive guise. Finance Minister Miyazawa proposed a 'regional currency support mechanism' to complement the IMF, not supplant it; Fred Bergsten endorsed an Asian Pacific Monetary Fund to provide an early warning and early action system in the face of incipient crises (Miyazawa 1998; Bergsten 1998b). Regional solutions might better reflect the interests of smaller, more open developing economies. Asia may have suffered because of its lack of a regional option before and during the crisis. Regional collaboration offers one promise of exit from the cycle of recurrent financial crises.

Conclusion: The New Financial World and the Developing Economies

Although it may be oversold, the new financial architecture is unlikely to do harm. Greater transparency in governments, private financial institutions and IFIs may reduce the information asymmetries that plague cross-border financial transactions. Strong banking systems may shield economies from some future crises as well as serving important development ends. Even with a new financial architecture in place, however, the international financial environment will not be a friendly one for developing countries. Rather than embracing the new architecture as a reliable insurance policy against the risk of a major financial crisis, these governments would be better served by a defensive strategy, particularly while implementing the proposed reforms. Such a strategy would emphasise a shortlist of recurrent vulnerabilities (such as a buildup of short-term debt), a longer-term strategy of making national banking and financial systems more resilient, and a realisation that neither the IFIs, the G-7 nor international bankers can guarantee that an economy will escape the next financial downdraft.[9]

Such a modest and differentiated strategy, accompanied by regional support that is now lacking, would contrast with the global and harmonised vision of the IMF and might be more likely to maintain financial stability. As long-time IMF staff member Jacques Polak contends, the thinness of knowledge about the new environment points to the value of an experimental attitude in governments rather than the 'adoption of new dogma' (in Fischer et al. 1998: 53).

Since the new financial architecture is likely to be incremental, however, emphasising a strategy of realistic and defensive steps should not obscure the larger questions that remain. The need for consideration of regional options to complement the new architecture's globalism has been described: regional clubs dealing with regional financial and monetary externalities may provide a more effective means of monitoring and enforcing necessary reforms. A second lacuna concerns the global financial markets. A common feature in diagnoses of the Asian economic crisis and the global financial turmoil of the past few years is the alarming gap in knowledge of financial market dynamics. Since the autumn of 1998, the uncertainties of financial markets are no longer an issue only for emerging markets. From an early (and continuing) emphasis on changing national policy regimes, attention has shifted to the financial markets themselves. Former US Treasury Secretary Robert Rubin urged the development of measures to reduce the volatility of capital flows produced by dangerously wide swings in confidence: 'What we need are mechanisms to induce appropriate focus on risk during good times; reducing the excesses of booms will reduce the likelihood and severity of busts' (Rubin 1999). That agenda is barely an outline.

Finally, although the IMF forms the institutional core of the new financial architecture, as it did in the old, an architectural alternative is likely to resume a position of prominence that it gave up fifty years ago. During the era of global financial integration before World War I and the failed reconstruction of that system during the 1920s, management of the 'market-led international monetary system' was awarded to central banks and their private financial allies. Financial and monetary diplomacy was theirs, until they were ejected from their central position by war, capital controls and a new 'government-led international monetary system'.[10] As a market-led system has been reconstructed since the 1980s, central banks and their agent for cooperation, the BIS, have assumed a greater role in international financial management. Whether their central position as lenders of last resort and regulators of their banking sectors can be wielded accountably in tandem with the IMF and its political masters is a final and critical issue in architectural design.

Notes

1 Causes and Consequences of the Asian Financial Crisis

1 Thailand's exports had grown in dollar terms by 22 per cent in 1994 and 25 per cent in 1995; in 1996, however, they declined by 2 per cent (Bhanupong 1998: 311).

2 From the viewpoint of individual investors, such herd-like behaviour can be entirely rational. Failing to move quickly when others are withdrawing funds might leave them at best with substantially reduced returns, and at worst with totally worthless assets.

3 In some countries where banks were saddled with large quantities of non-performing loans that weighed heavily on the negative side of their balance sheets, the international financial markets offered an apparent opportunity to make substantial profits, albeit from relatively high-risk investments (such as the Brady bonds issued by Latin American debtors).

4 For instance, some governments introduced an incentive structure that encouraged short-term rather than long-term borrowing, for example Thailand's promotion of the Bangkok International Banking Facility and Korea's maintenance of controls on long-term but not short-term borrowing.

5 The *Economist*, 'The vice of thrift' (21 March 1998), reported a study by J.P. Morgan that showed that returns on capital fell sharply in East Asian economies in the first half of the 1990s, particularly in South Korea, Thailand and Malaysia, and a study by McKinsey that found that capital in Korea was used less than half as productively as capital in Brazil. These studies appear to provide some confirmation for arguments that suggested that the 'Asian miracle' had occurred because of an increase in the volume of resources applied rather than through improvement in total factor productivity in East Asian economies. For a pessimistic assessment of Asia's performance in total factor productivity see Young (1994) and the popularisation of the argument by Krugman (1994).

6 Some also appeared unable to resolve critical issues relating to the supply of public goods, such as infrastructure and education. This was particularly the case in Thailand (see Doner 1992; Doner & Ramsay 1993; Warr 1998).

7 Unlike Thailand and Korea, Indonesia moved quickly to float its currency when it first came under speculative attack. This attempt at pre-emption was insufficient, given the country's combination of political and economic problems, to prevent the currency from going into freefall.

8 In the fundamentalist camp were international financial institutions, the US government and prominent academics such as Paul Krugman (1998a) and Jeffrey Frankel (1998), and a large number of authors associated with right-wing think-tanks in the United States. The panic-stricken camp included most East Asian governments: see especially the speeches of Malaysian Prime Minister Mahathir and Japan's Vice-Minister of Finance for International Affairs, Eisuke Sakakibara. Prominent academic representatives of the panic-stricken camp were Wade and Veneroso (1998a) and Chang et al. (1998).

9 For a representative selection of these arguments see the special issue of the *Cato Journal* (1998, vol. 17, no. 3), especially the article by Charles W. Calomiris (1998). See also Simon, Shultz and Wriston (1998). For an argument that IMF support for the crisis-hit Asian economies did not contribute to moral hazard problems (on the grounds that any such support would inevitably involve conditionality, and speculators *ex ante* could not be sure of what response would come from the international community) see Mussa (1999).

10 'That is, circumstances that are largely beyond the member's control and stem primarily from adverse developments in international capital markets consequent upon developments in other countries' (IMF 1999b).

11 See, for instance, the Australian Treasury assessment of transparency in the Australian economy (Australia 1999).

12 A detailed study suggested that the hedge funds were not a major factor in the currency depreciations of 1997 (Brown, Goetzmann & Park 1997), a conclusion shared by studies conducted by the IMF (see Eichengreen & Mathieson et al. 1998). For a contrary view that highlights the role of hedge funds in speculation against the Hong Kong dollar in 1998 see Yam (1999).

13 For a positive assessment of ASEAN's response to the crisis see Soesastro (1998).

14 The Japanese government is providing 7.5 billion yen in cash for assistance with interest payments and to finance technical assistance, and 360 billion yen in Japanese government notes to guarantee loans by crisis economies.

15 A new grouping of 'systemically significant economies', the G–20, founded at a meeting of G–7 finance ministers in September 1999, includes only three East Asian economies – China, Japan, and Korea.

2 Capital Flows and Crises

1 Special thanks to Gordon de Brouwer and Amanda Thornton for their help in preparing this chapter.

2 The sort of volatility discussed here is not day-by-day or week-by-week 'noise', but big disruptive swings.

3 This is not to take sides in the Krugman debate on whether Singapore's productivity came from more capital or from total factor productivity; the result, in terms of higher living standards, is not in dispute.

4 Foreign direct investment has been the key form of capital inflow for Singapore in its rapid development since the 1970s. Foreign direct investment

accounted for around 50 per cent of net capital inflows in the 1970s and formed the bulk of capital inflows in the 1980s, largely in manufacturing, trade and financial and business services. Direct investment flows surged from 1987 onwards, spurred by Japanese and European investment, particularly in financial and business services and, to a much lesser extent, in electronics manufacturing, reflecting the changes in Singapore's industrial structure and comparative advantage. Foreign direct investment as a proportion of investment accelerated during the late 1980s. That was also the period of the great surge in Singapore's share accumulation index, which captures capital and income gains from shares. Excluding cyclical effects, the incremental capital-output ratio for Singapore fell steadily from the 1970s to the 1990s, which suggests that the marginal efficiency of capital was still rising and investment opportunities were there to be exploited. Moreover, real interest rates were relatively high. During the 1990s, however, real interest rates came down and, in recent years, Singapore's incremental capital-output ratio has started to rise. At the same time, portfolio flows rose substantially, in both an absolute and relative sense.

5 In thirteen of the twenty quarters to mid 1997, the yen-carry trade for yen/baht was profitable (exchange rate changes did not outweigh the interest differential). Equivalent yen/US dollar transactions were profitable in eighteen of the twenty quarters (IMF 1998a: 44).

6 Foreign direct investment from Japan tripled in the decade to 1997, rising from $US22.3 billion in 1986 to $US66.2 billion in 1997. Although the United States and Europe remain important destinations for Japan's foreign direct investment, Asian destinations involved the largest rise, increasing from around 10 per cent of the total in 1986 to 25 per cent in 1997. The rise is most spectacular in foreign direct investment into China, whose share jumped from 1 to almost 9 per cent over the period. Indonesia was another important beneficiary. These flows were very important to the countries concerned: Japanese total foreign direct investment to Korea, Malaysia, the Philippines, Singapore and Thailand accounted for around 46 per cent of total net foreign direct investment to those countries between 1990 and 1995.

7 For example, the index of capital controls calculated by the IMF fell significantly in 1992–94 (see IMF 1997: 242).

8 The usual rule is that diversification should match the capitalisation of equity markets. French and Poterba (1991) point out that at the end of the 1980s, US investors held 94 per cent of their equity wealth in US securities; for Japanese, the figure was 98 per cent. It was higher still for French, Germans and Canadians.

9 For the experience elsewhere, see IMF (1993) and World Bank (1997: 28).

10 Indeed, the constant revisiting of the Feldstein/Horioka result has found less correlation between domestic saving and investment rates over time, implying increasing international capital integration (Fujiki & Kitamura 1995; Ghosh 1995).

11 Some have described this process of fixed exchange rates as 'guarantees', but this misunderstands the nature of the problem. Certainly, investors did not expect the exchange rate to depreciate much, but they knew that depreciations had occurred in the past, and those who had exposures in currencies other than the US dollar (by far the majority: see Goldstein & Hawkins 1998) had continually experienced changes in the relevant exchange rates. But few

of them saw any reason, in a world in which capital flows were putting upward pressure on exchange rates, to take out expensive cover against the possibility of the exchange rate falling sharply.

12 The staunchest supporters of interest rate parity must have had their faith sorely tested by the extraordinary movements of the yen in the 1990s, in a climate of interest rate stability.

13 What of the hedge funds, the butt of both strong attack and spirited defence? It might once have been possible to argue that the funds were playing a useful role as stabilising speculators, buying cheap and selling dear, to help markets find equilibrium values and smooth the flows. That position is no longer tenable, at least as a generalisation. There are enough examples of hedge funds shorting already undervalued currencies, in the hope (assisted by vigorous self-serving market commentary) that the undervaluation can be pushed further. While they may not be big players in the immediate future, now may be the moment to emphasise that any arguments for disclosure of official market positions (reserves and forward positions) apply with equal force to large private players. If fully informed markets work better, we should aim to ensure that markets are fully informed about hedge funds.

3   The Political Economy of the Asian Financial Crisis: Korea and Thailand Compared

1 The authors gratefully acknowledge research grants from the International Center for the Study of East Asian Development (Kitakyushu, Japan) and the Institute on Global Conflict and Cooperation (University of California). We also thank our colleagues at the Graduate School of International Relations and Pacific Studies in the Asian Financial Crisis Reading Group.

2 The IMF's $US17.2 billion package was unveiled in Tokyo on 11 August.

3 The increase in foreign debt, particularly short-term debt, has led a number of analysts to conclude that the central policy failure in the Korean case was the liberalisation of the capital account or, more specifically, a pattern of liberalisation that favoured short-term capital movements over longer-term ones (Chang 1999).

4   The Good, the Bad and the Ugly? Korea, Taiwan and the Asian Financial Crisis

1 The real exchange rate of the Korean won to the dollar in the immediate pre-crisis period was little changed from the rate two years before (World Bank 1998a: Box 1.2, 11). Some sources suggest the won may even have been undervalued at that time. Although no grounds exist to suggest that the won, unlike some South-East Asian currencies, was overvalued, the government's misguided attempt to defend its value in September and October 1997 provided speculators with windfall gains. In contrast, Taipei kept the New Taiwan dollar virtually pegged to the US dollar from 1995 to mid 1997 then, in the face of overwhelming market pressures, allowed it to depreciate in October 1997. Taiwan's depreciation in that month exerted further pressure on the Korean currency.

2　All trade data unless otherwise noted are IMF and Taiwanese government data accessed through the International Economic Data Bank, Australian National University.

3　On the history of the chaebol see Kim (1988), Kim (1997) and Kim (1976).

4　In 1975, for instance, the rate of interest on loans from the National Investment Fund was less than half the rate of inflation (25 per cent in that year).

5　For a contrast between interest rates on policy loans and in the curb market see Cho (1994).

6　In 1996, for instance, the Bank of Korea reported that 69 per cent of facility investments by Korean manufacturing companies was for expansion of production capacity and only 21 per cent was for research and development. The comparable figures for Japanese companies were 44 per cent for production capacity and 43 per cent for research and development and production rationalisation ('Firms focus investments on production capacity', *Korea Herald*, 5 October 1997).

7　In 1980, Korea's GDP shrank by 2.7 per cent. Taiwan's GDP in that year grew by over 7 per cent.

8　Ilhae was President Chun's pen name. Chun's younger brother headed the New Community (Saemaul) Movement and was indicted for embezzlement of its funds. Contributions were also sought for the New Generation Education Foundation and the Heart Foundation, both headed by the president's wife (for details see Rhee 1994).

9　For discussion of the dilemmas governments faced and the consequent constraints on policy options see Leipziger and Petri (1993).

10　Samsung Electronics is the world's single largest producer of DRAMs. LG and Hyundai rank sixth and seventh respectively. Korean companies (Hyundai Heavy Industries, Daewoo Shipbuilding and Heavy Machinery, and Samsung Heavy Industries) were the world's three largest shipbuilders, and by the mid 1990s POSCO vied with Nippon Steel for the title of world's largest steelmaker.

11　In contrast to the Korean dependence on DRAMs, which constitute less than 30 per cent of total worldwide demand for semiconductors, Taiwanese companies produce more higher-value-added devices like EPROMs and ASICs. In some sectors of electronics (motherboards, notebook computers and monitors), however, Taiwanese companies have an even more commanding share of world market than Korean companies do in DRAMs. The crucial difference is that most of those products are made to order for final assemblers or marketers; they are less of a 'commodity' than DRAMs. For further discussion see Kim (1996) and Ernst (1998).

12　In 1995–96, the export price of DRAMs fell by more than 70 per cent and the export price of steel dropped by about 30 per cent.

13　The government maintained ownership of five specialised banks: the Industrial Bank of Korea, the Korea Housing Bank, the National Agricultural Cooperative Federation, the National Federation of Fisheries Cooperatives and the National Livestock Cooperatives Federation.

14　Korea did not operate a formal deposit insurance scheme until 1992, but the unwillingness of the government to allow a bank to fail provided a functional equivalent.

15　In July 1997, the top thirty chaebol owned sixty-four financial subsidiaries (including merchant banks and insurance companies) (OECD 1999: Table 23, 111).

16 Post-crisis (March 1999), the volume of non-performing loans in non-bank financial institutions (including merchant banks) exceeded that in commercial banks, and was more than twice the share of total loans than in the latter (OECD 1999: 91).

17 The government's willingness to come to the aid of the banks contributed to the speculative panic in November 1997 when it was discovered that the government had deposited a substantial portion of the country's foreign exchange reserves with private banks that were facing difficulties in repaying foreign loans.

18 The few modest exceptions included foreign banks and private banks owned by overseas Chinese. Local investors controlled credit cooperatives and a number of insurance and trust companies (see Cheng 1993).

19 Amsden (1992: 84) notes that at the end of the 1980s there were more than twice as many US-trained PhDs in economics in South Korea as in Japan.

20 Kang (1999: 29) cites estimates that the cost of National Assembly and presidential campaigns of 1992 amounted to 5 trillion won ($US5.1 billion), equivalent to 16 per cent of the government's budget. Each candidate in the 1996 National Assembly campaign was estimated to have spent the equivalent of $US1.5 million.

21 Seong Min Yoo (1998) cites a paper by Moon that quoted a warning by Cha Kyung Koo, chairman of the Federation of Korean Industries, that political contributions would be used to retaliate against politicians who supported moves against chaebol. Similar comments were made by Jong Hyon Chey, a former chair of the FKI, and Kyn Hee Lee, chairman of the Samsung grouping.

22 OECD (1999) provides a comprehensive analysis of the reform measures implemented in Korea.

23 'Government meddling, price gaps cloud outlook for "big deals"', *Korea Herald*, 2 October 1999. The Samsung auto plant is of particular political sensitivity for the Kim Dae Jung presidency as it is located in the political stronghold of his predecessor, Kim Young Sam.

24 'Spin-offs from 30 top conglomerates to face internal trading investigation', *Korea Herald*, 15 October 1999.

25 See, for instance, 'Seoul fears chaebol finance arms may use funds to prop up affiliates', *Korea Herald*, 23 July 1999.

5   Indonesia: Reforming the Institutions of Financial Governance?

1 Suharto's resignation is discussed in Forrester and May (1998).

2 Indonesia's monetary policy reflected a long-standing political bias that produced distributional gains for producers of traded goods and subsidised foreign exchange liabilities. See Cole and Slade (1996: 44, 78, 51). The state's institutional structure also supported an emphasis on monetary policy and the form of that emphasis (Root 1996: 98; Hamilton-Hart 1999: 149–57).

3 On the development of some forms of government capacity under Suharto see Anderson (1990: 94–120); on the different characteristics of the Philippine state see Anderson (1998: 192–226) and Hutchcroft (1998).

4 On the contrasting cost–benefit distributions for trade and financial liberalisation, see Helleiner (1994). On incentives for capital account liberalisation and certain types of financial deregulation see Haggard and Maxfield

(1996). On the potential for other types of liberalising reform to be supported by distributional coalitions, see Schamis (1999).

5 When a list of the largest state bank debtors behind in payments was leaked to the press in May 1993, it revealed the names of almost all the known business associates of the Suharto family, as well as other conglomerates that had thrived in the 1980s. Although some denied the accuracy of the report, most commentators consider it substantially correct (Robison 1994: 65–6; Schwarz 1994: 75). On the growth of Indonesian conglomerates in the 1980s see Sato (1994).

6 Indonesia's domestic regulatory capacities will thus have ramifications at the international level because any reform of the international 'financial architecture' will continue to rely on domestic implementation (Kapstein 1994).

7 Fry (1995) provides a review of both theory and evidence that is sympathetic to the pro-liberalisation case.

8 Only $US3 billion of IMF funds were released in the first six months of Indonesia's economic crisis.

9 Large nominal devaluations in the 1950s and 1960s reflected high domestic inflation.

10 Central bank emergency liquidity funds were later converted to equity, a move which was opposed by some parliamentarians on the grounds that it allowed tycoons to escape paying their debts to the government (*Business Times*, 6 January 1999, 9 January 1999).

11 Bank Indonesia liquidity support to BCA in May amounted to around Rp22 trillion (Johnson 1998: 51) and by the end of the year BCA debt to the central bank was Rp48 trillion (*Business Times*, 19 December 1998). By comparison, BCA's 1995 shareholders' equity was Rp1.5 trillion (Bank Central Asia, *Annual Report 1995*).

12 The IMF official statement notes only that conditions in Indonesia are not appropriate, but in press briefings the agencies all cited the Bank Bali scandal as the reason for suspending loans (see 'The situation in Indonesia and the IMF', IMF Press Release, 16 September 1999 [http://www.imf.org/external/ np/vc/1999/091699.HTM]; *Jakarta Post*, 14 September 1999).

13 BII is related to the Sinar Mas group of companies, one of the few Indonesian conglomerates to weather the economic crisis reasonably well.

14 The two men were Sofjan Wanandi and Arifin Panigoro, both supporters of opposition political groups. Earlier, Habibie was recorded asking the attorney-general to place pressure in a government corruption case against them (see note 29).

15 According to IBRA, Danamon's former shareholders agreed to assume the bank's non-performing loans to related parties, and agreed that the loans would be settled privately. The bank's other bad loans would be transferred to IBRA's Asset Management Unit (*Business Times*, 5 March 1999).

16 For example, IBRA reportedly now owns 44 per cent of Astra International, which has $US2 billion in foreign debt.

17 The sources for this paragraph are *Far Eastern Economic Review*, 10 June 1999: 91; *Jakarta Post*, 29 June 1999: 1; *Kapital*, 25, 12 July 1999; and personal interviews carried out in Jakarta in June and July 1999.

18 Bank Danamon, for example, the largest listed bank to be nationalised and put under IBRA management, was an active counter on the exchange as of August 1999 even though the listed portion of its stock represents an equity share of 0.25–1.5 per cent in the bank and the Jakarta Stock Exchange's

main publication, *JSX Statistics*, stopped providing data on trade in Danamon shares after the bank was nationalised.

19 The commitment to sell the nationalised banks by the end of 1999 appears to be the result of IMF pressure (*Business Times,* 21 July 1999).

20 On the origins and implications of the economic strength but political marginalisation of ethnic Chinese in Indonesia see Mackie (1991), Robison (1992) and T. Shiraishi (1997).

21 Bank Indonesia successfully resisted the attempt to remove its responsibility for bank regulation.

22 Hence the presence of a foreign consultant given the task of drawing up options for inflation targeting by the central bank seems to reflect the consultant's own previous experience (in Latin America) rather than any demonstrable need for an inflation targeting policy in Indonesia.

23 The inflationary consequences of central bank credits to domestic banks in late 1997 and early 1998 were severe but short-lived. In any case, withholding liquidity in the context of a loss of depositor confidence is not an obviously superior policy choice.

24 On HIID see Mason (1986); on the government's use of consultants and openness to outside influence see Winters (1996: 68, 148, 168), Higgins (1957: 40–5) and MacIntyre (1995).

25 This paragraph on Bapindo is drawn from Hamilton-Hart (1999: 135–47).

26 At one end of the spectrum are culturalist and Foucaldian analyses (for example, Mitchell 1999); at the other end are neo-institutionalist reformulations of principal-agent theory (for example, Solnick 1998).

27 Corruption, patrimonialism and bureaucratic incapacity have not been constant in the Indonesian state and its colonial predecessor, which was in many ways a highly organised bureaucratic state, but these traits have often been pronounced (Willner 1970; Smith 1971; Lev 1972; Sutherland 1979; McVey 1977). Along with increased state strength in the early years of the Suharto regime (Anderson 1990: 94–120), patrimonial systems were centralised and adapted to capitalist development rather than displaced (Robison 1986; MacIntyre 1993).

28 On bapakism see Feith (1962: 127) and Anderson (1972: 236). On the persistence of these norms in the New Order see S. Shiraishi (1997) and Hamilton-Hart (1999: 112–15).

29 The attorney-general eventually admitted that it was his voice on the recording (*Business Times,* 10 March 1999).

30 The continuity is suggested by a recent comment on 'the next batch of technocrats [who are] already positioning themselves' (Hendro Sangkoyo 1999: 176–7).

31 The inability of technocratic outsiders to eliminate abuses is not peculiar to Indonesia. Wedel's (1998) study of aid and 'technical assistance' to Eastern Europe and Russia provides evidence of how outsiders can become enmeshed in, and indeed feed, domestic systems of corruption and patronage.

6 Political Impediments to Far-reaching Banking Reforms in Japan: Implications for Asia

1 The author thanks Natasha Hamilton-Hart, Gregory Noble, Daniel Okimoto, John Ravenhill, Yves Tiberghien and Tetsuro Toya for helpful suggestions.

2 For example, in 1996 Japan absorbed 27.1 per cent of Indonesia's exports, 14 per cent of Malaysia's exports, 8.3 per cent of Singapore's exports, 18 per cent of Thailand's exports and 18.6 per cent of total exports from the Philippines.

3 Japan is the largest provider of ODA in the world.

4 A former Japanese Vice-Minister for International Finance serves as president of the ADB.

5 Japan's central bank exercised its powers under MOF supervision until 1 April 1998, when revisions in the Bank of Japan Law gave it greater legal autonomy and responsibility for monetary policy. In June 1998, inspection and supervisory functions in private finance were transferred from the MOF to a newly created Financial Supervisory Agency.

6 The number of former MOF officials in the Diet peaked in 1980 at thirty-two, but ranged between twenty-six and thirty in the 1990s. At the time of writing, prominent posts occupied by former MOF officials include Finance Minister, Minister for Financial Reconstruction and chairman of the LDP Policy Affairs Research Council.

7 The pervasiveness of these ties to the Diet reflects the centrality of politics in the passage of the annual budget, compiled by the MOF.

8 In the words of a former director-general of the Banking Bureau, '[obtaining] cooperation is preferential to legislating [change]' (*horitsu o tsukuru yori, kyoryoku mashi da*).

9 For a detailed examination of each of the MOF's relational networks across time, see Amyx (1998).

10 When government bonds had to be issued for the first time (in 1965), they were regarded as government investment bonds rather than deficit bonds to cover revenue shortfalls. In principle, the government only issued investment or 'construction bonds' to fund projects expected to pay for themselves over time. Legislative approval, renewed annually, was necessary for further government bond issues, signalling the government's desire to check the issue of such bonds. Only with the issue of deficit bonds after the oil shocks and the shift to slowed growth was this balanced budget principle clearly in jeopardy. For more on the historical roots of the balanced budget principle, see Ohkawa and Ikeda (1993).

11 For more on the main bank system, see Sheard (1985), Aoki and Patrick (1994) and Scher (1997).

12 Japan's Deposit Insurance Corporation lacked sufficient funds to bail out even a single regional bank.

13 In the presence of deposit insurance, stockholders and management have virtually nothing to lose in seeking out high-risk high-return investment opportunities when banks face large losses and stockholder equity nears zero or becomes negative. If the risky returns pay off, management and stockholders both win; if not, they have suffered no extra losses because deposits are guaranteed and stockholders are not liable for bank debts. For a more in-depth discussion, see Scott and Weingast (1992).

14 MOF officials were aware by 1993, for example, that certain banks were manipulating accounts through the transfer of bad loans to paper companies but permitted such practices to continue (see 'How ministry gambled in case of NCB', *Daily Yomiuri On-Line*, http://www.yomiuri.co.jp/newse/0729cr20.htm, 29 July 1999).

15 While the LDP was the greatest beneficiary of the nokyo vote, every major party in the 1996 lower house election won at least 50 per cent of its seats in non-heavily urban districts where the nokyo are strongest (*Nihon Keizai Shimbun*, 22 October 1996). Thus, even non-LDP parties had disincentives to pursuing aggressive recovery of delinquent loans.

16 Any RTC-like institution would have faced significant barriers to the collection of collateral for non-performing loans. Most collateral involved land and land values have been frozen at low levels, limiting the marketability of those assets.

17 Even more capital flowed to the region from the United States and Europe in this period, however, indicating that low Japanese interest rates and the snail-like pace of Japanese financial system reform were among many factors encouraging a global trend of investment in Asia.

18 The impact of the yen was more mixed for countries such as Thailand and Indonesia, whose low value added goods complemented rather than competed with Japanese exports.

19 In 1996, for example, the disparity in per capita spending between certain rural and urban districts was greater than twenty to one.

20 Arguably, either policy choice – which would have represented a major break with entrenched patterns – would have signalled a genuine government commitment to reforms.Thus, such policy choices might have boosted consumer confidence and helped reverse the trend of depressed demand. I am grateful to Gregory Noble for this observation.

21 Japan's financial year 1998 central government deficit was 10 per cent of GDP.

22 Calculation based on figures provided in Tachi (1995: 32).

23 From 1987 to 1996, Japan's largest banks earned an average of only 1.8 per cent return on equity, while those in the United States earned 8.4 per cent (*Economist*, 24 January 1998: 16).

24 Under the Hashimoto administration (January 1996–July 1998), plans for the privatisation of postal savings moved ahead, on the back of plans for large-scale financial system reform. But with the instalment of the Obuchi administration in July 1998, privatisation was dropped from the agenda. Obuchi and his first chief cabinet secretary Nonaka are among the most powerful LDP politicians representing MPT interests in the Diet.

25 The process of creating the FSA differed significantly from past instances in which the bureaucracy itself proposed the creation of new administrative structures. The decision to establish the FSA was made by elected officials and opposed by MOF bureaucrats.

26 According to IMF data, Japan's public debt in 1999 had reached 130 per cent of GDP.

27 In the absence of such clear effects on the real economy, the use of public funds was naturally interpreted to mean a tax hike in the future.

28 A key factor in the FSA's ability to separate itself from the MOF and regulate with greater independence has been the agency's political leadership. Overseen by the Minister of Financial Reconstruction, the FSA's status is more elevated than that of the Fair Trade Commission, long criticised for its lack of independence. The October 1998 reforms also established a Financial Reconstruction Commission to oversee the FSA, assume responsibility for decisions surrounding the injection of public funds and supervise the Deposit Insurance Corporation.

29 Even without the recall of loans, however, yen depreciation brought a decline in the dollar value of loans extended by Japanese banks to the region. In April 1995, the yen traded at ¥80 to the dollar; in 1998 it approached ¥150 to the dollar.

30 The unwillingness of Japanese banks to accept reductions or temporary suspensions of interest payments, however, is more puzzling and difficult to explain.

31 Although there were numerous Asian nations selling larger quantities of steel in the United States at extremely low prices in 1999, Japan was the primary target of US criticism.

32 Finance Minister Kiichi Miyazawa has made it no secret that the government hopes to establish an international guarantee institution focused primarily on Asian countries (see, for example, 'Statement' 1998).

33 Withdrawal from overseas operations is generally part of a larger restructuring plan banks must undertake in order to receive such funds and stabilise their fiscal positions.

34 'Beyond the Asian crisis', speech by Kiichi Miyazawa on the occasion of the APEC Finance Ministers Meeting in Langkawi, Malaysia, on 15 May 1999 (http://www.mof.go.jp/english/if/e1b068.htm). Further government-level responses of note include measures taken by MITI to provide direct subsidies to Japanese companies operating in ASEAN, in an attempt to decrease the number of lay-offs of locally hired workers (Kohno 1999).

35 In February 1999, a new Japanese government taskforce was established to draw up plans for such a fund in time for the G-8 global powers meeting in Tokyo in 2000 (Cornell 1999).

36 While the stage appears set for the sale of the nationalised Long-Term Credit Bank to a US consortium of financiers, conditions for the sale suggest that the government has not grappled fully with the problem of letting questionable borrowers be cut off from funds. The purchasers of the LTCB have pledged to maintain lending relations with all borrowers for a fixed period.

37 Of the imports Japan has absorbed, a large portion has always been from Japanese manufacturers in the region.

7 Dangers and Opportunities: The Implications of the Asian Financial Crisis for China

1 I would like to thank participants of the Melbourne conference for their comments and questions. I have especially benefited from written comments by Gregory Noble, John Ravenhill and Stephan Haggard. I take sole responsibility for any remaining mistakes.

2 According to one informed source, 'every year at least US$20 billion flow out of the country unrecorded' (*Business Times*, 24 July 1998: 9). Chinese companies funnel much of the foreign currencies they retain through bank transfers to the United States, skirting Chinese capital restrictions to do so (*Wall Street Journal*, 30 March 1998: A1). It is important to note that the problem of capital flight occurred even before the Asian financial crisis, as a result of unsafe property rights, fraud and corruption in China.

3 It is worth noting that some of the foreign investment in China is round-tripping capital that originated in China. In light of that, the discrepancy in

China's actual foreign currency reserve may be less significant than it appears.

4 In December 1998, the standing committee of the National People's Congress passed a supplement to the Criminal Law, imposing criminal penalties (including life sentences) on illegal activities in the realm of foreign exchange transactions.

5 In 1998, PRC exports to Indonesia went down 44 per cent, to South Korea 32 per cent, to Thailand 24.2 per cent and to Malaysia 17.1 per cent (US–China Business Council).

6 Domestic savings will not be able to provide sufficient funds, and will have to be complemented by international bonds (Graham & Liu 2000).

7 Between the beginning of 1998 and early 1999, the PBC slashed short-term interest rate by a total of 225 base points (Leung 1999).

8 The Bank of China said in July 1998 that it would increase 25 billion yuan worth of new loans to promote exports (*South China Morning Post*, 6 July 1998: 3; China News Service (CNS), 21 October 1998). The government has also increased export tax rebates in more than ten industries, benefiting many large companies (*Renmin Ribao*, 23 February 1998: 9; *People's Daily*, 17 August 1998: 10).

9 As usual, China's official statistics are almost certainly too optimistic. According to *Barclays Economic Review* (1998), China's growth rate for 1998 was 6.5 per cent.

10 This is an estimate by Hu Angang (*Washington Post*, 20 June 1998: A13). According to another report, China's leading economists and sociologists forecast that 11 million people will join the job-seeking army (*Zhongguo Maoyi Bao*, 7 January 1998).

11 Hong Kong citizens recognise their dependence on China. According to a well-known Hong Kong commentator, 'If in the run-up to the handover Hong Kong citizens were eager about erecting barriers against "interference" from Beijing, a radically different mind-set reigns today' (*South China Morning Post*, 1 July 1998: 6).

12 In this context, it is interesting to note that the Chinese government has been very sensitive to any political gains by Taiwan. In April 1998, when the Taiwan government proposed that both sides of the Taiwan Straits join forces to study ways to stabilise the regional crisis, China immediately pointed out that Taiwan does not have equal status with China. The Chinese government warned Taiwan not to take advantage of the crisis to try to improve its international status (*Straits Times*, 8 April 1998: 1).

13 By late 1999, more than two years after the onset of the Asian financial crisis, the Chinese government had become less vocal about its commitment to the 'no devaluation' pledge (Saywell 1999).

14 The Chinese government has also criticised the United States for not pressing Japan hard enough to prevent the depreciation of the yen (*Washington Post*, 21 June 1998: C01).

15 A recent example is the case of Xinguoda Futures Co. Top management took investors' money and fled, prompting investors to stage protests in central Beijing (*Washington Post*, 8 August 1998: A18).

16 For instance, the World Bank plans to help China in this regard (*South China Morning Post*, 11 April 1998: 1).

17 This was also a central theme of discussion during the National People's Congress (NPC) meeting in March (*People's Daily*, 17 March 1998).

18 Whether the new structure will actually function like the Federal Reserve system in the United States is, of course, an entirely different question.

19 They account for 90 per cent of the banking system's total loans, deposits and assets (Kazuhiko 1998: 84). These write-offs are quite insignificant given the enormous bad debts of Chinese banks, but they are a step in the right direction.

20 GITIC was closed in October 1998, when it had accumulated $US1.95 billion in foreign debt and failed to make interest payments on $US200 million of bonds. In January 1999, the superior court of Guangdong province declared the company bankrupt. The government also removed twelve futures companies from the market for engaging in illegal operations overseas, providing fake auditing materials, failing to meet registered capital requirements and other irresponsible behaviour.

21 In September 1998 the head of CSRC signed memoranda with Jiangsu, Shanghai and Anhui, which marked a transition for local China securities supervision agencies to vertical administration by the CSRC.

22 The decline of SOEs is somewhat less dramatic according to data used in Steinfeld (1998: 13) and Lardy (1998a: 25–6).

23 The net losses were 278 million yuan in 1996, 403 million yuan in 1997 and 82.5 million yuan in 1998 (*China Statistical Yearbook*, 1998; *Zongguo Tongji Zhaiyao*, 1999).

24 For a discussion of the predominance of policy lending see Lardy (1998a: 83–92).

25 As Steinfeld (1988) points out, this is far more important than any restructuring of ownership.

26 According to one estimate, there are 22–33 million workers 'off post' (Qiq Zeqi & Zheng Yongnian 1998: 227–47).

27 For instance, the government has decided to cut 1.1 million railway jobs and close 22 000 small coalmines (*Guardian*, 25 August 1998: 22). An estimated 12 million people lost their jobs in 1997 and 13 million more were expected to be laid off in 1998 (*Washington Post*, 20 June 1998: A13).

28 For instance, in March 1997, workers at Nanchong's largest silk factory took their manager hostage and paraded him through town, demanding back pay. Other workers joined in. In the end 20 000 people besieged the city hall for thirty hours (*Far Eastern Economic Review*, 26 June 1997). In Chongqing, according to the city's academy of social sciences, organised petitions and demonstrations occurred more than a hundred times in 1997 (*Washington Post*, 20 June 1998: A13).

29 As scholars of the politics of economic adjustment are careful to point out, the impact of social conflicts is limited by collective action problems and by the ambiguity of groups' policy interests (Nelson 1992; Haggard & Kaufman 1992).

30 In this discussion, the concept of the state refers to party (Chinese Communist Party) and government organisations at both the central and local levels. For a detailed discussion of the Chinese political system, formal and informal, see Lieberthal (1995: chs 6, 7).

31 The top leadership can be seen as having 'encompassing interest', in contrast to narrow group interests (Olson 1982).

32 As of 1997, SOE assets accounted for 90 per cent of the total assets in Qing Hai, but only 29 per cent in Guangdong (calculated from *China Statistical Yearbook*, 1998).

33 For a discussion of the decline of organised dependence, monitoring capacity and sanctioning capacity in China in the reform era, see Walder (1994). Although Walder's focus is on state–society relations, I find it useful to understand the changing relationship between the central and local governments.

34 In 1997, the government further increased the share of central government taxes in the financial sector (*People's Daily*, 5 January 1998: 10).

35 Huang Yasheng argues that throughout the reform era economic decentralisation has been accompanied by the strengthening of China's unitary political system. Institutional constraints force local governments to surrender revenues and curb demands for inflation (Huang 1996b).

36 There is a lot of information on the PLA's business activities (for example, Cheung 1996; Tanzer 1997; Mulvenon 1998).

37 This is what Miles Kahler calls the 'orthodox paradox' (Kahler 1990: 55).

38 Conventional wisdom views decentralisation of power as consistent with economic liberalisation and political democratisation (see, for example, Ter-Minassian 1997: 36–9). The US government also subscribes to this claim. For instance, the USAID actively promotes decentralisation in the former communist states of Eastern Europe (USAID 1997). Increasingly, scholars are challenging this wisdom. Empirical research demonstrates a mixed relationship between decentralisation and development (Zhang & Zou 1998: 221–40; Woller & Phillips 1998: 139–48).

8   The International Monetary Fund in the Wake of the Asian Crisis

1 This is a revised version of a paper prepared for the Monash University/ Australian National University Conference on Responses to the Asian Crisis, Melbourne, 17–18 December 1998. I am grateful to conference participants, especially Stephen Grenville and Benjamin Cohen, for helpful comments, and to the conference organisers for guidance regarding revisions. Financial support was provided by the Ford Foundation through the Berkeley Project on International Financial Architecture. This chapter draws in part on my book (1999a).

2 As national central banks have traditionally done for domestic financial intermediaries that are worth more in continued business than wound up. See, for example, the Federal Reserve's handling of long-term capital or even the Bank of England's management of the first Barings crisis (Eichengreen 1999a).

3 Two analyses of how much monetary autonomy countries with fixed exchange rates enjoyed in the past are Giovannini (1993) and Eichengreen and Flandreau (1996).

4 Smooth fiscal adjustment now can be more confidence-inspiring, in other words, than painful fiscal adjustment later (see Alesina, Perotti & Tavares 1998). Predictably, I prefer my formulation of their argument (Eichengreen 1998).

5 In addition, standing committees of creditors should be created to provide better communication between lenders and borrowers, jump-starting negotiations and diminishing the information asymmetries that encourage the two sides to fight a protracted war of attrition. The IMF could lend to countries in arrears on their external debts as long as the recipients are making a seri-

ous adjustment effort and are engaged in good-faith negotiations with creditors, providing the equivalent of the 'debtor in possession' finance available to US corporations under Chapter 11 of the US bankruptcy code. When the problem is defaulted corporate and bank debts, the solution lies not in unrealistic designs for an international bankruptcy court but in strengthening national bankruptcy statutes, reinforcing the independence of the judicial system administering them, and harmonising those laws across countries.

6 When these conditions do not hold, the policy will delay crisis resolution, not expedite it. This is why lending into arrears should be considered on a case-by-case basis.

7 For example, Dooley (1997) and Krugman (1998a). The point applies not just to the Asian crisis. Post-mortems on the 1992 EMS and 1995 Mexican crises, although focusing on other factors as the main source of financial difficulties, also point to the weakness of banking systems as an important reason why governments were unable or unwilling to defend their currencies when they came under attack (see, for example, Goldstein & Calvo 1996).

8 Thus, we could imagine the IMF withholding its approval of a capital import tax on these grounds in the case of a country that had not succeeded in meeting the Basle Capital Standards.

9 Taming the Phoenix? Monetary Governance after the Crisis

1 This chapter benefited from discussion at the Conference on the Asian Financial Crisis as well as the thoughtful comments of David Andrews, Michael Gordon, David McKay, Greg Noble and John Ravenhill. The assistance of Ben Pettit is also gratefully acknowledged.

2 The earliest example I can find of this change of tone was a column by *Financial Times* commentator Martin Wolf in March 1998. Ordinarily a firm champion of free markets, Wolf reluctantly concluded: 'After the crisis, the question can no longer be whether these flows should be regulated in some way. It can only be how' (Wolf 1998). Ten months later, at the annual World Economic Forum in Davos, Switzerland – always a useful means of tracking authoritative public- and private-sector opinion – it was clear that unrestricted capital mobility was no longer much in favour (see, for example, *New York Times*, 29 January 1999: C1).

3 The discussion in this section is based on arguments presented at greater length in Cohen (1998a).

4 In Krugman's words, in the confidence game economic policy 'must cater to the perceptions, the prejudices, the whims of the market. Or, rather, one must cater to what one *hopes* will be the perceptions of the market ... [Policy becomes] an exercise in amateur psychology' (1999: 113, original emphasis).

5 For a bitter post mortem, see Culp et al. (1999). Culp et al. dismiss the risk at the time of a rush to buy dollars as a 'nightmare scenario', suggesting that opposition to an Indonesian currency board, led by the US Treasury and the IMF, was motivated not by 'the fear that it would not have worked but rather that it would have worked too well – viz., saving Indonesia and postponing the end of the Suharto regime' (1999: 61, 64). This seems a bit strong in view of Washington's traditional support of Suharto.

6 A notable exception was the head of the Hong Kong Monetary Authority, Joseph Yam, who in early 1999 made a spirited plea for 'our own Asian currency' to reduce the region's vulnerability to speculative attack (quoted in *Financial Times*, 6 January 1999).

7 Perhaps most ambitious was EMEAP (Executive Meeting of East Asia and Pacific Central Banks), a self-described 'vehicle for regional cooperation among central banks' encompassing Australia, China, Hong Kong, Indonesia, Japan, Malaysia, New Zealand, the Philippines, Singapore, South Korea and Thailand. Other examples include SEACEN (South-East Asian Central Banks) and SEANZA (South-East Asia, New Zealand and Australia), both of which provide for regular meetings of central bank officials as well as various training programs.

8 Privately, Washington feared a loss of political influence in the region since the AMF, if implemented, would obviously have been dominated by Tokyo. In economic terms, Washington's response to the AMF proposal was remarkably reminiscent of a similar episode a quarter-century earlier, when an agreement to create a Financial Support Fund in the OECD (based in Paris) was torpedoed by the US government on almost identical grounds (Cohen 1998b).

9 In October 1998, for example, Finance Minister Kiichi Miyazawa offered $US30 billion in fresh financial aid for Asia in a plan soon labelled the 'New Miyazawa initiative', and two months later made it clear that Japan intended to revive its AMF proposal when the time seemed right (*Financial Times*, 16 December 1998).

10 Special Functions Minister Diam Zainuddin, as quoted in Wade and Veneroso (1998b: 20).

11 For an overview of recent debate, compare the contrasting views of Hale (1998) and Wade and Veneroso (1998b). A balanced analysis is provided by Cooper (1999).

12 Article VI, Sections 1 and 3 of the Articles of Agreement of the IMF.

13 'Post-war currency policy', a British Treasury memo dated September 1941, reprinted in Moggridge (1980: 31). For "'ole' read 'hole' – a handy place to hide money.

14 'Plan for an international currency (or clearing) union', January 1942, reprinted in Moggridge (1980: 129–30).

15 For more on Keynes' views and how they relate to the current crisis, see Cassidy (1998) and Kirshner (1999).

16 Interim Committee Communique, 28 April 1997: para. 7. Under the plan, two Articles were to be amended: Article I, where 'orderly liberalisation of capital' would be added to the list of the IMF's formal purposes; and Article VIII, which would give the IMF the same jurisdiction over the capital account of its members as it already has over the current account. The language would require countries to commit themselves to capital liberalisation as a goal.

17 For a statement of the same point, see Cohen (1965). In my bolder and more dogmatic youth, I was even willing to raise this observation to the status of an economic law – what I ambitiously labelled the Iron Law of Economic Controls: 'to be effective, controls must reproduce at a rate faster than that at which means are found for avoiding them' (Cohen 1965: 174). Today I am less inclined to be quite so categorical.

18 Admittedly, the distinction between FDI-like flows and more impatient investment categories may be easier to draw in principle than in practice. For some discussion of the practical difficulties involved, see Maxfield (1998).

10   The Vagaries of Debt: Indonesia and Korea

1 The following is partly based on official documents, press reports and confidential interviews.
2 I have modified the percentages for Indonesia to match the detailed debt data given above; they vary slightly from the percentages derived from the J.P. Morgan figure. The rough comparison highlights the dramatic difference between the external debt structure of the three countries.
3 When Korea was negotiating for OECD membership, it asked to become a member of the Paris Club but was refused. In fact, the term 'member' was not used formally until Russia was allowed to join in October 1997.

11   The New International Financial Architecture and its Limits

1 On one recent set of OECD cases, the Scandinavian economies, see Drees and Pazarbasioglu (1998).
2 On this distinction, see Noland et al. (1998: 3–29) and CEPR (1998: 5–14). 'Fundamentalists' is a term used in Noland et al.
3 A useful summary of the progress made (from the point of view of the IFIs) is given at 'Progress in strengthening the architecture of the international financial system' (8 October 1999); http://www.imf.org/external/np/exr/facts/arcguide.htm (with additional links).
4 By late 1999, forty-seven governments were subscribers to the SDDS.
5 The speaker is John Crow, chair of the external evaluation team. The complete report, *External Evaluation of IMF Surveillance*, is available at www.imf.org. The four countries examined closely were the Czech Republic, Brazil, Thailand and Korea (see IMF 1999d: Part 3, 67–70).
6 The Core Principles are reproduced in IMF (1998d: 52–71).
7 Opposing views on moving toward a bankruptcy model are given by Sachs (1998b) and Eichengreen and Portes (1995).
8 See the contributions to Fischer et al. (1998). As Krugman declares, 'As long as capital flows freely, nations will be vulnerable to self-fulfilling speculative attacks and policy-makers will be forced to play the confidence game. And so we come to the question of whether capital should really be allowed to flow so freely' (Krugman 1998b: 25; see also Krugman 1998c; Radelet & Sachs 1998b).
9 For a different version of a strategy of self-reliance, see Feldstein (1999).
10 The terms 'market-led' and 'government-led' international monetary system are drawn from Padoa-Schioppa and Saccomanni (1994).

Bibliography

Adams, Charles, Donald J. Mathieson, Garry Schinasi & Bankim Chadha (1998), *International Capital Markets: Developments, Prospects and Key Policy Issues* (Washington DC: International Monetary Fund).

Aditjondro, G. (1998), 'A new regime, a more consolidated oligarchy and a deeply divided anti-Soeharto movement' in G. Forrester & R.J. May (eds), *The Fall of Soeharto* (Bathurst, NSW: Crawford House Publishing).

AFP (1998), Paris Club (23 September).

Alesina, Alberto, Roberto Perotti & Jose Tavares (1998), 'The political economy of fiscal adjustments', *Brookings Papers on Economic Activity*, 1: 197–248.

Altbach, Eric (1997), 'The Asian Monetary Fund proposal: a case study of Japanese regional leadership', *JEI Report*, 47A (December).

Amsden, Alice H. (1992), 'The South Korea economy: is business-led growth working?' in Donald N. Clark (ed.), *Korea Briefing, 1992* (Boulder, Colo.: Westview).

Amyx, Jennifer (1998), 'Banking policy breakdown and the declining institutional effectiveness of Japan's Ministry of Finance', PhD dissertation (Stanford, Calif.: Stanford University [UMI]).

Anderson, B. (1972), *Java in a Time of Revolution: Occupation and Resistance 1944–1946* (Ithaca, NY: Cornell University Press).

Anderson, B. (1990), *Language and Power: Exploring Political Cultures in Indonesia* (Ithaca, NY: Cornell University Press).

Anderson, B. (1998), *The Spectre of Comparisons: Nationalism, Southeast Asia and the World* (London: Verso).

Aoki, Masahiko & Hugh Patrick (1994), *The Japanese Main Bank System* (New York: Oxford University Press).

Arndt, H.W. (1984), *The Indonesian Economy: Collected Papers* (Singapore: Chopmen Publishers).

Arndt, H.W. & N. Suwidjana (1982), 'The Jakarta dollar market', *Bulletin of Indonesian Economic Studies*, 18(2): 35–64.

Athukorala, Prema-chandra (1999), 'The Malaysian experiment' (Canberra: Paper presented to a Conference on Reform and Recovery in East Asia: The Role of the State and Economic Enterprise, Australian National University).

Australia, Commonwealth of, Department of the Treasury (1999), 'Making transparency transparent: an Australian assessment' (Canberra: Department of the Treasury, 25 March); http://www.treasury.gov.au/publications/MakingTransparencyTransparent-AnAustralianAssessment/download/full.pdf.

Bagehot, W. (1880), *Economic Studies* (London: Longman Green).

Bank Indonesia (1999a), *Laporan Tahunan 1998/99* (Jakarta: Bank Indonesia).

Bank Indonesia (1999b), *Statistik Ekonomi Keuangan Indonesia*, May (Jakarta: Bank Indonesia).

Barclays Economic Review (1998), 'International economy: Asia', 4th quarter.

Basle Committee on Banking Supervision (1988), 'International convergence of capital measurement and capital standards' (Basle: Basle Committee on Banking Supervision, July).

Basle Committee on Banking Supervision (1999), 'A new capital adequacy framework' (Basle: Basle Committee on Banking Supervision, June).

Bergsten, C. Fred (1998a), 'Missed opportunity', *International Economy*, 12(6): 26–7.

Bergsten, C. Fred (1998b), 'Reviving the Asian Monetary Fund', *International Economics Policy Briefs*, 98–8 (Washington DC: Institute for International Economics).

Bhagwati, Jagdish (1998a), 'The capital myth: the difference between trade in widgets and dollars', *Foreign Affairs*, 77(3): 7–12.

Bhagwati, Jagdish (1998b), 'Free thinker: free-trader explains why he likes capital controls', *Far Eastern Economic Review*, 15 October: 14.

Bhanupong, N. (1998), 'Economic crises and debt-inflation episodes in Thailand', *ASEAN Economic Bulletin*, 15(3): 301–18.

BIS (Bank for International Settlements) (1998a), *68th Annual Report* (Basle: BIS, June).

BIS (Bank for International Settlements) (1998b), *International Banking and Financial Market Developments* (Basle: BIS, August).

Bittermann, Henry (1973), *The Refunding of International Debt* (Durham, NC: Duke University Press).

Bordo, Michael & Barry Eichengreen (1999), 'Is our current international economic environment unusually crisis-prone?' (Sydney: Reserve Bank of Australia, paper for Conference on Capital Flows and the International Financial System, September).

Borensztein, Eduardo & Jong-Wha Lee (1999), 'Credit allocation and financial crisis in Korea' (Washington DC: International Monetary Fund, Research Department Working Paper WP/99/20).

Borsuk, Richard (1998), 'World Bank tries to explain Indonesian economic crisis', *Wall Street Journal*, 29 July.

Boyd, Tony (1998), 'Kamikaze looms at the end of a lost decade', *Australian Financial Review*, 22 December.

Brittan, Samuel (1998), 'Exchange controls: the economic trap', *Financial Times*, 1 October.

Brown, Gordon (1998), Statement at the Joint Annual Discussion (Washington DC: International Monetary Fund, World Bank Group, Board of Governors Annual Meeting).

Brown, Stephen J., William N. Goetzmann & James Park (1997), 'Hedge funds and the Asian currency crisis of 1997' (Cambridge, Mass.: National Bureau of Economic Research, Working Paper No. 6427, February).

Bruno, Michael & Stanley Fischer (1990), 'Senior age, operating rules and the
    high inflation trap', *Quarterly Journal of Economics*, CV: 353–74.
Buira, Ariel (1999), *An Alternative Approach to Financial Crises* (Princeton, NJ:
    Essays in International Finance No. 212, International Finance Section,
    Department of Economics, Princeton University).
Calder, Kent E. (1988), *Crisis and Compensation: Public Policy and Political Stability
    in Japan, 1949–1986* (Princeton, NJ: Princeton University Press).
Calomiris, Charles W. (1998), 'The IMF's imprudent role as lender of last
    resort', *Cato Journal*, 17(3); available on the web at http://www.cato.org.
Calvo, G.A. & M. Goldstein (eds) (1996), *Private Capital Flows to Emerging Markets
    after the Mexican Crisis* (Washington DC: Institute for International
    Economics).
Camdessus, Michel (1998a), Capital account liberalization and the role of the
    Fund (Washington DC: Remarks to the IMF Seminar on Capital Account
    Liberalization, 9 March).
Camdessus, Michel (1998b), 'Managing director's opening address, Board of
    Governors of the IMF, Washington DC, 6 October 1998', *IMF Survey*, 19
    October 1998.
Carey, J. & M. Shugart (1995), 'Incentives to cultivate a personal vote: a rank
    ordering of electoral formulas', *Electoral Studies*, 14(4): 417–39.
Cassidy, John (1998), 'The new world disorder', *New Yorker*, 26 October:
    198–207.
Castellano, Marc (1999), 'Japanese foreign aid: a lifesaver for East Asia?', *Japan
    Economic Institute Report*, 6A (12 February): 1–11.
Central Bank of China (Zhongyang Yinhang) (1996), *Zhonghua Minguo Taiwan
    Diqu Gongminying Qiye Zijin Zhuangkuang Diaocha Jieguo Baogao (Minguo 84
    Nian* (Report on the results of a survey of the financial situtation of public
    and private enterprises in Taiwan Area, Republic of China (1995)).
Central Bank of China (Zhongyang Yinhang) (1997), *Benguo Yinhang Yingyun
    Jixiao Jibao* (Quarterly report on the operational results of domestic banks),
    4th quarter.
CEPD (Council for Economic Planning and Development), Executive Yuan,
    Republic of China, *Taiwan Statistical Data Book* (Taipei: annual).
CEPR (Centre for Economic Policy Research) (1998), *Financial Crises and Asia*
    (London: CEPR).
Chang, Ha-Joon (1999), 'The hazard of moral hazard: untangling the Asian cri-
    sis' (New York: Paper presented to the American Economic Association
    Annual Meeting, 3–6 January).
Chang, Ha-Joon, Hong-Jae Park & Chul Gyue Yoo (1998), 'Interpreting the
    Korean crisis: financial liberalisation, industrial policy and corporate gover-
    nance', *Cambridge Journal of Economics*, 22(6): 735–46.
Chant, J. & M. Pangestu (1994), 'An assessment of financial reform in Indonesia,
    1983–90' in J. Caprio, I. Atiyas & J. Hanson (eds), *Financial Reform: Theory
    and Experience* (Cambridge: Cambridge University Press).
Chaudry, K.A. (1989), 'The price of wealth: business and state in labor remit-
    tance and oil economies', *International Organization*, 43(1): 101–45.
Chen, Mingtong (1995), *Paixi zhengzhi yu Taiwan zhengzhi bianqian* (Factional
    politics and the political transformation of Taiwan) (Taipei: Yuedan).
Cheng, Tun-jen (1989), 'Democratizing the quasi-Leninist regime in Taiwan',
    World Politics, 41(4): 471–99.

Cheng, Tun-jen (1990), 'Political regimes and development strategies: South Korea and Taiwan' in Gary Gereffi & Donald L. Wyman (eds), *Manufacturing Miracles* (Princeton, NJ: Princeton University Press).

Cheng, Tun-jen (1993), 'Guarding the commanding heights: the state as banker in Taiwan' in Stephan Haggard, Chung H. Lee & Sylvia Maxfield (eds), *The Politics of Finance in Developing Countries* (Ithaca, NY: Cornell University Press).

Cheung, Tai Ming (1996), 'Can PLA Inc. be tamed?', *Institutional Investor,* July.

Chinn, Menzie (1998), 'Before the fall: were the East Asian currencies overvalued?' (Washington DC: National Bureau of Economic Research Working Paper No. 6491).

Cho Kap Che & Pu Chi Yong (1998), 'IMF Sat'aeüi Naemak' (The inside story behind the IMF situation), *Wolgan Chosun*, March.

Cho Soon (1994), *The Dynamics of Korean Economic Development* (Washington DC: Institute for International Economics).

Claessens, Stijn, Simeon Djankov & Larry H.P. Lang (1999), 'Who controls East Asian corporations?' (Washington DC: World Bank, Working Paper No. 2054, February).

Claessens, Stijn, Simeon Djankov & Daniela Klingebiel (1999), 'Financial restructuring in East Asia: halfway there?' (Washington DC: World Bank, Financial Sector Discussion Paper No. 3, September).

Cline, William (1996), 'Crisis management in emerging capital markets' in Peter B. Kenen et al., *From Halifax to Lyons: What has been Done about Crisis Management?* (Princeton, NJ: Essays in International Finance No. 200, International Finance Section, Department of Economics, Princeton University).

Cohen, Benjamin J. (1965), 'Capital controls and the U.S. balance of payments', *American Economic Review*, 55(1): 172–6.

Cohen, Benjamin J. (1993), 'Beyond EMU: the problem of sustainability', *Economics and Politics*, 5(2): 187–203.

Cohen, Benjamin J. (1996), 'Phoenix risen: the resurrection of global finance', *World Politics*, 48(2): 268–96.

Cohen, Benjamin J. (1998a), *The Geography of Money* (Ithaca, NY: Cornell University Press).

Cohen, Benjamin J. (1998b), 'When giants clash: the OECD Financial Support Fund and the IMF' in Vinod K. Aggarwal (ed.), *Institutional Designs for a Complex World: Bargaining, Linkages and Nesting* (Ithaca, NY: Cornell University Press).

Cole, D. & B. Slade (1996), *Building a Modern Financial System: The Indonesian Experience* (Cambridge: Cambridge University Press).

Cole, D. & B. Slade (1998), 'Why has Indonesia's financial crisis been so bad?', *Bulletin of Indonesian Economic Studies*, 34(2): 61–6.

Cole, D. & R. McLeod (eds) (1991), *Cases on Financial Policy and Banking Deregulation in Indonesia* (Yogyakarta: Gadjah Mada University Press).

Cooper, Richard N. (1998), 'Should capital-account convertibility be a world objective?' in Stanley Fischer et al., *Should the IMF Pursue Capital-Account Convertibility?* (Princeton, NJ: Essays in International Finance No. 207, International Finance Section, Department of Economics, Princeton University).

Cooper, Richard N. (1999), 'Should capital controls be banished?', *Brookings Papers on Economic Activity*, 1: 89–141.

Cornell, Andrew (1999), 'Japan pushes for Asian version of IMF', *Australian Financial Review*, 12 February.

Corsetti, Giancarlo, Paolo Pesenti & Nouriel Roubini (1998), 'What caused the Asian currency and financial crisis? Part I: A macroeconomic overview; Part II: The policy debate', unpublished manuscript (revised edn, September), http://www.stern.nyu.edu/ nroubini/asia/AsiaHomepage.html.

Cottarelli, Carlo & Curzio Giannini (1997), *Credibility without Rules? Monetary Frameworks in the Post-Bretton Woods Era* (Washington DC: International Monetary Fund).

Cox, G. (1984), 'Strategic electoral choice in multi-member districts: approval voting in practice?', *American Journal of Political Science*, 28: 722–38.

Crouch, H. (1978 [1988]), *The Army and Politics in Indonesia*, revised edn (Ithaca, NY: Cornell University Press).

Culp, Christopher L., Steve H. Hanke & Merton H. Miller (1999), 'The case for an Indonesian currency board', *Journal of Applied Corporate Finance*, 11(4): 57–65.

Dai, Xianglong et al. (1997), *Zhongguo Jinrong Gaige yu Fazhan* (China's financial reforms and development) (Beijing: Zhongguo Jirong Chubanshe).

Dauvergne, Peter (1997), *Shadows in the Forest: Japan and the Politics of Timber in Southeast Asia* (Cambridge, Mass.: MIT Press).

Dean, J. (1996), 'Recent capital flows to Asia Pacific countries: trade-offs and dilemmas', *Journal of the Asia Pacific Economy*, 1(3): 287–317.

Delhaise, Philippe F. (1998), *Asia in Crisis: The Implosion of the Banking and Finance Systems* (Singapore: John Wiley & Sons).

DGBAS (Directorate-General of Budget, Accounting and Statistics), Executive Yuan, Republic of China (1998), *Quarterly National Economic Trends, Taiwan Area, The Republic of China*, 80 (February).

Diaz-Alejandro, C. (1985), 'Goodbye financial repression, hello financial crash', *Journal of Development Economics*, 19: 1–24.

Dickson, Bruce J. (1993), 'The lessons of defeat: the reorganization of the Kuomintang on Taiwan, 1950–52', *China Quarterly*, 133: 56–84.

Doner, Richard F. (1992), 'Limits of state strength: toward an institutionalist view of economic development', *World Politics*, 44(3): 398–431.

Doner, Richard F. & Ansil Ramsay (1993), 'Postimperialism and development in Thailand', *World Development*, 21(5): 691–704.

Doner, Richard & Daniel Unger (1993), 'The politics of finance in Thai economic development' in Stephan Haggard, Chung H. Lee & Sylvia Maxfield (eds), *The Politics of Finance in Developing Countries* (Ithaca, NY: Cornell University Press).

Dooley, Michael (1996), 'A survey of literature on controls over international capital transactions', *International Monetary Fund Staff Papers*, 43(4) (December): 639–87.

Dooley, Michael (1997), 'A model of crises in emerging markets' (Washington DC: National Bureau of Economic Research Working Paper No. 6300, December).

Drees, Burkhard & Ceyla Pazarbasioglu (1998), *The Nordic Banking Crises: Pitfalls in Financial Liberalization?* (Washington DC: International Monetary Fund).

Eichengreen, Barry (1997), 'International monetary arrangements: is there a monetary union in Asia's future?', *Brookings Review*, 15(2): 33–5.

Eichengreen, Barry (1998), 'Comment on Alesina, Perotti and Tavares' "The political economy of fiscal adjustments" ', *Brookings Papers on Economic Activity*, 1: 255–62.

Eichengreen, Barry (1999a), 'The Barings crisis in a Mexican mirror', *International Political Science Review* (forthcoming).

Eichengreen, Barry (1999b), *Toward International Financial Architecture: A Practical Post-Asia Agenda* (Washington DC: Institute for International Economics, February).

Eichengreen, Barry (1999c), 'Strengthening the international financial architecture: where do we stand?' (Honolulu: Paper prepared for the East-West Center Workshop on International Monetary and Financial Reform, 1–2 October).

Eichengreen, Barry & Marc Flandreau (1996), 'Blocs, zones and bands: international monetary history in light of recent theoretical developments', *Scottish Journal of Political Economy*, 43(4): 398–418.

Eichengreen, Barry & Richard Portes (1995), *Crisis? What Crisis? Orderly Workouts for Sovereign Debtors* (London: Centre for Economic Policy Research).

Eichengreen, Barry & Donald Mathieson et al. (1998), *Hedge Funds and Financial Market Dynamics* (Washington DC: International Monetary Fund).

Eichengreen, Barry, Michael Mussa & Staff Team (1998), *Capital Account Liberalization: Theoretical and Practical Aspects* (Washington DC: International Monetary Fund, Occasional Paper No. 172).

Eichengreen, Barry et al. (1999), *Liberalizing Capital Movements: Some Analytical Issues* (Washington DC: International Monetary Fund).

EIU (1998a), *Country Profile: Thailand* (London: Economist Intelligence Unit).

EIU (1998b), *Country Profile: Indonesia* (London: Economist Intelligence Unit).

Erie, Steven P. (1988), *Rainbow's End: Irish-Americans and the Dilemmas of Urban Machine Politics, 1840–1985* (Berkeley, Calif.: University of California Press).

Ernst, Dieter (1998), 'Destroying or upgrading the engine of growth? The reshaping of the electronics industry in East Asia after the crisis' (Washington DC: World Bank, background paper for World Bank, *East Asia: The Road to Recovery*, mimeo).

Evans, K. (1998), 'Survey of recent developments', *Bulletin of Indonesian Economic Studies*, 34(3): 5–35.

Evans, Peter (1995), *Embedded Autonomy: States and Industrial Transformation* (Princeton, NJ: Princeton University Press).

Fane, G. (1998), 'The role of prudential regulation' in R. McLeod & R. Garnaut (eds), *East Asia in Crisis: From Being a Miracle to Needing One?* (London: Routledge).

Feith, H. (1962), *The Decline of Constitutional Democracy in Indonesia* (Ithaca, NY: Cornell University Press).

Feldstein, Martin (1998), 'Refocusing the IMF', *Foreign Affairs*, 77(2): 20–33.

Feldstein, Martin (1999), 'A self-help guide for emerging markets', *Foreign Affairs*, 78(2): 93–109.

Feldstein, M.S. & C.Y. Horioka (1980), 'Domestic saving and international capital flows', *Economic Journal*, 90: 314–29.

Financial Times (1999), 'Lenders beware', editorial, 12 October.

Fischer, Stanley (1997), 'Closing remarks: what have we learned?' in Guillermo Perry, Guillermo Calvo, W. Max Corden, Stanley Fischer, Sir Alan Walters & John Williamson (eds), *Currency Boards and External Shocks: How Much Pain, How Much Gain?* (Washington DC: World Bank).

Fischer, Stanley et al. (1998), *Should the IMF Pursue Capital-Account Convertibility?* (Princeton, NJ: Essays in International Finance No. 207, International Finance Section, Department of Economics, Princeton University).

Forrester, G. (1999), 'Introduction' in G. Forrester (ed.), *Post-Soeharto Indonesia: Renewal or Chaos? Indonesia Assessment 1998* (Bathurst, NSW: Crawford House Publishing).

Forrester, G. & R.J. May (eds) (1998), *The Fall of Soeharto* (Bathurst, NSW: Crawford House Publishing).

Fox, Justin (1998), 'The great emerging markets rip-off', *Fortune*, 11 May: 68–74.

Fraga, Arminio (1996), 'Crisis prevention and management: lessons from Mexico' in Peter B. Kenen et al., *From Halifax to Lyons: What has been Done about Crisis Management?* (Princeton, NJ: Essays in International Finance No. 200, International Finance Section, Department of Economics, Princeton University).

Frankel, Jeffrey A. (1998), 'The Asian model, the miracle, the crisis, and the Fund' (Washington DC: US International Trade Commission, 16 April).

Frankel, Jeffrey (1999), 'The international financial architecture' (Washington DC: Brookings Institution, Policy Brief No. 51, June).

French, K.R. & J.M. Poterba (1991), 'International diversification and international equity markets' (Cambridge, Mass.: National Bureau of Economic Research Working Paper No. 3609).

Fry, Maxwell (1995), *Money, Interest and Banking in Economic Development*, 2nd edn (Baltimore: Johns Hopkins University Press).

Fujiki, H. & Y. Kitamura (1995), 'Feldstein-Horioka paradox revisited', *Bank of Japan Monetary and Economic Studies*, 13(1): 1–16.

Furman, Jason & Joseph Stiglitz (1998), 'Economic crises: evidence and insights from East Asia' (Washington DC: World Bank, unpublished manuscript).

Geddes, Barbara (1994), 'The politics of economic liberalization', *Latin American Research Review*, 30(2):195–214.

Ghosh, A.R. (1995), 'International capital mobility amongst major industrialised countries: too little or too much?', *Economic Journal*, 105: 107–28.

Giovannini, Alberto (1993), 'Bretton Woods and its precursors: rules versus discretion in the history of international monetary regimes' in Michael Bordo & Barry Eichengreen (eds), *A Retrospective on the Bretton Woods System: Lessons for International Monetary Reform* (Chicago: University of Chicago Press).

GOI (Government of Indonesia) (1998a), *Indonesia: Memorandum of Economic and Financial Policies*, 15 January (http://www.imf.org/external/np/LOI/011598.htm).

GOI (Government of Indonesia) (1998b), *Letter of Intent and Memorandum of Economic and Financial Policies*, 29 July (http://www.imf.org/external/np/LOI/072998.htm).

GOI (Government of Indonesia) (1998c), *Letter of Intent and Supplementary Memorandum of Economic and Financial Policies*, 11 September (http://www.imf.org/external/np/LOI/091198.htm).

GOI (Government of Indonesia) (1998d), *Letter of Intent and Supplementary Memorandum of Economic and Financial Policies*, 19 October (http://www.imf.org/external/np/LOI/101998.htm).

Goldstein, M. & J. Hawkins (1998), 'The origin of the Asian financial turmoil' (Canberra: Reserve Bank of Australia, Research Discussion Paper No. 9805).

Goldstein, Morris (1996a), 'The case for an international banking standard', *Policy Analyses in International Economics*, 47 (Washington DC: Institute for International Economics, April).

Goldstein, Morris (1996b), 'Avoiding future Mexicos: a post-Halifax scoreboard on crisis prevention and management' in Peter B. Kenen et al., *From Halifax to Lyons: What has been Done about Crisis Management?* (Princeton, NJ: Essays in International Finance No. 200, International Finance Section, Department of Economics, Princeton University).

Goldstein, Morris (1997), *The Case for an International Banking Standard* (Washington DC: Institute for International Economics).

Goldstein, Morris (1998), *The Asian Financial Crisis: Causes, Cures and Systemic Implications* (Washington DC: Institute for International Economics).

Goldstein, Morris & Guillermo A. Calvo (1996), 'What role for the official sector?' in Guillermo A. Calvo, Morris Goldstein & Eduard Hochreiter (eds), *Private Capital Flows to Emerging Markets after the Mexican Crisis* (Washington DC: Institute for International Economics).

Gong, Yan (1998), 'Zhengfu de Guodu Ganyu' (Excessive government intervention), *Shijie Jingji*, 5: 10–13.

Goodman, David & Gerald Segal (eds) (1994), *China Deconstructs: Politics, Trade and Regionalism* (London/New York: Routledge).

Graham, Edward M. & Li-Gang Liu (2000), 'Opening China's bond market: catalyst to further reform and a jumpstart to stalled WTO accession negotiations', *Journal of World Trade* (forthcoming).

Greenspan, Alan (1998), 'The globalization of finance', *Cato Journal*, 17(3): 243–50.

Grenville, Stephen & David Gruen (1999), 'Capital flows and exchange rates' (Sydney: Reserve Bank of Australia, paper for Conference on Capital Flows and the International Financial System, September).

Group of 7 (1999), *Strengthening the International Financial Architecture: Report of the G–7 Finance Ministers to the Köln Economic Summit* (Cologne, 18–20 June).

Group of 22 (1998), 'Summary of reports on the international financial architecture' (International Monetary Fund, 1 October; http://www.imf.org/external/np/g22/index.htm).

Group of 30 (1997), *Global Institutions, National Supervision and Systemic Risk* (Washington DC: Group of Thirty).

GSSB: Gongshang Shibao (Taipei).

Gwartney, James D. (1996), *Economic Freedom of the World, 1975–1995* (Vancouver: Fraser Institute).

Haggard, Stephan & Robert Kaufman (1992), 'The political economy of inflation and stabilization in the middle-income countries' in Stephan Haggard & Robert Kaufman (eds), *The Politics of Economic Adjustment: International Constraints, Distributive Conflicts and the State* (Princeton, NJ: Princeton University Press).

Haggard, Stephan & Sylvia Maxfield (1996), 'The political economy of financial internationalization in the developing world' in Robert Keohane & Helen Milner (eds), *Internationalization and Domestic Politics* (Cambridge: Cambridge University Press).

Hale, David D. (1998), 'The hot money debate', *International Economy*, 12(6): 8–12, 66–9.

Hamilton-Hart, Natasha (1999), 'States and capital mobility: Indonesia, Malaysia and Singapore in the Asian region', PhD dissertation (Ithaca, NY: Cornell University).

Hanke, Steve H. & Kurt Schuler (1994), *Currency Boards for Developing Countries: A Handbook* (San Francisco: Institute for Contemporary Studies).

Hanke, Steve H., Lars Jonung & Kurt Schuler (1993), *Russian Currency and Finance: A Currency Board Approach to Reform* (London: Routledge).

Harris, Elliott (1999), 'Impact of the Asian crisis on sub-Saharan Africa', *Finance and Development*, 36(1): 14–17.

Hastings, Laura A. (1993), 'Regulatory revenge: the politics of free-market financial reforms in Chile' in Stephan Haggard, Chung H. Lee & Sylvia Maxfield (eds), *The Politics of Finance in Developing Countries* (Ithaca, NY: Cornell University Press).

Helleiner, E. (1994), 'Freeing money: why have states been more willing to liberalize capital controls than trade barriers?', *Policy Sciences*, 27(4): 299–318.

Hellman, T., K. Murdock & J. Stiglitz (1997), 'Financial restraint: toward a new paradigm' in M. Aoki, H. Kim & M. Okuno-Fujiwara (eds), *The Role of Government in East Asian Economic Development: Comparative Institutional Analysis* (Oxford: Clarendon Press).

Hendro Sangkoyo (1999), 'Limits to order: the internal logic of instability in the post-Soeharto era' in G. Forrester (ed.), *Post-Soeharto Indonesia: Renewal or Chaos? Indonesia Assessment 1998* (Bathurst, NSW: Crawford House Publishing).

Herring, Richard J. & Robert E. Litan (1995), *Financial Regulation in the Global Economy* (Washington DC: Brookings Institution).

Hicken, Allen (1998), 'From patronage to policy: political institutions and policy-making in Thailand' (Chicago: Paper presented at the Midwest Political Science Association Annual Meeting, 23–25 April).

Higgins, B. (1957), *Indonesia's Economic Stabilization and Development* (Westport, Conn.: Greenwood Press).

Hill, H. (1996), *The Indonesian Economy since 1966: Southeast Asia's Emerging Giant* (Cambridge: Cambridge University Press).

Hill, Hal (1998a), 'An overview of the issues', *ASEAN Economic Bulletin*, 15(3): 261–71.

Hill, Hal (1998b), 'Southeast Asia's economic crisis: origins, lessons and the way forward' (Canberra: Department of Economics, Research School of Pacific and Asian Studies, Australian National University, October).

Ho, Szu-yin & Jih-chu Lee (1998), 'The political economy of banking in Taiwan' (Charlottesville, Va.: Paper presented at the 37th Annual Meeting of the Southeast Regional Conference, Association for Asian Studies [SEC/AAS], 16–18 January).

Huang Yasheng (1996a), 'The Statistical Agency in China's bureaucratic system', *Communist and Post-Communist Studies*, 29(1): 59–75.

Huang Yasheng (1996b), 'Central–local relations in China during the reform era: the economical and institutional dimensions', *World Development*, 24(4): 655–72.

Huntington, Samuel (1968), *Political Order in Changing Societies* (New Haven: Yale University Press).

Hutchcroft, P. (1998), *Booty Capitalism: The Politics of Banking in the Philippines* (Ithaca, NY: Cornell University Press).

IBRA (Indonesian Bank Restructuring Agency) (1999), Asset Management Investment Unit, downloaded 31 July (http://www.bppn.go.id/eng/bank.htm).

IMF (International Monetary Fund) (1993), 'Recent experiences with surges in capital inflows' (Washington DC: IMF, Occasional Paper No. 108, August).

IMF (International Monetary Fund) (1995), *International Capital Markets: Developments, Prospects and Policy Issues* (Washington DC: IMF, August).

IMF (International Monetary Fund) (1997), *International Capital Markets: Developments, Prospects and Key Policy Issues* (Washington DC: IMF, November).

IMF (International Monetary Fund) (1998a), *International Capital Markets: Developments, Prospects and Key Policy Issues* (Washington DC: IMF).

IMF (International Monetary Fund) (1998b), 'Republic of Korea: selected issues' (Washington DC: IMF, Staff Country Report 98/74, August).

IMF (International Monetary Fund) (1998c), *Capital Account Liberalization: What's the Best Stance?*, IMF Economic Forum, 22 October (text available from the IMF website).

IMF (International Monetary Fund) (1998d), *Toward a Framework for Financial Stability* (Washington DC: IMF).

IMF (International Monetary Fund) (1998e), *Report of the Managing Director to the Interim Committee on Strengthening the Architecture of the International Monetary System* (Washington DC: IMF).

IMF (International Monetary Fund) (1998f), *World Economic Outlook and International Capital Markets: Interim Assessment, December 1998* (Washington DC: IMF).

IMF (International Monetary Fund) (1999a), 'IMF takes additional steps to enhance transparency' (Washington DC: IMF, 16 April; http://www.imf.org/external/np/sec/pn/1999/PN9936.htm).

IMF (International Monetary Fund) (1999b), 'IMF tightens defenses against financial contagion by establishing contingent credit lines' (Washington DC: IMF, 25 April; http://www.omf.org/external/np/sec/pr/1999/PR9914.htm).

IMF (International Monetary Fund) (1999c), 'Press conference of Mr Boorman on "Involving the Private Sector in Forestalling and Resolving Financial Crises"', 15 April.

IMF (International Monetary Fund) (1999d), *External Evaluation of IMF Surveillance* (Washington DC: IMF; http://www.imf.org/external/pubs/ft/extev/surv/index.htm).

IMF (International Monetary Fund) (1999e), *A Guide to Progress in Strengthening the Architecture of the International Financial System* (Washington DC: IMF).

Inoguchi Takashi & Iwai Tomoaki (1987), *Zoku Giin no Kenkyu: Jiminto o Gyujiru Shuyakutachi* (Research on Diet members in tribes: the actors who control the LDP) (Tokyo: Nihon Keizai Shinbunsha).

Institute for International Finance (1999), 'Capital flows to emerging market economies' (Washington DC: Institute for International Finance, 27 January).

Jakarta Stock Exchange (1996), *JSX Statistics*: 108.

Japan, Government of (1996), *Organization of the Government of Japan 1996* (Tokyo: Prime Minister's Office, Government of Japan).

Japan, Government of, Ministry of Finance (1996), *Nihon no Zaisei* (Japan's public finance) (Tokyo: Toyo Keizai Shimnposha).

JETRO (Japan External Trade Organisation), International Communication Department (1999), *1999 White Paper on Foreign Direct Investment* (Tokyo: Government of Japan).

Ji, Donghyun (1998), 'Prudential supervision of Korean financial institutions' (Canberra: Australian National University, paper for a Conference on Financial Reform and Macroeconomic Policy and Management in Korea, November).

Johnson, Colin (1998), 'Survey of recent developments', *Bulletin of Indonesian Economic Studies*, 34(2): 3–60.

Kahler, Miles (1990), 'Orthodoxy and its alternatives: explaining approaches to stabilization and adjustment' in Joan Nelson (ed.), *Economic Crisis and Policy Choice: The Politics of Adjustment in the Third World* (Princeton, NJ: Princeton University Press).

Kahler, Miles (1992), 'External actors, conditionality and the politics of adjustment' in Stephan Haggard & Robert Kaufman (eds), *The Politics of Economic Adjustment: International Constraints, Distributive Conflicts and the State* (Princeton, NJ: Princeton University Press).

Kahler, Miles (ed.) (1998), *Capital Flows and Financial Crises* (Ithaca, NY: Cornell University Press).

Kaminsky, Graciela & Carmen M. Reinhart (1998), 'The twin crises: the causes of banking and balance of payments problems' (unpublished manuscript).

Kang, Dave (1999), 'Neither miracle nor meltdown: explaining the historical pattern of Korean government–business relations' (Atlanta: Paper presented at the American Political Science Association Convention).

Kang, Myung Hun (1996), *The Korean Business Conglomerate: Chaebol Then and Now* (Berkeley, Calif.: Institute of East Asian Studies, University of California Berkeley).

Kapstein, Ethan B. (1994), *Governing the Global Economy: International Finance and the State* (Cambridge, Mass.: Harvard University Press).

Kapstein, Ethan B. (1998), 'Global rules for global finance', *Current History*, 97(622): 355–60.

Kawai, Masahiro (1999), 'The resolution of the East Asian crisis: financial and corporate sector restructuring' (Canberra: Australian National University, paper for the Asia Pacific School of Economics and Management, Conference on Reform and Recovery in East Asia: The Role of the State and Economic Enterprise, September).

Kazuhiko Shimizu (1998), 'China's broken banks: the cleanup begins', *Institutional Investor*, August.

Kikkawa, Mototada (1998), *Manee Haisen* (Money defeat) (Tokyo: Bunshun Shinsho).

Kim, Eun Mee (1988), 'From dominance to symbiosis: state and chaebol in Korea', *Pacific Focus*, III(2): 105–21.

Kim, Eun Mee (1997), *Big Business, Strong State: Collusion and Conflict in South Korean Development, 1960–1990* (Albany, NY: State University of New York Press).

Kim, Kyong-Dong (1976), 'Political factors in the formation of the entrepreneurial elite in South Korea', *Asian Survey*, XVI(5): 465–77.

Kim, S. Ran (1996), 'The Korean system of innovation and the semiconductor industry: a governance perspective' (Brighton: University of Sussex, Science Policy Research Unit Working Paper, December).

Kirshner, Jonathan (1999), 'Keynes, capital mobility and the crisis of embedded liberalism', *Review of International Political Economy*, 6(3): 313–37.

Kohno, Masaru (1999), 'Recent changes in MITI and Japan–US relations' (Vancouver: Unpublished manuscript presented at the Conference on Japanese Business and Economic System, History and Prospects for the 21st Century, University of British Columbia, 12–13 February).

Korea, National Statistical Office (1997), *Major Statistics of Korean Economy* (March).

Kraay, Aart (1998), 'Do high interest rates defend currencies against speculative attacks?' (Washington DC: World Bank, unpublished manuscript).

Krause, Lawrence B. (1998), *The Economics and Politics of the Asian Financial Crisis of 1997–98* (New York: Council on Foreign Relations).

Krugman, Paul (1994), 'The myth of Asia's miracle', *Foreign Affairs*, 73(6): 62–78.

Krugman, Paul (1998a), 'What happened to Asia?' (Cambridge, Mass.: Massachussetts Institute of Technology, unpublished manuscript; see also http://www.stern.nyu.edu/nroubini/asia/AsiaHomepage.html).

Krugman, P. (1998b), 'The confidence game', *New Republic*, 5 October: 23–5 (see also http://web.mit.edu/krugman/www).

Krugman, Paul (1998c), 'Saving Asia: it's time to get radical', *Fortune Magazine*, 138(5): 74–80.

Krugman, Paul (1999), *The Return of Depression Economics* (New York: Norton).

Kumar, Anjali et al. (1996), *China's Non-bank Financial Institutions: Trust and Investment Companies* (Washington DC: World Bank).

Kuo, Shirley W.Y. & Christina Y. Liu (1998), 'Taiwan' in Ross H. McLeod & Ross Garnaut (eds), *East Asia in Crisis: From Being a Miracle to Needing One?* (London: Routledge).

Lane, Timothy et al. (1999), 'IMF-supported programs in Indonesia, Korea and Thailand: a preliminary assessment' (Washington DC: IMF mimeo, January).

Lardy, Nicholas R. (1998a), *China's Unfinished Economic Revolution* (Washington DC: Brookings Institution).

Lardy, Nicholas R. (1998b), 'China and the Asian contagion', *Foreign Affairs*, 74(4): 78–88.

Lee, Peter (1998), 'Korea stares into the abyss', *Business Week*, 15 March: 32–7.

Lee, Valerie (1999), 'Indonesia debt restructure gathers pace', Reuters, 28 January.

Lee, Yeon-ho (1996), 'Political aspects of South Korean state autonomy: regulating the chaebol', *Pacific Review*, 9(2): 149–79.

Leipziger, Danny M. & Peter A. Petri (1993), *Korean Industrial Policy: Legacies of the Past and Directions for the Future* (Washington DC: World Bank).

Leung, James (1999), 'Still searching for a cure', *Asian Business*, March: 42–3.

Lev, D. (1972), 'Judicial institutions and legal culture in Indonesia' in C. Holt (ed.), *Culture and Politics in Indonesia* (Ithaca, NY: Cornell University Press).

Lew, Seok-Jin (1999), 'Democratization and government intervention in the economy: insights on the decision-making process from the automobile industrial policies' in Jongryn Mo & Chung-in Moon (eds), *Democracy and the Korean Economy* (Stanford, Calif.: Hoover Institution Press).

Li Xianzhe & Zhuo Cuiyue (1997), 'Jinrong yujing xitong zhi yingyong: yi Taiwan Xinyong hezuoshe wei li' (Applications of financial warning systems: the case of Taiwan's credit cooperatives), *Taiwan Yinhang Jikan*, 48(1): 1–26.

Liddle, R. William (1991), 'The relative autonomy of the third world politician: Soeharto and Indonesian economic development in comparative perspective', *International Studies Quarterly*, 35(4): 403–27.

Lieberthal, Kenneth (1995), *Governing China: From Revolution through Reform* (New York: Norton).

Lincoln, Edward J. (1988), *Japan: Facing Economic Maturity* (Washington DC: Brookings Institution).

Lindsey, T. (1998), 'The IMF and insolvency law reform in Indonesia', *Bulletin of Indonesian Economic Studies*, 34(3): 119–24.

Lopez-Mejia, Alejandro (1999), 'Large capital flows: a survey of the causes, consequences and policy responses' (Washington DC: IMF, Staff Working Paper No. WP/99/17).

Lowi, Theodore (1985), 'The state in politics: the relation between policy and administration' in Roger G. Noll (ed.), *Regulatory Policy and the Social Sciences* (Berkeley, Calif.: University of California Press).

Lum, Linda (1999), 'Malaysia's response to the Asian financial crisis' (Washington DC: Testimony prepared for hearings before the Subcommittee on Asia and the Pacific of the House Committee on International Relations, US Congress, 16 June).

MacIntyre, Andrew (1993), 'The politics of finance in Indonesia: command, confusion and competition', in Stephan Haggard, Chung H. Lee and Sylvia Maxfield (eds), *The Politics of Finance in Developing Countries* (Ithaca, NY: Cornell University Press).

MacIntyre, Andrew (1994), 'Power, prosperity and patrimonialism: business and government in Indonesia' in Andrew MacIntyre (ed.), *Business and Government in Industrialising Asia* (Ithaca, NY: Cornell University Press).

MacIntyre, Andrew (1995), 'Ideas and experts: Indonesian approaches to economic and security cooperation in the Asia–Pacific region', *Pacific Review*, 8(1): 159–72.

MacIntyre, Andrew (1998), 'Political institutions and the economic crisis in Thailand and Indonesia', *ASEAN Economic Bulletin*, 15(3): 272–80.

Mackie, J. (1970), 'The Commission of Four report on corruption', *Bulletin of Indonesian Economic Studies*, 6(3): 87–101.

Mackie, J. (1991), 'Towkays and tycoons: the Chinese in Indonesian economic life in the 1920s and 1980s' in *The Role of the Indonesian Chinese in Shaping Modern Indonesian Life, Indonesia* (special issue).

Mackie, J. (1998), 'What will the post-Soeharto regime be like?' in G. Forrester & R.J. May (eds), *The Fall of Soeharto* (Bathurst, NSW: Crawford House Publishing).

Marshall, Andrew (1998), 'Indonesia tries to prime private debt talks', Reuters, 2 November.

Mason, E. (1986), *The Harvard Institute for International Development and its Antecedents* (Cambridge, Mass.: Harvard Institute for International Development and University Press of America).

Mathews, John (forthcoming), *Tiger Technology* (Cambridge: Cambridge University Press).

Maxfield, Sylvia (1998), 'Effects of international portfolio flows on government policy choice' in Miles Kahler (ed.), *Capital Flows and Financial Crises* (Ithaca, NY: Cornell University Press).

Mayer, Martin (1998), *The Bankers: The Next Generation* (New York: Truman Talley Books/Plume).

McKinnon, R. & H. Pill (1996), 'Credible liberalizations and international capital flows: the "overborrowing syndrome"' in T. Ito & A. Krueger (eds), *Financial Deregulation and Integration in East Asia* (Chicago: University of Chicago Press).

McLeod, Ross (1997), 'Survey of recent developments', *Bulletin of Indonesian Economic Studies*, 33(1): 3–43.

McLeod, Ross H. (1998a), 'Indonesia' in Ross H. McLeod & Ross Garnaut (eds), *East Asia in Crisis: From Being a Miracle to Needing One?* (London: Routledge).

McLeod, Ross H. (1998b), 'The new era of financial fragility' in Ross H. McLeod & Ross Garnaut (eds), *East Asia in Crisis: From Being a Miracle to Needing One?* (London: Routledge).

McLeod, Ross (ed.) (1994), *Indonesia Assessment 1994: Finance as a Key Sector in Indonesia's Development* (Canberra: RSPAS, Australian National University and Singapore: ISEAS).

McVey, R. (1982 [1977]), 'The Beamtenstaat in Indonesia' in B. Anderson & R. McVey (eds), *Interpreting Indonesian Politics: Thirteen Contributions to the Debate* (Ithaca, NY: Cornell Modern Indonesia Project).

Mehran, Hassanali et al. (1996), *Monetary and Exchange System Reforms in China: An Experiment in Gradualism* (Washington DC: IMF).

Migdal, J. (1988), *Strong Societies and Weak States: State–Society Relations and State Capabilities in the Third World* (Princeton, NJ: Princeton University Press).

Ministry of Finance, Government of Japan (1999a), 'Establishment of "Asian currency crisis support facility"' (Tokyo: Ministry of Finance, 23 March; http://www.mof.go.jp/english/gyousei/e1b056.htm).

Ministry of Finance, Government of Japan (1999b), 'Major tasks for the reform of the international financial system' (Tokyo: Ministry of Finance, 22 April; http://www.mof.go.jp/english/gyousei/e1b062.htm).

Mitchell, T. (1999), 'Society, economy and the state effect' in G. Steinmetz (ed.), *State/Culture: State-formation after the Cultural Turn* (Ithaca, NY: Cornell University Press).

Miyazawa, Kiichi (1998), 'Towards a new international financial architecture', Speech at the Foreign Correspondents Club of Japan (Tokyo: Ministry of Finance, 15 December).

Mo, Jongryn & Chung-in Moon (1999), 'Epilogue: democracy and the origins of the Korean economic crisis' in Jongryn Mo & Chung-in Moon (eds), *Democracy and the Korean Economy* (Stanford, Calif.: Hoover Institution Press).

Moggridge, Donald (ed.) (1980), *The Collected Writings of John Maynard Keynes*, vol. XXV (Cambridge: Cambridge University Press).

Montinola, Gabriella, Yingyi Qian & Barry R. Weingast (1995), 'Federalism, Chinese style: the political basis for economic success in China', *World Politics*, 48(1): 50–81.

Mulvenon, James (1998), 'Soldiers of fortune: the rise of the military–business complex in the Chinese People's Liberation Army, 1978–1998', PhD dissertation (Los Angeles: University of California).

Mundell, Robert A. (1997), 'Forum on Asian fund', *Capital Trends*, 2(13).

Mussa, Michael (1999), 'Reforming the international financial architecture: limiting moral hazard and containing real hazard' (Sydney: Reserve Bank of Australia, paper for the Conference on Capital Flows and the International Financial System, September).

Nasution, A. (1992), 'The years of living dangerously: the impacts of financial sector policy reforms and increasing private sector external indebtedness in Indonesia', *Indonesian Quarterly*, 20(4): 405–37.

Nelson, Joan (1992), 'Poverty, equity and the politics of adjustment' in Stephan Haggard & Robert Kaufman (eds), *The Politics of Economic Adjustment: International Constraints, Distributive Conflicts and the State* (Princeton, NJ: Princeton University Press).

Noble, Gregory W. (1998), *Collective Action in East Asia: How Ruling Parties Shape Industrial Policy* (Ithaca, NY: Cornell University Press).

Noland, Marcus, Li-Gang Liu, Sherman Robinson & Zhi Wang (1998), *Global Economic Effects of the Asian Currency Devaluations* (Washington DC: Institute for International Economics, Policy Analyses in International Economics No. 56, July).

Nukul Commission Report (1998), *Analysis and Evaluation on Facts behind Thailand's Economic Crisis*, English language edn (Bangkok: The Nation).

Nurkse, Ragnar (1944), *International Currency Experience: Lessons from the Inter-war Period* (Geneva: League of Nations).

Oatley, Thomas & Robert Nabors (1998), 'Redistributive cooperation: market failure, wealth transfers and the Basle Accord', *International Organization*, 52(1): 35–54.

Obstfeld, M. (1998), 'The global capital market: benefactor or menace?' (Cambridge, Mass.: National Bureau of Economic Research, Working Paper No. 6559).

Obstfeld, M. & A.M. Taylor (1997), 'The great depression as a watershed: international capital mobility over the long run' (Cambridge, Mass.: National Bureau of Economic Research, Working Paper No. 5960).

Obstfeld, Maurice (1994), 'Risk taking, global diversification and growth', *American Economic Review*, 84(5): 1310–29.

OECD (Organisation for Economic Cooperation and Development), Business Sector Advisory Group on Corporate Governance (1998), *Corporate Governance: Improving Competitiveness and Access to Capital in Global Markets* (Paris: OECD).

OECD (Organisation for Economic Cooperation and Development) (1999), *OECD Economic Surveys: Korea* (Paris: OECD).

OECD/BIS (1999), *Statistics on External Indebtedness: Bank and Trade-related Nonbank External Claims on Individual Borrowing Countries and Territories* (Paris/Basle: New Series, No. 22, January).

'Official creditor countries of Indonesia press release' (1998), Paris, 23 September.

Ohkawa, Masazo & Kotaro Ikeda (1993), 'Government bonds' in Tokue Shibata (ed.), *Japan's Public Sector* (Tokyo: University of Tokyo Press).

Olson, Mancur (1982), *The Rise and Decline of Nations* (New Haven, NJ: Yale University Press).

Padoa-Schioppa, Tommaso & Fabrizio Saccomanni (1994), 'Managing a market-led global financial system' in Peter B. Kenen (ed.), *Managing the World Economy: Fifty Years after Bretton Woods* (Washington DC: Institute for International Economics).

Park, Daekeun & Changyong Rhee (1998), 'Currency crisis in Korea: could it have been avoided?' (Seoul: Hanyan University, mimeo).

Park, Yung Chul & Dong Wong Kim (1994), 'Korea: development and structural change of the banking system' in Hugh Patrick & Yung Chul Park (eds),

The Financial Development of Japan, Korea, and Taiwan (New York: Oxford University Press).

Pasuk, P. & C. Baker (1998), *Thailand's Boom and Bust* (Bangkok: Silkworm Books).

Patrick, Hugh & Yung Chul Park (eds) (1994), *The Financial Development of Japan, Korea, and Taiwan* (New York: Oxford University Press).

Pauly, Louis W. (1997), *Who Elected the Bankers? Surveillance and Control in the World Economy* (Ithaca, NY: Cornell University Press).

Pearson, Margaret (1997), *China's New Business Elite: The Political Consequences of Economic Reform* (Berkeley, Calif.: University of California Press).

Phillips, Michael M. & Peter Fritsch (1999), 'US, IMF prod big banks to aid Brazil', *Wall Street Journal*, 9 March: A17.

Polak, Jacques J. (1998), 'The Articles of Agreement of the IMF and the liberalization of capital movements' (unpublished manuscript, Per Jacobsen Foundation).

Posen, Adam (1998), *Restoring Japan's Economic Growth* (Washington DC: Institute for International Economics).

Qiq Zeqi & Zheng Yongnian (1998), '*Xia Gang* and its sociological implications of reducing labor redundancy in China's SOEs' in Wang Gungwu & John Wong (eds), *China's Political Economy* (Singapore: Singapore University Press).

Radelet, Steven (1995), 'Indonesian foreign debt: headed for a crisis or financing sustainable growth', *Bulletin of Indonesian Economic Studies*, 31(3): 39–72.

Radelet, Steven & Jeffrey Sachs (1998a), 'The onset of the East Asian financial crisis' (Cambridge, Mass.: Harvard Institute for International Development, 30 March).

Radelet, Steven & Jeffrey D. Sachs (1998b), 'The East Asian financial crisis: diagnosis, remedies, prospects', *Brookings Papers on Economic Activity*, 1: 1–90.

Reinhart, Carmen M. & Vincent Raymond Reinhart (1998), 'Some lessons for policy-makers who deal with the mixed blessing of capital inflows' in Miles Kahler (ed.), *Capital Flows and Financial Crises* (Ithaca, NY: Cornell University Press).

Republic of China, Ministry of Finance, Bureau of Monetary Affairs (1996), 'The ROC financial market integration' (Financial Reference Series No. 17, April).

Republic of China, Ministry of Economic Affairs (Jingjibu) (1996), *Zhonghua Minguo Taiwan Diqu Gongshang Qiye Jingying Gaikuang Diaocha Gongsi Qiye Diaocha Jibao* (Quarterly report on the incorporated enterprises survey Taiwan-Fukien Area, the Republic of Taiwan) No. 25 (January–December).

Republic of China, National Science Council (NSC) (1995), 'Zhonghua Minguo Kexue Jishu Tongji Yaolan Minguo 84 Nianban' (Republic of China, Indicators of Science and Technology 1995).

Reuters (1998a), 'Indonesia ...', 21 September.

Reuters (1998b), 'Indonesia closer to recovery', 23 September.

Rhee, Jong-Chan (1994), *The State and Industry in South Korea: The Limits of the Authoritarian State* (London: Routledge).

Robison, Richard (1986), *Indonesia: The Rise of Capital* (Sydney: Asian Studies Association of Australia/Allen & Unwin).

Robison, Richard (1992), 'Industrialization and the economic and political development of capital: the case of Indonesia' in R. McVey (ed.), *Southeast Asian Capitalists* (Ithaca, NY: Southeast Asia Program, Cornell University).

Robison, Richard (1994), 'Organising the transition: Indonesian politics 1993/94' in Ross McLeod (ed.), *Indonesia Assessment 1994: Finance as a Key Sector in Indonesia's Development* (Canberra: RSPAS, Australian National University and Singapore).

Robison, Richard (1997), 'Politics and markets in Indonesia's post-oil era' in Garry Rodan, Kevin J. Hewison & Richard Robison (eds), *The Political Economy of South-East Asia: An Introduction* (Melbourne: Oxford University Press).

Robison, Richard (1998), 'Indonesia after Soeharto: more of the same, descent into chaos or a shift to reform?' in G. Forrester & R.J. May (eds), *The Fall of Soeharto* (Bathurst, NSW: Crawford House Publishing).

Robison, Richard & A. Rosser (1998), 'Contesting reform: Indonesia's New Order and the IMF', *World Development*, 26(8): 1593–609.

Rodrik, Dani (1998a), 'Who needs capital account convertibility?' in Stanley Fischer et al., *Should the IMF Pursue Capital–Account Convertibility?* (Princeton, NJ: Essays in International Finance No. 207, International Finance Section, Department of Economics, Princeton University).

Rodrik, Dani (1998b), 'The global fix', *New Republic*, 2 November: 17–19.

Rodrik, Dani (1999a), 'Governing the global economy: does one architectural style fit all?' (Washington DC: Paper presented at the Brookings Institution Trade Policy Forum Conference on Governing in a Global Economy, 15–16 April).

Rodrik, Dani (1999b), 'The Asian financial crisis and the virtues of democracy', *Challenge*, 42(4): 44–59.

Rogoff, Kenneth (1999), 'International institutions for reducing global financial instability', *Journal of Economic Perspectives*, 13(4): 21–42.

Root, Hilton L. (1996), *Small Countries, Big Lessons: Governance and the Rise of East Asia* (Hong Kong: Asian Development Bank/Oxford University Press).

Rosenbluth, Frances McCall (1989), *Financial Politics in Contemporary Japan* (Ithaca, NY: Cornell University Press).

Rowley, Anthony (1997), 'International finance: Asian Fund, R.I.P.', *Capital Trends*, 2(14).

Rubin, Robert E. (1999), 'Treasury Secretary Robert E. Rubin remarks before the World Economic Conference Davos, Switzerland' (Washington DC: US Treasury, 30 January).

Ruggie, John G. (1983), 'International regimes, transactions and change: embedded liberalism in the postwar economic order' in Stephen D. Krasner (ed.), *International Regimes* (Ithaca, NY: Cornell University Press).

Sachs, Jeffrey D. (1997), 'The wrong medicine for Asia', *New York Times*, 3 November.

Sachs, Jeffrey D. (1998a), 'Global capitalism: making it work', *Economist*, 12–18 September: 23–6.

Sachs, Jeffrey D. (1998b), 'Alternative approaches to financial crises in emerging markets' in Miles Kahler (ed.), *Capital Flows and Financial Crises* (Ithaca, NY: Cornell University Press).

Sadli, Mohammad (1998), 'The Indonesian crisis', *ASEAN Economic Bulletin*, 15(3): 272–80.

Sakakibara, Eisuke (1999), 'Speech by Dr Eisuke Sakakibara at the Manila Framework Meeting in Melbourne on 26 March 1999' (Tokyo: Ministry of Finance, March; http://www.mof.go.jp/english/daijin/e1e070.htm).

SaKong, Il (1993), *Korea in the World Economy* (Washington DC: Institute for International Economics).

Sato, Y. (1994), 'The development of business groups in Indonesia: 1967–1989' in T. Shiraishi (ed.), *Approaching Suharto's Indonesia from the Margins* (Ithaca, NY: Southeast Asia Program, Cornell University).

Savastano, M.A. (1996), 'Dollarization in Latin America: recent evidence and policy issues' in P.D. Mizen & E.J. Pentecost (eds), *The Macroeconomics of International Currencies: Theory, Policy and Evidence* (Brookfield, VT: Edward Elgar).

Saywell, Trish (1998), 'Baby steps ...', *Far Eastern Economic Review*, 30 April: 41–2.

Saywell, Trish (1999), 'Trade cheer, deflation gloom', *Far Eastern Economic Review*, 30 September: 75.

Schamis, H. (1999), 'Distributional coalitions and the politics of economic reform in Latin America', *World Politics*, 51: 236–68.

Scher, Mark (1997), *Japanese Interfirm Networks and their Main Banks* (New York: St Martin's Press).

Schwarz, A. (1994), *A Nation in Waiting: Indonesia in the 1990s* (Sydney: Allen & Unwin).

Scott, Kenneth & Barry F. Weingast (1992), *Economic Propellants, Political Impediments* (Stanford, Calif.: Hoover Institution).

Sender, Henny (1998a), 'A tale of why Indonesia never got a debt deal', *Wall Street Journal Interactive Edition*, file://A:\SB910122716433401000.htm, 4 November.

Sender, Henny (1998b), 'Indonesia's new proposal fails to impress its creditors', *Asian Wall Street Journal*, 10 October.

Sender, John (1998), 'Why Indonesia never got a debt deal: as crisis in Asia worsened, Japan's banks dithered over write-offs', *Asian Wall Street Journal*, 4 November.

Shafer, D. Michael (1994), *Winners and Losers: How Sectors Shape the Developmental Prospects of States* (Ithaca, NY: Cornell University Press).

Shari, Michael (1999a), 'Indonesia getting out from under: ad hoc deals may win Indonesia's key players much-needed relief', *Business Week*, 1 February.

Shari, Michael (1999b), 'Jakarta's Mr Workout', *Business Week*, 15 March.

Sheard, Paul (1985), *Main Banks and Structural Adjustment in Japan* (Canberra: Research School of Pacific Studies, Australian National University).

Shin, Inseok & Joon-Ho Hahm (1998), 'The Korean crisis: causes and resolution' (Hawaii: East-West Center, paper for the East-West Center/KDI Conference on the Korean Crisis, August).

Shin, Roy W. & Yeon-Seob Ha (1999), 'Political economy of policy reform in Korea: review and analysis', *Policy Studies Review*, 16(2): 65–97.

Shiraishi, S. (1997), *Young Heroes: The Indonesian Family in Politics* (Ithaca, NY: Southeast Asia Program, Cornell University).

Shiraishi, T. (1997), 'Anti-Sinicism in Java's New Order' in D. Chirot & A. Reid (eds), *Essential Outsiders: Chinese and Jews in the Modern Transformation of Southeast Asia and Central Europe* (Seattle: University of Washington Press).

Siamwalla, Amar (1997), 'Can a developing democracy manage its macroeconomy?' in Thailand Development Research Institute, *Thailand's Boom and Bust* (Bangkok: Thailand Development Research Institute).

Silberman, Bernard S. (1993), *Cages of Reason: The Rise of the Rational State in France, Japan, the United States and Great Britain* (Chicago: University of Chicago Press).

Simon, William E., George P. Shultz & Walter B. Wriston (1998), 'Who needs the IMF?', *Wall Street Journal*, 3 February: A22.

Siregar, R.Y. (1996), 'Inflows of portfolio investment to Indonesia: anticipating the challenges facing the management of the macroeconomy', (Singapore: ISEAS, Working Papers, Economics and Finance 2/96).

Smith, Heather (1998), 'Korea' in Ross H. McLeod & Ross Garnaut (eds), *East Asia in Crisis: From Being a Miracle to Needing One?* (London: Routledge).

Smith, T. (1971), 'Corruption, tradition and change', *Indonesia*, 11: 21–40.

Soesastro, Hadi (1989), 'The political economy of deregulation in Indonesia', *Asian Survey*, 29(9): 853–69.

Soesastro, Hadi (1998), 'ASEAN during the crisis', *ASEAN Economic Bulletin*, 15(3): 373–81.

Soesastro, Hadi & C. Basri (1998), 'Survey of recent developments', *Bulletin of Indonesian Economic Studies*, 34(1): 3–54.

Solnick, S. (1998), *Stealing the State: Control and Collapse in Soviet Institutions* (Cambridge, Mass.: Harvard University Press).

Soros, George (1998a), 'Towards a global open society', *Atlantic Monthly*, 281(1): 20–32.

Soros, George (1998b), *The Crisis of Global Capitalism* (New York: Public Affairs).

'Statement by the Hon. Kiichi Miyazawa, Minister of Finance of Japan, at the Fifty-Third Joint Annual Discussion' (1998), Ministry of Finance, Government of Japan, 6 October (http://www.mof.go.jp).

Steinfeld, Edward (1998), *Forging Reform in China* (Cambridge: Cambridge University Press).

Stiglitz, Joseph (1998), 'Boats, planes and capital flows', *Financial Times*, 25 March.

Stiglitz, J. & A. Weiss (1981), 'Alternative approaches to analysing markets with asymmetric information', *American Economic Review*, 73(1): 246–9.

Sugisaki, Shigemitsu (1998), 'The outlook for Japan and its global implications' (Kobe: Address at the Kobe University/IMF Symposium, Towards the Restoration of Sound Banking Systems in Japan: Its Global Implications, 14 July).

Summers, Lawrence H. (1996), 'Introduction' in Peter B. Kenen et al., *From Halifax to Lyons: What has been Done about Crisis Management?* (Princeton, NJ: Essays in International Finance No. 200, International Finance Section, Department of Economics, Princeton University).

Sutherland, H. (1979), *The Making of a Bureaucratic Elite: The Colonial Transformation of the Javanese Priyayi* (Singapore: Heinemann Educational).

Tachi, Ryuichiro (1995), *Zaisei Databook: zaisei no genjyo to tenbo* (Fiscal policy databook: present conditions and survey [of the past]) (Tokyo: Okura Zaimu Kyokai).

Tanzer, Andrew (1997), 'The People's Liberation Army, Inc.', *Forbes*, 24 March.

Ter-Minassian, Teresa (1997), 'Decentralizing government', *Finance and Development*, 34(3): 36–9.

Thoenes, Sander (1999a), 'Bakrie arm may swap debt of $1.15bn', *Financial Times*, 27 January.

Thoenes, Sander (1999b), 'Japanese banking dogma blocks Indonesian debt rescue', *Financial Times*, 23 February.

Tietmeyer, Hans (1999), 'Evolving cooperation and coordination in financial market surveillance', *Finance and Development*, 36(3): 20–3.

Tilly, C. (1985), 'War-making and state-making as organized crime' in P. Evans, D. Reuschemeyer & T. Skocpol (eds), *Bringing the State Back In* (Cambridge: Cambridge University Press).

Tomlinson, Richard (1998), 'Soldiers of fortune', *Accountancy*, September.

USAID (1997), 'Declaration on Local Governance', *Public Management*, April.

US–China Business Council, 'China trade update', http://www.uschina.org/press/tradememodec.html.

Velasco, Andres & Pablo Cabezas (1998), 'Alternative responses to capital inflows: a tale of two countries' in Miles Kahler (ed.), *Capital Flows and Financial Crises* (Ithaca, NY: Cornell University Press).

Wade, Robert (1998), 'The Asian crisis and the global economy: causes, consequences and cure', *Current History*, 97 (November): 361–73.

Wade, Robert & Frank Veneroso (1998a), 'The Asian crisis: the high debt model versus the Wall Street-Treasury-IMF complex', *New Left Review*, 228 (March/April): 3–23.

Wade, Robert & Frank Veneroso (1998b), 'The gathering support for capital controls', *Challenge*, 41(6): 14–26.

Walder, Andrew (1991), 'Workers, managers and the state: the reform era and the political crisis of 1989', *China Quarterly*, 127: 467–92.

Walder, Andrew (1994), 'The decline of communist power: elements of a theory of institutional change', *Theory and Society*, 23(2): 297–323.

Walder, Andrew & Gong Xiaoxia (1993), 'Workers in the Tiananmen protests: the politics of the Beijing Workers' Autonomous Federation', *Australian Journal of Chinese Affairs*, 29: 1–29.

Walter, Norbert (1998), 'An Asian prediction', *International Economy*, 12(3): 49.

Wang, Hongying (forthcoming), *Weak State, Strong Networks: The Institutional Dynamics of Foreign Direct Investment in China* (Hong Kong: Oxford University Press).

Wang, Yizhou (1998), 'Quanqiuhua Shidai de Guojia Jingji, Zhengzhi yu Anquan' (National economy, politics and security in the era of globalization), *Shijie Jingji*, 8: 15–18.

Warr, Peter G. (1998), 'Thailand' in Ross H. McLeod & Ross Garnaut (eds), *East Asia in Crisis: From Being a Miracle to Needing One?* (London: Routledge).

Weber, Max (1947), *The Theory of Social and Economic Organization* (ed. T. Parsons) (New York: Free Press).

Wedel, Janine R. (1998), *Collision and Collusion: The Strange Case of Western Aid to Eastern Europe, 1989–1998* (New York: St Martin's Press).

Weiss, Linda (1998), 'From miracle to meltdown: the end of Asian capitalism' (Perth, WA: Murdoch University, paper for Asia Research Centre Conference, August).

Whittaker, D. Hugh & Yoshitaka Kurosawa (1998), 'Japan's crisis: evolution and implications', *Cambridge Journal of Economics*, 22(6): 761–72.

Williamson, John & Molly Mahar (1998), *A Survey of Financial Liberalization* (Princeton, NJ: Essays in International Finance No. 211, International Finance Section, Department of Economics, Princeton University).

Willner, A.R. (1970), 'The neotraditional accommodation to political independence: the case of Indonesia' in L. Pye (ed.), *Cases in Comparative Politics: Asia* (Boston: Little, Brown & Co.).

Winters, J. (1996), *Power in Motion: Capital Mobility and the Indonesian State* (Ithaca, NY: Cornell University Press).

Wolf, Martin (1998), 'Flows and blows', *Financial Times*, 3 March.

Woller, Gary M. & Kerk Phillips (1998), 'Fiscal decentralisation and LDC economic growth: an empirical investigation', *Journal of Development Studies*, 34(4): 139–48.

Woo, Jung-en (1991), *Race to the Swift: State and Finance in Korean Industrialization* (New York: Columbia University Press).

World Bank (1991), 'Project completion report: Indonesia, Fifth Bank Pembangunan Indonesia (Bapindo) Project 16 August 1991' (Industry and Energy Operations Division, Asia Regional Office, World Bank).

World Bank (1997), 'Private capital flows to developing countries: the road to financial integration' (Oxford University Press for the World Bank, World Bank Policy Research Report).

World Bank (1998a), *East Asia: The Road to Recovery* (Washington DC: World Bank).

World Bank (1998b), *Global Economic Prospects and the Developing Countries 1998/99: Beyond Financial Crisis* (Washington DC: World Bank).

World Bank (1998c), 'Indonesia in crisis: a macroeconomic update' (Washington DC: World Bank, 16 July): I, 1.1, 1.3 (prepared for the July Consultative Group meeting in Paris).

World Bank (1999a), *Global Development Finance 1999* (Washington DC: World Bank).

World Bank (1999b), 'Managing the recovery in East Asia' (Washington DC: World Bank mimeo).

World Bank (1999c), 'Statement by Mark Baird, Country Director for Indonesia, on Bank Bali (Jakarta: World Bank, World press release, 20 August).

World Trade Organization (1999), 'World trade growth slower in 1998 after unusually strong growth in 1997' (Geneva: World Trade Organization, 16 April; http://www.wto.org/wto/intltrad/internat.htm).

Wyplosz, Charles (1998), 'Globalized financial markets and financial crises' (Amsterdam: Paper presented at the Conference on Coping with Financial Crises in Developing and Transitional Countries, Forum on Debt and Development, 16–17 March).

Yam, Joseph C.K. (1999), 'Capital flows, hedge funds and market failure: a Hong Kong perspective' (Sydney: Reserve Bank of Australia, paper for Conference on Capital Flows and the International Financial System, September).

Yang, Liehui & Xu Zhong (1998), 'Dongnanya Jinrong Dongdang de Shenceng Sicao' (Deep thoughts about the financial turbulence in Southeast Asia), *Shijie Jingji*, 4: 18–20.

Yoo, Seong Min (1998), 'Corporate restructuring in Korea: policy issues before and during the crisis' (Canberra: Australian National University, paper presented to a Conference on Financial Reform and Macroeconomic Policy and Management in Korea, November).

Young, Alwyn (1994), 'Lessons from the East Asian NICs: a contrarian view', *European Economic Review*, 38(3/4): 964–73.

ZGSB: Zhongguo Shibao (Taipei).

Zhang Tao & Zou Heng-fu (1998), 'Fiscal decentralization, public spending and economic growth in China', *Journal of Public Economics*, 67(2): 221–40.

Zhang Zhiwei (1998), 'Minying Jinrong Xin Jiyuan' (A new era in private finance), *Taiwan Jingji Yanjiu Yuekan*, 21(4): 55–61.

Zhong, Wei & Hu Songming (1998), 'Dongya Jinrong Weiji de Fansi' (Reflections on the financial crisis in Southeast Asia), *Shijie Jingji*, 6: 23–6.

Zou, Jiayi (1998), 'Hanguo Jinrong Weiji de Shencengzi Yuanyin' (Deeper causes of the financial crisis in Korea), *Shijie Jingji*, 5: 6–9.

Index